Westmoreland's War

Westmoreland's War

Reassessing American Strategy in Vietnam

BY GREGORY A. DADDIS

OXFORD
UNIVERSITY PRESS

OXFORD
UNIVERSITY PRESS

Oxford University Press is a department of the University of Oxford.
It furthers the University's objective of excellence in research, scholarship,
and education by publishing worldwide.

Oxford   New York
Auckland   Cape Town   Dar es Salaam   Hong Kong   Karachi
Kuala Lumpur   Madrid   Melbourne   Mexico City   Nairobi
New Delhi   Shanghai   Taipei   Toronto

With offices in
Argentina   Austria   Brazil   Chile   Czech Republic   France   Greece
Guatemala   Hungary   Italy   Japan   Poland   Portugal   Singapore
South Korea   Switzerland   Thailand   Turkey   Ukraine   Vietnam

Oxford is a registered trademark of Oxford University Press
in the UK and certain other countries.

Published in the United States of America by
Oxford University Press
198 Madison Avenue, New York, NY 10016

Library of Congress Cataloging-in-Publication Data
Daddis, Gregory A., 1967–
Westmoreland's war : reassessing American strategy in Vietnam / Gregory Daddis.
pages cm
Summary: "Gregory A. Daddis argues senior military leaders developed a comprehensive campaign
strategy in Vietnam, one not confined to 'attrition' of enemy forces."— Provided by publisher.
ISBN 978–0–19–931650–2 (hardback)
1. Vietnam War, 1961–1975—Campaigns.   2. Westmoreland, William C. (William Childs),
1914–2005—Military leadership.   I. Title.
DS557.7.D27 2014
959.704′340973—dc23
2013026839

3 5 7 9 8 6 4
Printed in the United States of America
on acid-free paper

To
My mother, Doris
My wife, Susan
And my daughter, Cameron

CONTENTS

Acknowledgements ix
Abbreviations used in the Text xiii
Abbreviations used in the Notes xv
Map of South Vietnam Administrative Divisions xvii
Preface xix

Introduction: A Word on War and Strategy 1

1. Conceiving Strategy for the Cold War Era 15

2. From Advice to Support to War 38

3. The Myth of Attrition in Vietnam 65

4. On Bewildering Battlefields: Implementing Westmoreland's Strategy 92

5. The Parallel War 120

6. Training an Uncertain Army 147

Conclusion: When Strategy May Not Matter 170

Notes 185
Index 245

ACKNOWLEDGMENTS

It seems best to begin with a genuine acknowledgment. This book is a work of historical revisionism. In one sense, all history is an act of revisionism, of reevaluating and improving our understanding of the past. No doubt, my conclusions will challenge many a reader's basic understanding of how the American phase of the Vietnam Wars unfolded. I conscientiously have sought to contest the standard narrative of what continues to be a highly contested war. My goal, however, in writing *Westmoreland's War* is not to be deemed simply a contrarian. Far from it.

In truth, I undertook this project because historical evidence continually forced me to question the traditional storyline of one of the United States' most painful military excursions in the twentieth century. Part of this questioning arose from my previous work on how the US Army sought to measure progress and effectiveness in such a complex war. Why, I asked more and more as my research progressed, did the army encumber itself with hundreds of reports and thousands of data points if its sole mission was "attrition" of the enemy? If army officers cared only about killing the enemy, why were "body counts" supplemented with metrics that measured population security, economic development, political stability, and scores of nonmilitary programs? Was it possible that Americans understood that victory or defeat in Southeast Asia turned on more than just military factors? Was it possible that US strategy in Vietnam was more than just one of attrition? These are the questions, ultimately, that this book asks.

Just as important, however, I find it essential to acknowledge the tremendous support offered to me by so many people. As a Vietnam War historian, I am continually humbled by how a community of scholars, students, and veterans—despite the contentiousness of the topic—is always willing to lend assistance, share research, offer advice, and provide perspective.

First off, I want to thank Dave McBride at Oxford University Press for continuing to place his faith in my interpretation of the Vietnam War. Dave has been a pleasure to work with over the last few years. Thanks also to Sarah Rosenthal, Kate Nunn, and Patterson Lamb for helping me through the publication process. Working with the professionals at Oxford has been a treat.

I have had the privilege of working in the Department of History at the United States Military Academy for the last three years. I can think of no better place to learn about, teach, and discuss military history than at West Point. My thanks goes out to the faculty in the department for making this a special place to work—Lance Betros, Greta Bucher, David Frey, Rob McDonald, Jason Musteen, Ty Seidule, John Stapleton, Steve Waddell, Sam Watson, and Gail Yoshitani all have been tremendous colleagues in helping me better understand the history of the "military art." Deb Monks and Melissa Mills aided me on more occasions than I can recall and continue to serve as the glue that holds our entire department together. Kevin Farrell assisted me with some of my early ideas on the war's popular narrative and I greatly value his friendship. Comrade Cliff Rogers also helped me work through defining strategy for a war that oftentimes lacked precise definitions. My good friend Gian Gentile, never one to shy away from a debate on counterinsurgency and historical mythmaking, read through a draft manuscript and offered constructive comments on the relationships between tactics and strategy. Our daily conversations have been both engaging and enjoyable. Jen Kiesling, a dear friend, not only read through portions of an early version and made invaluable suggestions but served as a near daily sounding board on more than just military history. I'm not sure how, but she continues to mentor better than any. It must be the cookies.

One of the unique, and truly wonderful, aspects of working at West Point is serving with a "rotating" faculty of officers and professors who continually bring fresh perspectives on the army, the state of the academic profession, and new approaches to teaching undergraduate students. Jackie Whitt, a lead "revolutionary" now at the Air War College, was first among equals in making fun of my "Great Wall of Outline." In spite of her biting sense of humor—no, very much because of it—she remains a true friend. I also have benefited immensely, both personally and intellectually, from my friendships with Beth Behn, Josiah Grover, and Casey Doss. Tom Moore and Rod Dwyer have been amazing colleagues in helping direct our core military history course at West Point. Wynne Beers, Geoff Earnhart, C. J. Kirkpatrick, Dwight Mears, Dave Musick, Bill Nance, Joe Scott, and Dave Siry equally have set high bars in the classroom and I am proud to have taught with all of them.

Beyond the Hudson Valley, I have profited from the advice and friendship of some remarkable historians and teachers. At Chapel Hill, Dick Kohn, Joe Glatthaar, Michael Hunt, and Wayne Lee continue to inspire. At Princeton, Paul Miles gave me more of his time and attention than I rightly deserved. I continue to build up a debt of gratitude that likely will go unpaid. This book would not have been possible without his invaluable support. I also am indebted to Bob Brigham (technically in the Hudson Valley) for his encouragement and insights on the Vietnam War. Bob is an incredible teacher and a top-notch scholar. So too are Lloyd Gardner, who read the entire manuscript, and Andy Wiest, who offered counsel early on in the project. Heather Stuhr made me rethink the role of the civilian population as the project proceeded. Marilyn Young graciously accepted an invitation to talk with my cadets at West Point on the role of the home front during the war and spent a delightful evening prior with friends and family. Darmouth's Ed Miller offered a unique Vietnamese perspective that kept me straight on a number of important parts of this story and I owe him greatly for his terrific feedback that came "just in the nick of time." William Rust graciously shared his own research material on Laos. At the University of South Carolina, I received wonderful assistance and support from Herb Hartsook, Brian Cuthrell, and Christine Nicol-Morris. My thanks also go to General Volney Warner who not only allowed me a full afternoon of his time and exchanged numerous emails with me but shared his personal papers during a research trip to Washington, DC. Ken Burns, Geoffrey Ward, Lynn Novick, and Sarah Botstein offered enormous encouragement as they traveled their own paths through the Vietnam War. I look forward to their final work as much as any new interpretation of the conflict.

Once again, I am humbled by the support from the US Army's official historical community. At the Center of Military History at Fort McNair, Andy Birtle opened up his personal files and gave me an incredibly thoughtful critique of my work in its final draft form. Andy is a true professional. So too are Dale Andrade, John Carland, and Erik Villard whose own works reassessing Westmoreland helped me reconsider not only the general but the war as a whole. At the Military History Institute at Carlisle Barracks, Conrad Crane, Richard Sommers, Dave Keough, Rich Baker, Louise Arnold-Friend, and Terry Foster all helped with my research and with my framing of the historical question that this book hopes to answer. Con's insights on counterinsurgency were particularly helpful. Finally, at Fort Leavenworth I have benefited from my relationships with Jim Willbanks and Roger Spiller. Both offered priceless comments that improved the end product. Roger especially challenged me with several larger observations that helped me rethink my views on grand and military strategy and kindly allowed me to incorporate his comments into the final narrative.

The Omar N. Bradley Foundation graciously granted me a fellowship that allowed me to complete my research and I am grateful for their support. A General and Mrs. Matthew B. Ridgway Military History Research Grant also permitted me to conduct invaluable archival research at the US Army Military History Institute.

Finally, I want to thank my friends for making the time spent away from Westmoreland and his war over the last few years so special: Cotton and Robyn Puryear, Rob Young, Beth Bailey, Martha Beltran, Rob Citino, Joseph "Chip" Dawson, Sheila Farrell, Beth Frey, Gee Won Gentile, Mike and Alison Gillette, Jill Gregory, Darien Grover, Richard Immerman, Peter Law, Hayley Moore, Mike "Hippie" and Barbara Neiberg, David O'Connor, Shelley Reid, Julie Shappy, Chuck and Bridget Steele, and John Walmsley. Moreover, I can't thank enough all the support from my family, Robert "Raging Bull" Castronova and the Chittick, Hays, and Tarvestad clans. They all are incredibly special to me. As are our cats George and Lucky. But not nearly as much as the three amazing women to whom this book is dedicated.

ABBREVIATIONS USED IN THE TEXT

ARCOV	United States Army Combat Operations in Vietnam
ARVN	Army of the Republic of Vietnam
CAP	Combined Action Platoon
CGSC	Command and General Staff College
CIA	Central Intelligence Agency
CINCPAC	Commander in Chief, US Pacific Command
CIP	Counterinsurgency Plan
CJCS	Chairman of the Joint Chiefs of Staff
COMUSMACV	Commander, United States Military Assistance Command, Vietnam
CORDS	Civil Operations and Revolutionary Development Support
COSVN	Central Office of South Vietnam
CTZ	Corps Tactical Zone
DMZ	Demilitarized Zone
DoD	Department of Defense
DRV	Democratic Republic of Vietnam
FLN	Algerian National Liberation Front
FM	Field Manual
FWMAF	Free World Military Assistance Forces
GVN	Government of South Vietnam
HES	Hamlet Evaluation System
ICP	Indochinese Communist Party
JCS	Joint Chiefs of Staff
JUSMAPG	Joint United States Military Advisory and Planning Group
KIA	Killed in Action
LZ	landing zones
MAAG	Military Assistance Advisory Group
MACV	Military Assistance Command, Vietnam

MCP	Malayan Communist Party
NCO	Noncommissioned Officer
NLF	National Front for the Liberation of South Vietnam
NSC	National Security Council
NSAM	National Security Action Memorandum
NSSM	National Security Study Memorandum
NVA	North Vietnamese Army
OCO	Office of Civil Operations
PAVN	People's Army of Vietnam; see also NVA
PLAF	People's Liberation Armed Forces; see also VC
PRC	People's Republic of China
PROVN	Program for the Pacification and Long-Term Development of South Vietnam
RD	Revolutionary Development
RF/PF	Regional Forces/Popular Forces
RVN	Republic of Vietnam
RVNAF	Republic of Vietnam Armed Forces
TCK-TKN	*Tong Cong Kich-Tong Khoi Nghia* (General Offensive-General Uprising)
VC	Vietnamese Communist, Vietcong; see also NLF
VCI	Vietcong Infrastructure
USAID	United States Agency for International Development
USIA	United States Information Agency

ABBREVIATIONS USED IN THE NOTES

CARL	Combined Arms Research Library. Fort Leavenworth, Kansas
CMH	US Army Center of Military History. Fort McNair, Washington, DC
FRUS	*Foreign Relations of the United States*. US Department of State.
LBJL	Lyndon B. Johnson Library Oral History Collection. Austin, Texas.
JCSHO	Joint Chiefs of Staff History Office. The Pentagon, Washington, DC
MHI	US Army Military History Institute. Carlisle Barracks, Pennsylvania.
NARA	National Archives & Records Administration. College Park, Maryland.
OSDHO	Office of the Secretary of Defense Historical Office. Washington, DC
TTUVA	The Vietnam Archive, Texas Tech University. Lubbock, Texas.
USAASL	US Army Armor School Library. Fort Knox, Kentucky.
USAAWCL	US Army Aviation Warfighting Center, Aviation Technical Library. Fort Rucker, Alabama.
USMA	United States Military Academy, West Point, New York.
VNIT	Vietnam Interview Tape Collection, CMH. Fort McNair, Washington, DC
WCWP	William C. Westmoreland Papers
WPUSC	William C. Westmoreland Papers, South Caroliniana Library, University of South Carolina, Columbia, South Carolina
WPSC	Special Collections, United States Military Academy Library. West Point, New York.

MAP OF SOUTH VIETNAM
ADMINISTRATIVE DIVISIONS

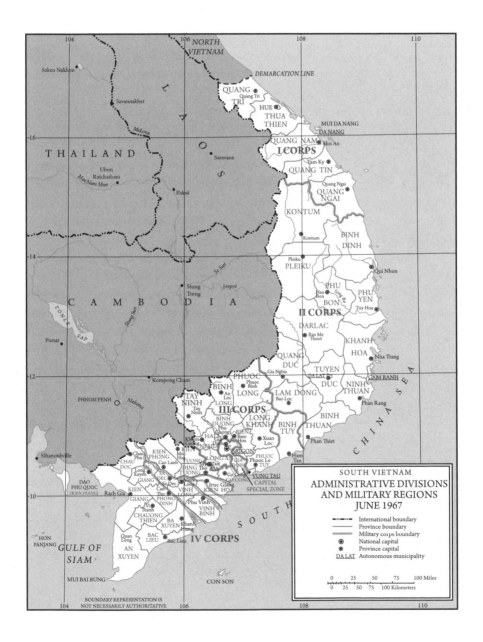

SOUTH VIETNAM

**ADMINISTRATIVE DIVISIONS
AND MILITARY REGIONS
JUNE 1967**

- - - · - International boundary
——— Province boundary
——— Military corps boundary
⊛ National capital
⊙ Province capital
DA LAT Autonomous municipality

| 0 | 25 | 50 | 75 | 100 Miles |
| 0 | 25 | 50 | 75 | 100 Kilometers |

BOUNDARY REPRESENTATION IS
NOT NECESSARILY AUTHORITATIVE

PREFACE

Attrition. In the last five decades, the word has become synonymous with American strategy in the Vietnam War. The word conjures sinister images of the First World War, when sturdy young men, guided by distant, phlegmatic generals, hurled themselves to their deaths against unseen trench-bound enemies. Attrition is wasteful, inhuman, bloody. It is a strategy for the unimaginative. Blundering generals, so the popular conception goes, prosecute strategies of attrition simply to kill the enemy, to bleed their opponents white. For those seeking inspiration from war, attrition is baldly unheroic. Soldiers find no glory on the battlefield in this type of war, only senseless destruction and too often meaningless death. In the modern era, it is a mechanical strategy in which brawn trumps brains. Attrition is embodied in generals like Ulysses S. Grant in the 1864 Wilderness Campaign during the American Civil War and Erich von Falkenhayn at Verdun during World War I. It also is William C. Westmoreland in the Vietnam War—or so the accepted narrative wants us to believe.[1]

Popular histories of the Vietnam War largely have been unkind to General William Westmoreland, the commander of the United States Military Assistance Command, Vietnam (MACV) from 1964 to 1968. They argue he presided over a narrow strategic concept that placed a premium on killing the enemy at the cost of other, more important, missions such as pacification and the training of South Vietnamese armed forces. Such histories recycle shopworn phrases like "search and destroy," "big unit war," and "body counts" to simplify for their readers an immensely complex war.[2] In truth, the military lexicon of the day was unsuited for fully articulating the intricacies of a broadly defined political-military strategy in Vietnam. Attrition thus served as a convenient short-hand for journalists, politicians, and even military commanders during the 1960s. In the process, the term became so embedded into the war's narrative, and into Westmoreland's role as a wartime commander, that over the years attrition evolved into an unquestioned truth for explaining the war's outcome. The US Army failed in Vietnam because a misguided general had implemented a wrong-headed strategy.

Perhaps, however, such explanations are overly reductive. Certainly, the Vietnam War presented American officers and soldiers with experiences that looked far different from combat in Korea or the Second World War. The enemy in Vietnam proved frustratingly elusive while social and political factors frequently eclipsed military operations. The host-nation government in Saigon and the South Vietnamese army often seemed to many Americans more a liability than an asset. Developing a coherent strategic concept for such an unfamiliar environment proved immensely difficult for military and civilian leaders alike. Moreover, emphasizing political constraints under which MACV planners worked begs the question whether any approach could have achieved victory against a committed nationalist-communist enemy given that all strategy—grand and military—is contextual and interactive. Yet to argue as some historians have that the US Army under Westmoreland, wedded to a conventional concept of warfare, lost the war in Vietnam because of a flawed strategy of attrition seems wildly simplistic.[3] Perhaps the time has come for a reassessment of William Westmoreland's role in the making of strategy during the Vietnam War.

This work offers such a reassessment. At its core, it argues that Westmoreland developed a comprehensive military strategy for Vietnam, one not confined to simple attrition of enemy forces. The implementation of that strategy, however, failed to resolve the underlying issues of the war and, in the process, highlighted the limits of American military power abroad during the Cold War era. Without question, comprehensiveness does not equal strategic excellence. Above all, strategy must be effective. Here an important question arises. If the execution of a strategic concept is unattainable, does that not mean the conception was flawed from the outset? What a strategy produces surely is as important as the context in which it is formulated. In short, results matter. But outcomes should not be the *only* basis of judgment. It is possible, as in the case of the American war in Vietnam, to devise a sound strategy and still lose.[4]

Central to this work's argument is the contention that Westmoreland not only devised a sound military strategy but that the general was not the unthinking officer who is presented so contemptuously in many history books. Because Westmoreland's name has become synonymous with a lost war, we have tended to forget how much he was admired and how much he seemingly incorporated America's strengths in the early 1960s. Named *Time*'s "Man of the Year" in January 1966, Westmoreland was described by the weekly news magazine as the "sinewy personification of the American fighting man in 1965." As the United States expanded its war in Southeast Asia, the former Eagle Scout and West Point First Captain appeared emblematic of all that was good and virile in American society. *Time* painted him as a modern-day heroic warrior: "A jut-jawed six footer, he never smokes, drinks little, swims and plays tennis to remain at a flat-bellied 180 lbs.—only 10 lbs. over his cadet weight."[5]

But beyond the physical qualities, *Time* assured its readers that Westmoreland was more than just a plodder who cared only about killing his enemy. "Wherever he goes," the article noted of the general's frequent visits with his soldiers, "he reminds them that Viet Nam is not only a military operation, but a 'political and psychological' struggle as well."[6] Westmoreland's ideas therefore seemed appropriate to a new form of warfare in which political sensitivity mattered as much as physical strength.

Decades later, however, the general often ranks high on lists evaluating America's worst military commanders. A 1982 broadcast by *60 Minutes*, "The Uncounted Enemy: A Vietnam Deception," demonstrates how far Westmoreland had fallen since the heady days of early 1966. Not only had the general lost the Vietnam War through a misguided strategy but worse, he had attempted to "suppress and alter critical intelligence on the enemy" in order to make false claims of progress.[7] The heroic icon was not just a failure but a fraud. When Westmoreland sued CBS for libel, the ensuing court case, ultimately settled before going to jury, seemed only to further critiques that the general had egregiously mishandled his war. Somehow Americans had been lied to, not only by their elected officials but their military leaders as well.

But what if this convenient storyline, in reducing a lost war to blaming a failed commander, erases the nuances of the prolonged American experience in Vietnam? What if Westmoreland devised a strategy that in fact encompassed more than just attrition of the enemy? Just as important, what if the army Westmoreland led in Vietnam learned from its experience with unconventional warfare and adapted accordingly during the crucial years of 1964 to 1968? Such questions are more than just hypothetical musings. In reality, their answers, when based on a thorough investigation of historical evidence rather than on a search for blame, offer a new reality to what actually transpired in Vietnam during Westmoreland's tenure as the MACV commander.

Far from being wedded to conventional strategic concepts of annihilation or attrition, many US Army officers in the early 1960s, Westmoreland included, proved capable of revising their views on how military power might achieve larger political objectives. They incorporated new ideas on countering local insurgencies, on the potential of civic rather than military action, and on the importance of gaining some semblance of political support from the population. Putting these new ideas into practice unquestionably achieved only modest results. The lure of battle was ever present in Vietnam and destructive military operations too often nullified social and political progress within the countryside's rural villages. Yet, even despite mistakes, too often factors outside of the army's purview vitiated its progress.

Indeed, many historians, Americans in particular, have written Vietnam War history with the view that the conflict was the United States' to win or lose. In such examinations, the US Army failed to shape local factors in a war that had begun decades before American involvement. Some "revisionist" historians in particular maintain that an ineffective military strategy led to stalemate, a loss of will on the American home front, and thus ultimate defeat. Other "orthodox" scholars have subscribed to the notion that the war in Vietnam, because of unique historical circumstances, was somehow "unwinnable." In a futile attempt to challenge Vietnamese nationalism, American civil and military leaders failed to realize that no amount of force short of complete destruction of North Vietnam could defeat Ho Chi Minh's bid for national independence. In one sense, orthodox historians critique US strategy as roundly as their revisionist counterparts. They suggest that American strategists miscalculated by backing a corrupt and largely illegitimate South Vietnamese government, thus squandering resources that might have been better employed elsewhere in the global war against communism.[8]

Despite how one evaluates these competing interpretations of the Vietnam War's outcome, the role of strategy remains an unavoidable, and oftentimes controversial, topic. If strategy is the way in which a country's armed forces achieve the nation's political objectives, then understanding how such concepts were formulated and applied in Vietnam is necessary for truly appreciating the war's outcome. In short, this book hopes to correct some persistent misconceptions of how American officers conceived military strategy. It also aims to fill a longstanding void in the literature of the war. Most histories of Vietnam assess American strategy through the lens of White House officials. In particular, they consider the deliberations of President Lyndon B. Johnson and his key advisors, such as Secretary of Defense Robert S. McNamara and national security advisor McGeorge Bundy. Such works focus on what best can be termed "grand strategy." To date, however, no single work has concentrated on how the commander of MACV and senior staff officers developed a broad military strategy for US troops fighting in Vietnam. This book consciously shifts the strategic focus from Washington to Saigon.

Dissecting American military strategy in Vietnam seems best approached thematically, rather than from a strict chronological narrative of the US Army's experiences in Vietnam between 1964 and 1968. The complex environment of South Vietnam did not lend itself to military operations isolated from political, social, and economic realities. Vietnam was both a multifaceted and convoluted war. For instance, search-and-destroy missions aimed at defeating National Liberation Front (NLF) insurgents frequently undercut nonmilitary programs in civil affairs and revolutionary development that sought to build governmental support in the countryside. Each chapter thus will focus separately on the multiple yet interconnected aspects of American military strategy in Vietnam—combat operations, pacification, nation building, and the advising and training of South Vietnamese armed forces. A common thread within these chapters emphasizes how the US Army learned to conduct itself in the relatively new areas of counterinsurgency and unconventional warfare.

In truth, both Westmoreland and the army he led conscientiously approached the problems of Vietnam and developed a comprehensive strategy that appreciated the war as something more than just killing enemy soldiers. The main point in assessing this strategy should not focus on what Westmoreland ought to have done. Rather, we should examine why MACV's commander developed the strategy that he did and how the army attempted to implement his vision on the complex political and military battlefields of Vietnam. The actions that the US Army performed on a daily basis (and, as an organization, how it adapted to its environment) offer some of the best insights into how Westmoreland formulated his strategic concepts and what he hoped to achieve. In this sense, a study of American strategy in Vietnam should be based on the advice offered by Prussian military theorist Carl von Clausewitz. As Jon Sumida perceptively notes, Clausewitz believed that the proper study of the past "required consideration of why decisions were hard, rather than whether they had been right or wrong."[9] This story, thus, concentrates less on placing blame for a failed strategy in Vietnam and more on actual decision making at the strategic level of war.

In the process, this work considers three main questions. First, was Westmoreland's own approach to strategic planning consistent with the Johnson administration's grand strategy? While the political leadership in Washington placed limitations on Westmoreland—President Johnson refused any requests to "broaden" the war—larger strategic objectives forced the MACV commander to view the war in expansive terms. As the president noted in October 1966, "we recognize that success cannot be equated entirely on military victories, important as they are, but must also be brought about through the effective application of broad and comprehensive politico-economic-sociological-psychological programs designed both to improve the well-being of and to orient the population toward the central government."[10] Tasked to create conditions that would demonstrate to the enemy that the odds were against winning, Westmoreland had to fulfill national policy in a manner acceptable to the administration but also suitable to the conditions of South Vietnam. A sole focus on military operations would have been out of step with guidance from administration authorities and would have challenged the doctrine of civilian supremacy in military affairs.[11]

Second, was there a logical relationship between the military means available to Westmoreland and the goals implicit in MACV's mission? "No strategy can be effective," John Lewis Gaddis has maintained, "if it fails to match means with ends." Under the Johnson administration, US policy rested on the ability to "maintain the independence and territorial integrity of South Viet-Nam."[12] Breaking the enemy's will served as the chief intermediate objective in achieving that aim. Yet the war seemed to suggest that the enemy's will was not fully accessible to the means at Westmoreland's disposal. For MACV, the problem consistently remained one of raising the costs to North Vietnam within acceptable, anticipated costs to the US government and home front, while simultaneously reducing the risks of a wider war outside of Vietnam. Moreover, an independent, noncommunist state required not just a military victory, but a political one as well. As Westmoreland concluded in 1967, the enemy was "waging against us a conflict of strategic political attrition in which, according to his equation, victory equals time plus pressure."[13] If annihilation of the North Vietnamese armed forces proved infeasible given the political constraints of the early and mid-1960s, how well did Westmoreland develop a strategy that matched available means to larger administration aims given the resources at hand?[14]

Finally, was Westmoreland's strategic concept not only logical but realistic? In other words, what was the probability of success? General Bruce Palmer claimed that MACV's commander recognized that any strategy in Vietnam "meant a long, protracted struggle and that demonstrating progress in such an indefinite conflict to an impatient American people was extremely difficult."[15] Breaking the enemy's will required a military focus on both enemy main-force units and guerrillas, on "searching and destroying" as well as "clearing and holding." Given the troops allotted for these missions, did Westmoreland conceive of a strategy that reasonably augured success? He certainly had to determine how best to apply limited resources to particular problems in the environment of South Vietnam. As Westmoreland remarked to his key commanders in May 1967, the main-force war was competing for the same resources required by revolutionary development and the challenge was "to allocate resources properly so that both can proceed without slighting either one."[16] This tension in effectively distributing limited resources to achieving one's strategic aims highlights an important aspect in evaluating strategy: if a strategic concept cannot be implemented, it hardly can be deemed satisfactory.

Embracing such a critical approach when reassessing the American war in Vietnam leads us away from one-dimensional conclusions that Westmoreland almost single-handedly lost the war in Southeast Asia.[17] A sound strategy alone does not guarantee success, just as one general cannot control all the forces at play in a time of war. The enemy always has a vote, as do one's allies and even the population among which the struggle is being fought. In few other wars was this truer than in Vietnam. Narrowly considering the war's outcome ignores multiple interdependent variables (and the weights of these variables), many of which fell outside the US Army's ability to affect. In September 1965, as American combat troops were expanding from their enclaves in South Vietnam, journalist James "Scotty" Reston ran a thoughtful piece in the *New York Times*. Reston found that Americans officials in Saigon had discovered they could influence the course of the war, but others, especially in Washington, were uncertain of what that influence might provide in the long term. In the process, a sense of false optimism was spreading among those running the war in Vietnam. The veteran correspondent concluded that these officials had "seen the power of America to influence the military situation. But they cannot control it without the support of the South Vietnamese Government and people, and so far they are not assured of either."[18] For a strategy aimed at preserving the independence and territorial integrity of a noncommunist South Vietnam, Reston's findings held inauspicious portents for the future.

Westmoreland's War

Introduction

A Word on War and Strategy

When Maxwell D. Taylor, the famed World War II commander of the 101st Airborne Division, became the US Army Chief of Staff in June 1955, he recruited Brigadier General William Westmoreland for the position of secretary of the General Staff (SGS). According to Taylor, the SGS was a "traditional stepping stone to senior rank" and afforded the 44-year-old Westmoreland a unique opportunity to consider the problems of strategy at the national level.[1] The assignment came at a time when senior military leaders were clashing with President Dwight D. Eisenhower over a host of strategic questions—deterrence of a perceived global communist threat, the role of nuclear weapons in national security, and the implications of burgeoning defense budgets. Westmoreland thus held a front-row seat as Taylor developed his views on a "National Military Program." Rather than relying primarily on nuclear weapons for national security, the army's chief argued the United States should have enough "political, military, economic, and moral strength sufficient to induce the Communist Bloc to renounce or refrain from all forms of aggression."[2] Sound strategy rested on more than just military muscle. In the aftermath of the Korean War, Taylor advocated a flexible force structure capable of defeating local wars of aggression while also fighting on potential nuclear battlefields. For the next three years, Westmoreland was "associated with virtually all of the Chief of Staff's activities," gaining a practical education not found in the army's school system of the day.[3] Few officers, in truth, had the chance to glimpse the process of developing national strategy from such a close distance.

Westmoreland's education in strategy took a different form when he assumed command of Taylor's old outfit in the spring of 1958. Leading the 101st Airborne Division entailed putting strategic theory into practice for an officer who had just spent the last three years working at the highest levels inside the Pentagon. Taylor's advocacy of more flexible army formations led to the development of "Pentomic" divisions, units no longer based on the triangular concept of three regiments but on five independent "battle groups." Westmoreland took over the 101st just as it was preparing for the final shakedown exercise that would mark it as a combat-ready Pentomic. (With an atomic-armed rocket battery, the 101st was the first US Army division to have an organic nuclear capability.)[4] Because of the division's designation as a rapid deployment force requiring movement within six hours of an emergency notification, Westmoreland stressed constant readiness as he watched the Lebanon crisis unfold in the summer of 1958. He kept a close eye as well on the rising levels of violence in Indochina over the next two years. These emerging local threats helped spur the general to create a special "Recondo" school that focused training on "counterinsurgency warfare, with an emphasis on small-unit operations."[5] In short, Westmoreland's command of the 101st provided him the chance to put abstract strategic theories into concrete operational practice.

Westmoreland's final assignment before heading to South Vietnam served as a sort of strategic finishing school for the future Military Assistance Command, Vietnam (MACV) commander. In the summer of 1960, Westmoreland relinquished command at Fort Campbell and assumed the post of superintendent of the United States Military Academy. For the next three years, the general met with foreign dignitaries, congressional delegations, senior military leaders, Vice President Lyndon Baines Johnson, and President John F. Kennedy. Johnson, who gave the commencement address in 1961, was followed by Kennedy in 1962. In his remarks, Kennedy told the commissioning class they could no longer focus on "strictly military responsibilities." Their future assignments, taking them across the globe, would "require a versatility and an adaptability never before required in either war or peace."As the president put it, service in such places as Vietnam would place unprecedented "burdens" on a new generation of military leaders.[6] Just two years later, Kennedy's message would prove to have special meaning for not only the graduating cadets but also Westmoreland himself.

The three years at West Point were busy ones for Westmoreland and illustrated his growing appreciation of the challenges young army officers would face in the early 1960s. He oversaw revision of the academic curriculum aimed at promoting the intellectual development of cadets across a wide range of topics, from math and engineering to history and philosophy. Drawing upon his experience with the 101st, Westmoreland instituted Recondo training for cadets and formed a committee whose recommendations led to the adoption of 54 hours of instruction on counterinsurgency over a cadet's four-year West Point experience. Given the growing number of US advisors being sent to South Vietnam, the superintendent hosted a senior British general who had fought against the communist insurgency in Malaya. He also refocused cadet summer training and sponsored a counterinsurgency conference that featured Walt W. Rostow, a special national security advisor in the Kennedy White House, as the keynote speaker.[7] While at West Point, Westmoreland was exposed to the question of strategy as an intellectual problem that required serious professional study.

In three successive assignments—on the Pentagon staff, as a division commander, and as academy superintendent—the general thus grappled with distinct, yet corresponding, aspects of US strategy in the Cold War era even though he had little experience with strategic planning per se.[8] But what did strategy really mean to American military officers and civilian policymakers in the decade before William Westmoreland departed for command in Vietnam? Clearly the general had taken part in discussions and training that reflected contemporary strategic concerns, whether they be debates over force structure or the best way to train for conflict in the post–World War II period. But what were the implications of these forays into the realm of strategy? It seems reasonable to suggest that both Westmoreland and the US Army as a whole in the late 1950s and early 1960s understood that strategy meant more than just leadership or tactical skill on the battlefield. We should also consider the prospect that many army officers went to Vietnam with a more expansive definition of strategy in mind than is generally realized. Reassessing Westmoreland's war in Vietnam therefore first requires a broader reconsideration of how American military leaders came to think about the word "strategy" in the early 1960s.

Strategy is more than just how a nation and its armed forces think about and discuss war. Language, as was the case in Vietnam, often can prove insufficient for fully articulating strategic concepts like attrition or annihilation. Even the word itself, strategy—first used in antiquity to describe the art and skill of a general—can disorient and confuse when applied in modern contexts. (One student of the subject during the Vietnam years called it "a loose sort of a word.")[9] In large part, this potential for confusion stems from the fact that strategy is both a concept and a process. It is an idea—and a highly contingent one—for how military force should be used to achieve political objectives, as well as the way such force actually is employed in a time of war. Thus, in evaluating strategy, historians arguably are best served when exploring not only what an army discusses but what it does. Contemporary lexicon, of course, can be inadequate when attempting to explain the intricacies of complex wars, and incongruities almost always exist between what is being done and said. One must also consider the climate in which the definition is being used and for what purpose. Moreover, the concept of strategy has evolved over time.[10]

Take, for instance, how Carl von Clausewitz, writing in the aftermath of the Napoleonic Wars, approached the topic. In *On War*, the Prussian theorist defined strategy as "the use of the engagement for the purpose of war."[11] Such a limited conception of the word centered on the commander's ability to shape individual campaigns, what is called "operational art" in today's military vocabulary, for achieving a political objective. In this sense, strategy focused on the conduct of battles and its results. A commander aimed to achieve tactical successes in such a way that led directly to a political goal. Clausewitz's ideal found no better expression than in Napoleon's stunning victory at Austerlitz. The emperor's 1805 masterpiece battle not only crushed the Third Coalition but compelled Austria to sign the Treaty of Pressburg and effectively forced the Hapsburg Empire out of the war. Battle, and the planning behind its execution, had resulted in a tangible political outcome.

A close read of *On War*, however, suggests that Clausewitz believed the interplay between military means and political aims encompassed more than simply using battlefield engagements for a specific political purpose. "It is only in the highest realms of strategy," he argued, "that intellectual complications and extreme diversity of factors and relationships occur. At that level there is little to no difference between strategy, policy and statesmanship." Strategy, in this sense, became more than "the art of skillfully exploiting force for a larger purpose."[12] Clausewitz thus used the term in two different senses, one for what we might consider today operational design, the other for general war planning. In some contexts he used the more limited, restrictive definition and in others employed the term to impress upon his readers a much broader meaning. In both versions of the concept, though, Clausewitz emphasized that war was a function of interdependent variables, whether they be the unique capabilities of the commander or the oftentimes shifting political intentions of the government. Consequently, fixed rules and prescriptions were unsuited for a fuller understanding of strategy.[13]

In the wake of the First World War, British military theorist Basil H. Liddell Hart rendered a severe, and highly tendentious, criticism of Clausewitz's supposed glorification of battle as the principal element of strategy. Surely there were other means to one's political ends than the wholesale killing of a generation of young men. Liddell Hart thus strove to broaden strategy's definition, emphasizing not only the application of force but its distribution and allocation over space and time. Strategy therefore meant "the art of distributing and applying military means to fulfill the ends of policy."[14] Liddell Hart certainly concerned himself with the conduct of military operations as well as their effects, yet found a narrow focus on military instruments dangerous. A nation's armed forces had to serve a sensible policy, one that properly allocated and coordinated national resources in such a way that regulated the use of force "to avoid damage to the future state of peace." Here was the art of "grand strategy," a concept that encompassed more than just fighting power. Liddell Hart argued that other instruments of power—financial, diplomatic, commercial, even ethical—could be brought to bear for weakening an opponent's will. Strategy was more than "the pure utilization of battle."[15]

Liddell Hart's expanded definition of strategy implied that a nation's leaders establish priorities when establishing political objectives in a time of war, a topic highlighted by more recent commentators like Colin Gray. Gray's contributions to the literature have in part concentrated on the civil-military relationships required for the successful prosecution of strategy. If strategy "seeks control over an enemy's political behaviour" it also serves as the "bridge that relates military power to political purpose; it is neither military power *per se* nor political purpose."[16] Good strategists and policymakers thus not only need a vision but a policy that provides aim and direction for those waging war. In Gray's formulation, the strategic bridge helps "connect policy purposefully with the military and other instruments of power and influence."[17] In an age of nuclear weapons, such a definition made patent sense. Yet Gray's observations are hardly novel. General Matthew B. Ridgway, writing in the Korean War's aftermath, maintained that civilian leaders needed "to work closely with military authorities in setting attainable goals and in selecting the means to attain them."[18] Strategy was not the exclusive preserve of uniformed officers.

These few examples of strategic definitions, far from comprehensive, underscore the elasticity of the word "strategy" and how different characterizations can serve very different needs. Yet it would be misleading to propose that civilian and military leaders always develop strategy based on well-laid plans. Strategy can be, and too often is, a matter of improvisation. Given the sheer complexity of the topic, this should not be surprising. Recall Clausewitz's interdependent variables which strategists must address not only when planning for war but when directing it as well. Systematic analysis is not always possible in the fog of war, whether it be a conventional or unconventional conflict. The eminent British historian Michael Howard well articulated this phenomenon in his exploration of Anglo-American Mediterranean strategy in the Second World War. As Howard maintained, the "development of British—and Allied—strategy was a piecemeal affair, in which military leaders had often simply to do what they could, where they could, with the forces which they had to hand."[19] Is it possible that strategists more often than not extemporize when it comes to war?

In part, such improvisation fulfills an important role in strategy. War is an undertaking of chance, uncertainty, and reciprocal action between actors who make choices before and during actual conflict. In this environment, strategy cannot be stagnant. Field Marshal Helmuth Graf von Moltke, writing in 1871, believed strategy was a "system of expedients...the continued development of the original leading thought in accordance with constantly changing circumstances."[20] Learning and adaptation thus seem essential considerations for those planning and prosecuting war at the strategic level. The trouble, of course, is that military commanders often find it difficult to make momentous changes to their doctrine and units' organizational structures once committed to open hostilities. Few soldiers tend toward self-examination in the heat of battle. Military organizations, traditional in nature and hierarchical in structure, also are inclined to be constrained by cultural preferences that circumscribe leaders' visions of what might be possible outside of normal routine. "Nevertheless," von Moltke claimed, "the conduct of war does not lapse into blind, arbitrary action."[21]

This appears to be the case at the two most recognized levels of strategy— grand strategy and military strategy. While the two terms are not synonymous, they most certainly are interdependent. Policy influences both levels but remains a separate entity unto itself. The term grand strategy, evoking the multidimensional definition of strategy promoted by Liddell Hart, includes the relationships among a nation's allies, enemies, and neutral countries. It entails the coordination of military and nonmilitary means that support long-term political interests and attempts to tailor theater, if not larger regional, operations to realistic national security objectives.[22] In the context of the Vietnam War, contemporary critics protested that an overly ambitious military strategy inside South Vietnam was forcing the United States to cut back on its global commitments in the larger Cold War effort. Seasoned diplomat George Kennan, for instance, complained in 1965 that Washington had lost "almost all flexibility of choice" in Vietnam and in its "approach to the communist world generally."[23] American political and military leaders consequently found themselves limiting their military strategy in Southeast Asia to better support the nation's grand strategy for the overarching Cold War.

As with strategy, definitions abound for the term grand strategy. Barry Posen, as an example, describes grand strategy as "a political-military, means-ends chain, a state's theory about how it can best 'cause' security for itself." Other commentators have classified the term as the "art and science of employing national power" or of relating a nation's instruments of power and influence to its vital interests.[24] For evaluating US strategy in Vietnam, however, it seems best to use contemporary terminology. American military leaders and civilian policymakers might not have benefited from more recent explorations into the complex topic of strategy but they certainly wrestled with its conceptual and theoretical problems during the Cold War. Thus, for the purposes of this study, the US Army's 1962 *Field Service Regulations* provides a useful definition for what was then called "national strategy." The army's doctrine opined that "national strategy is the long range plan through which a nation applies its strength toward the attainment of its objectives." In line with Liddell Hart's concept, the army included all elements of national power into this broad description: "political, economic, psychological, and military and... other national assets such as geographic location and spiritual attitudes."[25]

Supporting this grand vision, army doctrine defined military strategy as the "development and use of the military means which further national strategy though the direct or indirect application of military power."[26] While this work focuses on American strategy inside South Vietnam from 1964 to 1968, such a definition proves too narrow for fully evaluating how William Westmoreland sought to fulfill American objectives in the Vietnam War. The ground war over which Westmoreland exercised command and influence included much more than strict military means. Instead, this study relies on the more general definition of strategy published as part of a 1961 *Dictionary of United States Army Terms*. The army characterized strategy as the "art and science of developing and using the political, economic, psychological, and armed forces of a nation, during peace and war, to afford the maximum support to national policies, in order to increase the probabilities of victory and to lessen the chances of defeat."[27] As will be argued, Westmoreland embraced this broader definition of strategy instead of focusing strictly on destruction of the enemy's military forces. It is important to note, however, the constraints MACV's commander faced in developing his campaign plans and concepts of operation. As Westmoreland recalled, his "responsibilities and prerogatives were basically confined within the borders of South Vietnam."[28] American strategy in Vietnam paradoxically was as comprehensive as it was limited.

Assessing Strategy

So how should one assess strategy? Is victory or defeat the only true metric for evaluating a strategy? Is it possible to develop a sound strategy and still lose? It seems problematic to assess any strategy without reference to its successes and failures. Even if strategy is more a process than an outcome, ideally it should evolve in the direction of success. Should one assess strategy through an evaluation of the strategist alone? Field Marshal Bernard L. Montgomery's quip that the right man with the right plan would suffice for British victory in Malaya seems unsatisfactory for explaining the outcome of a war as complex as Vietnam. Strategy entails both purpose and the design for achieving that purpose and, as was the case in Vietnam, the man on the ground does not always devise the overarching purpose for strategy.[29] Westmoreland certainly conceived his own strategic plan but the president and secretary of defense assigned the general his military and political objectives. As will be argued, the Johnson administration made few if any grand strategic reassessments as the war evolved.

Moreover, defining victory in Vietnam became just as thorny a problem as articulating strategy itself. As US combat forces deployed to Southeast Asia in mid-1965, Secretary of Defense Robert S. McNamara listed nine fundamental elements for achieving a "favorable outcome" in Vietnam, among them reducing incidents of terror and sabotage, ensuring the Saigon government remained independent (and "hopefully pro-US"), and forcing North Vietnam to withdraw its forces from the south. Also at play, of course, was the will of the enemy.[30]

Would a successful strategy account for all of these elements or rather determine which among these numerous political and military objectives actually were achievable? Were all elements necessary for achieving the strategic end-state and thus victory?

The conventional answer to these questions posits that Westmoreland failed to understand his environment, neglected new ideas, and implemented a narrow strategy of attrition that led ultimately to failure. Unquestionably, recent scholarship by the likes of Graham Cosmas, Andrew Birtle, and John Prados has moved beyond this rather oversimplified picture. Notwithstanding these new contributions, the conventional narrative continues to shape not only popular but more scholarly literature.[31] Eventual defeat in Vietnam reinforced arguments that MACV's commander presided over a flawed strategy. Constrained by an organizational culture favoring firepower and enemy-centric operations, Westmoreland, along with most of the US Army officers he led, "devoted insufficient attention to pacification" in their quest for high body counts. One American journalist further claimed that US strategists "misgauged the North Vietnamese and Vietcong by applying their own values to them."[32] For such critics, the causal chain effortlessly linked poorly conceived strategy, implemented in a heavy-handed manner, to failure in Vietnam.

Yet is seems plausible to argue that every army responds to stimuli, both internal and external, when developing and carrying out its strategic concepts. Admittedly, reactive change does not equal institutional learning. Still, even armies slow to learn in new environments must act in response to their surroundings. A proper strategy is one that responds to local, regional, and even international conditions. Culture may help explain organizational choices but it by no means dictates those choices. Accordingly, the longer an army is involved in war, searching for victory, one should expect to find an evolution of strategic thinking over time. In this sense, strategy is a process steeped in problem solving. For the US Army in Vietnam—confronting military, political, social, and economic issues all simultaneously—the chief difficulty came from finding the proper relationships between and among these diverse problem sets. The path to victory hardly ran in a straight line through the destruction of enemy forces, a point well understood by William Westmoreland.[33]

Thus, this study assumes that to properly evaluate strategy one must assess how armies draw conclusions from their environment, from their own experiences, and from the experiences of others, particularly those of the enemy. An evaluation of strategy also must consider how armies draw upon their own history. Perceived lessons from the past often are interpreted within existing intellectual and doctrinal constructs. The US Army of the 1950s and 1960s (or, more accurately, military intellectuals within the army) learned lessons from World War II and Korea that confirmed many officers' preexisting visions of war.[34]

Victory came from defeating the enemy in the field. Yet the legacy of these wars did not straightjacket officers into viewing strategy as simply using battlefield engagements for achieving a political purpose. Change may have been unnatural for veterans of the Second World War and Korea, but they did realize that the conflict in Southeast Asia diverged significantly from their past experiences. Despite their cultural affinity toward conventional warfare, many US Army officers in the 1960s, Westmoreland included, embraced a wider definition of strategy that appeared better suited to the environment of South Vietnam.[35]

The point here is that observing the process of strategy is as important as assessing the theory behind it. Enticing as it is to judge war simply through the lens of victory or defeat, such evaluations suffer from reduction. Outcome cannot solely explain process. This is particularly true for a war as multifaceted as Vietnam. Officers like Westmoreland wrestled with the thorny problems of translating American power into feasible strategic concepts for a conflict that was at once a revolutionary war, a limited-scale conventional war, an internal political struggle, and a contest within the larger Cold War. As one observer recalled, in "intellectual terms, understanding the war in Vietnam demanded a great deal more than had prior US overseas conflicts. In military terms alone, it was a complicated shifting war, without a front line to signal progress."[36] General Maxwell Taylor, who served as ambassador to Vietnam in 1964 and 1965, found equal challenges in bridging the gap between policy and performance. "One of the facts of life about Vietnam," Taylor recalled, "was that it was never difficult to decide what should be done but it was almost impossible to get it done, at least in an acceptable period of time." In short, merely ascertaining success or failure is insufficient *alone* for judging strategy.[37]

Reconsidering Strategy in Vietnam

In the process of assigning blame for a lost war, histories often have overlooked the nonmilitary aspects of American strategy in Vietnam. For decades, critics of the war have relied on catchphrases like "attrition," "body counts," and "search-and-destroy," all of which have become mainstays within Vietnam War literature. One historian has even described Westmoreland's "strategic equation" as "mobility + firepower = attrition."[38] Strategy could not be made any simpler. Yet attrition, "a word commonly employed but rarely defined," has helped distort the historical record of the Vietnam War. German academic Hans Delbrück first used the term *Ermattungsstrategie* (a "wearing out" or "attrition" strategy) in the early 1900s when defining an alternative to an annihilation strategy and the concept soon took hold for explaining the destructiveness of World War I.[39] In the aftermath of the slaughter on the Western Front, attrition assumed an ominous meaning. Critics argued an attrition strategy lacked aim, was unimaginative or used as a last resort, and, in the extreme, was "irrefutable proof of the *absence* of strategy." Journalist Ward Just, writing in 1969, maintained attrition was "an ugly word, signifying a long-drawn-out struggle with many dead and one side or the other exhausted and beaten at the end."[40]

Pundits further claimed that the US Army's attraction with killing the enemy flowed directly from its experiences in World War II when generals viewed military strategy only as a matter of attacking the enemy in the most efficient and effective manner possible. Guided by the political aim of forcing the Axis powers to accept an "unconditional surrender," senior American officers sought to place "unremitting pressure" on the enemy. Destruction of German and Japanese armed forces thus ranked high among US strategic objectives.[41] In Vietnam, however, applying overwhelming military power to destroy the enemy seemed out of place. Ambassador Henry Cabot Lodge, himself a critic of Westmoreland's strategy, wrote to Secretary of Defense McNamara in 1966 that " 'Seek out and destroy' should not be an end unto itself, as it rightly was in World War II. This war will not be won by killing Viet Cong or soldiers of North Viet-Nam, but by destroying terrorist organizations in South Viet-Nam." While Westmoreland retorted that Lodge did "not have a deep feel of military tactics and strategy" and was "inclined to over-simplify the military situation," the ambassador's critique represents a particular commentary on US strategy in Vietnam.[42]

Lodge's assessment, however, presumed American strategic thought had remained stagnant in the wake of World War II. Yet many US Army officers well understood the changes wrought by the Second World War, chief among them the advent of atomic weaponry and the process of decolonization in Africa, India, and Southeast Asia. Warfare seemed at once more constrained and comprehensive. If no political objectives were worth fighting a general nuclear war, then localized aggression, ostensibly sponsored by communist agents, required a credible response beyond just military means. Strategies of annihilation risked just that—obliteration not only of opposing armed forces but of entire nations.[43] In this context, it should be unsurprising that contemporary definitions of strategy evolved to encompass more than just battlefield engagements. If one aim of war was to achieve "some measure of control over the enemy," then strategists had to incorporate elements of power besides military into their planning, a point not lost on US Army officers. One lieutenant colonel, writing his student thesis for the Army War College in 1963, noted that "the number of situations requiring a strategy coordinating military, political and economic factors seems always increasing." The officer went on to argue that "the effective study of military strategy [could] be accomplished only within the broader framework of political and economic relationships."[44]

Such a broad approach seems best for understanding American strategy in Vietnam. Westmoreland, for instance, did not subscribe to a narrow strategy of attrition, just as he did not subscribe exclusively to a counterinsurgency approach. In fact, American strategy proved much more expansive; consequently, Westmoreland exercised influence in a variety of ways, both directly and indirectly. True, the compartmentalized nature of the Vietnam War ensured that the MACV commander's authority paled in comparison to that of Dwight D. Eisenhower, the Supreme Allied Commander of the European theater in World War II.[45] Westmoreland recalled, for example, that his "interest in the air war was somewhat incidental" because of the "dichotomy in organization between the air war and the ground war." Still, as will be seen, the general had to accommodate, integrate, and direct a wide array of activities inside South Vietnam.[46]

Westmoreland's chief intelligence officer drew attention to MACV's diverse undertakings. As Phillip B. Davidson recalled, the general "had not one battle, but three to fight: first, to contain a growing enemy conventional threat; second, to develop the Republic of Vietnam's Armed Forces (RVNAF); and third, to pacify and protect the peasants in the South Vietnamese countryside. Each was a monumental task."[47] Westmoreland thus had to develop a concept of operations for the employment of US forces in South Vietnam, provide advice and assistance to the RVNAF, support civil operations and pacification, and advise both the Commander in Chief, Pacific (CINCPAC) and the Joint Chiefs of Staff on strategic issues. It is equally important to note Westmoreland's occasional direct interaction with the commander in chief. Military success alone would not suffice for achieving US objectives in Vietnam. As Westmoreland himself argued in early 1967, "Political, economic, and psychological victory is equally important, and support of Revolutionary Development is mandatory."[48]

The first section of this work provides context on Cold War strategy and doctrine and the growing US involvement in Vietnam. Thematic chapters then analyze Westmoreland's multiple tasks as MACV's commander. The first reassessment concentrates on the strategic concept for the ground war devised by Westmoreland, a topic as hotly contested today as it was in the early 1960s. Critics argued, and still do, that MACV misjudged the nature of the war, focusing on the symptoms and not the cause of the problem in South Vietnam. As one colonel claimed, military professionals in Vietnam incorrectly focused on the guerrilla threat and thereby confused tactics with strategy.[49] Certainly, the nature of the threat looms large in any conversation on strategy. The chapters on Westmoreland's strategy and the tactics employed to support strategic objectives thus highlight the discord among political and military officials over whether internal subversion or external aggression posed the greatest threat to South Vietnam's independence. The war, of course, did not fit easily into a standard framework. Westmoreland consequently had to discern not only the nature of the threat but of the war as a whole. "The real question," one senior officer recalled, "was *not* what was the proper strategy to guide the ground war in South Vietnam, but *what kind of war was the United States fighting in Vietnam at any given period.*"[50]

The second section focuses on the role the US Army played in supporting civil operations and pacification. As with the ground war, this topic engenders strong disagreement among historians. Most critics contend that Westmoreland gave little notice to pacification and one recent biography even dismisses the topic whole cloth, apparently to suggest that MACV ignored fully the war's non-military aspects. Under Westmoreland, however, pacification—what one study termed "the establishment of internal security, political stability, and economic viability"—became an integral part of MACV's concept of operations.[51] Most army officers in Vietnam understood the importance their adversaries placed on political activity, especially in the countryside. MACV equally appreciated the relationships between territorial security and the need for reviving the Saigon government's rural administration and services. The problem, one of implementation, arose from imbalances between the constructive efforts of pacification and the destructive results of military operations.[52] As the US embassy reported in early 1965, the limited effectiveness of pacification programs following "on the heels of military clearing operations" served as a major "cause of lack of progress against the insurgency."[53] If pacification efforts were to succeed, MACV had to find balance in its approach to both the political and military struggles then being waged in South Vietnam.

The final area in which to reconsider Westmoreland's strategy falls within the realm of MACV's advice and assistance to the RVNAF, particularly the South Vietnamese Army (ARVN). The general realized early on that while US forces might be able to "dislodge the Communists from local areas"—itself a dubious prospect—they "would not have a 'lasting effect' unless the South Vietnamese were able to retain control over such areas."[54] Westmoreland accordingly conferred often with his counterpart General Cao Van Vien and urged RVNAF leadership to correct persistent shortcomings that appeared to be hampering the war effort. As with pacification, the challenge Westmoreland faced lay in implementation. The decision to deploy US forces to South Vietnam rested on the conclusion that the RVNAF was on the verge of collapse in early 1965. How best to divide responsibilities between Americans and South Vietnamese remained a matter of debate throughout the war. While Westmoreland conceived of using American forces primarily in an offensive role, MACV recognized that for "political and psychological reasons the conflict must retain primarily a Vietnamese character at all times."[55] Clearly, that goal would be difficult to achieve with nearly 400,000 Americans serving in South Vietnam by the end of 1966, a number that

Figure 0.1 REUNION. General Westmoreland visits his family in Hawaii, 1965, after President Lyndon Johnson ordered the evacuation of more than 1,800 American dependents from Vietnam in February 1965. (WPUSC, Westmoreland Family Photos)

would rise to more than 530,000 troops by the time Westmoreland left command in mid-1968.

One could reason that few historical precedents existed for a military commander juggling a comparable array of responsibilities. Journalist Robert Shaplen, perhaps overstating his case in mid-1967, argued that it was "doubtful if any commander in the history of warfare has ever faced such a complicated combination of tasks as Westmoreland." Still, fellow correspondent Hanson Baldwin agreed, characterizing the general as a "theater commander with more responsibility and less authority than any in our history."[56] Surely single declarative words like "attrition" were, and are, insufficient for communicating the intricacy of Westmoreland's war. The conflict was a synthesis of political and military action, pacification efforts and conventional tactics, and technological advances and deep historical imperatives that bedeviled those seeking straightforward explanations of strategy and tactics. As General Frederick C. Weyand remarked in late 1968, efforts to categorize the war using terms like "search-and-destroy" or "massive sweeps" failed to convey accurately the situation in the field. "The truth is that the strategy I was directed to pursue during the past two and a half years involved every type of military operation I have ever heard of and some I hadn't heard of."[57] If attrition truly steered Westmoreland's strategy, one might expect a professional such as Weyand to be more certain of the role he played as a senior officer in Westmoreland's command.

In the last 30 years, however, Westmoreland has become a caricature, an incarnation of Gilbert and Sullivan's "Modern Major General" from *The Pirates of Penzance*. Surely, he was not as obtuse as some historians and other critics would have us believe.[58] Hence, this work makes the argument that William Westmoreland, and the organization he led, not only learned and adapted in Vietnam but also developed a comprehensive strategy best suited for the multifaceted environment in which the US Army was operating. Many officers, Westmoreland included, understood the problems associated with rising nationalism and decolonization in the 1950s and 1960s. Their strategy, while comprehensively planned and faithfully implemented, was not sufficient in itself for securing victory in Vietnam. It seems that the one common failing of most military officers and senior civilian officials—among them MACV's commander—was their faith that military power, broadly defined, could achieve political objectives in post-colonial states during the Cold War era. This, of course, presents an uncomfortable truth, especially for those who served, and continue to serve, in uniform.[59] Talented American generals can develop and implement a comprehensive political-military strategy and still lose a war.

1

Conceiving Strategy for the Cold War Era

If most US Army officers serving in the 1950s and 1960s shared an overabundance of faith in military power achieving political ends, the larger intellectual aspects of fighting wars in an age of national liberation did not escape them. While one need take care when speaking of the "officer corps" as a single entity, arguments that the US Army was institutionally incapable of fighting unconventional wars in the aftermath of World War II and Korea seem overblown.[1] In truth, many officers realized the nature of war might be changing. The advent of atomic weaponry certainly altered perceptions of how combat would be fought on modern battlefields. Just as important, however, were concerns generated by global decolonization in the wake of the Second World War. Both events held significant implications for army officers and how they plied their trade. In particular, military means became intertwined with political, social, and economic action during the often violent process of decolonization. Uniformed leaders did not miss the point. One former officer, writing in 1957, recognized this new era of "limited war" as a "complex problem, but an unavoidable one...in which the moves are primarily political, though they involve measures of an economic or psychological nature, and though some of the pawns are military."[2] Less than a decade later, another officer declared that the world was "being threatened by a new form of war. Its founder Mao Tse-tung and his disciples call it 'protracted revolutionary warfare.'"[3] War for Americans no longer resembled Europe in 1944 or 1945.

To many officers, decolonization and revolutionary warfare created a new challenge which arguably fell outside of the army's traditional warfighting skill set—countering local insurgencies. Mao's victory in the Chinese Civil War became the model for this "new" form of warfare. Or so a number of US military leaders believed. As the 1949 communist triumph rippled throughout the globe, the US Army became captivated by Maoist theory and ways to combat his "armed liberation" strategy. Far from being wedded solely to conventional warfare, officers delved into the writings of Mao, Lenin, Ché Guevara, and Vo Nguyen Giap. As one lieutenant colonel quipped, the "ability to quote from Mao and Guevara became the unquestioned mark of the specialist."[4] In embracing the Maoist model as accepted wisdom, officers likely underestimated the possibility that other revolutionaries, like those in Indochina, might modify Chinese methods to suit their own needs. Still, the quest for understanding protracted, revolutionary warfare led to an appreciation of the nonmilitary aspects of strategy. One captain, writing on the "communist long war," argued that the enemy intended "to explore every possible means of waging war." Thus, following one single strategy or tactic made little sense against communists who prized flexibility and achieving balance between military and political action.[5]

The surplus of commentary on Maoist theory in the post–World War II era suggests that officers in the US Army were not seduced entirely by the prospects of conventional war in Europe. Without question, the army saw the Soviet threat in Western Europe as most dangerous to national, if not global, security. Throughout the 1950s and 1960s, the United States shaped its strategic framework around Cold War conceptions of communist Russia and China and worried consistently about war escalating across the nuclear threshold. Yet the problems of countering revolutionary wars found expression in this same strategic framework. Officers, in fact, were open-minded and progressive when it came to unconventional warfare. Prevailing doctrine increasingly viewed insurgency and counterinsurgency as "political, social, and economic rather than military problems" and "struggles for men's minds, rather than territory."[6] A review of this doctrine, the military education system, and professional journals indicates that the US Army found the topic of unconventional warfare worthy of intellectual energy. In their relationship to Cold War strategy, insurgencies and irregular "guerrilla" warfare, especially after 1960, became a fundamental element of professional investigation and debate.[7] This study ultimately would hold important consequences for Westmoreland and his staff as they constructed their own strategy for the war in South Vietnam.

Conceptualizing Cold War Strategy

Any discussion of strategy in the 1950s and 1960s must begin—and perhaps even end—with the policy of containment. A sweeping national security plan derived in the late 1940s to counter supposed Soviet expansionism, containment guided Cold War strategy for decades. George F. Kennan, one of the principal forefathers, argued in early 1947 that "only by the exertion of steady pressure over a period of years" could the United States modify Soviet behavior.

By 1949, a National Security Council paper warned that the USSR, "now an Asiatic power of the first magnitude," was expanding influence throughout Asia and the Pacific.[8] The Americans' hard line against Soviet growth derived from two key sources, one practical, the other ideological. First, the United States enjoyed impressive economic and military advantages vis-à-vis the Soviet Union in the aftermath of World War II, persuading Washington officials to accept a more interventionist foreign policy. Second, Americans, self-possessed from their role in defeating totalitarianism abroad, convinced themselves that liberal, democratic governance offered the surest means of defeating communism in nations seeking to throw off the yoke of colonial rule.[9] Army doctrine supported such assertive foreign policy goals. The army's principal field service regulations noted that "military forces [had] important cold war functions." The manual advised that such forces "may be used to encourage a friendly government in difficulty, to stabilize an unsettled area, to maintain and restore order, or to protect personnel and property."[10]

Such counsel implied a full range of responsibilities for military forces, especially in an age when decolonization threatened to undermine global stability. Revolutionary nationalism, spurred in part by the First World War, gained full steam after the Second. Local resistance movements against colonial rule and oppression profited from the support of populations eager for political, social, and economic change. In the process, political and social structures buckled under the revolutionary strain. This forced dismantling of European rule—what one scholar has dubbed "the liquidation of colonial empires"—worried American foreign policy leaders who feared the Soviet Union would rush into former colonies to fill the political vacuum.[11] Students of local rebellions argued that these "transitional societies" were "vulnerable to insurgency," and few doubted these insurgencies were vulnerable to communist subversion. Nearly everywhere the Americans turned, communists seemed to be fomenting insurrection—in Cyprus, Greece, Czechoslovakia, Yugoslavia, and Indochina. The future of the free world looked bleak indeed.[12]

If World War II had weakened European colonial powers in the eyes of local insurgent leaders, the conflict also elevated the United States to the position of preeminent global power. Given contemporary beliefs that the communist menace threatened the very existence of democracy, President Harry Truman encouraged the nation to "support free peoples who are resisting attempted subjugation by armed minorities or outside pressures."[13] Truman's rhetoric found expression in National Security Council paper 68. NSC 68, which called for a national military buildup to respond militarily to communist aggression, put into question when and how the United States should respond to overseas threats. The army, unsurprisingly, welcomed the strategic emphasis on preparedness, for it justified a revitalization of its force structure in the years following World War

II.[14] Critics, however, suspected the president was rejecting diplomacy in favor of military solutions. Even George Kennan advised that decisions on interventionism should consider American capabilities. (Truman himself worried about the costs of implementing NSC 68.) Such counsel made patent sense given the prevailing view that an international communist movement was replacing the Soviet Union as the chief threat to national security.[15] If the United States needed to respond to challenges in Asia, Europe, and Indochina—all simultaneously—perhaps there were limits to what American power could achieve overseas.

Few questioned potential American inadequacies after Mao Tse-tung's stunning victory in the Chinese Civil War. While domestic critics blamed Truman for the "loss" of China, civilian policymakers and military officers alike vowed that communist expansion could be tolerated no longer. In the process, both camps rushed to uncover the secrets of Mao's success. New students of revolutionary warfare pored over Mao's writings, most notably "Problems of Strategy in China's Revolutionary War" (1936), "On Guerrilla Warfare" (1937), and "On Protracted War" (1938). Recently proclaimed Sino "specialists" quoted the now famous dictum that guerrillas were fish swimming in the sea of the people. Other observers believed communist success emanated from some specific strategy in which men could defeat machines, failing to notice that communist attempts at guerrilla warfare in Southeast China often had met with mixed results.[16] For those in uniform, Mao's writings revealed the necessity for viewing strategy more holistically. Here, the Chinese revolutionary leader made an enormous impact that would influence how Americans conceived military strategy in Vietnam. Following Mao's victory, US Army officers spoke increasingly on the importance of building comprehensive strategies that did not isolate military power from other elements of national power. One Army War College student, writing in 1963, found Mao's theories and doctrine momentous because they were "integrated, encompassing and relating various fields: military, political, economic, sociological and psychological."[17] Wars could no longer be won by military means alone.

The Korean War, fought from 1950 to 1953, forced Americans to face this uncomfortable truth. Following on the heels of Mao's victory in China and pitting US soldiers against Chinese in open combat, the conflict placed Americans directly into a local, if not civil, war with the aim of blunting communist expansionism. The war's results, however, caused concern. Three years of fighting produced what many believed was a draw, hardly the clear-cut victory of World War II. Military officers chafed under limits imposed by a White House concerned about upsetting the global balance of a world now firmly entrenched in an ideological cold war. Foreshadowing events in Vietnam, the Korean conflict also highlighted the linkages between domestic policy and its influence on military strategy. General Matthew Ridgway, who commanded the United Nations forces in Korea, advised that "civilian authorities... need to work closely with military authorities in setting attainable goals and in selecting the means to attain them." The future Chief of Staff of the Army further presaged the difficulties of strategic decision making in Vietnam. "A war without goals would be most dangerous of all," Ridgway argued, "and nearly as dangerous would be a war with only some vaguely stated aim, such as 'victory' or 'freedom from aggression' or 'the right of the people to choose their own government.'"[18] The general's concerns underscored those many officers had of fighting limited wars in a nuclear era. Melding "police action" concepts into the realities of conventional combat potentially imposed handicaps on those waging war against communist aggression.[19]

Concerns over the long-term economic viability of pursuing containment through continual military preparedness matched officers' worries about fighting and winning limited wars. The Eisenhower administration, anxious over rising defense budgets and hesitant to embroil US ground troops in overseas conflicts, sought to rely more heavily on airpower and low-yield tactical nuclear weapons for national security. This "new look" at US military strategy met with sharp criticism from soldiers and scholars alike. General Maxwell Taylor, soon to be an important voice in debating Vietnam strategy, wrote in 1960 that relying on massive retaliation by nuclear weapons had "reached a dead end" and that there was "an urgent need for a reappraisal of our strategic needs."[20] Other skeptics worried that an overreliance on technology undermined the army's ability to respond effectively to communist threats below the nuclear threshold. Prominent academics seemed to agree. The University of Chicago's Robert Osgood admitted the value of being able to deter a "total war" but warned that "unless the nation can also wage limited war successfully, Communist aggression may force the United States to choose between total war, non-resistance, or ineffective resistance."[21] Henry Kissinger equally expressed concern over the inability to relate military power to political purpose in an "all-out war." As the Harvard professor advised, a "limited war, by contrast, is fought for specific political objectives which, by their very existence, tend to establish a relationship between the force employed and the goal to be attained."[22]

Criticism of the New Look policy appeared justified by the numerous wars of national liberation fought during Eisenhower's administration. American officers already had gained experience advising the Greek National Army in their civil war during the late 1940s. Rebellions opposing colonial powers soon followed—against the US-backed government in the Philippines, the British in Malaya, and the French in Indochina and Algeria. By 1956, roughly 20 percent of US Army officers had served as military advisors to foreign armies battling insurgencies. Few doubted the role of communism in these conflicts. When, in January 1961, Soviet premier Nikita Khrushchev pledged support for these "wars in which oppressed peoples rise against their oppressors," most all

Americans agreed a communist hand was directing this global threat to democracy.[23] If Khrushchev's bellicose rhetoric helped illuminate the threat, army officers remained less certain on how best to respond. The conventional conflict in Korea in fact had not placed blinders on the US Army and, increasingly throughout the Eisenhower administration, officers wrestled with the problems of parrying communist advances through unconventional means. Those in uniform studied the wars of decolonization from a surprisingly nonmilitary perspective. Certainly, battlefield tactics garnered much attention but so too did other aspects of these struggles. One lieutenant colonel, writing on the failure of the communist insurgency in Greece, opined that if "a people's war is to be successful, it must appeal to the fundamental political, moral, and ethical values of the people among whom it is waged."[24] Such reflections, matched by officers in the mid-1960s, would hold important consequences for the development of US military strategy in South Vietnam.

These same officers confronting wars of national liberation experienced firsthand the difficulties of matching military strategy to grand strategy throughout the 1950s. Constrained in their use of absolute force, military leaders struggled to implement containment in a way that did not unintentionally involve the nation in nuclear war. Based on their experiences in Korea, officers recognized that limited wars might be protracted affairs that tested the will of both army and nation. Moreover, civilian leaders appeared more apt to curtail the number of strategic options from which generals could choose. As early as 1951, Ridgway embraced a strategy of attrition in large part because US and United Nations forces had no alternatives. Forbidden by Truman from attacking China, Ridgway's forces emphasized inflicting heavy costs on the enemy to force them to the negotiating table.[25] A strategy of bleeding the enemy also favored American advantages in firepower and technology. Still, the experience left many in uniform unsatisfied. Henry Kissinger likely spoke for most officers when arguing that limited war, by its very nature, was "more ambiguous" than an all-out conflict and that victory offered "no final solution....As a result, the psychological correlation of forces in a limited war is not stable; it depends on a series of intangibles."[26] The challenge for those conceptualizing strategy in the Cold War era thus became one of managing these intangibles. If national policy decisions precluded the annihilation or unconditional surrender of an enemy, how best could military strategists achieve the political aims of their civilian masters?

These experiences in the late 1940s and throughout the 1950s demonstrated the strong linkages between military action and political decision making. Wars of national liberation also revealed the growing importance of the sociopolitical struggle over operational and technological factors. Officers realized the need to adapt to such changing circumstances. One major, writing in 1959, cautioned against any "preoccupation with science and technology, especially in discussions of war and the nature of war." Instead, he argued, "it may be well to take a broader and more comprehensive view of some basic definitions and concepts of war, and the place of war in the scheme of things, for war does not exist in a vacuum. It is caused by the social, economic, and political climate of the contending societies, and it is affected by this climate and by its physical environment."[27] If the US Army as a whole paid less attention to counterinsurgency than to nuclear warfare in this period, the institution still felt a need to prepare for war along a "spectrum of conflict" that ranged from the conventional to the unconventional. In the process, many officers looked to recent historical examples in hopes of learning from the mistakes of colonial powers like Great Britain and France.[28]

While the US Army grappled with the intellectual problems of formulating military strategy in the Cold War era, Washington policymakers questioned whether Eisenhower's New Look was best suited for containing the global communist threat. President John F. Kennedy's 1961 inauguration heralded a new approach, coined "flexible response," to US grand strategy. As Maxwell Taylor described it, the term suggested "the need for a capability to respond across the entire spectrum of possible challenge, for coping with anything from general atomic war to infiltrations and aggressions such as threaten[ed] Laos and Berlin in 1959."[29] Though many conventional-minded officers distrusted Kennedy's visible infatuation with Special Forces and counterinsurgency, official army publications soon fell in line with the new administration's thinking. One pamphlet, quoting the secretary of defense, noted that wars of national liberation were "often not wars at all. In these conflicts, the force of world Communism operates in the twilight zone between political subversion and quasi-military action." More notably, the army's primary doctrinal manual, *Field Service Regulations 100-5, Operations*, acknowledged the Kennedy administration's concerns over preparing for nuclear, conventional, *and* insurgency warfare. The 1962 version of the manual codified the phrase "spectrum of warfare," indicating that army training requirements would expand in support of flexible response.[30]

Perhaps most important for the coming war in Vietnam, the army's embrace of flexible response—no doubt reluctant at first—forced a serious reevaluation of how the US Army defined strategy. Though some senior officers resisted any deemphasis of high intensity conflict on the grounds that it undermined the army's ability to defeat the conventional Soviet threat in Europe, Americans on the eve of the Vietnam War were viewing strategy in increasingly inclusive terms. By 1964, the US Army officially defined strategy as the "art and science of developing and using the political, economic, psychological, and armed forces of a nation, during peace and during war, to afford the maximum support of national policies, in order to increase the probabilities and favorable consequences of victory to lessen the chances of defeat."[31] A mouthful to be sure, this comprehensive definition spoke volumes to how the US Army viewed the problem of strategy during the Cold War era. Given that military strategy was derived from, and an integral part of, national strategy, intelligent officers surely appreciated that war comprised more than simply stringing battlefield engagements together.[32] As the wars of decolonization, for the Americans at least, came to a head in Vietnam, the problem became one of constructing a doctrinal framework for such an expansive definition of strategy.

Crafting Doctrine for Unconventional War

For decades detractors of the US Army's performance in Vietnam have unleashed virulent criticism on an organization that presumably was unable or unwilling to adapt to its environment. Former West Point superintendent Dave R. Palmer contended in the late 1970s that "many professional officers did not even recognize the term 'counter-insurgency,' much less were they prepared to practice it." Another commentator claimed, in the face of countervailing evidence, that the "U.S. Army's doctrine in Vietnam was not integrated with the nation's grand strategy." More recently, John Nagl has argued that the "army had neither the knowledge nor the desire to change its orientation away from conventional warfare."[33] Unsurprisingly, soon after the war critics would paint William Westmoreland in similar brushstrokes, condemning the general for his intellectual rigidity and his general ignorance on the topic of counterinsurgency. A closer examination of contemporary doctrine, however, implies an alternate view. Although often careless use of terms like insurgent, guerrilla, and irregular forces revealed a lack of theoretical rigor, soldiers clearly struggled with the practical aspects of how to develop strategic concepts and doctrine for unconventional warfare.[34]

Though competing with more traditional forms of conflict, interest in unconventional warfare grew steadily throughout the 1950s. By the early 1960s, the topic necessarily became imbedded in the army's doctrine and, in truth, matched well with the army's more inclusive definition of strategy. Certainly, field manuals on "irregular warfare" frequently emphasized military considerations over political ones and contended that population security was the sine qua non of counterinsurgency success. Yet doctrine also highlighted the nonmilitary aspects of Cold War era warfare. In describing the operational environment, the army's principal manual on irregular conflict spoke directly on the ideological basis of rebellions. "The fundamental cause of large-scale resistance movements stems from the dissatisfaction of some portion of the population, whether real, imagined, or incited, with the prevailing political, social, or economic conditions."[35] *Field Service Regulations 100-5* plainly stressed the ideological nature of modern conflict. The manual noted that in the Cold War particularly, "the struggle for influence over the minds of men makes unconventional warfare a key element."[36] If few officers comprehended the genuine social and cultural underpinnings of revolutionary movements overseas, they at least appreciated that counterinsurgency held an increasingly important position within army doctrine.[37]

Undoubtedly, the Kennedy administration's fascination with unconventional warfare helped spur interest in the topic among uniformed officers. In January 1962, the president created a new NSC committee designated the Special Group (Counterinsurgency) for coordinating US assistance to foreign governments threatened by rebellion. Administration officials, however, placed relatively light emphasis on military action. Rather, they concentrated on economic development and political reform. Attorney General Robert F. Kennedy, the president's brother, believed the use of force should be considered carefully. "A military answer," he wrote, "is the failure of counterinsurgency.... Any effort that disregards the base of social reform, and becomes preoccupied with gadgets and techniques and force, is doomed to failure and should not be supported by the United States." State Department official Roger Hilsman went further, arguing that insurgency "isn't a war; it's a political struggle with military aspects."[38] Thus, Kennedy administration officials focused on solving political and social problems at the village level. Contemporary officers clearly recognized the value of such reforms yet viewed the physical security of these villages in equally important terms. Good government and economic growth were crucial for success against insurgencies, but few military men believed development could proceed in an insecure environment. If the attorney general defined counterinsurgency as "social reform under pressure," most officers saw their role as relieving that pressure so the population living in rural villages could prosper.[39]

The army's doctrine matched these officers' sentiments. In fact, the development of counterinsurgency principles underscored the tensions between political reform and population security. This friction arose partially from the way the army distilled its own experiences in the aftermath of World War II. As one perceptive student has noted "the creation of military doctrine is an exercise in highly selective historical interpretation."[40] Since the early 1950s, army doctrine writers acknowledged the role of politics not only in preventing insurgencies from arising, but in defeating them once in bloom. Because of politics' crucial role, field manuals and planning guides recognized that the "primary responsibility for conducting counterinsurgency operations must rest with the local government."[41] In an internal, ideological struggle, any attempt by an external power to assume control of the war effort and impose security likely would be counterproductive. No local leader wished to be seen as a puppet of American leadership. Here, US officers faced a dilemma. If a local insurgency had progressed to a point requiring American intervention, it seemed obvious that indigenous

military forces were incapable of providing security for their civilian population. In the coming years, Westmoreland and his planners would wrangle over
this very problem once US Army and Marine Corps ground troops deployed to
South Vietnam.

While unconventional warfare doctrine considered the tensions between
reform and security, the army's field manuals defined counterinsurgency in similar fashion to strategy. Official publications described the term as "those military,
paramilitary, political, economic, psychological, and civic actions taken by a government to defeat subversive insurgency." Much like strategy, counterinsurgency
covered a wide swath of recommended activities. Just the phrase civic action
involved a multitude of undertakings—construction of schools, hospitals, and
churches; assistance in agricultural planting, harvesting, and processing; and
the furnishing of food, clothing, and medical supplies. Simultaneously, doctrine
advised commanders to play a role in police operations and the maintenance of
order. (Manuals quietly left aside how the local population might react to US
forces engaging in censorship and the setting of curfews.)[42] One contemporary
officer highlighted a noteworthy critique of counterinsurgency doctrine, arguing
that "the very definition of the word is not clear. Unfortunately, it signifies many
things to different people."[43] Written in late 1964, this assessment portended one
of the chief shortcomings with American strategy in Vietnam. If Westmoreland
followed doctrinal recommendations—and he most certainly did—the resultant strategy risked confusing those charged with implementing such a broadly
defined political-military design. In their search for comprehensiveness, army
doctrine writers had elevated the potential for misinterpretation.

Surely it made sense to view strategy and unconventional warfare through a
broad lens. Resistance movements prospered from social, political, economic,
and religious discontent so any plan to oppose these rebellions required a generally comprehensive approach. The basic field manual on the topic emphasized such a methodology. *Counterguerrilla Operations*, published in 1963 and
revised and expanded in 1967, discussed the historically nonmilitary roles of
political and psychological action in defending against insurgencies. Military
action, doctrine suggested, was "only a part of the overall internal defense and
development effort."[44] While the manual stressed the importance of small-unit
patrolling and reconnaissance, especially since fighting in this type of environment largely would be decentralized, it also recommended that commanders
establish "pacification committees" to coordinate military, paramilitary, and
civilian efforts. Equally important, intelligence planning should concentrate
not only on the enemy force's strengths and weaknesses but on the society as
well. *Counterguerrilla Operations* proposed that intelligence staffs identify and
exploit matters such as "popular hunger for social improvement." Of course, the
source of this information created new challenges for military planners. "Since

the major source of military information available to a force conducting coun-terguerrilla operations is the civilian population, every effort is made to develop a reliable informant network utilizing civilian personnel."[45] The implications of this doctrinal recommendation inferred larger issues with deploying US forces in support of local governments under siege. If American troops relied on the population for their information, what happened if civilians refused to accom-modate their foreign benefactors?

The army's counterinsurgency doctrine contained other limitations that would influence the conduct of fighting in Vietnam. The very title of Field Manual (FM) 31-16, *Counterguerrilla Operations*, indicated that many officers often conflated terms like insurgent, guerrilla, and revolutionary. The manual defined a guerrilla force as the "armed combatant element of a resistance move-ment," insinuating an institutional preference for defeating the military threat in a political-military conflict. Doctrine thus urged commanders to "orient their efforts continually on the destruction or neutralization of the guerrilla rather than the terrain."[46] Phrases like "continuous pressure," "vigorous combat patrol-ling," and "aggressive" action saturated the field manuals. Inherent in such word-ing was the assumption that population security led directly to governmental stability. Here US Army doctrine mimicked contemporary theorists like David Galula who viewed counterinsurgency as a sequential process. While Galula, a French officer with experience in China and Algeria, argued that "no opera-tion can be strictly military or political," he nonetheless established a theoreti-cal framework in which security both preceded and stimulated political, social, and economic development. US Army doctrine writers seemed to agree. As FM 31-16 maintained, the "primary reason for the use of armed forces...is to assist the host country in insuring its internal security by countering subversion, law-lessness, and/or insurgent activities."[47] Thus, if contemporary doctrine charac-terized insurgencies in broad political-military terms, it also considered armed force as a catalyst for governmental reform.

Without question, some contemporary officers believed the army was exaggerating the significance of unconventional warfare. Such conventionally minded men disapproved of their peers' arguments that "guerrilla warfare is something special." One 1961 newspaper report, for instance, quoted Chairman of the Joints Chiefs Lyman Lemnitzer as stating that "the new administra-tion was 'oversold' on the importance of guerrilla warfare and that too much emphasis on counter-guerrilla measures would impair the ability of the South Vietnamese Army to meet a conventional assault by the ten or more regular North Vietnamese divisions."[48] Another general officer wrote the following year that the "military commander, if he is wise, will realize that he can only beat these guerrilla gangs by a system of continuous, unrelenting patrolling and ambush-ing."[49] As the war in Vietnam progressed, the experience of some field officers reinforced these early counterarguments. One infantry lieutenant colonel, penning his observations as a battalion commander in 1967, felt war had changed little, if at all. "Despite the many comments that the war in Vietnam is different from WW II and Korea, I do not believe that this is true at Battalion level, and it is certainly not true at Company and below.... An Infantry Unit need only do as it has been trained to do in order to survive and win."[50]

Success absolutely depended on some measure of tactical excellence in combat, a point on which all officers agreed. Arguing, however, that the US Army failed to comprehend the political and nonmilitary aspects of unconventional warfare because of some institutional obsession with conventional war fighting seems widely off the mark. Despite critics' claims, neither doctrine writers nor the officers who read their manuals ignored the complex topic of counterinsurgency in the 1950s and 1960s. Doctrine indeed possessed certain shortcomings. Many an officer in Vietnam would abide by the recommendations of being aggressive and maintaining the initiative against the guerrilla. In the process, heavy doses of firepower destabilized the very foundation of Vietnamese society and contradicted doctrinal prescriptions that "effective local government is vital to carry effective counterinsurgency programs to the local populations."[51] In general, though, the army's field manuals genuinely valued the role nonmilitary programs played in defeating insurgencies. As the army approached the war in Vietnam, its doctrine for countering internal rebellions and insurgencies provided constructive advice for commanders in the field—advice reinforced by a professional education system equally coming to grips with the challenges of balancing conventional and unconventional warfare.

Educating Officers for Brushfire Wars

As the United States gradually shifted its foreign policy focus to Southeast Asia in the early 1960s, US Army schools added more and more instruction on counterinsurgency into their curricula. In 1961, the Continental Army Command ordered the subject taught at every level of officer education. While hours of instruction varied by school, students encountered an increasing number of theoretical works like Galula's *Counterinsurgency Warfare* (1964), Robert Taber's *The War of the Flea* (1965), and Vo Nguyen Giap's *People's War, People's Army* (1961). A 1962 lecture at the Industrial College of the Armed Forces highlighted the similarities between the army's broad-based doctrine and classroom pedagogy. Professor Ralph Sanders, a well-regarded faculty member, noted that counterinsurgency programs had to "prompt the people to identify themselves with the national government," "promote economic and social improvement at a rate fast enough to convey an image of progress," and "improve internal security by strengthening the armed forces, intelligence services, and the police."[52] Few reading the army's doctrine would have found anything surprising in Sanders's lecture. More important, the topic seemed increasingly worth studying given the focus of the armed forces. As Army Chief of Staff Harold K. Johnson asserted in October 1964, counterinsurgency would be "the major mission in the foreseeable future."[53]

A full decade before Johnson's declaration, the US Army War College began probing the topic of revolutionary warfare. In 1951, the faculty assigned roughly one-fifth of the college class to study US policy in Southeast Asia. The following year more than a few students wrote critical papers on the army's response to revolutionary wars. One officer argued that "industrial warfare had become too costly and destructive to achieve political goals"; thus "unconventional warfare becomes a vital and possibly decisive instrument of national policy." Colonel Bruce Palmer noted the same year that combating "guerrilla warfare" required more than mere tactical modifications since it was "the sum of all military, political, psychological and economic operations carried on by irregular forces behind enemy lines."[54] Throughout the remainder of the decade War College students watched the ongoing French campaigns in Indochina and Algeria with interest, exploring the ways in which communist forces were seeking to destabilize the Third World. By the 1961–1962 academic year, the college featured a discussion period that examined the army's role in counterinsurgency operations. Recognizing rebellion as a "cultural and political competition," the discussion guide pointed out that all facets of national power had to be brought to bear in battling insurgencies. Evidence clearly demonstrated, even to "the most parochially minded," that counterinsurgency was a "national struggle [and] not a single-agency effort."[55]

War College students took heed and their papers in the early and mid-1960s revealed a body of officers increasingly comfortable with the nuances of unconventional warfare. Writing on civic action, Colonel Kenneth Kennedy maintained that any "successful program must be a cooperative venture between the local military forces and the community inhabitants, giving a challenge and stake to every man, woman, and youth." (Unfortunately for Americans, South Vietnamese peasants rarely viewed government forces as participating in a cooperative venture.) Other officers explored the role of propaganda in bending public opinion and the ways in which Mao Tse-tung's political-military doctrine "demonstrated its practicability in underdeveloped lands to overthrow established governments and destroy established socio-political systems."[56] By 1964, officers were incorporating the army's experiences in South Vietnam into their student theses. One field artillery colonel wrote a long exposé on the strategic hamlet program which, in its proper focus on the people, he believed might establish a "foundation for victory." Another artilleryman, Lieutenant Colonel

Robert M. Montague Jr. concentrated his 1966 student essay on pacification. Montague would become a leading staff officer in Westmoreland's efforts to incorporate pacification into the American war effort and called for an "integrated strategy" that "recognized [the] complex interrelationships of military, economic, social, psychological, and political aspects of any counterinsurgency campaign."[57]

If Westmoreland profited from the intellectual forays of officers like Montague, he also personally contributed to the study of unconventional warfare in the army's education system. As the West Point superintendent from 1960 to 1963, the future MACV commander mandated counterinsurgency instruction be included in the core curriculum. Westmoreland, mirroring doctrinal advice, took a holistic approach. The Military Academy created a Counterinsurgency Committee that assessed the integration of new instruction into cadet learning and coordinated the interdisciplinary approach across all academic departments. Cadets soon encountered the topic in their history and international relations classes while performing counterguerrilla tasks during summer training. In 1962 the Department of Social Sciences published a handbook titled "Readings in Counterinsurgency" that covered a myriad of topics—the revolutionary strategy of Mao Tse-tung, objectives and methods of communist guerrilla warfare, and the role of the rural population in Vietnam. An integrated bibliography recommended such wide-ranging works as *American Guerrilla in the Philippines, La Guerre Révolutionnaire,* and *Strategic Problems of China's Revolutionary War.*[58] The Academy's Department of Tactics followed suit, publishing the instruction manual "Counterinsurgency: First Class Fundamentals." The booklet advised senior cadets about to graduate to make maximum use of existing civil agencies and police forces and to incorporate "civilian assistance into operational planning." When Westmoreland departed West Point in the summer of 1963 for assignment in Vietnam, the Counterinsurgency Committee judged that the graduating class successfully had "acquired a general understanding of this many faceted subject."[59]

West Point, of course, comprised only a portion of the army's pre-commissioning training and education. The Reserve Officers' Training Corps (ROTC) program similarly reviewed its approach to teaching future officers who likely would be at the sharp end of unconventional combat. Surveyors of both West Point and ROTC questioned the academic relevancy of math and engineering courses to the new counterinsurgency environment and increasingly argued that more resources be applied to the behavioral and social sciences. The 1964 ROTC Vitalization Act sought not only to improve the quality of junior officers but to broaden their academic experience while in college. Cadets were encouraged to take courses in psychology, political science, history, and even anthropology. Senior officers largely supported the shift in emphasis.[60] In March

1962, the army even sponsored a symposium titled "The US Army's Limited War Mission and Social Science Research." One lieutenant colonel, writing on the topic in *Military Review*, concluded that "*expertise* in the various social and behavioral sciences" was required for any type of success against subversive insurgencies.[61] Whether ROTC or West Point could instill such expertise into young officers for their war in Vietnam remained to be seen.

These newly graduated officers first reported to their respective branches' basic officer courses where they learned the technical and tactical skills of their new profession. Critics long have vilified the army's officer education program, one arguing that "the attention given to counterinsurgency studies was paltry."[62] Evidence, however, suggests a more nuanced learning environment. The US Army Armor School at Fort Knox, for example, doubled the hours of instruction devoted to unconventional warfare between 1963 and 1964. At Fort Bragg, a Military Assistance Training Advisor (MATA) course was established in early 1962. Such courses drew heavily on historical case studies like the Philippines Huk campaign, the French Algerian war, and German operations in the Ukraine during World War II. "Lessons Learned" reports from Vietnam reinforced the need for improved counterinsurgency education at home. One published summary from August 1965 recommended that all platoon leaders and enlisted soldiers receive additional training since recent experiences demonstrated "a lack of understanding when it comes to civic action visits to villages."[63] Less than one year later the army was dispatching teams to Vietnam to evaluate how well the school system was serving those actively in combat. Certainly army schools fell short in preparing officers and soldiers for dealing with a hostile population or wrestling with the moral pressures of fighting among civilians.[64] Yet, as an organization, the army recognized that the environment in which its young men were operating differed from the battlefields of World War II and Korea.

In fact, the US Army during the early 1960s fostered a good deal of intellectual study and debate on the topic of counterinsurgency. Most officers realized theirs was a profession requiring study and reflection and recommended reading lists flourished. In March 1962, the Joint Chiefs' Special Assistant for Counterinsurgency and Special Activities issued a bibliography of works that emphasized military, political, and economic considerations in underdeveloped countries. The collection included studies in such far-flung areas as Cyprus, Malaya, Africa, and Egypt. Two months later the editors of *Military Review* compiled a list of the "most significant studies on unconventional warfare" that the journal had published in the last six years. Interestingly, other organizations followed suit.[65] American University published a research compendium on insurgent, revolutionary, and resistance warfare that examined a number of case studies: France and Yugoslavia in the early 1940s; the Philippines and Palestine in the mid to late 1940s; and Malaya and Algeria in the 1950s. The

Rand Corporation offered a related survey of literature on the relations between foreign advisors and their local counterparts.[66] US Army officers thus came into contact with a host of foreign writers, such as Britain's Robert Thompson and Frenchmen David Galula and Roger Trinquier. Those reading Trinquier no doubt pondered his assertion that since the end of World War II "a new form of warfare has been born." According to the French officer, warfare had become "an interlocking system of actions" that included political, economic, psychological, and military aspects.[67]

Such definitions matched well with the US Army's own broad-based conceptions of strategy and slowly made their way from the schoolhouse to Southeast Asia. In fact, the army's experience in Vietnam featured a rather symbiotic relationship between professional military education faculty and senior officers in the field. Westmoreland openly brought perspectives gained from his tenure at West Point to his command of MACV. Lieutenant General Lionel C. McGarr made a similar transition, serving as the commandant of the US Army Command and General Staff College (CGSC) before being named chief of the Military Assistance Advisory Group (MAAG), Vietnam in late 1960. McGarr oversaw an aggressive overhaul of the college's curriculum that included increased counterinsurgency instruction. Course topics covered regional subjects in Latin America and Southeast Asia, examined patterns of communist aggression, and evaluated the social and economic aspects of strategy. McGarr recalled that the "1958 rewrite of the entire course" came about because faculty began "to face the fact that we had such a thing as unconventional warfare."[68] When McGarr moved to take command of the advisory group in Vietnam, college officials, seemingly mimicking Trinquier, noted that "the very nature of war is changing."[69]

As with doctrine, one key factor inhibited the professional military education system from embracing more completely the topic of counterinsurgency. Army schools still found it necessary to concentrate on the Soviet threat in Western Europe and the problems of nuclear war. General George H. Decker, the army chief of staff from 1960 to 1962, highlighted the concerns of many officers when he argued that "our primary interest must be in Europe. With the exception of Japan, the areas of the East have nothing to contribute toward our survival."[70] Civilian policymakers equally worried that military action in Asia might weaken the United States' position in Europe. One need take care, however, in arguing that culturally constrained officers, mesmerized by conventional battle, ignored counterinsurgency. They did not. Decker's comments arguably say less about the army's willingness to familiarize itself with unconventional warfare but rather more about the complexity of the Cold War environment. Organizational biases no doubt were present. Serving officers easily could have seen Vietnam and counterinsurgency as a threat to the army's professional identity. Why learn about a form of war that distracted from the real danger of the Red Army in Europe? As one officer wrote in 1962, "Increased attention to strategic guerrilla operations should not…detract from the principal combat role of conventional units."[71] The army thus found itself caught between two competing forms of warfare. Yet to their credit, officers recognized the need to contemplate both high-intensity conventional combat and the sociopolitical nature of unconventional conflict. Their writings on the latter subject conveyed genuine interest in a subject professional soldiers historically had found intimidating.

Through the Lens of Professional Discourse

By the early 1960s, US Army officers were increasingly and openly wrestling with the problems of unconventional warfare in professional journals and student papers. While these writings failed to inspire any intellectual revolution within the army's ranks—it is unlikely they were intended to do so—the discourse indicated that officers were reflecting seriously on how best to win in an unconventional environment. Officers remained assured that communism in general, and Moscow in particular, lay behind most all rebellious activity. One colonel, for example, pointed to "the sinister strategy and danger of guerrilla warfare as another means used by the Communists to achieve political change."[72] Though evoking comic images of Boris Badenov, such commentary nonetheless encouraged fellow officers to view strategy from a political perspective. One lieutenant colonel, writing his 1963 War College student thesis on Mao, believed the Chinese leader's strategy rested on "a unity and correlation of political and military action. Military and political action are clearly complementary; one flows into the other smoothly and without hiatus. There is no pronounced division of war and peace or military theory and political theory."[73] Two years later, Westmoreland would be pondering similar correlations as he devised his own strategy for allied forces in South Vietnam.

Mao, perhaps unsurprisingly given the global impact of the Chinese Civil War, ranked first among historical case studies examined in professional journals. Westmoreland himself recalled that the Viet Minh struggle against French colonialism "was predicated on three phases in keeping with precepts developed by the Chinese Communist leader Mao Tse-tung."[74] War College students wrote extensively on Maoist strategy, which theoretically moved from a defensive phase, during which political mobilization took precedence over military action; to an equilibrium phase, which balanced political subversion and military raids; to a final counteroffensive phase in which conventional forces brought final victory to the revolutionary cause. Mao's writings influenced a generation of US Army officers. Not only did many see parallels between Ho Chi Minh and Mao Tse-tung but Americans generally assumed that all Asian insurgencies would follow precisely the three-stage Chinese model.[75] When, in late 1964, Hanoi sent North Vietnamese regulars into South Vietnam, US officials in both Washington and Saigon convinced themselves that the war was proceeding toward its final conventional, counteroffensive phase. Historical comparisons could prove useful but constraining as well. Too few Americans in the mid-1960s considered the possibility that Hanoi borrowed from the Chinese only that which was relevant to the unique situation unfolding in Southeast Asia.

While officers held a special reverence for Maoist theory, they studied other recent historical examples of guerrilla warfare and insurgency movements. The successful campaign against the communist-led Huks in the Philippines generated much interest and commentary. Liberation from Japanese rule in World War II solved few, if any, economic problems as the wealthy landholding class continued to exploit local farmers. Though Filipino officials largely viewed the Huks as bandits employing terror tactics, officials in the Truman administration believed the growing rebellion could be derailed only by political, economic, and social reforms. The American position solidified with Ramon Magsaysay's appointment as the secretary of national defense in 1950. Magsaysay had fought against the Japanese occupation and found a kindred spirit in his American advisor, Air Force Colonel (and CIA operative) Edward Lansdale. With uncommon efficiency, the new secretary revitalized the Filipino armed forces, melded civic action programs into military operations, and enhanced the government's image among the population. Surveyors of the rebellion found "lessons" in civilian cooperation, psychological warfare, and political-military planning.[76] More reflective officers, though, noticed potential limitations in the Filipino response. Lansdale noted that "commanders were not always willing to undertake civic action with their soldiers because they viewed this action as 'political' and therefore outside their military domain." Another American officer hit upon a more crucial point. Given that foreigners would be less welcome among the people, "native troops would be more effective than foreign forces in operations against native communist conspirators."[77]

The French experience in Indochina seemed to reinforce such counsel. Though critics long have argued that Americans ignored the French-Indochina War in approaching Vietnam, both civilian academics and military officers in fact studied the protracted colonial conflict. Certainly, the defeat at Dien Bien Phu in 1954 colored examinations of the French Army, as did strained Franco-American relations throughout much of the 1950s. Still, careful observers saw utility in studying the war. Academician Robert Osgood reasoned that the French Army failed, only in part, because of "faulty military tactics" that depended heavily on static defensive positions and on mechanized equipment. "But, more fundamentally," Osgood insisted, "they failed for lack of the proper political and psychological foundation for effective military action."[78] Colonel Charles Biggio's

Military Review article "Let's Learn from the French" highlighted similar themes. Biggio noted the misguided political decision to reinstitute colonial rule after the Second World War, which was "out of step with the surge of nationalism" sweeping through Indochina. Ho Chi Minh conversely saw the struggle as an ideological one. As Biggio argued, the "French underestimated the potency of this ideological offensive. They saw the problem as one which simply required military suppression in the conventional colonial manner."[79] Such criticism no doubt caused many officers to dismiss the French counterrevolutionary struggle as irrelevant to future American strategy. The focus on the French Army's political missteps, however, attested to the growing comfort among officers in seeing unconventional war as a largely political act.

If Americans tended to minimize the lessons of the French Indochinese experience, they still reviewed the theoretical works written by French officers who fought in Vietnam and Algeria. The doctrine of *guerre révolutionnaire* garnered the most attention. Seeking ways to counter anti-colonial insurrections, French officers with experience in Indochina devised *guerre révolutionnaire* with two interdependent components in mind. While "destruction" efforts aimed at dismantling the insurgency's political-military framework, officers performing "construction" tasks sought to organize the population into a new political and social system. The doctrine rested on the inherent belief that communist conspirators were inciting anti-colonial sentiments.[80] Americans took notice. In late 1960, *Military Review* ran an essay titled "Revolutionary War and Psychological Action" in which the editors declared that the "French experience of *la guerre révolutionnaire* and its contingent problems are worthy of detailed scrutiny by qualified military experts." The author believed the French approach to be "*total* war on a *limited* scale, because it utilizes propagandistic appeal to whole populations and all economic, social, and political levers it can avail itself of."[81] The Rand Corporation came to similar conclusions, holistically examining the problems of insurgency and counterinsurgency in Algeria in a 1964 document of more than 300 pages. Lieutenant Colonel Donn A. Starry, then serving in Vietnam, offered his own thoughts on the topic in early 1967 with an insightful essay in *Military Review*. Starry argued that *guerre révolutionnaire* "was aimed at the right target—people, and it dealt with the key problem—public administration. But," the colonel added, "there are surely other ways of implementing programs without turning solely to military services."[82]

Starry's critique of French heavy-handedness came about, ironically, when American actions in Vietnam faced similar condemnation. British officers, especially those with experience in Malaya, led the charge, arguing that their own focus on civil affairs resulted in a successful counterinsurgency campaign against the Malayan Communist Party (MCP). Americans studied the British experience for sure. *Military Review* published a case study on Malaya in

1963 written by a British officer with practice in resettling villagers away from insurgent-controlled areas. In 1964, the US Army Command and Staff College hosted a lecture by British Lieutenant General Sir Kenneth Darling who spoke on counterinsurgency and the importance of "winning the people's minds."[83] Critics shouted that Americans were missing key lessons by not following in their allies' footsteps. Students of Vietnam, however, expressed caution in over-estimating the parallels between Malaya and Indochina. Bernard Fall believed the physical environments analogous, yet insisted that the two countries were "totally different in the sociological, political, and ethnic factors so crucial to winning such a battle." One War College student came to similar conclusions. "Vietnamese officials and U.S. advisors have been criticized, on occasion, for their refusal to adopt more of the successful Malayan strategies and tactics." His study, however, found "that the seeming likenesses are greatly outweighed by the definite divergencies."[84] Westmoreland himself agreed after visiting Malaya en route to Vietnam in 1964.

These historical examinations of the Philippines, Indochina, Algeria, and Malaya demonstrated that US Army officers in the 1950s and 1960s actively sought perspectives on fighting unconventional warfare, even if their profession's main interests lay on conventional European battlefields. Through their case studies, officers soon distilled themes relevant to countering insurgencies. First, many uniformed leaders increasingly saw the importance of viewing revolutionary movements in more than simply military terms. Political reform mattered. This, of course, posed potential difficulties given American military traditions. As one colonel noted, "the chief obstacle to development of the ability of the US Army to get close to a people and engage in effective civil affairs and civic action is what we have always treasured as one of our virtues—the apolitical nature of the officer corps."[85] Still, many officers recognized the need to consider the political aspects of insurgencies. Even professional journals normally consigned to tactical matters took a more comprehensive approach to the topic. A 1966 article in *Infantry* journal recommended that campaigns against insurgent forces "consider the cause for which the guerrillas claim to be fighting, the reasons why they are receiving support, and the basic conditions which justify or seem to justify the guerrilla movement."[86] Clearly there was more to defeating an insurgency than merely killing the enemy.

While officers spoke more and more on the role of political reform, they concurrently discussed the need for social reform in countries facing revolutionary threats. Lansdale's concept of "civic action," used to seemingly good effect in the Philippines, progressively found its way into professional literature. One lieutenant colonel, who viewed civic action as both a counter to and a cure for insurgencies, defined the term as "military programs directed at the promotion of economic-social development, civilian good will, and resultant political stability necessary for underdeveloped countries in their progress toward nationhood."[87] The very definition alluded to an expanded role for the US Army and how it might fight on an extended political-military battlefield. As two officers contended, "Civic action is a weapon of war and, to be effective, it requires the same accuracy, coordination, and support given any other weapon." As war in Vietnam loomed, military leaders clearly understood the limits of force in overcoming a revolutionary movement. They spoke of social reform, of economic development, and of how indigenous forces were best suited for building projects useful to the local population. If their professional education provided them with little expertise in the fields of public works, transportation, or agriculture, officers at least realized the worth of these programs. Civic and military action had to progress hand in hand in any successful counterinsurgency.[88]

The confluence of political and social reform found expression in "revolutionary development," a phrase used regularly during the Vietnam era. Lieutenant Colonel Samuel Smithers Jr. defined the term as "those civilian, military, and police actions taken to eliminate [enemy] political and military activity and to enhance the economic, political, and social development of a community."[89] The definition—akin to civic action and even contemporary conceptions of strategy—presumed any revolutionary movement spread well beyond military boundaries. Officers' understanding of revolutionary development actually fit well with larger strategic notions of Cold War policymakers. Most all Washington officials believed that poverty and political-economic backwardness made former colonial countries susceptible to communist influence. Here, US Army officers saw a way to influence unconventional warfare through more conventional means. If troops could instill order and stability in an embattled country, they could provide an opportunity for social and economic growth. As Secretary of Defense Robert S. McNamara explained it, in "a modernizing society security means development. Security is not military hardware, though it may include it; security is not military force, though it may involve it; security is not traditional military activity, though it may encompass it. Security is development, and without development there can be no security."[90]

McNamara's assumptions on the interrelationship between security and development formed the bedrock of American military strategy in Vietnam. If US Army officers viewed strategy through a broader lens than they did in World War II or Korea, they still retained their faith in military force for achieving nonmilitary aims. This conjecturing—embraced by William Westmoreland, if not all commanders in Vietnam—proved to be one of the most unfortunate preconceptions held by contemporary officers. Believing the Third World under assault by a unified communist front, American civilian and military leaders grappled with how best to accommodate the role of nationalism in their approach to strategy.[91] While officers rightly developed strategic concepts in a comprehensive fashion, they took for granted that securing a country's rural population would lead directly to political stability and thus social and economic progress. As the internal situation in South Vietnam deteriorated in the wake of the 1954 Geneva Accords (which ended French colonial rule in Indochina) Americans believed they could confront the communist menace with a balanced program of military force, political management, and economic development.[92] Defeating the insurgent threat would promote government stability. This stability, in turn, would undercut the communists' position in the eyes of the population, thus leading to a more democratic nation able to withstand the pressures of totalitarianism. Or so the assumption went.

From the Schoolhouse to the Battlefield

US Army officers in the 1950s and 1960s most certainly deemed the Soviet threat in Europe as most dangerous to global peace in the Cold War era. They likely preferred to prepare for war there as well. (Americans rarely have been comfortable fighting against unconventional enemies.) Yet arguments that the US Army in general, and Westmoreland in particular, lost the war in Vietnam because of an inability to see the conflict as more than a contest of arms distort the historical record. True, officers serving in Vietnam tended to emphasize military considerations over political ones. True, the army's faith in military force to solve political problems too often went unquestioned. Nonetheless, uniformed leaders demonstrated a genuine willingness to study the unconventional side of war even while they were maintaining their proficiencies in conventional war. Organizational culture is not so constraining as some scholars would have us believe. If the army, in fact, had been wedded to a conventional concept of warfare it seems doubtful that Chief of Staff Harold K. Johnson would have claimed in late 1965 that "activities to promote stability and progress in the modernization process of emerging nations" had become one of the army's principal missions. Tasks derived from this mission included "combat service support, advisory operations, civic action, civil affairs activities and peacekeeping operations."[93] This was not an army blindly devoted to combat alone.

A review of the army's doctrine, education system, and professional journals on the eve of the Vietnam War seems crucial for understanding how both the US Army and William Westmoreland approached the development of strategy in the early and mid-1960s. Officers throughout the army accepted the strategic realities and demands imposed by decolonization in the wake of World War II. They equally realized that war encompassed more than just military might. While Westmoreland grew up in an army that defined itself largely by its conventional war fighting skills, he, along with many of his peers, understood the competing ideas of confronting revolutionary movements. Even if the army's organizational culture shaped individual officers' visions, that same culture did not limit individual possibilities.[94] In short, to claim that a conventional mindset caused defeat in Vietnam is at very least incomplete. Such an argument removes the possibility of individual choices in the development and implementation of strategy. It also dismisses the truth that many US Army officers appreciated the changing nature of the Cold War environment.[95] Neither the army nor its surroundings remained static on the eve of Vietnam.

Theoretical ruminations meant nothing, of course, if not replicated in practice on the battlefield. As the US Army stepped on the path to war in Southeast Asia, its ability to implement new doctrinal concepts in the field arguably mattered most. Knowledge, framed in doctrine and propagated in schoolhouses, could only establish a foundation for strategic success in Vietnam.[96] Officers and soldiers serving in the field would have to translate these new ideas into concrete action. The conduct of war, however, rarely follows the plans for war.

From Advice to Support to War

The United States did not rush frantically to war in 1965. Rather, involvement in Southeast Asia transpired gradually, over a series of presidential administrations. These incremental steps toward open hostilities allowed American civilian and military leaders to consider strategy for several years before the introduction of ground combat troops to South Vietnam. By the time William Westmoreland arrived in Saigon in mid-1964, key US officials had been debating strategic issues for nearly five years and most understood that any policy for Vietnam required more than simply military might. Vice President Lyndon B. Johnson, for instance, reported on the importance of "responsible political institutions" after his trip to South Vietnam in 1961. "Most important," the vice president averred, "there must be a simultaneous, vigorous and integrated attack on the economic, social and other ills of the Vietnamese peoples. The leadership and initiative in this attack must rest with the Vietnamese leaders."[1] Notably, Johnson would persist in such beliefs when he assumed the presidency in late 1963. Thus, well before Westmoreland's arrival, top American officials were viewing the Indochinese struggle in more than just military terms.[2]

Suppositions on the need for an integrated strategic approach increasingly mattered as both civilian policymakers and military officers viewed the survival of South Vietnam as critical to Cold War containment. As early as 1954, before the climactic battle at Dien Bien Phu, the US National Security Council declared that "Communist domination...of all Southeast Asia would seriously endanger in the short term, and critically endanger in the longer term, United States security interests."[3] Military officers concurred. One argued in early 1962 that "South Vietnam represents a proving ground for democracy in Asia." Four years later, with US forces engaged in open combat against a resilient enemy, another officer believed that American prestige was riding on "the preservation of the independence of the South Vietnamese people." Vietnam's alleged importance to US national security certainly influenced military strategy and its evolution from advice to support to war. Underwriting the "democratic experiment" in South Vietnam meant senior officers would need to craft their military strategy in such a way that supported both presidential objectives and constraints.[4] Thus, the gradual transition from peace to war highlighted the interrelationships between grand and military strategy. All the while, senior military leaders reporting from Saigon influenced Washington perceptions on the viability of a South Vietnamese state.

These early ideas on grand and military strategy—and maturing conceptions on how to win in an environment that looked nothing like World War II or Korea—set an important intellectual foundation for Westmoreland and his staff officers in MACV headquarters. Taking their cues from army doctrine and, perhaps more important, civilian policymakers, officers realized that stopping communism abroad meant building indigenous political foundations. In late 1951, for example, Senator John F. Kennedy commented that checking aggression in Indochina could not be achieved "through reliance on the force of arms. The task rather is to build strong native non-Communist sentiment within these areas and rely on that as a spearhead of defense." Unsurprisingly, the January 1962 "Outline of Counterinsurgency Operations," prepared by the Task Force in Vietnam during Kennedy's presidency, highlighted the role of political, economic, and psychological operations.[5] The incremental nature of American escalation thus not only promoted a certain amount of strategic continuity but also allowed senior military officers the chance to consider revolutionary warfare in Southeast Asia as something more than conventional battle. By the time Westmoreland took command in Vietnam, both he and the army he led already had profited from a decade's worth of experience advising South Vietnamese forces on a war that required an expanded definition of the word "strategy."

Vietnam at War

The Vietnamese, of course, had been at war long before the arrival of American military advisors in the early 1950s. Roughly 2,000 years prior, "Viet" ethnic leaders rallied their people against Chinese domination. Resistance to Chinese belligerence helped stimulate a growing cultural identity among the Vietnamese, even as they incorporated Chinese innovations into their own political and social structures. Seeing themselves as victims of perpetual aggression became, according to Douglas Pike, a "national syndrome."[6] Yet while a separate ethnic identity grew out of these early wars of resistance, Vietnamese leaders contemporaneously struggled with internal dissension. Geography served as a major impediment to national unity; the Nguyen dynasty, for instance, (founded 1802) was really the first Vietnamese dynasty to extend its rule over Saigon and the southern Mekong Delta. Thus, the relatively recent and incomplete nature of the Vietnamese conquest of the south helped foster a political culture that facilitated resistance to external authority. Moreover, strong familial ties made the village, and not any central government, the basis of social, if not political, authority. These competing cultural notions of national resistance to foreign control and internal antagonism to central government led to civil war in the 1600s. For the next two centuries, a divided Vietnam wrestled with domestic strife before a new challenge to Vietnamese independence arrived in the mid-1800s.[7]

French colonialism in Indochina added a completely new dimension to the struggle over Vietnamese national identity. Swept up by mid nineteenth-century imperial ambitions, France sought Asian possessions for economic gain and political prestige. French military expeditions landed in the late 1850s and, despite local partisan resistance, soon replaced the Confucian-based imperial government with an all-embracing French colonial apparatus in Cochinchina. (The French never removed the imperial government in the center (Annam) and always preserved at least the monarchy's nominal rule over Tonkin.) Still, Vietnamese life for many changed dramatically.[8] The new European administration altered governance structures, recast the social order, and sought to reform Vietnamese literature and culture. The economic transformation of the countryside not only extracted raw materials for French profit but created a new social class of landlords and merchants who, though styling themselves as defenders of the traditional conceptions of family relationships and responsibilities, seemingly challenged long-established customs and institutions. This economic exploitation and attempt at social reconstruction predictably met with resistance from Vietnamese already attuned to the threats of foreign occupation. While some local leaders saw value in assimilating modern Western methods into Vietnamese norms and traditions, many other nationalists chafed under French rule. For those leading the anti-colonial movement, French rule meant little more than humiliation and political and cultural dependence.[9]

European colonialism intensified the struggle over competing conceptions of Vietnamese nationalism. By the 1920s, the revolutionary movement against French rule had made tentative strides in melding peasant concerns with those advocating national independence. The challenge became one of creating a disciplined organizational structure to guide the disparate elements of revolution. In 1927, Vietnamese intellectuals created the Viet Nam Quoc Dan Dong (VNQDD), or Vietnam Nationalist Party, to organize the French opposition movement. While the party recruited students, women, and soldiers, the VNQDD lacked rural support, and its attempts to spark armed rebellion met with a brutal French response. Still, rebellion seemed the only way to break the cycle of economic hardship and political disillusionment caused by colonial rule.[10] By 1930, an increasing number of Vietnamese revolutionaries found refuge in the Indochinese Communist Party (ICP), a new group organized in large part by Nguyen Ai Quoc, a forty-year-old activist soon to be called Ho Chi

Minh. The ICP sought to carefully weave issues of class warfare into the struggle for national independence. There seems little doubt, however, that communist ideology remained subordinate to the anti-colonial effort. By the time Ho Chi Minh took control of the Viet Nam Doc Lap Dong Minh Hoi (Vietnamese Independence League) in the spring of 1941, the Vietnamese revolutionary movement had enlarged its appeal to create a broad coalition of anti-French groups.[11]

While the ICP had struggled to gain external support against French rule, the Vietnamese Independence League, popularly known as the Viet Minh Front, benefited from the early French defeat in World War II. The Japanese occupation of Indochina followed closely behind the German defeat of France in 1940. Vietnamese watching the French yield to fellow Asians saw confirmation that France, its legitimacy already in question, no longer had the capacity to rule in Vietnam.[12] The Viet Minh wasted little time. Instead of combating the Japanese directly, Vietnamese nationalists concentrated on organizing the countryside and extending their strength among the rural population. Ho Chi Minh understood the risks entailed in forfeiting the cities to Japanese occupation but realized the opportunity global war afforded the Vietnamese in building a viable revolutionary movement for the future. Ho was far from passive. The Viet Minh carried out a guerrilla campaign against the Japanese, provided intelligence to allied forces, and spread propaganda throughout the civilian population. All the while, Western political leaders warily surveyed the collapse of colonialism unfolding in Southeast Asia. For those looking past the fighting of World War II, Vietnam's independence movement portended a lengthy period of violent decolonization and global instability.[13]

For Ho Chi Minh and fellow nationalists, World War II more importantly provided the long awaited opportunity to declare independence. Following Japanese defeat in 1945, Ho proclaimed the Democratic Republic of Vietnam (DRV), invoking the American Declaration of Independence at a rally before hundreds of thousands of supporters. Given the widening ideological divide between American and Soviet allies, it did not take long for US policymakers to question Ho Chi Minh's legitimacy as a national leader. French authorities, seeking a return to colonial-era influence in Southeast Asia, eagerly fueled American anxieties over Ho's communist credentials. By late 1946, US diplomats already were expressing fear that Ho Chi Minh might establish a "communist-dominated, Moscow-oriented state."[14] The Truman administration thus cautiously acquiesced in the French return to Indochina. US policymakers no doubt struggled with the competing ideals of opposing a restoration of colonial rule and resisting communist influence at home and abroad. As war broke out once more in Indochina, the Americans seemed to have little choice in backing their French allies. In early 1947, Secretary of State George C. Marshall spoke for many

Washington officials when he emphasized that "we do not lose sight [of the] fact that Ho Chi Minh has direct Communist connections and it should be obvious that we are not interested in seeing colonial empire administrations supplanted by philosophy and political organizations emanating from and controlled by the Kremlin."[15]

Marshall's warning ensured that the outbreak of war in December 1946 would remain a largely French-Vietnamese affair. The French expeditionary corps, better equipped than General Vo Nguyen Giap's forces, found "la guerre sans fronts" frustrating in the extreme. Viet Minh troops once more conceded urban areas to their enemy while building support in the countryside for a protracted war of resistance. Guerrilla attacks slowly eroded French strength and by 1949 French strategy already had shifted to the defensive. As Giap parried his enemy's thrusts, he moved progressively from guerrilla hit-and-run tactics to more large-scale campaigns. As he recalled, the move was necessary "to annihilate big enemy manpower and liberate land."[16] All the while, the Viet Minh emphasized the political struggle which built up a "counter-state" that levied taxes, recruited soldiers, and disseminated propaganda. When Giap widened the war to Laos in 1953, the die was cast for a climactic battle at the border town of Dien Bien Phu. There, besieged French forces capitulated in early May 1954, a decisive battle (of which there had been few during the war) that fortuitously preceded a peace conference in Geneva that had been scheduled months before. French rule in Indochina would soon come to an ignominious end. Ho Chi Minh, enthused with success, spoke glowingly of the resistance struggle. "For the first time in history a small, weak colony has defeated a powerful colonial country. That was a glorious victory of the Vietnamese people and was also a victory of the forces of peace, democracy and socialism in the world."[17]

The peace conference, however, left Vietnam a divided state. Ho Chi Minh, though perhaps a disappointed revolutionary, realized that Dien Bien Phu had been a near run thing and that his communist forces were in need of a respite. Naturally, he had hoped for more at Geneva but other forces were at play, both home and abroad. China, fearing US military intervention in Indochina should the communists be seen as dominating Southeast Asia, helped limit DRV control of Vietnam to territory north of the seventeenth parallel. Communist allies had forced Ho to accept less than a complete victory. The Viet Minh, though, blamed US "imperialists" as the "principal obstacle to the restoration of peace in Indochina." While Ho set about consolidating his power in the north, the area south of the seventeenth parallel was, according to one CIA official, "in a state of political chaos bordering on anarchy."[18] Ngo Dinh Diem certainly faced greater challenges in preparing for elections that supposedly would unify Vietnam based on popular referendum. Unlike Ho Chi Minh, Diem confronted numerous competing religious sects, a displaced refugee population from the north, and a governmental structure weakened by decades of colonial rule. One CIA officer recalled that the "South Vietnamese government existed in name only, a collection of French-trained civil servants who didn't have a clue what to do without the French giving them orders. We didn't know if Diem would survive or even if South Vietnam would survive."[19]

When it became apparent that Diem would survive after his internal rivals' defeat during the 1955 battle of Saigon, the United States put its full weight behind the South Vietnamese leader. Though President Eisenhower financially had backed the French in Indochina, both civilian and military leaders resisted outright military support. Cold War imperatives, however, now forced the US administration's hand. Having "lost" the northern half of Vietnam to the communists, senior administration officials resolved to halt any further expansion. In short, a colonial struggle had become immersed in the larger Cold War conflict.[20] The implications for US grand strategy were enormous. For the next fifteen years, few Americans questioned the basic necessity of propping up the South Vietnamese government. Successive presidential administrations qualified Saigon's problems as inevasible to the larger goal of confronting communism. Eisenhower's team realized Diem held little purchase over the rural population yet acted as if the United States could render legitimacy on another government. Though an honest, dedicated man, Diem ineptly handled administrative duties, remained suspicious of subordinates, and rarely delegated authority. Most important for Americans, though, Diem committed himself to building an anti-communist South Vietnam. Given such credentials, US Ambassador Frederick E. Nolting Jr. believed "the Diem regime was the best available to govern South Vietnam."[21] In truth, Nolting, though a staunch supporter of Diem, saw few alternatives.

Diem soon would be tested, for the Geneva Convention produced no enduring solution to Vietnam's internal struggle over national identity. As the South Vietnamese president struggled to impose security across a politically fractured landscape, southern revolutionaries resisted using both political and military means. Increasingly, however, it became apparent that political defiance would be insufficient for contesting Diem's policies. In 1959, Le Duan, the Hanoi Politburo's First Secretary, lobbied successfully for a strategy that increased military action in the south. Competing factions inside the Politburo hotly debated the strategic alternatives, many North Vietnamese officials worrying that an emphasis on military action would draw the United States more deeply into the struggle.[22] Le Duan's views prevailed though the debate over Hanoi's strategy remained a constant for the war's remainder. More urgent for Diem's regime, Le Duan sponsored the formation of the National Front for the Liberation of South Vietnam (NLF). Pejoratively dubbed the Vietcong (VC or, more accurately, Vietnamese Communist traitor) by Diem, the broad-based front aimed for national unification through a tightly interwoven strategy of political influence, military engagement, and diplomatic initiatives. Almost immediately, Diem's governmental structure suffered terrorist attacks and political agitation from an enemy that inherited both experience and infrastructure from the Viet Minh.[23]

Thus, by the time American combat troops entered war, the Saigon government had been battling a full-fledged insurgency for nearly five years. Without question, Hanoi and the southern insurgency held the ideological advantage. They were the defenders of nationalism, propagandists trumpeted, not the "puppet" Diem who survived only because of the imperialistic Americans' largesse. As Giap noted of the French-Indochina conflict, the "Vietnamese people's war of liberation was a just war, aiming to win back the independence and unity of the country, to bring land to our peasants and guarantee them the right to it, and to defend the achievements of the August Revolution."[24] Political education, so important to a "people's war" approach, rested on a message that foreigners could not possibly counter. How, as an example, could Americans respond to NLF proselytism that extolled local histories of the Viet Minh and Front movements? How could American officers fully understand the patience of Vietnamese revolutionary leaders who already had been at war for 20 years by 1964? One colonel in the North Vietnamese Army well expressed the difficulties US Army officers soon would face in Vietnam. "The Vietnamese Communists and the Americans had very different ideas about the war. When the Americans came to Vietnam, they didn't bring with them a hatred for the Vietnamese people. But we had it for them!"[25]

Enter the Americans

Americans brought to Vietnam an unquestioned faith that halting further communist expansion in Southeast Asia served US national security interests. The United States' credibility as a global power rested on the successful defense of South Vietnam. As Harry C. McPherson, special counsel to President Johnson, recalled, "losing to the new mode of aggression, or failing to resist it, would raise doubts in the minds of others with whom we were allied."[26] Vietnam thus fit easily into the grand strategy of containment. If the United States acted weak in one area of the globe, inaction would encourage aggression elsewhere. Perhaps ironically, many military officers did not share the alarmist views of the "domino" theorists. Senior military men questioned whether Laos, Indonesia, and India all would fall if South Vietnam crumbled under communist pressure. The Joint Chiefs of Staff Strategic Plans Committee argued as early as 1951 that "even limited involvement in Vietnam 'could only lead to a dilemma similar to that in Korea, which is insoluble by military action.' "[27] Fear of appearing ineffectual against the global communist threat, however, overwhelmed such warnings.

In August 1950 a small military advisory group arrived in Saigon to assist French efforts against the Viet Minh. A formal US Military Assistance Advisory Group (MAAG) was formed the following month. As American military aid funneled into French and allied units, US military advisors took their first steps toward training Vietnamese forces. After the Geneva Conference, the MAAG assumed far greater responsibilities, yet immediately faced challenges. As one US official recalled, "When we started the war there was no American in the embassy in Saigon who could speak Vietnamese."[28] More significantly, MAAG officers found their host army in disarray. The Vietnamese had no centralized planning staff, an insubstantial logistical system, and a command structure controlled by numerous region commanders. Worse, the Americans saw a need to train local forces to defend against an external attack from the north while also defeating an internal insurgency in the south. To be successful, the MAAG had to reform an entire nation's armed forces to combat a multifaceted political-military threat without being seen as a colonial surrogate by the local population. Unsurprisingly, Vietnamese officers viewed their early American advisors with suspicion. As one US Army colonel noted: "Their recent freedom from French domination, and considering themselves combat experienced veterans, made the majority of the military reluctant to accept any MAAG recommendations or advice."[29]

The Army of the Republic of Vietnam (ARVN) garnered most of the Americans' attention. Officially created in December 1955, the ARVN was, in essence, a renamed version of the Vietnamese National Army that fought alongside the French Expeditionary Corps against the Viet Minh. (The fact that these troops were linked to Vietnam's colonial past was not lost on the civilian population.) MAAG recommended a force structure of 150,000, consisting of four conventional infantry divisions and six "territorial" divisions. The breakdown hinted at the ARVN's dual role—defending the country from outside aggression and establishing internal security. US Army officers, fresh off their experiences in Korea, leaned naturally toward preparing for an invasion from the north.[30] Yet these same officers did not narrowly define the ARVN's mission solely in conventional terms. Lieutenant General Samuel T. Williams, MAAG's chief from 1955 to 1960, recognized "that any attack from the north would certainly be accompanied by flaming guerrilla activity from guerrilla forces already in place." While MAAG staff planners surveyed possible invasion routes into South Vietnam (their main concern), they concurrently developed ARVN training programs for counterinsurgency operations. Debate over the nature of the enemy threat would persist throughout the coming decade and bedevil American strategists in Vietnam. It seems unmerited, however, to argue that US Army officers in the

1950s cared only about conventional warfare. They could not ignore the main force threat from the north. But they also grasped the domestic insurgent threat against Diem's regime.[31]

Williams's tenure at MAAG serves as a relevant case study. Known as "Hanging Sam" to his peers, Williams assumed command from Lieutenant General John W. O'Daniel in November 1955. Within a month, the new MAAG chief prepared a paper on "Guerrilla Operations" that echoed contemporary US doctrine. "Military operations alone are not sufficient for success as there are really two objectives: the destruction of the guerrilla force and the elimination of the Communist influence on the civilian population." Williams added that an "over-all plan at Government level embracing political, psychological, economic, administrative and military action is necessary for success."[32] Five years later, MAAG's chief spoke in similar, holistic terms when discussing the unconventional aspect of warfare in South Vietnam. Williams opined in early 1960 that to be "successful, anti-guerilla operations must be based on a broad, realistic plan that coordinates political, administrative and military phases of the operations." Few doctrine writers at the time would have disagreed. Without question, MAAG concentrated more on creating an ARVN capable of meeting a conventional North Vietnamese threat, one likely to be subsidized by China and the Soviet Union. Throughout his term, though, "Hanging Sam" backed initiatives to counter the revolutionary menace inside South Vietnam's borders even while his eyes remained fixed on the threat from beyond those borders.[33]

South Vietnam's internal political situation surely prompted such initiatives. Senior Americans reported in late 1954 and early 1955 on the "chaotic" nature of Saigon's government and suggested that internal turmoil, not external aggression, was destabilizing South Vietnam. Once more taking their cue from US counterinsurgency doctrine, MAAG officers sponsored programs aimed at providing population security while Diem sought to gain control over a tumultuous political scene. The creation of the Self-Defense Corps and the Civil Guard revealed the importance of domestic security. Both forces—the former a static village militia, the latter a mobile militia for district patrolling—gained increasing attention, and funding, from the US mission in Vietnam.[34] MAAG hoped these paramilitary forces might provide local security, allowing ARVN divisions to concentrate on the North Vietnamese main force threat. In one sense, Westmoreland later would attempt to replicate this division of labor in his own strategic concept, with American troops providing a protective shield behind which South Vietnamese troops could tackle territorial security missions. In short, both Williams and his successors understood full well the distinct characteristics of this new conflict. The war for South Vietnam's survival was at once a civil war and a cross-border attempt by Hanoi to unify the country.[35]

Predictably, Diem focused most of his efforts on policing insurrectionists who sought to topple his unsteady regime. In the process, the ARVN became an indispensable tool for suppressing political opposition, allowing Diem to favor security issues over social concerns and economic development. The South Vietnamese president tellingly insisted that work on pacification be called "national security action," a term coined by Lansdale. (A new law in 1959 even allowed roving military tribunals to sentence to death anyone convicted of sabotage.) Diem's focus partly reflected American notions of countering insurgencies in which population security preceded any governmental reform efforts. The president's heavy-handed approach produced results, yet at a high cost. As one NLF official recalled, by the end of 1958 "Diem had succeeded brilliantly in routing his enemy and arrogating power. But he had also alienated large segments of the South Vietnamese population, creating a swell of animosity throughout the country."[36] Americans equally took notice. Acknowledging both the enemy's rising terrorist campaign and potential coup threats against Diem, US officials still worried that the Saigon government was "placing increasing reliance on military measures for producing stability and relatively less emphasis on popular political, economic and social measures." Ellen Hammer, a Southeast Asia scholar, well summarized contemporary concerns. "Political stability," Hammer wrote in late 1957, "in the long run requires more than the suppression of political opposition."[37]

Diem, of course, was fighting not only for his own political (if not personal) survival but that of South Vietnam as well. Le Duan's support for a more active approach to the southern revolutionary movement kept South Vietnamese security forces occupied throughout the late 1950s. A Saigon newspaper reported at the end of 1957 that, "the menace is heavier than ever with the terrorists no longer limiting themselves to the notables in charge of security. Everything suits them—village chiefs, chairman of liaison committees, simple village guards and even former notables."[38] Diem, thus, could ill afford to ignore the growing threat inside his country's borders. In one sense, each side escalated military action in response to the other. The ARVN, however, did little to endear Diem to his people. Colonel Edward Lansdale, reporting in mid-1958, described how the South Vietnamese "man in uniform was not the best representative of the new government—he was accustomed to mistreating civilians at check-points and to obtaining his food gratis from civilians by the weapons he carried." Lansdale went on to depict the insurgent who, in sharp contrast, "conscientiously made friends with civilians as a helpful comrade." Most MAAG officers, full from a diet of Maoist theory, appreciated the magnitude of the insurgent "fish" being able to swim freely in the "sea" of the people. Even latent sympathies from the population afforded revolutionary forces vital advantages in shelter and intelligence.[39]

By the time Lieutenant General Lionel C. McGarr replaced Williams as the MAAG chief in September 1960, few if any American officers viewed the conflict in South Vietnam solely through conventional lenses. McGarr, fresh from his assignment at the Command and Staff College, brought to Saigon an extensive study from the Fort Leavenworth staff on the southern insurgency. (Notably, the study detailed the French experience against the Viet Minh.) Despite his conventional service in World War II and Korea, the general well understood the importance of countering the internal challenge to Diem's regime. McGarr, however, arrived only a few months before the NLF's official formation and confronted an enemy increasingly committed to military action.[40] The rise in violence presented a dilemma for the new MAAG chief. It would have been "erroneous," McGarr recalled, to place "the pacification wagon before the security horse." While realizing the necessity for political and social reforms, the general also saw clearly that the "army was the only power of government which had [an] infrastructure throughout the country to any degree at all." To make matters worse, Diem's inchoate command structure meant the ARVN, Civil Guard, and Self Defense Corps rarely operated in a cohesive manner.[41] South Vietnamese realities plainly were limiting American strategic designs.

Undeterred, McGarr pushed forward with a focus on counterinsurgency. As he noted soon after leaving Vietnam, "My concept at that time was clearing and holding, and I never changed that concept. I felt that you had to clear and hold the areas in between your villages, your hamlets, your big cities, and your ports." McGarr worked mightily to reorganize, retrain, and employ the Civil Guard for "anti-insurgency operations." At the same time, he codified his approach to US advisors with a meticulous publication titled "Tactics & Techniques of Counter-Insurgent Operations." Echoing doctrine—unsurprisingly given McGarr's previous assignment—"Tactics & Techniques" argued that "Guerrilla Warfare needs to be viewed in the overall 'Political-Military' context, as the primary answer to its *military* success is the basic fact that it has its roots in *prior psycho-political* action."[42] In other documents, the MAAG chief spoke of the struggle for gaining control of the population and of population security requiring "more than an initial sweep of the area to drive out the terrorists." McGarr also addressed the problems of force structure and the need for creating a national organization to confront the insurgency.[43] It seems unlikely that President Kennedy could have found a more loyal servant to apply counterinsurgency theories so in vogue in the early 1960s. Yet despite MAAG's genuine focus on combating the NLF's combined political-military threat, conditions inside South Vietnam seemed only to worsen. By October 1961, the Joint Chiefs soberly remarked that Southeast Asia was "now critical from a military viewpoint."[44]

Given President Kennedy's approval of a "Basic Counterinsurgency Plan for Viet-Nam" ten months earlier, the Joint Chiefs' assessment highlighted the limitations of what the United States could achieve in South Vietnam. The CIP, as it was called, had three broad aims: to defeat the insurgency while maintaining the ARVN's capacity to meet external aggression; to establish political stability and improve economic conditions; and to stop infiltration flowing across South Vietnam's borders.[45] As will be seen, Westmoreland's own concept of operations included all three CIP objectives. At the time, however, McGarr failed to persuade Diem into fully supporting the plan and possessed little capacity to match the NLF's advantages in ideology and propaganda. MAAG had no answer to the Front's claim that it was the "sole legitimate representative of the South Vietnamese people." While Kennedy officials initially viewed the CIP with optimism, by late fall reports from Vietnam suggested a deteriorating situation. In September, MAAG reported "mounting indications of [a] significant increase in Viet Cong capabilities" and an "increase in size and aggressiveness of Viet Cong actions."[46] Equally crucial, the NLF appeared to be effectively opposing Diem on the political front. One Party treatise, "Needs of the Revolution," suggested cadres "choose the right moment to act…when the people's rights have been endangered." Such threats from the Saigon government included "corruption, high taxation, forced money donations, land robbing, [and] military draft."[47] Thus, while the CIP envisioned a comprehensive approach to combating the NLF insurgency, the plan failed to gain traction against an enemy well-positioned to parry American thrusts.

By 1962, McGarr found his support among Washington officials fading. Frustrated with ARVN inefficiencies and governmental ineptitude, the MAAG chief's relationship with Diem soured. Few Americans on the ground seemed all that surprised. Lieutenant Colonel John Paul Vann, advising the ARVN 7th Division, found that ARVN operations merely "pushed the guerrillas into hiding or flight, in the way a ship displaced water. The moment they departed, the guerrillas flowed back." One sympathetic CIA analyst also appreciated McGarr's political difficulties, noting that the "absence of a visible political rationale to undergird the Saigon government's counterinsurgency effort plagued American efforts throughout the war."[48] The CIP's failure thus suggested to the Kennedy administration that South Vietnam's survival required more than just American guidance on how to counter insurgencies. A massive escalation of US advisors denoted the change in strategic approach. The number of military personnel in South Vietnam climbed from 3,200 in December 1961 to 11,325 by the end of 1962. There seemed, however, to have been no serious strategic reappraisal leading to this decision. The only US response to this situation seems to have been "more." McGarr later recalled that when he left for Vietnam he was "briefed on a peace time situation," yet when he arrived he "found that there was a war time situation. Actually we had a brutal, vicious hot war against President Diem."[49] As the outgoing MAAG chief departed Saigon in July 1962, most all US Army officers realized the "hot war" in Vietnam was entering a new, even more vicious phase.

An Abortive Strategy for a Hot Cold War

Prior to McGarr's departure, President Kennedy authorized formation of the US Military Assistance Command, Vietnam (MACV). The headquarters, established on 8 February 1962, subsumed MAAG due to its responsibility "for all U.S. military policy, operations and assistance" in South Vietnam. Intensified pressure on Diem from the NLF no doubt helped birth the new command. So too—and perhaps more important—did reports from Maxwell Taylor and Walt Rostow, who returned from an October 1961 trip to Vietnam with a bleak assessment and a call to reverse the "present downward trend of events." General Paul Harkins, a protégé of Taylor who had served as Patton's chief of staff in World War II, took the reins at a time when US advisors were focusing nearly all their efforts on the NLF insurgency. The mission bestowed upon MACV, however, demonstrated once more the multifaceted nature of the threat to South Vietnam. Harkins was to "assist and support the Government of Vietnam in its efforts to provide for its internal security, defeat communist insurgency, and resist overt aggression."[50] While the new commander acknowledged the value of winning the allegiance of the people, critics expressed their doubts. One journalist felt Harkins "lacked curiosity about his war," while a Kennedy administration official believed the MACV head "never saw that the central principle of the concept was the need to subordinate military measures to a political and social program." No doubt the American organizational structure in Vietnam—in which the US ambassador held responsibility for political matters, while MACV concentrated on the war's military aspects—drove Harkins's focus toward combating the enemy in the field.[51]

Rising NLF attacks across South Vietnam also placed pressure on Harkins to respond in kind. Population security, the mantra of counterinsurgency doctrine, necessitated a martial approach to the guerrilla and terrorist threats. Harkins may not have been the most thoughtful of officers, but clearly his enemy in Hanoi was intensifying the fighting. As the MACV commander claimed, in what would become a popular refrain among US officers, "the main thing was the infiltration from Laos and Cambodia."[52] Diem's fears of a coup nevertheless prevented a unified response to the dual threat of insurgency and infiltration. Worse, it appeared that Diem failed to appreciate the relationship between the insurgency and his often repressive response to it. In such an environment, MACV struggled mightily to develop—and persuade the Saigon government to pursue—a coherent strategy against National Liberation Front and Hanoi forces. Harkins and his staff in truth were at odds on how to proceed. Lacking unanimity over strategy, MACV officers debated the relative values of counterinsurgency, ARVN command arrangements, pacification, and border control. It would be erroneous, though, to assume contemporary officers viewed these strategic challenges in strict military terms. As one American advisor, assigned to the Mekong Delta region, maintained, "Most of us are sure that this problem is only fifteen per cent military and eighty-five per cent social and economic. It's not just a matter of killing the Viet Cong but of coupling security with welfare."[53]

MACV thus began a study of strategic options with the foundational notion that any approach required a wide-ranging set of political, social, economic, and military initiatives. True, Harkins himself seemed disoriented by this new form of war. The resultant National Campaign Plan for 1963, however, called for a series of undertakings aimed at destroying enemy strongholds, clearing and holding key areas dominated by the NLF, and achieving some degree of border control. These undeniably were military tasks, yet the MACV commander accepted that the problem was "complex" and involved "almost the whole of human endeavor."[54] Harkins envisioned "full-scale coordinated operations exploding at every level from the rice roots to the national level." The ambitious plan, dubbed "Operation Explosion," rested on the assumption that the NLF ran "the gamut of all governmental functions from the political to military to economic and sociological. Action against him, then, must also be all-inclusive to be successful." Harkins also acknowledged that "control of the people is a matter of extreme importance" and sought to wrestle NLF influence away from the population. Whether the ARVN and Saigon political leadership could support such a nationwide offensive remained to be seen. Harkins, a perpetual optimist, supposed—without much evidence—that US training and assistance efforts over the last two years had left an ARVN ready for the challenge. And he seemed to have been left to his own devices, with little guidance from Washington, DC.[55]

In fact, Harkins's strategic plans quickly became overwhelmed by the complexities of the South Vietnamese political-military battlefield. Critics charged that Harkins was at fault, one officer accusing the MACV chief of being "totally insensitive to all the political considerations" of the war effort. Yet clearly other issues were at play, even if Harkins spent much of his time on the "Three M's" of men, money, and materiel. A January 1963 CIA report found the US-backed counterinsurgency effort "blunted by the [Saigon] government's political modus operandi" and concluded provincial administration was a "major weakness."[56] Other US officials observed substantial problems within South Vietnam's armed forces. Roger Hilsman, director of the State Department's Bureau of Intelligence and Research, reported that the ARVN continued to rely on "large-scale operations and conventional tactics"— partially a byproduct of the American advisory effort—and that "political interference by the Vietnamese leadership" was restricting initiative in the field. (Many American advisors did discourage their ARVN counterparts from undertaking large operations, with only marginal success.) Hilsman also criticized GVN pacification efforts which had been "precipitous and uncoordinated" and "slow to be implemented." Further frustrating MACV's strategic approach, South Vietnamese economic growth had not matched the large amounts of external aid provided by the United States.[57] If Harkins tended to view South Vietnam's problems through a military lens, he also confronted a host of problems well outside the military sphere.

Few, if any, of these strategic problems could be assessed with any level of certainty. Harkins traveled the countryside frequently to evaluate the condition and effectiveness of the Vietnamese armed forces and complained personally to Diem about serious officer shortages and problems with army leadership. Yet the status of the RVNAF, and even the enemy's own force structure, defied easy explication. Auguring future debates over the National Liberation Front's "order of battle," CIA analysts and MACV intelligence officers sparred over how to "count" enemy militia elements, political cadre, and part-time soldiers. Reports from the field on pacification efforts likewise created more confusion than clarity. The MACV staff later noted that "pacification reports from the beginning were in a constant state of flux because of a continuing search for meaningful basis of comparison between past and present."[58] How, as an example, should Harkins and his team evaluate political corruption at the village or district level? If the nature of the conflict truly was political, were military successes against insurgent forces more or less important than political reform if population security remained the starting point for any effective counterinsurgency plan? All the while, it seemed doubtful that American officers could strengthen Diem's popular support among the rural peasantry. The rising number of US military personnel serving in South Vietnam—over 11,000 by the end of 1962—exposed Saigon officials to NLF propaganda claims of being little more than American "puppets."[59]

Nowhere were these problems more appreciable than in the strategic hamlet program. Ostensibly modeled on the British approach of resettling civilians into government-protected strongholds during the Malayan emergency, Diem and his brother Ngo Dinh Nhu also drew heavily from French counterinsurgency theories when they launched the program in late 1961.[60] The basic concept centered on extending the government's authority and services throughout the countryside while concomitantly protecting the civilian population from NLF influence. Harkins had little choice but to back the strategic hamlets which totaled over 4,000 by early 1963. The sudden upsurge of numbers worried advisors, one of whom noted that if Nhu's strategic villages were "*all* strategic, *none* are strategic."[61] To Southeast Asia expert Bernard Fall, provincial chiefs, eager to display progress, too often "declared a hamlet 'strategic' when it had received a few strands of barbed wire and a few old hunting guns; while others had exerted dire pressure on the population to provide free construction services for jobs that should have been remunerated."[62] Equally problematic, the NLF more easily could target relocated civilians who had been uprooted from their ancestral homelands. The strategic hamlets decidedly limited the insurgents' freedom of movement, but only temporarily. Nhu simply had set unrealistic goals. In attempting to do "all things at all places at the same time," the strategic hamlet program crumpled from lack of focus and from governmental overreach.[63]

Harkins, ever the optimist, tended to downplay the difficulties in South Vietnam typified by the strategic hamlet program. While Diem continued to alienate influential segments of the population like the Buddhists, and the NLF increased its ranks through local recruitment, MACV stressed the positive. An early 1963 MACV summary claimed that "barring greatly increased resupply and reinforcement of the Viet Cong by infiltration, the military phase of the war can be virtually won in 1963."[64] Impatient White House officials no doubt placed pressure on Harkins to demonstrate progress and many US civil and military officials in fact shared the general's optimism. The MACV chief also had to consider how bad news might cause political problems for his South Vietnamese allies. Yet Harkins's unbound confidence helped to cloud the strategic decision-making process. How could the war truly be won militarily if neither the ARVN nor their US advisors had been able to confront the infiltration problem? If South Vietnam's borders remained porous, what strategic changes did the White House and MACV headquarters need to consider? Harkins's subordinates certainly asked these questions and challenged the sanguine reporting, but the commander paradoxically downplayed any criticism while telling Diem that the "VC are still everywhere." Worse, Harkins allegedly edited intelligence reports "so as not to convey any lack of 'headway' in the war effort."[65] The battle over reporting "progress" would not lessen in the coming years.

For now, the debate revolved increasingly around the Buddhist crisis that erupted in the spring and summer of 1963. Challenging not only Diem's oppressive domestic policies but the very presence of Americans in Vietnam, the Buddhists' protests validated for many Americans the lack of political stability in Saigon. Henry Cabot Lodge, who had succeeded Nolting as ambassador, tended to view Diem as an obstacle, arguing that the Nhu brothers had lost the confidence of the army and, more important, the country's rural population. The South Vietnamese president fired back, howling that "They can send ten Lodges, but I will not permit myself or my country to be humiliated, not if they train their artillery on this Palace."[66] By September, the ambassador and MACV commander visibly were at odds. Lodge cabled President Kennedy that the NLF was "steadily gaining in strength" and that the "Heart of the Army is *not* in the war." Harkins retorted that "All is not black. No, far from it." In a message to Pacific Command, the general noted that he remained "as optimistic as ever, particularly on the military side, and I firmly believe there is reason for optimism in some of the other spheres." Harkins observed that Diem had lifted military law and relaxed press censorship while the ARVN had done well in "countering several larger than usual VC attacks."[67] (How these larger attacks represented progress, Harkins did not say.) It seems doubtful that any officer watching the Lodge-Harkins debate unfold judged the war simply as a conventional affair between armies. Politics unquestionably was driving the war.

The political crisis came to a head in early November 1963 with the overthrow and murder of Ngo Dinh Diem. While Lodge had indirectly supported the coup after obtaining the president's reluctant approval for a change in Saigon leadership, US officials were ill prepared to deal with the political fallout that followed. Kennedy, visibly shaken by Diem's death, would be assassinated in Dallas, Texas, only three weeks later. Inside South Vietnam, the NLF reaped the rewards by exploiting the political chaos. Coup followed coup in Saigon. Over the next eighteen months, US advisors struggled to find constancy as twelve different governments assumed nominal control of the country. Pacification efforts screeched to a standstill. One MACV officer believed the coup equally had "discredited and demoralized" the GVN police forces. "The Viet Cong, in consequence, had gained greater freedom of action in all but strictly military endeavors. The field was open for increased Viet Cong emphasis on sabotage, terrorism, proselytizing and other forms of political subversion."[68] The coup's aftermath surely discredited Harkins's upbeat reporting, even if the MACV chief warned Diem's overthrow would have dire consequences. More important, the coup convinced Kennedy's successor that American advice alone no longer could sustain a noncommunist South Vietnam. Diem's death thus had a tremendous impact on US strategy. If Lyndon B. Johnson was to maintain American prestige in Southeast Asia, Americans would need to revise their strategic concepts of simply advising indigenous civil and military leaders.[69]

Johnson wasted little time in reinforcing the grand strategic objectives for South Vietnam. On 26 November 1963, the president issued National Security Action Memorandum (NSAM) 273 which opened with a clear commitment to containing the communist threat in Southeast Asia. "It remains the central object of the United States in South Vietnam to assist the people and Government of that country to win their contest against the externally directed and supported Communist conspiracy."[70] While devaluing the southern-based insurgency, NSAM 273 unmistakably obliged the United States to deeper

Figure 2.1 THE TRAINING OF AN ARMY. CPT Eugene J. Wyles, Senior Advisor to the 2nd Battalion, 33rd ARVN Infantry, assists a South Vietnamese soldier with his weapon in Choung Thien Province, 22 July 1964. (RG 111-CV, NARA, 56)

responsibilities that would lead to war. Was this a reconceptualization of grand strategy or simply escalation? Assessments from Saigon spoke of mounting terrorist attacks, serious economic issues, and unrelenting political factionalism. After a two-day trip to Vietnam in December, Secretary of Defense McNamara reported on a "very disturbing" situation in which current trends, "unless reversed in the next 2–3 months, will lead to neutralization at best and more likely to a Communist-controlled state." Deputy MACV Commander William Westmoreland concurred with McNamara's assessment, recalling that politically "we were operating on a shoestring." Of the post-coup atmosphere, Harkins's second cracked that it "was like pushing a piece of spaghetti to get anything done."[71]

To the last, however, the MACV chief put a positive spin on South Vietnam's internal affairs. In June 1964, Harkins departed Saigon, handing command over to his deputy. Maxwell Taylor assumed the ambassadorship the following month, cleaning the slate for a fresh approach to the war effort. (The relationship between Harkins and Ambassador Lodge had become so dysfunctional by early 1964 that the two virtually had no official contact with each other.)[72] The *New York Times* announced that the retiring Harkins retained "the confident and optimistic tone he has employed throughout his service here in the face of military reverses and press criticism." Other senior officers, speaking anonymously with the press, offered a more uncertain outlook, one noting that the "Vietcong are better armed, more competent and more ornery." While Harkins agreed that the NLF had improved over the course of his command, he believed, with questionable justification, the South Vietnamese government was "in a better position" to counter the threat. Additionally, the outgoing commander expressed in a news conference that MACV ought to resist assuming full control of the ground war in Vietnam. The American military command's function, Harkins claimed, should continue to be one of advice and support. "We've just got to keep on doing what we have been doing," the general insisted.[73] President Johnson and worried policymakers in Washington thought otherwise.

Toward War with Westmoreland

By June 1964, William Childs Westmoreland had been serving in South Vietnam for nearly six months. As Harkins's deputy, the South Carolina native and former West Point first captain spent much of his time serving as a mediator between the embassy and MACV headquarters. He saw firsthand the ramifications of overoptimistic reporting and took note of senior officers' criticisms of American policy in Vietnam. Most important, Westmoreland learned of the war's political nature. "Despite the military nature of my assignment in South Vietnam," he recalled, "it was impossible to keep my activities entirely separate from the political turmoil that soon gripped the country, in large measure because most of those in the center of the turmoil were the military leaders with whom I had to deal."[74] The deputy position afforded Westmoreland an opportunity to develop his own strategic ideas, study the relationship between civil and military action in a wartime environment, and weigh the possibility of increased American authority in South Vietnam. In one sense, Westmoreland agreed with Harkins on enlarging the US role. Given that he was "astonished at the state of affairs" when he first arrived in Saigon, the new MACV commander warned against American escalation until US leaders were assured that the GVN was "established on [a] reasonably firm political, military, and psychological base."[75]

Westmoreland's initial assessments as MACV commander belie allegations of a simple-minded officer who failed to grasp the complexities of the war in which he found himself. True, the general's service in conventional units during World War II and Korea had influenced his professional outlook. He saw combat in North Africa and Europe in the Second World War and commanded an infantry regimental combat team during the Korean conflict. In the 1950s, Westmoreland's star continued to rise; he became secretary of the Army General

Staff under Maxwell Taylor before taking command of the 101st Airborne Division.[76] Duty with combat units, however, was matched by assignments that broadened Westmoreland intellectually. He taught at the Army War College in 1951 and attended the Advanced Management Program at Harvard University in 1954. A peer depicted the general as "more than just a fine physical specimen; he was thoughtful, sensitive, and very shrewd."[77] If Westmoreland was preoccupied with his public image, he also had demonstrated from his days at West Point an ability to both manage and lead in an effective manner. True, like the army in which he served, he had little to no practical experience in counterinsurgency. Yet Westmoreland watched carefully the events in Southeast Asia and prepared himself and his units for what increasingly seemed an unavoidable war.

Nowhere was this truer than at West Point, where Westmoreland served as the superintendent from 1960 to 1963. The new academy head took a special interest in revolutionary and insurgency warfare, not only overseeing the creation of the Counterinsurgency Committee but seeking advice from peer academic institutions. In June 1962, the superintendent wrote to MIT's Lucien W. Pye, a leading Asia scholar, asking him to serve as a consultant on counterinsurgency instruction. As Westmoreland noted, an "emphasis at the national level" necessitated a review of the academy's current instruction. The academy also hosted a spring 1963 conference, "New Nations and Their Internal Defense," during which Walt Rostow and a number of other national policymakers spoke to cadets and faculty.[78] Brigadier Richard G. Stilwell, the academy's commandant, further ensured that cadets came into contact with officer alumni who were gaining experience in Southeast Asia. As Stilwell remarked, the "antennae of the graduates are highly sensitized to the realities of the world scene and to the comprehensive, integrated nature of the Communist threat." Westmoreland, aware of these realities, even helped David Galula, later recognized as "the U.S. Army's patron saint of counterinsurgency," secure a research position at Harvard University's Center for International Affairs.[79] Clearly, this was not a senior American officer wedded to narrow, conventional concepts of warfare.

Westmoreland, only 49 when he reached Saigon, brought the same intellectual inquisitiveness he displayed at West Point to MACV headquarters. He visited Malaya as Harkins's deputy, yet rightly found the British experience there "had some but not much relevance to ours." If the social and economic conditions of Malaya did not match those of Vietnam, the conflict's length did impress Westmoreland. When asked in early 1965 how long the war against Hanoi might take, the general warned "It could be a long, drawn-out campaign. In Malaya it took twelve years."[80] Warnings of a lengthy war would be one of Westmoreland's constant refrains as MACV's commander. So too were his concerns over political instability in South Vietnam and the role of pacification in the allied war effort. Only a few days after Westmoreland's arrival, General Nguyen Kanh

overthrew Duong Van Minh in one of the many coups crippling Saigon politics. The incoming general needed little more proof that US-South Vietnamese
military cooperation rested on a shaky political foundation. Still, senior US
Army officers tendered their advice. From Fort Bragg's Special Warfare Center,
General William Yarborough, himself a top candidate for the MACV position,
wrote Westmoreland in February 1964 that "I cannot emphasize too greatly that
the entire conflict in Southeast Asia is 80 percent in the realm of ideas and only
20 percent in the field of physical conflict."[81]

Westmoreland thus had much to consider as he prepared to take charge of
MACV. Most important, the new commander wrestled with the problems of
redefining military strategy to support the Johnson administration's objectives
laid out in NSAM 273 and MACV's mission statement. Westmoreland recalled
that pacification was "the ultimate goal of both the Americans and the South
Vietnamese government," yet worried that an increased US presence would create friction "between our forces and the very people we were trying to help."[82]
Maxwell Taylor agreed. The US ambassador, along with the Joint Chiefs who
recognized that chronic political instability threatened future military success,
held deep reservations about committing ground forces to Southeast Asia. In a
November 1964 paper, Taylor thought it "highly unlikely" he would see a GVN
capable of reversing the "downward trend of events." Presciently, the ambassador admitted that the "objective of an improved counterinsurgency campaign
will depend for its feasibility upon the capacity of the South Vietnamese government."[83] The concerns of Westmoreland and Taylor, however, while making an
impression on Johnson and senior administration officials, already had become
overshadowed by events in South Vietnam.

In early August, US destroyers had engaged North Vietnamese torpedo
boats in the Gulf of Tonkin. The incidents, still controversial to this day, enabled
Johnson to secure from Congress a resolution taking "all necessary measures to
repel any armed attacks against the forces of the United States and to prevent
further aggression."[84] The resolution gave the president an expedient justification for showing strength against Hanoi during an election cycle, while also
demonstrating solidarity with his South Vietnamese allies. More important,
the Tonkin incident compelled Johnson to accept greater responsibility for the
south's survival. From all quarters, the news in Vietnam seemed discouraging.
Pacification efforts were bogged down. NLF units continued to rebuild. Saigon
politics remained chaotic. Reports from the Secretary of Defense, who had visited South Vietnam earlier in the year, verified the worsening situation. While
McNamara underscored the limits of present policy—"the South Vietnamese
must win their own fight"—he did recommend plans for increased US pressure
against North Vietnam. As he recalled, the administration was nearing a point
where it "had to choose between two alternatives: either expand our military

support of Vietnam or withdraw." If Johnson was not to "lose" South Vietnam like Truman "lost" China, escalation seemed the only option.[85]

Events in the aftermath of Tonkin substantiated the president's belief for greater US involvement. In large sense, administration strategists did little more than react to the deteriorating situation in Vietnam. Throughout 1964, the enemy held the initiative, a point made clear from numerous sources. An October National Intelligence Estimate portrayed the conflict in "quite pessimistic" terms. Chairman of the Joint Chiefs Earle Wheeler cautioned that time was "indeed running out for us in South Vietnam with such speed that we should undertake some dramatic military action without delay...with the objective of assisting in creating a more stable political and military situation." From a senior US advisor came the recognition that NLF strategy derived "its greatest support from the political instability which plagued the Republic of Vietnam."[86] Between 1962 and 1964 alone, insurgents had assassinated over 6,000 governmental officials and kidnapped another 30,000 among the civilian population. Even the Front's claims of progress worried American policymakers. Westmoreland's headquarters noted that "enemy radio claimed at the end of 1964 that three-fourths of SVN had been 'liberated,' and forecast 'new and greater victories.'" Communist leaders seemed intent on escalating the war as rapidly as possible and forcing the Americans' hand to abandon their South Vietnamese allies.[87]

Westmoreland well appreciated the difficulties he faced. Gradually, the MACV staff, taking its cue from Washington, underwent a transition, becoming increasingly more involved with the military aspects of ARVN operations as the number of US military personnel inside South Vietnam rose. Still, Westmoreland's focus remained on the political aspects of the growing conflict. In June 1964, he cabled the Joint Chiefs on "an urgent need to coordinate pacification efforts in the provinces surrounding Saigon."[88] Three months later, Westmoreland forwarded an honest assessment to Taylor that spoke of morale and leadership problems within the ARVN, the difficulties of finding an "equitable division of responsibility between the national government and the local community," and the "orientation and training of military units for their pacification tasks." MACV's commander even sent a request to the Rand think tank to "study the evolution of a rural Vietnamese village as it passes from insurgent control through pacification to government control."[89] If the US mission was moving toward full-scale intervention, Westmoreland at least was emphasizing to his superiors and his staff the political nature of the war. In fact, both Ambassador Taylor and the MACV commander resisted the introduction of American ground forces because of their appreciation of the political atmosphere. In an October cable to the JCS chairman, Westmoreland expressed his concern that unless a "fairly effective government" existed in Saigon, "no amount of offensive action by the United States either in or outside of South Vietnam has any chance by itself of reversing the deterioration underway."[90]

The deteriorating political and military situation in South Vietnam, however, was driving strategy at the national level. By early 1965, the president, conscious of pessimistic CIA and MACV estimates, neared his decision to escalate the war through increased US commitment. Johnson worried that American passivity would damage his Cold War credibility abroad and diminish Republican support for his Great Society program at home. When NLF forces raided a US base at Pleiku on 7 February, killing eight Americans and wounding another 60, administration officials believed they had no choice but to retaliate. Johnson ordered air strikes against North Vietnamese targets—codenamed Operation Flaming Dart—that set the foundation for a 44-month air campaign against North Vietnam. The retaliation, though, appeared ineffectual.[91] In March, MACV reported the presence of an NVA battalion in Kontum province, intelligence that suggested "the possibility that other such units have also been infiltrated into the area." The Americans and their South Vietnamese allies no longer faced just NLF insurgents, but a combination of regular units from the north and revolutionary forces from the south. Westmoreland, sensing the change, began to lay the groundwork for a logistical buildup that ultimately would establish the foundation for a massive introduction of US ground troops. It was an impressive, if too often underappreciated, feat.[92]

While Westmoreland initially focused on building a supply and basing infrastructure, the reactive nature of US grand strategy forced him to respond in kind to the enemy's escalation. Johnson administration officials realized by early spring that Rolling Thunder, the bombing campaign that succeeded Flaming Dart, was proving inadequate for forcing Hanoi into negotiations. The president's response, however, appeared muddled. Assistant Secretary of State William Bundy later remarked that Johnson's strategic guidance "seemed much more like a series of *ad hoc* decisions" than the result of a deliberate decision-making process.[93] Westmoreland, hoping for some "stop-gap measure to save the ARVN from defeat," reluctantly requested the deployment of US ground forces to Southeast Asia. Clearly, MACV's commander in the spring of 1965 was doing little more than reacting to the evolving strategic situation. In Westmoreland's estimation, with the introduction of NVA regulars into South Vietnam the war had "moved out of the purely guerilla phase and into a more formalized military conflict." (Maoist theories still held sway over many an American officer.) For now, the MACV chief could employ only a "fire brigade" approach to meet enemy concentrations and respond to allied forces under attack.[94] Hanoi most definitely held the upper hand.

In early March, Johnson, still hoping that Rolling Thunder air strikes might hold the line in Vietnam, authorized the landing of two US Marine Corps battalions at

Da Nang to secure the local air base and installations. Westmoreland intended to use these initial American units for base security around the Da Nang "enclave." It did not take long, however, for the mission, and the troops to support that mission, to rapidly expand.[95] As Lieutenant General Victor Krulak, soon to be a critic of Westmoreland's strategy, recalled, the almost immediate call for additional manpower arose "because the Marines' concept, from the start, involved fighting the Vietnam battle as a multipronged effort. They aimed to bring peace and security to the people in the highly populated coastal regions by conducting aggressive operations against the guerrillas and expanding the pacified areas as rapidly as they were totally secured." Krulak also noted that the Marines planned to train and support local South Vietnamese forces against enemy insurgents while going "after the larger organized units whenever they could be definitely located and fixed." Despite later Marine criticisms of Westmoreland's concept of operations, this "balanced strategy," as Krulak dubbed it, would look remarkably similar to the MACV commander's own "multipronged" approach to the war in South Vietnam.[96]

The introduction of American ground troops heralded a clear break in US military strategy. From the spring of 1965 forward, MACV planners no longer concentrated solely on offering advice and support to the South Vietnamese but rather on waging war alongside their allies. Few if any senior officers believed the ARVN could hold the line any longer. In April, Secretary of Defense McNamara authorized the deployment of additional ground units to Vietnam, to include the 173rd Airborne Brigade. By early June, Westmoreland was asking for further reinforcements—44 combat maneuver battalions—because "force ratios" were changing in favor of the enemy. He was convinced that US troops could "successfully take the fight to the VC" and "give us a substantial and hard-hitting offensive capability on the ground to convince the VC that they cannot win."[97] The assumptions behind the rapid increase in American troops were many: the enemy was abandoning guerrilla warfare in favor of larger battles along the lines of Maoist theory; US force could influence Hanoi's will; and, perhaps most significant (and fallacious), population security would lead to political stability inside South Vietnam.

Westmoreland, along with most of Johnson's top advisors, presupposed that American military power could effect political change in a foreign land. Yet these senior leaders also believed military power alone could not sustain the Saigon government. The South Vietnamese, they rightly understood, bore primary responsibility for the political and social transformations so necessary for defeating the NLF insurgency. In a large sense then, the American view of South Vietnam rested on a contradiction. On one hand, most Americans never questioned their faith in military force being able to achieve larger political goals. On the other hand, they well accepted that force alone could not achieve their objectives. Such inconsistencies soon would be played out on the political-military battlefields south of the seventeenth parallel. Worse, only a small minority of key US decision makers suspected in mid-1965 that Hanoi's leaders might not be as easy to convince as the Americans had hoped.[98]

On the Tiger's Back

Lyndon Johnson believed he had little choice but to make a stand in Southeast Asia. The president, and far too many of his senior advisors, refrained from any serious reevaluation of Cold War containment policies or South Vietnam's assumed importance to US national security. As Johnson noted, in an oft-used historical analogy, "We know, from Munich, that when you give, the dictators feed on raw meat. If they take South Vietnam, they take Thailand, they take Indonesia, they take Burma, they come right back to the Philippines."[99] American policymakers thus took it as a matter of faith that US prestige would collapse and Southeast Asian countries would fall if the communists won in Vietnam. Honest evaluations of what truly could be accomplished in Vietnam, however, did not accompany the Johnson administration's deliberate march to war. At the grand strategic level, decision making more often focused on troop deployments and force levels rather than on how military strategy should be crafted to induce Hanoi into abandoning its nationalist objectives. Columnist Joseph Alsop spoke for many critics in early 1965 when he proclaimed that the "aimless drift that afflicts our Vietnamese policy making calls out for explanation."[100]

Certainly, concerns over national prestige go far in helping explain Johnson's decision for war. So too, of course, does the enemy's escalation. The MACV official history admitted that "the VC were winning the war" as 1965 began. "Throughout the country, the military and political initiative was with the enemy." Withdrawing from the communist challenge seemed unthinkable to the commander in chief and his cabinet officials. The volatility of Saigon politics equally played a role. As National Security Advisor McGeorge Bundy wrote the president in January, "the uncertainty and lack of direction which pervade Vietnamese authorities" meant that the US mission could "not go further until there is a stable government, and no one has much hope that there is going to be a stable government while we sit still."[101] Even Under Secretary of State George Ball, one of the few dissenters in Johnson's inner circle, believed the South Vietnamese were losing the war. Ball, though, worried the United States was heading toward a "long-term catastrophe" given its involvement in an Asian civil war. "Once on the tiger's back," he warned, "we cannot be sure of picking

Figure 2.2 A SUNDAY WITH WESTMORELAND. The MACV commander meets with a young private during one of his many tours of US Army bases in South Vietnam, August 1966. (Photograph by Thomas R. Koeniges with his permission)

the place to dismount." The administration's Vietnam policy might seem adrift, but no other options besides commitment looked palatable to a White House readying itself for war.[102]

The narrowing of strategic options that accompanied US troop deployments held significant implications for how William Westmoreland would devise a military strategy that he believed best positioned the United States for achieving its goals in South Vietnam. From mid-1965 on, decisions made at the grand strategic level would inform how the MACV commander developed and implemented military strategy. (Westmoreland, however, took little part in deliberations of grand strategy.) Yet importantly, the general was able to profit from the US Army's 15-year experience in Indochina. The strategy the MACV's chief developed benefited from the extended American advisory period which saw the French defeat, the rise of the National Liberation Front, and persistent political problems seemingly inherent in South Vietnamese society. A decade plus of American frustrations left Westmoreland under no illusions as he began to craft his strategy. As he told Army Chief of Staff Harold K. Johnson on 24 June 1965, "we are in for the long pull." Two days later he declared, "We are deluding ourselves if we feel some novel arrangement is going to get quick results. We must think in terms of an extended conflict; be prepared to support a greatly increased effort; give the commander on the scene the troops that he requires and the authority to deploy these troops in accordance with his best judgment."[103] Westmoreland's pleas made sense given the political and military difficulties of fighting such a complex war. Most notably, his conception of how to use American ground troops over the "long pull" would determine how the US armed forces fought inside South Vietnam for the next seven years.

3

The Myth of Attrition in Vietnam

If continuity best described American military strategy in Vietnam, the same could be said of US grand strategy. In March 1964, just two months after Westmoreland arrived in Saigon, the Johnson administration published NSAM 288 which established the "objective" in South Vietnam as a "stable and independent noncommunist government." Highlighting the interrelationships between Indochina and the larger Cold War, the national security memorandum maintained that the Republic of Vietnam (RVN) was a "politico/military keystone in Southeast Asia and is symbolic of U.S. determination in Asia as Berlin is in Europe—to prevent Communist expansion."[1] Though Johnson had approved escalating the war effort against Hanoi, he denied that the larger objectives had changed. The new strategy, the president explained, did not signify a change in "purpose," but only in "what we believe the purpose requires." The American advisory effort clearly had proved insufficient for achieving Johnson's larger objectives of removing North Vietnamese support and influence from the south. The implications of this failure were clear to the president. As Johnson pronounced in mid-1965, "If we are driven from the field in Vietnam, then no nation can ever again have the same confidence in American promises, or in American protection."[2]

The White House's decision to escalate the war, however, was not accompanied by deliberations over developing a coherent strategy for the employment of ground forces. In short, the Johnson administration concentrated on the scale and timing of troop deployments and the question of how many might be needed in 1965 and 1966, rather than on how to utilize those forces once they arrived in Vietnam. Robert S. McNamara later confessed that he had "erred by not forcing...a knock-down, drag-out debate over the loose assumptions, unasked questions, and thin analyses underlying our military strategy in Vietnam."[3] Certainly, the secretary of defense realized at the time the difficulties of fighting a war in Southeast Asia. His post-trip report to the president in July 1965 painted a dismal picture. The South Vietnamese economy was deteriorating. Pacification programs were making little progress. The secretary saw no signs that the inflow of supplies to the National Liberation Front (NLF) had been throttled. "Indeed more and better weapons have been observed in VC hands," McNamara reported. Yet despite these difficulties, the defense chief recommended the deployment of additional US ground troops and the approval of supplemental appropriations to finance the growing war effort. Nowhere did McNamara suggest a comprehensive strategy for tackling the political-military crisis in South Vietnam.[4]

Perhaps McNamara's reticence in recommending strategic options reflected the tradition of deferring to army commanders in the field once engaged in battle. Perhaps Johnson's inner circle, though wary of uniformed officers, believed it best to leave the details of warfighting to MACV and Pacific Command. Or perhaps, more plausibly, the problems of conceiving a larger strategy for Vietnam illustrated the complexities of defining the very word "strategy" for a war like Vietnam. As the United States edged toward open conflict, how to characterize the war upon which Johnson had decided posed numerous difficulties. As the president himself recalled, Vietnam "was a war of subversion, terror, and assassination, of propaganda, economic disruption, and sabotage. It was a political war, an economic war, and a fighting war—all at the same time."[5] To make matters worse, as soon as US troops entered South Vietnam, Johnson conceded a tremendous political advantage to Hanoi's leaders who portrayed the Americans in stark colonial terms. Thus, as Westmoreland set about his task of constructing a concept for the war inside South Vietnam, the Johnson administration had done little more than affirm US objectives and approve MACV's troop requests. Devising a strategy for gaining the political loyalty of the South Vietnamese population and securing military defeat of communist subversion and external aggression would be left to the general in the field.[6]

Critics who lambast the president for failing the test of strategic vision arguably conflate grand and military strategy in their evaluations of Johnson. Should the president and his inner circle have deliberated over how to employ US forces in Vietnam, or should that task have fallen to the MACV commander and his staff? (Ideally, any strategic deliberations should have been conducted without such rigid divisions of labor.) Surely, Johnson believed he was following a wise middle course by refusing the extremes of withdrawal or total escalation. Detractors at the time, and there were many, doubted the president's claim that an independent, noncommunist South Vietnam was vital to US national security. Even critics inside the administration worried that those deciding on war had not deeply concerned themselves with how the application of military force would achieve Johnson's political objectives. Could North Vietnam truly be pressured given the inherent weaknesses inside South Vietnam? Without question, the administration had failed to sustain a coordinated political-military-diplomatic effort to force Hanoi to abandon its quest for unification—if such an objective even was possible.[7] Yet to condemn Johnson for not developing a more sophisticated strategy for the war's *actual conduct* seems misplaced. The president's focus, rightfully so, was on grand strategy as defined by Liddell Hart. Recall that the British theorist believed good strategists allocated and coordinated national resources so the use of force would "avoid damage to the future state of peace." Johnson may have believed maintaining the territorial integrity and independence of South Vietnam essential, at least up to a point, but geopolitical fears of a wider war limited the resources he was willing to apply in Indochina.[8]

Johnson's ultimate decision for war, and his focus on larger aspects of the conflict, left Westmoreland to devise a military strategy for achieving the president's goals. While the Joint Chiefs remained in regular contact with the MACV commander, they deferred to the field commander in matters of strategy. It would be wrong to assume, however, that neither the White House nor the JCS influenced Westmoreland as he developed and adjusted his approach to war between 1964 and 1968. Strategy was a negotiated process throughout. In fact, MACV's mission statement induced Westmoreland to take a holistic approach to the problem of strategy. In 1965, as the general drafted his concept of operations, the mission of US forces in South Vietnam "was to assist and support the RVNAF [South Vietnamese Armed Forces] in their efforts to defeat communist subversive insurgency, and to accelerate effective GVN control over the country."[9] MACV thus confronted a military and political problem, one that few officers would have found surprising given the decade-long American experience in Vietnam. Because of this mission, Westmoreland did not subscribe to an attrition strategy aimed solely at killing the enemy. Engaging enemy forces, especially in unpopulated areas, formed a key pillar of MACV's operational concept. Still, given their understanding of the political dimensions of revolutionary warfare, Westmoreland and his staff unmistakably incorporated nonmilitary means into their strategic planning.[10]

The problem for Westmoreland, however, was identifying an approach, given the resources at hand, which raised the war's costs for North Vietnam within acceptable limits for both the United States and South Vietnam. Finding the enemy's repository of resistance, its "Achilles' heel," eluded the Americans for the war's duration. As one senior MACV officer noted, "after several months of combat in Vietnam, experience taught that there was no single element of the enemy's organization that, if attacked alone, would cause the collapse of his force structure or the reduction of his will to resist."[11] In classic strategic terms, a nation's capital was thought to be the storehouse of national will, yet Hanoi was off limits to Westmoreland. The MACV commander thus had to devise an alternate strategy which convinced his enemy that victory was impossible. In the process, Westmoreland acknowledged that defeating the enemy's ground forces served only as a means to the larger end of securing the south's population. He held no illusions that US operations to dislodge communists from local areas would have a "lasting effect" unless the ARVN could retain control of these areas. Nor did he hold much faith in the Saigon government's ability to confront Hanoi from a political or ideological position.[12] On the whole, however, most Americans in 1965 retained their faith in US military power being capable of achieving Johnson's grand strategic goals. Westmoreland's acumen as a commander and strategist certainly remains a key factor in helping explain the United States' failure in Vietnam. Yet so too, and perhaps more important, do the general inadequacies of American military force abroad in the Cold War era.

Negotiating Strategy

The development of US strategy for Vietnam was an interactive process between civilian and military leaders. Faultfinders of LBJ's policies, many in uniform, argued both during and after the war that the president unduly constrained the war effort by limiting the role of the US armed forces. The Joint Chiefs bemoaned the "self-imposed restrictions" while Admiral U.S.G. Sharp, Commander in Chief, Pacific, condemned civilian decision makers who had "no business ignoring or overriding the counsel of experienced military professionals in presuming to direct the day-to-day conduct of military strategy and tactics from their desks in Washington, D.C."[13] Johnson, though, did not have to look far back in history for warnings about creating an inadvertent wider war. The Chinese intervention in Korea served as a cautionary tale for the president. A CIA briefing paper in mid-1965, suggesting that China would commit sizable forces if the United States invaded North Vietnam, hardened Johnson's stance on limiting the war. The president would not "lose" South Vietnam like Truman lost China, but neither would he be responsible for risking general war with the PRC or the Soviet Union. Johnson's concerns were not unreasonable, especially given his domestic agenda; yet uniformed officers, Westmoreland included, believed "unwise political decisions" crippled the implementation of military strategy in Vietnam.[14]

While political constraints have become a fixation in American-centric Vietnam War narratives, less emphasized is the president's influence on spurring MACV to consider more deeply the nonmilitary aspects of the war for South Vietnam's population. Johnson believed the United States could transport the Great Society's social engineering agenda to Southeast Asia. Economic development in South Vietnam not only would cure the ailments of a weak society but also help provide security to a population experiencing civil war. Domestic programs to end poverty, provide better health care, and improve education all could undermine the insurgency's appeal in South Vietnam without risking a wider war with the greater communist powers.[15] While Johnson did not instruct Westmoreland to fight the war in any particular manner, he made clear his preferences for using social and economic programs to bolster the Saigon government in its time of need. It seems unlikely then that the MACV commander would have been permitted to develop a strategy that did not comply with the president's wishes. More to the point, Westmoreland would have had to have been completely out of step with his commander-in-chief if he focused only on the attrition of enemy forces.[16]

Further, Westmoreland's appeal for additional troops in mid-1965, and the muted debate within the White House, is best viewed within the context of Johnson's domestic agenda. Here, politics on the home front influenced questions of grand strategy which then shaped decisions of military strategy. Throughout the summer of 1965, the president downplayed the costs of intervention in hopes of maintaining political support for his Great Society. The resulting consensus-building approach to strategic decision making came at a price.[17] Most administration officials—of whom Under Secretary of State George Ball remained an exception—too often left unanswered the crucial strategic question: "For what purpose?" Ball doubted the assumptions on which the domino theory was based. More directly, he questioned whether Johnson should "commit US manpower and prestige to a terrain so unfavorable as to give a very large advantage to the enemy." Ball even challenged the president's key assumption that US stature and influence would diminish if the United States failed to act in Vietnam. "If the war is long and protracted, as I believe it will be," he said, "then we will suffer because the world's greatest power cannot defeat guerrillas." For a president seeking consensus, Ball's arguments caused concern—but only temporarily. Johnson acknowledged Ball's views but found ready support from McNamara, National Security Advisor McGeorge Bundy, and Secretary of State Dean Rusk who all advocated meeting head-on the communist challenge to United States credibility.[18]

McNamara, of course, held a special place among Johnson's advisors, at least in 1965. A Harvard Business School alumnus and former executive at Ford Motor Company, McNamara brought to the Pentagon a rational, even scientific, approach to decision making. His intellectual disciples in the Defense Department lauded the new principles of systems analysis which offered a "reasoned approach to highly complicated problems of choice in a context characterized by much uncertainty." Senior officers in the Pentagon, perhaps inevitably, cast a wary eye on these "whiz kids" who seemed intent on replacing seasoned judgment with computer statistics. Even McNamara himself argued that military "judgments" could no longer be "intuitive," nor could they be based on past "experience" alone.[19] This managerial revolution, however, was not matched by an equally radical reconceptualization of strategy. With little background at the strategic level of war, McNamara conceded his ignorance and left those in uniform to set their own agenda. As one student has described it, he was in "many ways a superb Secretary of Defense" and yet an "ineffectual minster of war." True, McNamara would offer his assessments on strategy to the president but rarely if ever did he dictate to those running the war inside South Vietnam.[20]

The secretary's early views on Vietnam strategy thus presented less of a challenge to Westmoreland or the JCS than a summary of the military's recommendations and McNamara's outlook on future actions. For example, in a 26 June memorandum, McNamara composed a wide-ranging missive on MACV's recommendations for 1965. He weighed the American escalation against potential Hanoi reactions, economic and political initiatives in the south, and likely international responses from the Soviet Union and China. McNamara warned that the military effort depended on "whether the South Vietnamese hold their own in terms of numbers and fighting spirit, and on whether the US forces can be effective in a quick-reaction reserve role, a role in which they have not been tested." Mirroring Westmoreland's own concerns, the secretary cautioned that the "tide almost certainly cannot begin to turn in less than a few months, and may not for a year or more; the war is one of attrition and will be a long one."[21]

Figure 3.1 ESCALATING THE WAR IN SOUTH VIETNAM. US Ambassador to Vietnam Maxwell D. Taylor chats with General William C. Westmoreland at Tan Son Hut airport, Saigon while overseeing part of the evacuation of civilian dependents from Vietnam, 11 February 1965. (RG 111-CV, NARA, 282)

In late July, McNamara reiterated to the president that "even in 'success,' it is not obvious how we will be able to disengage our forces from Vietnam." Far from directing military strategy in these crucial months of American escalation, the secretary of defense reflected the views of the commanding general at MACV headquarters.[22]

The MACV commander also conferred with Pacific Command and the Joint Chiefs of Staff. The service chiefs, however, had seen their collective role diminished over the course of the Kennedy administration and in the early years of Johnson's term. Both presidents generally sought advice from trusted civilian counselors rather than military officers. It is important to note, however, that the JCS legally held "no executive authority" and served only in an advisory role. The Joint Chiefs did not command troops or craft military strategy. Service rivalries and a constant call for "expanded military actions both in SVN and North Vietnam" absolutely limited the chiefs' ability to offer the president sound strategic advice.[23] Yet the JCS, like McNamara, echoed many of Westmoreland's concerns about the inherent problems of fighting in Vietnam. Army Chief of Staff Harold K. Johnson, in a December 1964 trip report, believed the conflict could "be brought to some successful conclusion in a military sense, providing some semblance of a national governmental structure can be maintained." Confirming MACV trepidations, Johnson concluded that "we must reconcile ourselves to a prolongation of activity and a high probability of an increased casualty rate as more advisors occupy exposed positions at the sub-sector level." The Joint Chiefs may have failed to evaluate, in a comprehensive manner, the strategic issues of war in Southeast Asia, but their roles as military advisors left them caught between the White House and Saigon with little direct influence over the actions of either the president or the MACV commander.[24] At very least, the service chiefs drew attention to Westmoreland's apprehensions over fighting a long war.

Given their relatively limited function as advisors, it seems plausible that the failure of the Joint Chiefs of Staff has been somewhat overplayed by historians. The chiefs were not so naïve as to believe military power alone would solve South Vietnam's problems. Throughout 1965, the JCS provided their estimations to the secretary of defense which discussed the "lack of a viable politico/economic structure in the RVN" and the need to "improve the combat effectiveness of the RVNAF." While they clearly sought to expand the war into North Vietnam despite difficulties in the south, they acknowledged the need to "deter Communist China from direct intervention." The JCS also recognized "that the lack of stability in the central government, the low state of morale of the leadership, and the poorly trained civil service in the Republic of Vietnam (RVN) militate against early success and that the solutions, primarily political, to these problems are also critical to the eventual termination of the insurgency."[25] If the advice President Johnson received appeared conflicting, it likely arose from the Joint Chiefs struggling to find ways to effectively implement American military power in such a complex environment. The decision to make a stand in Vietnam came with an undefined price. Save George Ball, few advisors, civilian or military, could have deduced in 1965 the ultimate costs of assisting the South Vietnamese government in defeating an insurgent and external enemy and extending control over a country ravaged by civil war.[26] Faith in the utility of force simply was too ingrained in a generation that believed the United States could achieve its foreign policy goals once committed to war.

The Joint Chiefs thus were no less derelict in their role as advisors as Westmoreland was in his as field commander. They presented their views to the president—true, with a preference for military action outside the confines of South Vietnam—while serving as a conduit between the White House, Pentagon, and MACV headquarters. The key for Westmoreland was using the JCS structure to help gain support for his own strategic concept while ensuring that he acquired the resources to implement his plans. Here it seems important to note that Westmoreland was not a unitary actor when it came to devising or implementing military strategy. Both Pacific Command and the Joint Chiefs concurred with the MACV commander's strategy for South Vietnam, Admiral Sharp recalling "it to be both well conceived and entirely appropriate to the ground-battle conditions under which he was compelled to fight."[27] Westmoreland, of course, suffered from the compartmentalized nature of the war. In one sense, command and control arrangements never adjusted to the realities of the conflict. CINCPAC, not MACV, controlled air and naval assets in Southeast Asia, while the US ambassador served as the nominal senior American representative in South Vietnam. Westmoreland thus had to negotiate strategy not only with the Joint Chiefs and their political masters but with numerous military and civilian agencies as well. The complex command structure impeded information flow and complicated the synchronization of the vast political-military programs required to deal successfully with any insurgency.[28]

Equally important, Westmoreland held no authority for imposing his will on the South Vietnamese government and armed forces. Despite its increasing role in combat operations, MACV retained its advisory role with ARVN military leaders. Westmoreland opted against a joint US-South Vietnamese command because he believed such a move would confirm Hanoi's charges of the GVN being an American "puppet." The general also worried that a shared headquarters would make it more difficult to disengage when the time came to do so.[29] This fragmented command structure certainly undercut MACV's ability to prosecute the war and illustrated a widening gap between responsibility and authority. As the principal US commander in South Vietnam, Westmoreland was accountable for developing a comprehensive military strategy yet too often found himself unable to influence factors outside of his reach. MACV Chief of Staff William B. Rosson recalled that the lack of a "higher strategy" left his boss without a "master concept governing the weight, priority and nature" of military and nonmilitary endeavors. MACV officers understood the political, economic, and social aspects of revolutionary war but possessed only a limited ability to shape South Vietnamese programs to account for these nonmilitary factors.[30] If the Joint Chiefs deserve criticism, it seems best focused here, on their inability to assist Westmoreland in coordinating the diverse elements of US agencies prosecuting a multifaceted war inside Vietnam.

Recent scholarship reveals that Hanoi's leaders faced similar challenges in orchestrating a cohesive strategy that accounted for numerous political and military factors. The North Vietnamese plan for reunification included an equally broad swath of supporting objectives—carrying out land reform, implementing a rational social policy, and developing the economy and increasing production. How best to coordinate domestic reconstruction with revolutionary war bedeviled Politburo strategists throughout the war. Far from being a unified enemy, the North Vietnamese hotly debated whether to fight a protracted war or seek a rapid military victory. Hanoi leaders might agree with Ho Chi Minh's axiom that the "military without the political is like a tree without a root," but few concurred on the best mix of armed and political *dau tranh* (struggle).[31] Facing a massive American buildup complicated strategic deliberations. In December 1965, Hanoi's leadership, increasingly under the influence of First Secretary Le Duan, promulgated Lao Dong Party Resolution 12 which outlined a basic strategy to defeat the Americans "under any circumstances." The resolution placed greater emphasis on the military struggle as domestic priorities receded into the background. Evidence suggests, however, that even from Hanoi's perspective, developing and implementing strategy in Vietnam was not a straightforward task. Le Duan battled with senior military officials like Vo Nguyen Giap over the pace of military operations and the building of forces for a general offensive against the southern "puppets." Escalation proved challenging for both sides.[32]

The strategic debate in Hanoi held crucial implications for Westmoreland. As Le Duan crafted a strategy balancing southern revolutionaries and northern regular forces, the MACV commander needed to fashion a response that not only accounted for the dual nature of the threat but integrated military, political, social, and economic aspects of a war whose purpose remained guaranteeing the independence of an already unstable country. Even as escalation posed special problems for Le Duan and Hanoi's leadership, the US response enhanced the National Liberation Front's legitimacy. Westmoreland and his staff, though, realized that "counterinsurgency was too narrow a focus to cope with the arrival of the North Vietnamese army in the south."[33] Furthermore, MACV's commander had to oversee the construction of a vast logistical support network capable of supporting the thousands of Americans entering country. As Westmoreland's chief operations officer noted, "We had a difficult time in determining exactly the sizing of our logistic force because it was hard to predict what the consumption of gasoline, diesel, and ammunition would be."[34] How that support base might impact the South Vietnamese economy remained to be seen in the early days of American escalation.

One final point of negotiation remained. Westmoreland's strategy, focused as it was on the ground war in South Vietnam, necessarily reflected the political choices made within the larger international context of the Cold War. Never did the combatants in Vietnam fight the war in a vacuum. Johnson's political limitations, and his preoccupation with Chinese intervention, not only drew the ire of military leaders but restricted Westmoreland's strategic options. MACV grasped the vital role of external assistance to Hanoi's war effort yet chafed under the constraints of having to contain the fighting inside South Vietnam's borders. Westmoreland, however, had little choice but to navigate within the political boundaries. Johnson had placed obvious limitations on military strategy yet had made clear the American commitment at a higher level. "Despite our desire to limit conflict," the president maintained in early 1966, "it was necessary to act: to hold back the mounting aggression—to give courage to the people of the South—and to make our firmness clear to the North."[35] With the decision to act, Westmoreland thus contended with a vast assortment of strategic obligations in the summer of 1965. His resultant strategic concept accorded with the political and military realities not only inside South Vietnam, but with regional and global truths as well.

Westmoreland and the Limits of Attrition

In August 1965, roughly three months before the Ia Drang battles in which US Army ground forces first clashed with North Vietnamese regulars, the *New York Times* ran a page one story titled "The Undefinable War." Reporting from Saigon, correspondent James Reston argued that the war in Vietnam was "so alien to American experiences" that it defied "precise definition and [was] almost beyond comprehension." Conventional language failed to capture the political, cultural, religious, and regional complexities of a country and a conflict that were unfamiliar to contemporary Americans. The article further underscored the difficulties of accurately portraying the violence then escalating within South Vietnam's borders. As Reston pronounced, "This war needs a new vocabulary."[36]

Reston's advice suggests that catchphrases like "attrition strategy," "counterinsurgency strategy," and "pacification strategy"—while mainstays of the war's literature—fail to convey the true nature of Westmoreland's approach. In fact, as MACV's commander formulated his strategic concept in 1965, he appreciated fully the complexity of the threat to the South Vietnamese government and population. As Westmoreland directed his commanders in September, the "war in Vietnam is a political as well as a military war. It is political because the ultimate goal is to regain the loyalty and cooperation of the people, and to create conditions which permit the people to go about their normal lives in peace and security."[37] American forces might struggle in the years that followed to implement such an expansive strategic concept, but Westmoreland realized the importance of relating military power to political purpose. So too did he appreciate the mission of strengthening the ARVN and coordinating his efforts with the US embassy in Saigon. Ambassador Henry Cabot Lodge, writing in the fall of 1965, noted that Westmoreland's "broad strategy," crafted in "close coordination with the Vietnamese High Command," not only sought to destroy enemy forces but aimed to "restore progressively the entire country to GVN control" and to "support 'rural construction' with comprehensive attention to the pacification process."[38]

In short, Westmoreland's strategy rested on the three pillars of attrition, pacification, and ARVN training. Broad in nature, it was difficult to define. Journalists, and future scholars, turned increasingly to the word "attrition" as convenient shorthand despite Reston's warnings about imprecise definitions. One part of the three-pillared strategy was being mistaken for the whole. Westmoreland, of course, used the phrase attrition in both private memoranda to senior officials and in public, yet he early on recognized that killing the enemy was not an end unto itself. More important, attrition served as a means to express concern over maintaining morale during the "long pull." As Westmoreland wrote the Joint Chiefs in June 1965, "It is difficult, if not impossible for me to imagine how we can commit and sustain US forces, air, surface and naval, without backing them up for the long pull by mobilization of manpower, industrial and training resources at least to a limited degree."[39] The following year, the general gave a public appraisal of the war in which he warned "there had been no lessening of North Vietnam's resolve to prosecute the war." (At the same briefing, the president declared that the American people "must know that there will be no quick victory.")[40] The MACV commander's concerns over staying power, not a myopic adherence to killing enemy forces, thus helped propel the word "attrition" to the forefront of dialogue on the American war.

US Army officers, Westmoreland included, believed killing the enemy to be an important aspect of fighting in South Vietnam. No doubt cultural preferences for conventional operations influenced the army's conceptions of fighting. The army's doctrine spoke plainly of wresting the initiative away from the insurgency and avoiding "purely defensive measures [which] only allow the guerrilla force to grow strong."[41] Still, neither Westmoreland nor the American forces he led were blind to the realities of unconventional warfare. The claim that "several years were to pass before the American command began to accept the crucial role of population security" simply does not hold up when one scrutinizes the documentary evidence.[42] As MACV's commander formulated his strategic concept in the spring and summer of 1965, he appreciated fully the complexity of the threat to the South Vietnamese government and population. That threat, rather than an inane commitment to attrition warfare, goes far in explaining Westmoreland's approach to strategic planning.[43]

As seen in the previous chapter, most American estimates of the situation inside South Vietnam in early 1965 painted a grim picture. Political instability wracked the Saigon government. NLF insurgent forces increasingly showed a willingness to confront South Vietnamese Army units in battle. Political subversion, assassination of government officials, and attacks on infrastructure continued at an alarming rate. Equally grave, American intelligence analysts picked up indications of regular army units from North Vietnam infiltrating into the south.[44] On 26 June 1965, Washington officials gave Westmoreland permission "to commit U.S. ground forces anywhere in the country when, in his judgment, they were needed to strengthen South Vietnamese forces." The number of American forces rose precipitously. At the opening of 1965, 23,000 US troops were in Vietnam. One year later the number had soared to 184,000 troops.[45]

The troop escalation mirrored the growing concerns of Westmoreland and his staff. Their analysis of the operational environment and the nature of the threat led them to believe the enemy was doing all it could "to destroy the [South Vietnamese] government's troops and eliminate all vestiges of government control."[46] In fact, this assessment struck close to the mark. Responding to US intervention, planners in Hanoi became convinced, albeit not without disagreement, that only by escalating the struggle inside South Vietnam could they eventually defeat the "American aggressors." In March 1965, Hanoi's Party Central Committee decided to "mobilize the soldiers and civilians of the entire nation to strengthen our offensive posture and to attack the enemy." It is important to note, however, that this strategic offensive encompassed more than just military escalation. Communist leaders in South Vietnam spent considerable energy on "a wide-ranging political campaign throughout the armed forces and the civilian population" to minimize the impacts of US intervention.[47] This combined political-military campaign aimed at orchestrating the efforts of regular and insurgent forces, as well as coordinating the activities of political cadres and military units.

While Westmoreland and Johnson administration officials debated whether the enemy was moving into the third and final phase of Maoist revolutionary warfare—the largely conventional, counteroffensive stage—the general still appreciated the multifaceted characteristics of the developing war. A June 1965 cable outlining his concept of operations noted clearly that the "insurgency in South Vietnam must eventually be defeated among the people in the hamlets and towns."[48] The population thus had to be secured from both insurgents and regular military formations. Westmoreland likened the political subversives to "termites" which unrelentingly were eating away at the foundation of the Saigon government. Concurrently, main force units, or "bully boys," waited for the opportune moment to strike at the weakened structure with crowbars. As Westmoreland recalled, if the Americans and their South Vietnamese allies were to be successful, "Neither facet could be ignored."[49]

Westmoreland's analogy of termites and bully boys might easily be dismissed as simplistic, but MACV's commander realized that attrition of enemy main force units could not be achieved at the expense of pacification or counterinsurgency. The opposite also held true. Westmoreland could not simply conduct operations against insurgents while ignoring the conventional threat. All the while, the Americans needed to aid their South Vietnamese allies in pacifying the countryside and provide some sense of security to the rural population. Certainly, Westmoreland used the word "attrition" in both his memoirs and in his correspondence with senior and subordinate commanders. Such communications, however, suggest the general was focused not just on killing the enemy but also on intimating to those directing the war effort that the conflict in Vietnam would not be concluded in a swift manner. Attrition underlined the problem of fighting a protracted war. As Westmoreland wrote to the chairman of the Joint Chiefs of Staff in June 1965, "the premise behind whatever further actions we may undertake . . . must be that we are in for the long pull. This struggle has become a war of attrition. . . . I see no likelihood of achieving a quick, favorable end to the war."[50]

Westmoreland's sobering appraisal, so early in the war, reveals a commander deeply concerned about the staying power of his own armed forces and nation for fighting such a complex war. As his chief intelligence officer recalled, "Westmoreland had not one battle but three to fight: first, to contain a growing conventional threat; second to develop the Republic of Vietnam's Armed Forces (RVNAF); and third, to pacify and protect the peasants in the South Vietnamese countryside."[51] Both the threat and the mission required a broad concept of the operations, one that a simple word like attrition could not fully characterize. Indeed, the military lexicon of the day was unsuited to the myriad tasks required of Westmoreland's command. Lacking precise terminology to describe the three battles MACV simultaneously fought, any broad strategic concept came with the risk of ambiguity. In fact, a postwar survey concluded that 70 percent of army generals managing the war were "uncertain of its objectives."[52] If attrition of enemy forces had been the guiding light of American strategy in Vietnam, one might expect more certainty among the army's senior leaders. Westmoreland's panoptic strategy—and in truth, his own shortcomings in better communicating his strategic concepts and approach to his subordinates—left many American field commanders in doubt about the United States' main purpose in South Vietnam.

In fact, political stabilization of South Vietnam would form the bedrock of what would become Westmoreland's "three-phase sustained campaign." Phase I visualized the commitment of US and allied forces "necessary to halt the losing trend by 1965." Tasks included securing major military bases, defending major political and population centers, and preserving and strengthening the RVNAF. In Phase II, Westmoreland sought to resume the offensive to "destroy enemy forces" and reinstitute "rural construction activities." In this phase, aimed to begin in 1966, American forces would "participate in clearing, securing, reserve reaction and offensive operations as required to support and sustain the resumption of pacification." Finally, in Phase III, MACV would oversee the "defeat and destruction of the remaining enemy forces and base areas." It is important to note here that Westmoreland's official report on the war included the term "sustained campaign."[53] The general was under no illusions that US forces were engaged in a war of annihilation aimed at the rapid destruction of the enemy. Attrition suggested that a stable South Vietnam, capable of resisting the military and political pressures of both internal and external aggressors, would not arise in a matter of months or even a few years.

Nor should Westmoreland's use of the word "attrition" validate assertions that the American campaign strategy in Vietnam was singularly focused. In fact, it seems plausible to argue that MACV's commander formulated a "one war" approach without using the label later popularized by his successor. Creighton Abrams understood the war's political-military interrelationships, but so too did Westmoreland. "Probably the fundamental issue is the question of the coordination of mission activities in Saigon," the general opined in early 1966. "It is abundantly clear that all political, military, economic, and security (police) programs must be completely integrated in order to attain any kind of success in a country which has been greatly weakened by prolonged conflict and is under increasing pressure by large military and subversive forces."[54] True, more effective coordination alone would not have led MACV to achieve its strategic objectives. Yet contrary to the popular narrative of an officer consumed by racking up enemy body counts, Westmoreland thoughtfully considered the issues of land reform, improving the South Vietnamese armed forces, limiting civilian casualties, and facilitating population security in the countryside.[55] All the while, he worried that such a prolonged war might destabilize the very foundations on which his strategy was built.

This uneasiness over fleeting national willpower also led Westmoreland to dismiss what would become two controversial alternatives—some alleged missed opportunities—to MACV strategy. The first, dubbed an "enclave strategy," rested on the belief that Americans could help secure key population centers near the coast and then gradually expand outward like "blowing out a balloon."[56] Retired General James M. Gavin led the challenge in early 1966, claiming that MACV was spreading its forces too thin in an ill-advised effort to secure all of South Vietnam. Gavin argued the key to American success was limiting the scope of US operations. If a "village is fought over five or six times," he reasoned, "a great many civilians will die. The whole pattern of life in the village will be altered. If our objective was a better life for the people in that village, as the war continues to drag on we ourselves destroy the objective for which we fight. Destruction is a function of time as well as weapons and area."[57]

The US mission, however, had entertained similar proposals as early as 1964 and found critical deficiencies. Senior officers worried the enclaves would become "magnets" for NLF attacks. The concept also seemed to concede the initiative, "the most fundamental principle to be applied to counterinsurgency warfare," to the enemy, especially in areas outside of GVN influence. As JCS Chairman Earle Wheeler quipped, "No one ever won a battle sitting on his ass." Westmoreland, perhaps indicating a predilection for military force to stem the tide against enemy main force units, similarly believed that the enclave approach represented "an inglorious, static use of U.S. forces in overpopulated areas with little chance of direct or immediate impact on the outcome of events." Once more, the element of time influenced the MACV commander's strategic thinking. For Westmoreland, the enemy already held the upper hand. Consequently, to position American troops in a "series of unconnected beachheads, their backs to the sea, essentially in a defensive posture," did little to wrest initiative away from the NLF or NVA.[58] Even influential journalists sided with Westmoreland at the time. Joseph Alsop, noting the dual nature of the threat, believed the enclave strategy meant "surrendering all the rest of South Vietnam to the Viet Cong and the North Vietnamese, immediately after the American retreat to Gen. Gavin's coastal enclaves."[59] Alsop's derogatory use of the word "retreat" said much about the attitude of many Americans who believed there were few alternatives to confronting communist aggression.

The US Marine Corps (USMC) in Vietnam, however, offered what would become the most contentious alternative to Westmoreland's strategy in 1965 and 1966. Situated in I Corps, near the demilitarized zone between North and South Vietnam, the Marines initially devoted their attention to defending the large US air base at Danang. As Westmoreland sought to expand from these defensive positions to confront the growing NVA threat, Generals Lewis Walt, the Marine commander in Vietnam, and Victor Krulak, commander of the Fleet Marine Force in the Pacific, expressed concern over operating farther and farther away from population centers. Krulak argued that "victories in the search-and-destroy operations were not relevant to the total outcome of the war."[60] Instead, the

Marines advocated a combined action program in which American platoons would amalgamate with Vietnamese regional and popular forces to provide local security for the population. These combined action platoons, or CAPs, deployed to the fields to protect harvesters, organized local intelligence networks, and participated in civic action programs to aid in economic and social development. When compared to Westmoreland's "attrition strategy," the Marine approach appears enlightened in its holistic approach to countering the southern insurgency. Yet when evaluated against the true nature of MACV's approach, one finds more similarities than differences.[61]

In November 1965, Walt wrote Westmoreland that he understood his "primary mission to be to defend the established bases...to support the RVNAF effort, and to provide a security shield behind which the ARVN can develop a reliable rural construction program." In fact, Marines spent the bulk of their time on security-related issues. Westmoreland worried consistently that localized operations left the "enemy free to come and go as he pleased throughout the bulk of the region."[62] The same month that Walt sent his assessment to Westmoreland, the MACV operations officer, Brigadier General William E. DePuy, visited I Corps and conveyed a dismal picture. DePuy was "disturbed by the fact that all but a tiny part of the I Corps area is under the control of the VC who have freedom of movement east and west—north and south—outside the Marine enclaves." While NLF forces appeared to be gaining in strength, the ARVN was barely holding its own. DePuy perceptively noted that "the Vietnamese cannot adequately fill in behind the Marines in their expanding enclaves and for this reason, the Marines are stalled a short distance south of Danang. If they move out farther, they will have insecure areas behind them for which there are no Regional or Popular Forces or pacification cadre to provide long term hamlet-by-hamlet security."[63]

DePuy's bleak assessment seemed to confirm Walt and Krulak's criticisms of MACV strategy yet in truth underscored the problems of focusing only on one aspect of the war. Like US Army units, the Marines found it near impossible to "isolate" the battlefield from the enemy so pacification programs could proceed. Most all Americans lacked the linguistic skills necessary for effective combined operations and too often were contemptuous of their allies. For instance, one USMC captain noted that "officers were aware from their own surveys that over 40 percent of the Marines disliked the Vietnamese."[64] Moreover, both the army and Marine civic action programs rested on similar approaches. One infantry lieutenant colonel believed "the concept of civic action as adopted by the US Army and US Marine Corps is identical. It is aimed at advising and assisting the indigenous military forces in local assistance projects and thus enhancing their reputation and relationship with the local populace."[65] Perhaps unexpectedly, both services faced identical problems. Those Marines serving in combined action units ultimately spent most of their time trying to secure the population and, in doing so, failed to facilitate popular support for the government. In the end, Walt and Krulak failed to demonstrate the wisdom of their approach. As one Marine captain noted, the CAPs "seemed too fragile, the American role too temporary, other demands for U.S. manpower too powerful."[66]

The challenges to Westmoreland's strategy thus appear less compelling if one considers the MACV concept as more than one of simple attrition. Westmoreland reflected on the war as a whole before devising a strategy he felt best positioned American forces to achieve the president's goals. His dismissal of alternatives like those from the Marines stemmed from the need to confront multiple dangers to the stability of South Vietnam, threats which encompassed political, unconventional, and conventional aspects of a revolutionary war. Convincing the enemy that victory was impossible required more than military solutions. Westmoreland undeniably understood this. He also assumed, as did most Americans, that Hanoi in due course would recognize its inability to endure in a long war. This notion clearly misread Vietnamese history and misjudged the will of Hanoi's leaders to persist against one of the world's superpowers. In early 1966, few American leaders believed North Vietnam had the capacity to support Ho Chi Minh's claim that "So long as the U.S. army of aggression still remains on our soil, our people will resolutely fight against it."[67] The problem for Westmoreland was whether South Vietnam had a similar capacity to provide a moral, political, and military foundation upon which to implement an otherwise sound US military strategy.

An Evolving Strategy

By mid-1966, Hanoi arguably had lost, though not irretrievably, the military initiative to American and allied forces, forcing Politburo leaders to reassess their strategy. MACV's offensives had disrupted NLF operations and engendered fierce strategic debate in Hanoi. Military pressure on the enemy served not as an end, however, but a means to a larger political objective, one that Westmoreland realized. As the MACV commander noted in the summer of 1966, the growing strength of US and Free World Forces would "provide the shield that will permit ARVN to shift its weight of effort to an extent not heretofore feasible to direct support of revolutionary development."[68] Thus, in 1966 and 1967, Westmoreland sought to find linkages between pacification, combat operations, and ARVN training. But in one sense, US strategy changed little from 1965. MACV still aimed at using military offensives to upset the enemy's plans and provide space and time for GVN policies to take hold inside South

Vietnam. "After all," Westmoreland stated, "the main purpose of defeating the enemy through offensive operations against his main forces and bases must be to provide the opportunity through RD [revolutionary development] to get at the heart of the matter, which is the population of South Vietnam."[69]

Without question, the Johnson administration pressured Westmoreland—and the South Vietnamese leadership—in 1966 and 1967 to incorporate more fully nonmilitary means into their respective strategies. Reports in early 1966 indicated that the NLF controlled nearly three-fourths of South Vietnam. (Perhaps Hanoi had not relinquished the initiative. In a war without fronts, it was so hard to tell.) MACV might have stabilized the military situation but the government's foothold in the countryside seemed tenuous at best. When American and South Vietnamese leaders met at Honolulu in early February, President Johnson focused his comments on GVN political stability. While Prime Minister Nguyen Cao Ky and Chief of State Nguyen Van Thieu pledged a "social revolution" in Vietnam, Johnson ordered a reorganization of the US mission to facilitate an expansion of the "other war," a term increasingly in vogue to describe allied pacification efforts.[70] Concurrently, McNamara and Secretary of State Rusk defined Westmoreland's goals for the coming year. MACV would increase the South Vietnamese population living in secure areas by 10 percent, multiply critical roads and railroads for use by 20 percent, and increase the destruction of VC and PAVN base areas by 30 percent. To make sure the president's directives were not ignored, Westmoreland was to augment the pacified population by 235,000 and ensure the defense of political and population centers under government control. The final goal directed MACV to "attrite, by year's end, VC/PAVN forces at a rate as high as their capability to put men in the field."[71]

The Honolulu conference exemplified the immense array of tasks Westmoreland had to accomplish. Physical attrition of enemy forces unquestionably ranked high among these undertakings as MACV relied heavily on the "spoiling attack" to disrupt NLF and NVA concentrations and drive the enemy away from population centers. Westmoreland praised, perhaps unjustly, the effectiveness of these attacks, especially in light of evidence which showed the enemy had increased its combat numbers through infiltration and recruitment. The use of firepower also came with a price. As journalist Charles Mohr noted in June 1966, it was "difficult to bring the impressive weight of United States power to bear in rural South Vietnam without killing and maiming civilians as well as the guerrilla enemy."[72] Try as they might, US forces could not separate the fish from the sea as Westmoreland intended. Still, the MACV commander believed few reasonable alternatives presented themselves given Hanoi's own escalation of the military conflict. Furthermore, while body counts captured the attention of the Johnson administration and the American media, they constituted only one of many statistical indicators MACV employed for tracking the progress of an extremely complex war.[73]

The supposed single-minded commitment to accumulating high body counts led many pundits to suggest that Westmoreland foolishly dismissed yet another alternative, one outlined in the March 1966 PROVN report. Army Chief of Staff Harold K. Johnson assigned a small working group in mid-1965 the task of developing "new sources of action" that might lead to "successful accomplishment of US aims and objectives."[74] The findings of PROVN, shorthand for *A Program for the Pacification and Long Term Development of South Vietnam*, placed strong emphasis on nonmilitary means and argued that "victory" could only be achieved by "bringing the individual Vietnamese, typically a rural peasant, to support willingly the Government of South Vietnam (GVN)." The report's authors condemned the US mission for its "marginally effective" methods which grew from a "lack of understanding of the nature of the conflict." Chief among PROVN concerns was the apparent preoccupation "with purely military activities" and a lack of a unified command to coordinate diverse counterinsurgency operations.[75] Westmoreland's critics later would charge that the MACV commander, contemptuous of those challenging his strategic concepts, muted the report and failed to incorporate any of PROVN's sensible recommendations on elevating the political side of the war. In truth, the report provided few truly new ideas.[76]

The PROVN authors delineated "critical programs" that should demand MACV attention: defeat of PAVN and main force VC, rural construction, commercial import programs, and effective GVN functioning. Other recommendations included civil service and fiscal reform, destroying in-country safe havens, and providing refugee relief.[77] Few, if any, of MACV's staff officers or commanders would have disagreed with any of these suggestions. As Westmoreland later remarked to his executive officer, Volney Warner (incidentally one of the report's authors), we "were already doing pretty much all of what was recommended by PROVN." Far from dismissing the study, Westmoreland oversaw the incorporation of a number of its proposals. A report in early 1967 stated "that of the 140 recommendations in the PROVN report, 53 had been implemented and 45 had been partially implemented."[78] Of course, not all suggestions made sense. The authors advocated that Americans "perform as social innovators" and exercise a "greater degree of US influence in Vietnamese affairs." Given Hanoi claims that the Saigon government already served as a "puppet" to its American masters, such counsel surely failed to impress Westmoreland. So too did PROVN's conviction that US combat operations "be directed against enemy base areas and against their lines of communication in SVN, Laos, and Cambodia as required."[79] The president's decision to restrict the ground war to South Vietnam made unfeasible proposals like this which senior military officers already had advocated to the White House.

In the end, PROVN presented no remarkable alternatives for Westmoreland. By mid-1966, civil affairs and nonmilitary programs had evolved into key elements of MACV strategy. The MACV official history noted that the "basic objectives of the campaign for 1966 were to clear, secure, and assist in the economic development of the heavily populated areas around Saigon, in the Mekong Delta, and in selected portions of the coastal plain." Linking military operations to pacification, however, remained problematic. As Westmoreland wrote in August, the "essential tasks of revolutionary development and nation building cannot be accomplished if enemy main force units can gain access to the population centers and destroy our efforts."[80] Thus, the general sought to focus US efforts on clearing territory of enemy influence while the ARVN would be "in direct support of the revolutionary development program." In none of his directives or special communications in 1966 or 1967 did Westmoreland ever claim that attrition of enemy forces encompassed the whole of his military strategy. In delineating his concept of operations for 1967, Westmoreland informed Sharp and Wheeler that his mission included not only "defeating the communist insurgents and aggressors from the North," but also "expanding security in populated and productive areas, and encouraging and supporting all aspects of nation building."[81]

These interdependent undertakings—what one historian has described as a "parallel wars concept"—laid bare the rising importance of pacification in MACV strategy. In short, the whole purpose of "the protective shield of containment and offensive forces [was] to support the GVN pacification program."[82] Throughout his tenure, however, Westmoreland struggled to keep pace with Hanoi's infiltration of enemy forces into South Vietnam via Cambodia, Laos, and the famous Ho Chi Minh Trail. The general estimated at a press conference in early 1966 that "the North Vietnamese are infiltrating at the rate of approximately 4500 a month." The following year MACV projected the number had risen to over 6,000 personnel per month. Westmoreland reported to his chain of command that large main force and NVA units had "not been contacted for many months, some of which are in sanctuaries in Cambodia, Laos or the DMZ, thus making it difficult to get at them."[83] The porous borders, long a concern of US military officers, held deep implications for MACV strategy. Because Westmoreland's staff could only approximate enemy troop strength figures— one report noted "infiltration rates are very indefinite"—few if any Americans confidently could assess US military operations in support of GVN pacification efforts. "How big is the enemy?" remained a constant question among those in the US mission. The answers to this inquiry diverged greatly between MACV, the CIA, and critics at home, suggesting deeper issues with American strategy inside South Vietnam.[84]

The resultant "order of battle" controversy eventually led Westmoreland to court in 1985 countering accusations that he had deliberately misled the public on the enemy's strength so as to maintain support for a flawed attrition strategy. The truth proved much more complex. MACV staff officers struggled with quantifying NLF local defense forces who farmed by day and fought by night. Was a political cadre or an enemy propagandist, for instance, to be counted or not? How should MACV quantify the enemy's political-military infrastructure?[85] Without question, the Pentagon pressured Westmoreland to demonstrate progress, especially in 1967 as the war seemed locked in stalemate. Yet consensus eluded the US mission. While CIA analysts advocated more inclusive, and thus higher, numbers, MACV staffers balked. The command would count maneuver and combat support units but consider covert NLF forces beyond the scope of its assessments. Claims of a conspiratorial coverup by Westmoreland, however, ring hollow. President Johnson, Secretary McNamara, and the Joint Chiefs all were well aware of the CIA-MACV debate.[86]

With Westmoreland in the United States in August 1967, deputy MACV commander Creighton Abrams wrote Wheeler that including "self-defense" and "secret self-defense" forces in "an estimate of military capabilities is highly questionable. These forces contain a sizable number of women and old people.... They are rarely armed, have no real discipline, and almost no military capability." Abrams surely missed the point about the political struggle's role in Hanoi's strategy, but the controversy continues to offer worthwhile insights into the difficulties of drawing sharp lines between enemy main force units, self-defense forces, and part-time guerrillas. More problematically, Abrams, mirroring concerns of nearly all senior military officers at the time, warned that "the press reaction to these inflated figures is of much greater concern." As the deputy commander cautioned the JCS chairman, accepting and releasing the CIA's higher numbers would cause those at home to draw an "erroneous conclusion" as to the upsurge. "When we release the figure of 420–431,000, the newsmen will immediately seize on the point that the enemy has increased about 120–130,000."[87] In September, Westmoreland and the CIA agreed to a halfhearted compromise of approximately 235,000 enemy combatants then operating inside South Vietnam.[88]

The order of battle controversy indicated that Westmoreland's war continued to perplex those eager to demonstrate progress yet simultaneously be candid about the limits of US power abroad. Nearly all observers realized the war's outcome rested largely (though not solely) on the Vietnamese and the war in the villages. The rural conflict, though, comprised a subtle mixture of security, governmental reform, and social revolution which further complicated the problems of assessing enemy infiltration rates and strength levels. Mimicking US counterinsurgency doctrine, a 1966 *Los Angeles Times* editorial argued that "until ground is held and security is guaranteed to the local populace, there will be no peasant cooperation with the government."[89] Westmoreland clearly fretted over the fragility of the countryside's villages, locales that Americans found "subtle, incomprehensible" and even "impenetrable." Still, the MACV commander argued, revolutionary development could proceed only if allied forces prevented enemy main force units from gaining access to and disrupting population centers.[90]

Westmoreland's aims to place increased emphasis on pacification programs thus confronted a dilemma. If population security could not be achieved, how would fostering a common cause with the Saigon government be at all possible? Critics charged the US command with focusing too heavily on conventional operations while an undermanned ARVN and "inadequately trained paramilitary forces" made only limited gains in the pacification arena. Yet evidence also suggested that Westmoreland's strategy had hurt the enemy badly. Ambassador Ellsworth Bunker reported in mid-1967 that Hanoi's "time schedule has been disrupted" and that "General Westmoreland's strategy of anticipating enemy threats has paid off handsomely."[91] New research reveals similar attitudes within the enemy camp. The war's costly stalemate engendered a heated strategic debate among Hanoi's leaders with some influential party members calling for direct peace talks. Westmoreland, for his part, continued to temper such optimism, expressing his concern that the enemy was prolonging the war through continued efforts to "discredit and erode GVN political authority at all levels." The attrition piece of MACV's strategy thus cut both ways. While allied efforts indeed had kept the enemy "off balance," the monthly average of 816 American deaths in the first half of 1967 suggested Westmoreland's strategic concepts might be untenable in the long run.[92]

Perceptions of stalemate, even failure, not only triggered increasing criticisms of American strategy in Vietnam but a reappraisal at MACV headquarters as well. Despite roughly 470,000 US troops in country, Westmoreland feared he had insufficient numbers to secure his base areas, maintain the initiative in the field, and expand security in populated areas. Enemy infiltration persisted at near alarming rates. The MACV chief thus proposed a plan to isolate the South Vietnamese battlefield by blocking the Ho Chi Minh Trail in Laos. Worried over flagging domestic support for a prolonged and indecisive war, Westmoreland believed, as did the Joint Chiefs, that only through disruption of the enemy's Laotian sanctuaries could the allies force Hanoi to accept a negotiated peace.[93] Such an alternate military strategy, however, came with unacceptable political costs at the grand strategic level. Johnson, already uneasy about the war's ascendancy over his prized Great Society programs, could not sanction the additional 200,000 troops that MACV requested. Nor could the president in 1967 answer satisfactorily why Americans continued to bear a heavy load

Figure 3.2 ALLIES AT WAR. The 25th Infantry Divisions of the United States, Republic of Korea, and South Vietnam hold a "Fraternity for Freedom" ceremony in Cu Chi, 20 August 1966. Left to right: LTG ChaeMyung Shin, CG of ROK forces in RVN; Westmoreland; Jonathan O. Seaman, CG III FF; and COL PhanTrongChinh, CG of the ARVN 25ID. (RG 111-CV, NARA, 310)

while Saigon's leaders seemed unwilling to make necessary political and social reforms. Nearing an election year, Johnson refuted any widening of an increasingly unpopular war. A stoic Westmoreland returned to implementing, as best he could, his original strategic objectives for 1967: pressing a major pacification effort, conducting anti-main force spoiling offensives, limiting infiltration, mounting a national reconciliation program, and pressing for the emergence of a popularly based GVN.[94]

The rejection of Westmoreland's alternate strategy left MACV few options for reconceptualizing the allied war effort. In a large sense, Westmoreland had not offered much that was new. The Combined Campaign Plan for 1967 already included programs to improve the ARVN, care for civilian refugees, and train the national police. One field commander even reported to Westmoreland the effectiveness of his "rice denial operations" which also included "plans for security of harvesting and for disposition of the rice itself."[95] Yet the war's end seemed no closer in sight. American officials in both Saigon and Washington fretted they were losing support of the home front. Venerable journalist Walter Lippman asked if the war was "insoluble," while other correspondents increasingly used words like "stalemate" and "unwinnable" to describe the conflict. Assistant Secretary of Defense Alain Enthoven saw the war "as a race between, on the one hand, the development of a viable South Vietnam and, on the other, a gradual loss in public support, or even tolerance, for the war."[96] In Saigon, MACV's commander expressed similar concerns. Westmoreland wrote Wheeler in August, not without a touch of irony, that "a vocal segment of the news profession is equating a lack of major combat operations...with a stalemate at best, or a loss of the initiative on our part at worst."[97] Time, one of the general's earliest worries, seemed to be running out.

Unfortunately for Westmoreland, the president equally agonized over the apparent lack of progress and pressured his war managers to highlight the advances being made in Vietnam. MACV's strategy, according to Walt Rostow, might be "working, slowly but steadily" but Johnson needed more evidence to shore up support at home.[98] Westmoreland obliged. At a news conference at the White House on 17 July 1967, the general announced that the "statement that we are in a stalemate is complete fiction. It is completely unrealistic. During the past year tremendous progress has been made." In November, once again called back to the United States to sell the war on the administration's behalf, Westmoreland stated on *Meet the Press* that "constant, real progress" was being made.[99] Only two months before the climactic Tet offensive, the optimism seemed unfounded at best, misleading at worst. Westmoreland's public comments stood at odds with his longstanding beliefs. The war could be won only through a prolonged process of wearing down the enemy physically, politically, and psychologically. There was no light at the end of the tunnel, yet Westmoreland, loyally serving the president, helped widen what would soon become a yawning credibility gap. In supporting Johnson, the general had helped delude the American home front. His unduly optimistic public comments arguably ranked among the most unfortunate strategic missteps of Westmoreland's entire tenure as MACV commander.[100]

It is important to note, however, that Westmoreland was not alone in making these public statements of progress. In late 1967, General Harold K. Johnson, the army chief of staff, spoke at the Association of the US Army's annual meeting in Washington, DC and offered his own assessment of the war in Vietnam. Johnson first made it clear that "failure to continue to support South Vietnam would be just as dangerous in today's environment as when Chamberlain went to Munich." Obviously, appeasement was not the answer. The general then listed a number of points that demonstrated "clear and concrete evidence of progress." Both the morale and performance of the RVNAF had improved steadily in the last two years. The ARVN was capturing four communist weapons for each one it lost. To highlight success on the battlefield, Johnson noted that the "Communists are losing in combat more than four times as many men as all the allied forces." And, as debate continued to swirl over the now infamous cross-over point, the general declared that the "Viet Cong, all over the country, are experiencing severe manpower problems."[101] Either the "honorable warrior" Johnson believed MACV was making real headway against the enemy or he too felt obliged to back the president's agenda of garnering domestic support for a seemingly stalemated war.

In part, Westmoreland's own comments seem all the more regrettable given his overview of the war within MACV's 1968 campaign plan. The report delineated three principal roles for US and allied forces—pacification (a mission of "paramount importance"), offensive operations, and containment to prepare for the eventual withdrawal of US forces. Of note, the plan placed emphasis on the "dispersion of battalion size units for expansion of effective territorial security for pacification."[102] In a broad sense, little had changed in Westmoreland's strategy for South Vietnam. MACV throughout deemed military pressure on the enemy as essential to promoting nation building in a secure environment. Westmoreland also continued to speak on the importance of political, economic, social, and psychological programs supporting the larger war effort. Far from being condemned, the plan garnered broad support by senior officers. Each of the service chiefs wrote the president in February 1968 that they backed Westmoreland's strategy, which represented a "well-conceived and balanced approach toward freeing the South Vietnamese countryside from the domination of organized military units." Still, the MACV staff and commander realized they had yet to win the population's support, the sine qua non for maintaining an independent, noncommunist South Vietnam.[103]

This inability to gain popular support, arguably *the* underlying shortcoming in MACV's strategy, came into sharp relief with the early 1968 Tet offensive. In a nationwide attack, some 84,000 NLF troops and North Vietnamese regulars struck 36 of the 44 provincial capitals, the US embassy in Saigon, and the six largest cities in South Vietnam. Tet quite simply altered the trajectory of the war. As one US senator exclaimed, "What happened? I thought we were supposed to be winning this war."[104] Incoming Secretary of Defense Clark M. Clifford, after a full strategic review, recommended against additional troop deployments and any further expansion of the war. Despite gargantuan efforts on the part of Americans, Clifford had found "no diminution in the will of the enemy." (Tet, of course, had shaken the Hanoi leadership and resulted in significant political and diplomatic setbacks.)[105] Westmoreland had requested extra troops to take advantage of the horrendous casualties suffered by the enemy, but events away from the battlefield already had trumped any tactical successes made by US and South Vietnamese combat units. Political leaders in Washington, journalists reporting from Saigon, and even those prosecuting the war in South Vietnam no

longer could defend the costs of a conflict in which victory was so hard to deci-
pher. Time, the most fundamental aspect in Westmoreland's concept of "attrition," had run out.

Elusive Objectives

In the aftermath of Tet, General Creighton Abrams, soon to be the MACV commander, met with President Johnson and JCS Chairman Earle Wheeler on 26
March 1968. After a wide-ranging discussion on the war, the president asked
"Is there anything we should be doing that we aren't doing?" Wheeler believed
not, arguing that "Our basic strategy is sound." Abrams concurred. "I don't feel
we need to change strategy," the presumptive commander stated.[106] It seemed
clear, however, that despite years of effort, the US mission in South Vietnam
had failed to achieve its objective of breaking Hanoi's will to continue the war.
Westmoreland and the American forces he led had fallen short. Yet it is doubtful that any alteration to MACV's strategy would have resolved the deep-seated,
if not intractable, problems of fighting such a complex war in Southeast Asia.
While an uncomfortable truth, there were limitations to what US power could
achieve overseas during the Cold War era. One senior officer recalled that most
Americans assumed the enemy would quit if hit hard enough and long enough.
"But that assumption was totally wrong. The enemy was not going to quit, no
matter how good our statistics looked. We had made it a war of wills, rather than
a war of power. The problem was, while we had the power, it turned out they had
the will."[107]

The Americans' inability to break Hanoi's will reflected a fundamental flaw
in the logic of nearly all US civilian and military leaders during the Vietnam
War. These leaders recognized the basic factors responsible for political turmoil
in South Vietnam: "chronic factionalism, civilian-military suspicion and dis-
trust, absence of national spirit and motivation, lack of cohesion in the social
structure, lack of experience in the conduct of government."[108] In spite of these
realities, Americans held faith that military power, applied in a holistic manner,
would overcome the intrinsic weaknesses of South Vietnamese society. The
basic assumption that population security would lead to support for the GVN
proved incorrect. And without this support, breaking Hanoi's will would remain
outside of Westmoreland's reach. Here lay the truth of American military strategy in South Vietnam. The MACV commander had failed, not because of some
blind faith in attrition, but rather because of incongruities within the widely held
conviction that US military power could remedy social and political ills abroad.
When the reality of war discredited this belief, wounded critics, still true believ-
ers in American supremacy, turned on Westmoreland, blaming him for a lost war.

Arguably, what Westmoreland lacked, as did the entire US Army during the Vietnam War, was a way not only to link the various aspects of strategy into a coherent whole but also a way to articulate broad military concepts for such a complex environment as South Vietnam. Both the reality and the rhetoric of war had proved insurmountable for American leaders in the early and mid-1960s. An impoverished strategic language left uniformed officers and their civilian leaders unable to communicate fully their intentions and the means to achieve their objectives. Westmoreland's strategy was more nuanced and sophisticated than the language available to describe that strategy. Words like attrition, while useful for critics, remain unsatisfying in expressing the complexity of the tasks facing Americans and their South Vietnamese allies in the 1960s. Westmoreland's "three-phase sustained campaign," with its multitude of subordinate political and military tasks, in short, defied easy explication. No less easy was finding a way to implement such an all-encompassing strategy on the battlefields of South Vietnam.[109]

4

On Bewildering Battlefields

Implementing Westmoreland's Strategy

In September 1965, as American combat troops plunged into South Vietnam, Admiral U. S. Grant Sharp, the Commander in Chief, Pacific, cabled the JCS chairman to comment on the expanding role of US forces. Sharp noted that in a counterinsurgency the "primary object is to restore security to the population....If we are to succeed we must do a number of things at the same time and do them differently than we did in past conflicts."[1] Just over a year later, with Americans long since bloodied from battling a determined enemy, Westmoreland spoke on a similar topic at the October 1966 Manila Conference. The MACV commander's remarks, however, hinted at the limits of American strategy in Vietnam. "The fact is," Westmoreland observed, "that all of the military power which we can bring to bear can achieve only one thing: a state of security in which the people of South Vietnam can develop their institutions of government, their natural resources, and their potential for production."[2] In short, US strategic aims meant nothing unless the local population and government consummated the arduous process of nation building.

Both Sharp's and Westmoreland's comments highlighted the importance of strategic implementation. Success at the tactical level facilitated, if not permitted, strategic success. Yet critics of American strategy in Vietnam long have castigated Westmoreland for directing his troops toward traditional combat operations of finding, fighting, and destroying the enemy. One contemporary observer believed firepower was the "backbone" of American tactics, a point embraced by historians for the last 40 years.[3] John Nagl, for instance, has argued that the US Army's "employment of excessive firepower" and "reliance on large unit operations" made it "ineffective in a counterinsurgency role." In Nagl's account, military leaders in Vietnam rejected suggestions on improving their counterinsurgency doctrine and instead concentrated on tactical and technological innovations "all designed to assist in bringing conventional firepower to bear." Excluded from such analyses were officers like Major General Arthur S. Collins, the 4th Infantry Division commander in late 1966 and early 1967, who argued that the "tactical problem is determined by the attitude of the population." American troops most certainly used firepower—sometimes to excess—on the battlefields of South Vietnam, but many officers and soldiers also realized that tactics equated to politics within the larger paradigm of revolutionary warfare.[4]

When one considers Westmoreland's strategy from a more holistic perspective, the army's tactical approach seems less wedded to the conventional concepts of firepower and maneuver. Arguably, far too many critics have discounted the war's context when assessing how MACV chose to confront the political-military threat to South Vietnam's independence. In 1965, the American command believed, correctly so, that the National Liberation Front "retained complete control over areas of SVN and maintained their grip over other areas by terrorism."[5] The war clearly had progressed beyond limited guerrilla attacks against government officials and infrastructure. It was in this atmosphere, one in which Saigon risked collapse, that Westmoreland devised his strategy and supporting concept for operations. Accordingly, a September MACV directive on the tactics and techniques for the employment of US forces began with the premise that the "war in Vietnam is a political as well as a military war." The edict advised unit commanders that a "conscious effort must be made to minimize battle casualties among those non-combatants who must be brought back into the fold in the course of time." While the directive spoke of offensive search and destroy operations against "VC base areas and forces," commanders still needed to embrace the conflict's political and psychological aspects. Only through the combination of military force and "an imaginative and aggressive civic action program" could the war be won.[6]

By investigating what the army did throughout the mosaic of Vietnam one finds evidence of learning and adaptation in a Cold War era political-military conflict. Without question, the army found it difficult adjusting to the new realities of revolutionary warfare. As correspondent Ward Just noted in 1968, the "Vietnamese atmosphere, both of the people and of the land, varied from province to province and region to region. What held true in one part of the country was irrelevant in another." Yet to argue, as some historians have, that "the body count... drove strategic and tactical decision making at all levels," quite simply reduces the US Army in Vietnam to a machine wired only for killing.[7] Such claims ignore the *process* of planning, implementing, and sustaining a strategy that considered much more than destruction of enemy forces. These accusations equally discount how MACV regarded "military operations" as the mutually supporting tasks of military offensives, pacification, and nation building. The army's actual experience in war, it seems, has become distorted by historians' unquestioning acceptance that attrition drove all aspects of the American military experience in South Vietnam.[8]

Exploring how various US Army divisions attempted to carry out MACV's strategy surfaces an organization willing to experiment with new ideas and tactical approaches. Fighting obviously mattered. (The army defined "tactical" as actions "pertaining to the employment of units in combat.") Yet even in the aftermath of the November 1965 Ia Drang battle, the MACV commander warned against the tendency to exaggerate the magnitude of battlefield engagements. Westmoreland announced that most tactical actions were "small, involving relatively small numbers of troops and from these successes there may be a tendency to draw a conclusion that a battle or series of battles may end the conflict thru a single or a combination of military victories." As the general cautioned, "This is not that type of war."[9] Rather, the type of war in which American troops engaged depended on each unit's location, the predilections and talents of individual commanders, and the varying nature of the enemy threat. Generalizing the army's conduct of the war as simple "attrition" oversimplifies what one officer more accurately described as a "virtual kaleidoscope of apparently unrelated actions [that were] bewildering to many observers."[10]

The New Face of War

In 1986, more than a decade after the fall of Saigon, the publication of Andrew F. Krepinevich's *The Army and Vietnam* met a warm reception from reviewers. Among his core arguments, the former West Point instructor and then army major argued that the 1st Cavalry Division's November 1965 battle in the Ia Drang valley validated the "army concept" of conventional warfare in Vietnam. To Krepinevich, the bloody clash (later popularized in the memoir *We Were Soldiers Once…and Young*) represented for Westmoreland "the successful application of the attrition strategy.... Standard operations were working; therefore, no alternative strategies need be explored. No more feedback was required for MACV save the body counts that measured the attrition strategy's progress."[11] Firepower, a cultural imperative in Krepinevich's army, still won wars. An officer corps blinded by their quest for high body counts thus failed to appreciate the role counterinsurgency played in defeating the internal threat to South Vietnam. In large measure, *The Army and Vietnam* was a goldmine for those seeking evidence that heavy-handed tactics supporting a flawed strategy of attrition led to failure in Southeast Asia.[12]

Krepinevich, however, overstated his case that the army's conventional culture impeded organizational learning. In part, the argument failed to consider fully the context in which MACV had planned the 1st Cavalry Division's deployment. Possessing 435 helicopters, the new "airmobile" unit carved out a base in

An Khe, a relatively unpopulated area in South Vietnam's Central Highlands. Westmoreland intended the 1st Cavalry to screen the neighboring Cambodian border while protecting the vital Highway 19 which ran from Pleiku eastward to the coast.[13] Far from making this decision based on a cultural preference for battle, the MACV commander felt obliged to deploy his first division-sized unit in-country to An Khe because of the enemy threat. North Vietnamese regulars already had been crossing into South Vietnam from Cambodia. By early October 1965, Le Duan and Nguyen Chi Thanh had committed three NVA infantry regiments to the area, two of which struck the US Special Forces camp at Plei Me and throttled the South Vietnamese army column sent to relieve the beleaguered defenders. Westmoreland fretted that a major communist offensive would isolate the northern provinces from Saigon. Added to the MACV commander's concerns, Westmoreland expected the 1st Cavalry Division, thanks to its air mobility, to help guard critical lowland rice harvests from NLF disruption.[14]

This combination of main force and insurgent threats, rather than some instinctive desire for conventional battle, guided the deployment of US forces. Writing in August 1965, Ambassador Lodge concurred with Westmoreland's assessment. "While the Viet Cong regard the densely populated and rice-rich Mekong Delta as the prize in South Vietnam, they consider the highlands as the major battleground, since the difficult terrain, dense vegetation, and limited lines of communication tend to minimize RVNAF ground and air superiorities."[15] Recent evidence suggests that Hanoi aimed to isolate the highlands from Saigon by luring American and South Vietnamese troops onto ground more favorable to the communists. Given US advantages in firepower, such a strategy was fraught with risk. Still, NVA leaders believed that the annihilation of five or six American companies would reverberate far from the battlefield. As Major General Chu Huy Man recalled, "It was our intention to draw the Americans out of An Khe. We did not have any plans to liberate the land; only to destroy troops."[16]

Man's strategy, along with Westmoreland's requirement to protect the civilian population and its rice harvests, forced the 1st Cavalry into intensive patrolling throughout much of the Central Highlands. For an airmobile unit conceived to operate and survive on a high-intensity (and possibly nuclear) European battlefield, the division necessarily experimented with new techniques in airlift, coordinating air and artillery fire, and operating in a dispersed fashion. As one cavalry veteran remembered, the airmobile "concept now seems so elemental and commonplace; but in October 1965 it was revolutionary." While critics derided the fascination with helicopters—one believed they "exaggerated two great weaknesses of the American character in counter-insurgency—impatience and aggressiveness"—Westmoreland took special notice of the problem associated with noncombatant casualties caused by US firepower.[17] The general realized that even in the relatively underpopulated area of the Central Highlands, it was "the nature of the VC to live in villages and hamlets among the people." Westmoreland time and again stressed to his commanders that "casualties among the civilian population will tend to frustrate the attainment of US/GVN goals."[18]

In early October, Westmoreland visited the 1st Cavalry Division's command post to touch upon a similar theme. After receiving a briefing from the staff and unit commanders, the general turned the discussion to the role of US troops in South Vietnam, "emphasizing that our mission was to support the Vietnamese in defeating the communist insurgents and aggression and at the same time and of equal importance, make friends among the local people and hopefully earn their respect and admiration." The MACV chief wanted the behavior of American troops to be in "direct contrast to that of the French forces whose conduct was deplored by the Vietnamese."[19] Yet Westmoreland equally was aware that the main threat to the Central Highlands came from North Vietnamese regulars infiltrating across the Cambodian border into South Vietnam. Thus, while the 1st Cavalry grappled with the novel challenges of fitting airmobile tactics into the unique environment of South Vietnam, commanders also wrestled with how best to exploit their technological dominance while limiting collateral damage among the rural population and hopefully gaining support from local villagers. Air power, not surprisingly, often worked at cross purposes with the goal of gaining popular support for the Saigon government.

Though the role of air power largely falls outside the purview of this book—Westmoreland held no authority over the air campaign against North Vietnam—it is worth noting that MACV relied on tactical air support from the US Air Force and Navy throughout the war. (Complicating the US command structure, the Marine Corps retained control of its own aircraft.) Air superiority offered Americans distinct advantages when it came to battling North Vietnamese regular formations. Moreover, MACV planners hoped that interdiction missions against the Ho Chi Minh Trail would limit enemy infiltration into South Vietnam.[20] Coercing Hanoi through aerial attack, however, proved frustratingly elusive. The enemy devised elaborate countermeasures to offset American bombing missions and results never matched the aspirations of air advocates. Worse for Westmoreland, the use of air power undermined the larger goals of building a stable community inside South Vietnam. The introduction of B-52 strategic bombers in the summer of 1965 against suspected Vietcong base complexes and the creation of "free fire zones" brought an unprecedented level of destruction to the countryside. In truth, US bombing altered the very living patterns of Vietnamese villagers. One Phu My resident noted that farmers in his village were "afraid of air strikes, so they have to work at night." Thus, while US officers hoped that command of the air would contribute defeating the enemy,

Figure 4.1 THE AIRMOBILE CONCEPT IN ACTION. UH-1D helicopters airlift members of the 14th Infantry Regiment, 25th Infantry Division to a new staging area during Operation Wahiawa, northeast of Cu Chi, 16 May 1966. (RG 111-CV, NARA, 97)

the war among the villages left few opportunities for American airmen to distinguish between friend and foe. A big reason that MACV could not win over the populace was fomented, at least in part, by the disruptive force of American air strikes across Vietnam.[21]

Certainly, the November 1965 battle in the Ia Drang valley appealed to those US Army officers looking for opportunities to fight a recognizable enemy on a clearly defined battlefield away from civilians. Since October, Major General Harry W. Kinnard's cavalrymen had been sparring with PAVN forces, each side bloodying the other through sporadic firefights. In early November, Man planned for another attack on the Plei Me camp. Kinnard, however, struck first, landing a battalion directly into the enemy's staging area. Within hours of disembarking at Landing Zone X-Ray, Lieutenant Colonel Harold G. Moore's 1st Battalion, 7th Cavalry became engulfed in "fighting as fierce as any ever experienced by American troops." One trooper portrayed the battlefield as "smoke, artillery, screaming, moaning, fear, bullets, blood, and little yellow men running around screeching with glee when they found one of us alive, or screaming and moaning when they ran into a grenade or a bullet."[22] For three days Moore's unit gallantly held off waves of NVA assaults, arguably saved only by the B-52 bombing strikes which the US Air Force employed for the first time in a tactical role.

On 17 November, Man decided he had seen enough and withdrew back across the Cambodian border. Body counts revealed Moore's troopers killed 634 NVA soldiers—the unit "estimated" it had taken the lives of another 1,215—compared to losing 75 killed and 121 wounded.[23]

As with most all Vietnam engagements, body counts told only a portion of the story. Westmoreland publicly considered Ia Drang an "unprecedented victory" marshalling as his evidence that "more enemy were killed in this engagement than in any thus far." Privately, however, the general cabled Washington that based on estimates of increasing enemy infiltration numbers he would require a larger number of troops than initially anticipated. McNamara, concerned over additional force requests, already was on his way to Vietnam for a personal assessment. The visit shook the increasingly disillusioned defense secretary. McNamara recalled that while he was impressed by the valor and courage of American soldiers, he "saw and heard many problems. The U.S. presence rested on a bowl of jelly: political instability had increased; pacification had stalled; South Vietnamese Army desertions had skyrocketed."[24] Even Moore's presumably successful battle revealed complications with implementing MACV strategy. The North Vietnamese, not the Americans, decided when to open and disengage from the fighting. The battle seemed to make little impact on enemy infiltration rates. Nor did Hanoi appear at all fazed by either the ground war in South Vietnam or the intensified bombing of North Vietnam. As McNamara told reporters before heading back to Washington, "It will be a long war."[25]

While 1st Cavalry commanders grappled with the tactical lessons from Ia Drang and the secretary of defense struggled with his own "grave doubts" on the overall war effort, the enemy too responded to their first true encounter with US ground troops. The American advantages in firepower were obvious. Conceding this point, both NVA and NLF units sought to "grab the enemy by the belt" during tactical engagements. By getting in close with American soldiers, they hoped to mitigate the destructiveness wrought by US attack helicopters and airplanes.[26] The practice of "clutching the people to their breast" also served the Front's ends by making it exceedingly difficult for American and South Vietnamese forces to protect the civilian population. In truth, most US Army commanders did not like firing on populated areas. As one 1st Cavalry "lessons learned" report noted, "search and destroy operations where the enemy and innocent civilians are intermingled continues to present problems." The report advised using Vietnamese interpreters to help identify noncombatants, but in the heat of battle many soldiers found such recommendations impracticable.[27]

Far from focusing solely on search and destroy operations, the 1st Cavalry placed equal emphasis on civic action and rural construction programs, even in the lightly populated region of the Central Highlands. The division constructed schoolhouses, provided medical treatment to local citizens, assisted farmers in agricultural activities, and distributed food and clothing to "needy families and war victims." This emphasis corresponded with Westmoreland's own philosophy. Just three days before Moore's bloody clash with the North Vietnamese, the MACV commander cabled Wheeler, noting that "in operations which are designed to return an area which has been under VC domination to full time governmental control, civic action in the form of food, medical care and other assistance is a central feature of the operation and is accomplished as soon as the tactical situation permits and common sense indicates."[28] One month later, with the dust settling in the Ia Drang valley, Westmoreland sent a similar directive to the newly arrived 1st Infantry Division. The general directed that US advisors work with their South Vietnamese counterparts to establish a "realistic and consistent" rural construction plan. Westmoreland believed that the US troop buildup permitted not only an increased emphasis on civic action, but also allowed the "release of a far greater number of ARVN units for clearing and securing operations." Most important, the process facilitated the GVN's ability "to take early action to restore its presence in newly secured areas."[29]

The 1st Infantry Division's arrival into country exemplified the difficulties in extending US and GVN influence into areas considered "VC dominated territory." The unit set up base camps at Di An, Phuoc Vinh, and Lai Khe with the intent of guarding the approaches to Saigon and disrupting enemy movement north and northwest of the capital. Newly arrived US troops quickly found their movements canalized along roads and trails thanks to the area's dense vegetation. As with their cavalry brethren, the Big Red One's infantrymen confronted an enemy employing "bear hug" tactics aimed at reducing the effectiveness of US artillery and air power.[30] Worse, the very nature of combat appeared to upset the sensibilities of young American soldiers. One "lessons learned" report warned that "Females actively support VC activities and have been encountered in battle. Also young children have been used to hurl grenades into vehicles or commit other acts of sabotage. These tactics present problems for Americans who are not usually wary or alert for encounters of this nature." The division aimed to incorporate ARVN units into their pacification operations with the hopes of tackling this new threat, but commanders soon realized that success depended on the too often uneven quality of the South Vietnamese army.[31]

While the 1st Infantry sought ways to combine US-ARVN operations, the unit's commander, Major General William E. DePuy, endeavored to gain some semblance of initiative over a well-entrenched yet elusive enemy. DePuy had served previously as Westmoreland's chief operations officer and long had studied the problem of hindering NLF activities in populated areas. In a series of "Commanders Notes" in early 1966, the North Dakota native directed his battalions to engage in "saturation patrolling" missions, highlighting his personal preference for aggressive offensive action. By inundating locales with American infantry companies and platoons, DePuy hoped to force NLF withdrawals and assist populations in regaining "a sense of security achieved from the ever present network of patrols about the area."[32] Immersing himself in the finer points of tactical operations, the division commander offered advice on how squads should travel in rough terrain, how units should attack enemy fortified positions, and how rifle companies should anticipate "meeting engagements" with the Vietcong. No operation was to be planned outside the range of American artillery support. In DePuy's mind, expertise at the tactical level of war and in wielding US advantages in firepower offered the best chance of separating the NLF's insurgents from the rural population.[33]

The 1st Division commander's tactical observations made eminent sense. The problem, however, lay in Americans finding an enemy that blended so well into the countryside. As such, the word "ambush" appeared time and again in references to the fighting inside South Vietnam. Malcolm W. Browne of the Associated Press believed it "probably safe to say that the primary distinguishing feature of the Vietnamese war is the ambush." DePuy and other commanders lamented over their units' inability to find the enemy, one division going so far as to set up an "ambush academy" to train their soldiers, yet NVA and Liberation Front forces seemed always to hold the upper hand.[34] Far too often, the enemy rather than American troops initiated contact. One US soldier, graphically illustrating many of his peers' frustrations, inscribed on his helmet "War is hell, but contact is a mother fucker." The vicissitudes of combat wore heavily on young infantrymen. Clearly the NVA and NLF were not everywhere, but they were "apt to be met anywhere." As one veteran reflected, "a soldier in the counter-insurgency war of Vietnam could never know when violence would run amok and peace would interpose its fragile reign. Vietnam was the unexpected war, an alien world ruled by its lack of rules, totally at the mercy of its unexpectedness."[35]

The tactical frustrations of constant yet fruitless patrolling held deep ramifications for Westmoreland's strategy. How could American forces help protect the population and usher in GVN presence if they could not even find the enemy? Commanders at all levels strained to collect accurate intelligence on a foe that moved continuously and blended easily into the population. For the 1st Infantry Division, though, the problem seemed one of too few troops deployed in too large an area. With thirteen maneuver battalions, DePuy found it nearly impossible to defend the major cities in his tactical zone of responsibility, launch offensive operations to keep the enemy off balance, and at the same time support civic action and rural construction projects.[36] Westmoreland, still hoping to reverse the losing trend in South Vietnam, worried that his units were not "engaging the VC with sufficient frequency or effectiveness to win the war." As he explained to his senior leaders in mid-1966, "we have not yet proved that we have mastered the art of finding and destroying major VC forces through sustained campaigns against them in a given area."[37] Later critics would admonish Westmoreland for this focus on engaging enemy forces, yet any strategy founded on the principles of population security required the allies to defeat an enemy intent on controlling the Vietnamese people.

Despite the attention MACV placed on search and destroy operations, units like the 1st Infantry Division still carried out the accompanying nonmilitary tasks of Westmoreland's strategy. MACV directed that commanders "consider both the military and psychological objective of each operation" and plan them "in coordination with province and district chiefs." Moreover, a "civic action plan should be developed to support each operation even if the area has been controlled by the VC."[38] The Big Red One adhered to these guidelines and in June 1966 carried out Operation Lam Son II. Divisional units conducted a "seal and search" mission in Tan Phuoc Khanh before kicking off a hamlet festival that included speeches by candidates running for local office, medical treatment by army doctors and dentists, and National Police screening of all males between the ages of 15 and 45. To put a Vietnamese face on the operation, the 5th ARVN Division assisted with interviewing local villagers and checking identification cards. Lam Son II undoubtedly fell short of its main objective of eliminating the NLF infrastructure in Tan Phuoc Khanh. Still, the 1st Infantry Division's leadership believed it essential to incorporate psychological operations and civil affairs teams into their missions if they held any prospect of swaying the local population.[39]

Other operations demonstrated that MACV was paying more than just lip service to civic action and rural construction programs. According to its mission statement in 1966, the 1st Infantry Division "continued to conduct combat and Revolutionary Development operations designed to further extend and consolidate RVN control throughout the III Corps Tactical Zone."[40] Nowhere did divisional leaders speak of attrition simply for the sake of killing the enemy. One operation, Rolling Stone, highlighted how the Big Red One aimed to combine search and destroy missions with the larger objective of reinstating effective governmental presence in the countryside. The division's First Brigade constructed a road between Routes 13 and 16 "to open the area to RVN economic and military influence." Resting on contemporary counterinsurgency principles, the operation incorporated the "interrelated fields" of civic action, psychological warfare, and ground combat operations. 1st Infantry Division commanders ensured they included South Vietnamese officials into "Rolling Stone" and appreciated the importance of leaving a military force permanently based in the area to provide long-term security to the population. As one post-operation report stated, the "people must see stability and the capability of the GVN to maintain peaceful and improving conditions."[41] Even with DePuy's emphasis on firepower, his division understood winning the war required more than conventional combat.

Rolling Stone equally highlighted the often misplaced optimism American officers expressed for their operations. The commander's final evaluation report anticipated that the area encompassed by Rolling Stone "could become pro GVN in a relatively short period of time."[42] Given that the 1st Infantry Division continued to battle enemy forces in the III Corps region for the remainder of its tour in Vietnam, such confidence now seems imprudent. At the time, however, DePuy and his men believed they had blunted the 9th PLAF Division's aim of breaking governmental control over the countryside. Yet the problem remained of how best to translate tactical successes into strategic advantage. In Operation Attleboro, which consumed much of the division in October and November, 1st Infantry soldiers handled themselves well in numerous small-unit actions. Still, by the end of 1966 the division had made no significant inroads in helping link the local population to the central government in Saigon. Nor were American commanders even certain how much they had damaged the enemy in combat. Throughout South Vietnam, NLF and NVA forces continued to prove elusive. Westmoreland's headquarters recorded in December 1966 that the allies had failed to make contact with 56 enemy battalions identified in the MACV order of battle. Divisions like the 1st Cavalry and 1st Infantry might be adapting to a new way of war, yet the US Army's effectiveness in the political-military environment of South Vietnam remained incomplete. Population security, itself an illusory goal, did not lead inevitably to political stability.[43]

The Extended Battlefield

Unsurprisingly, other American units faced similar challenges despite fighting a very different type of war than their counterparts in III Corps or the Central Highlands. In early 1966, the 25th Infantry Division arrived in Hau Nghia province. Though a brigade had been posted in Pleiku at the end of 1965, the remainder of the division moved into positions near Saigon and the Cambodian border to provide security for a key area surrounding South Vietnam's capital. Swampy terrain made the region well suited to rice cultivation and the heavily populated province put Americans into close, sustained contact with civilians. Division leaders, however, considered Hau Nghia "politically unstable because of its long history of rebel activity." As one pacification report noted in mid-1966, before the 25th Infantry arrived effective government control "extended only to the maximum range of supporting weapons located in the Vietnamese military installations immediately surrounding the 4 district capitals and the province capital." Thus, as American soldiers moved into Hau Nghia, they faced a National Liberation Front organization already deeply entrenched within the local population. MACV estimates calculated that the NLF controlled 60 percent of the population with another 15 percent living in "contested areas."[44]

Communist forces proved more than willing to contest Hau Nghia. The province served as a key link between the Mekong Delta and nearby Cambodian sanctuaries and provided a main avenue of approach into Saigon via Highway 1. As proof that Hau Nghia ranked among the least pacified in all of South Vietnam's provinces, the 25th Infantry later found that its divisional headquarters at Cu Chi sat atop a major NLF tunnel system. The rural political system was just as complex. American troops entered a society torn apart by a generation of civil war, with provincial officials unable to move freely through their own hamlets and villages. As one 25th soldier recalled, "our military presence was tenuous. We didn't know what to expect from the enemy or where he was, at least not at my level."[45] At higher levels, US commanders equally appreciated the difficulties. Westmoreland admitted that the 25th ARVN Division, co-located with its American counterpart, was "hanging on by its teeth in Hau Nghia" and believed the province was "almost completely under VC control and has been for many years." To make matters worse, the 25th ranked as the "weakest division in the ARVN," crippled by high desertion rates and a strong NLF organization which had pushed the South Vietnamese forces back on their heels.[46]

In Hau Nghia, the Americans thus faced a much less conventional threat than did the 1st Cavalry Division in the Central Highlands. Major General Fred C. Weyand, the 25th's division commander, accordingly altered how his soldiers operated among the local population. Weyand directed that units engage in "area security" missions aimed at providing continuous protection to the province's villages and hamlets. Far from being formulaic, the command realized that the word "security" oftentimes depended on perception and that it was possible both US and South Vietnamese forces might constitute a threat to a villager's security. The division therefore discouraged the forced movement of refugees and limited the use of firepower. Leaders taught classes on the civil and military structure of South Vietnam and how provincial leaders interacted with AVRN units and local popular forces.[47] Weyand recognized that clearing Hau Nghia of enemy influence would be slow and tedious and thus reproved those expecting "spectacular results or large VC losses." In fact, in discussions with the province chief, Weyand found that successful military operations against NLF base areas and lines of communication were "having no measurable effect on the local civilians, and [were] not especially helpful to that official in carrying out his mission of Revolutionary Development." The general hoped that close coordination with both the 25th ARVN Division's commanders and local provincial leaders would lay the groundwork for an effective, long-term program of security. Unfortunately for Weyand's team, the complexities of operating in Hau Nghia undercut such aspirations.[48]

In early May 1966, Westmoreland directed both the 1st and 25th Infantry Divisions to "start working more closely" with their ARVN counterparts "in order to improve their morale, efficiency and effectiveness." The 25th, modeling the Marines' combined action program, instituted the Combined Lightning Initial Project to help achieve the division's pacification goals. While the division concentrated on training local popular forces, units assigned to the Lightning Project conducted clear and hold missions to "help expand the security 'oil spot' around the division's Cu Chi base camp."[49] The results were marginal. Not only did the NLF adjust its methods to deal with the increased American presence, but heavy fighting north of Saigon in mid-1966 forced Weyand to abandon the combined concept so he could focus on the main force threat to the capital. US soldiers also quickly became frustrated in their dealings with the local Vietnamese. One 25th Infantry soldier bluntly described the cultural divides between American soldiers and rural civilians. "I think one of the biggest disappointments over there was the attitude of the Vietnamese peasants. None of them seemed to give a shit about us. The feeling was mutual: We didn't even think they were people."[50] While certainly not all Americans viewed the population in such stark terms, it seems unlikely that sentiments like this one facilitated improvements in Vietnamese morale or efficiency.

Cultural misunderstandings in fact limited the 25th Infantry's effectiveness given its area security mission and close proximity to a population already weary of war. Despite gaining the military advantage in some areas of Hau Nghia, problems persisted in wresting the political initiative away from the NLF. Weyand's soldiers made few inroads in attacking the Front's infrastructure, what one officer described as "the central junction that makes the whole enemy system of warfare and political subversion work."[51] In large part, lack of intelligence upset the division's plans. Without a true understanding of the NLF's social and political organizational structure, far too many soldiers participated in operations without the benefit of intelligence willingly provided by the local peasantry. The results proved infuriating. As one platoon leader complained, "You could never tell who was the enemy and who was not. Therefore, you treated everybody with suspicion and mistrust."[52] Such misgivings made it immensely difficult for 25th Infantry soldiers to translate military action into pacification progress. In mid-1967, for instance, the division conducted three major operations in a three-month period compared to 1,198 small unit actions during the same quarter. Not only did these operations fail to advance governmental and economic reform in the province, but only 191 of the small unit actions resulted in enemy contact.[53]

Despite these difficulties, the division's leaders, as well as Westmoreland's senior officers, appreciated the importance of the NLF political infrastructure. Brigadier General William A. Knowlton of the MACV Revolutionary

Development Support Directorate recorded in early 1967 that "the omnipresence and influence in the rural areas of the VC political infrastructure" was one of the main obstacles to achieving victory inside South Vietnam.[54] NLF insurgents not only abducted and assassinated government officials, but established a network of personal contacts that proved impenetrable to American soldiers. A July 1967 Rand study concluded that "Viet Cong power derives from its superb organization in the countryside.... To counteract the VC we must disrupt this organization, develop counterpart organizations, and use family ties to develop support for the GVN."[55] Left unstated were examples of how US soldiers might help build family ties with a people held in such contempt by far too many young Americans. In truth, divisions like the 25th Infantry struggled mightily to engage the enemy in ways that affected this political infrastructure. The problem throughout was finding ways to match the NLF's fundamental understanding of the population's economic, personal, and community needs.

Though enlightened officers like Weyand and Knowlton valued the political struggle in achieving MACV's strategic aims, it would be disingenuous to suggest that the entire US Army in Vietnam grasped the meaning of the NLF's infrastructure. Learning had its limits. Battle still captivated, and thus narrowed the vision of, many American soldiers. Even in the 25th Infantry Division, leaders found combat alluring. One brigade commander felt that "commanders are too prone when we go into an area that's dominated by the VC to want to move all the civilians out, destroy the villages, and make it a free fire zone." While this colonel felt pacification offered a more effective way of dealing with the people, battle remained compelling. As one officer noted, to "most tactical commanders, civic action is a dull subject because it doesn't have the excitement and glamour of combat operations."[56] Soldiers received from their leaders both tangible and subtle rewards for killing the enemy. In a letter home, one platoon leader wrote of the benefits battle bestowed on its participants. "Last night I killed and everyone has been patting me on the back, including the battalion commander." Even President Johnson quipped that he regarded military men with suspicion given the appeal of war. "It's hard to be a military hero without a war. Heroes need battles and bombs and bullets in order to be heroic."[57] Soldiers surely realized that winning the support of the people was just as important as winning battles against the enemy, yet many still were drawn to the exhilaration of combat.

While soldiers may have been captivated by combat, Westmoreland deemed battle useful for the larger goal of breaking the enemy's hold in the countryside north of Saigon. (US Army tactics sometimes were reliant on firepower and large-unit operations because of the enemy's own commitment to winning the war militarily.) Known as the "Iron Triangle," the base area long had housed an NLF logistics center and headquarters for Military Region IV which controlled insurgent activity in and around the South Vietnamese capital. Westmoreland believed, according to one subordinate, that "the Communists *had* to fight for their critical base areas. When they attempted to defend them superior American power would destroy the defenders and base areas alike."[58] Thus, in early January 1967, the 25th Infantry Division, along with the 1st Infantry Division and 11th Armored Cavalry Regiment, launched Operation Cedar Falls. The multidivisional operation was the largest search and destroy mission to date. Intending to annihilate enemy forces and infrastructure, American and ARVN forces evacuated the population and turned the Iron Triangle into a "free fire zone." Engineer teams followed with bulldozers, clearing over 2,700 acres of jungle to deny the enemy a sanctuary so close to Saigon. In just under three weeks, Cedar Falls racked up impressive statistics—750 confirmed enemy dead, 60,000 round of small arms ammunition captured, and 3,700 tons of rice seized. The contribution to the war effort, however, remained unclear. One post-operation analysis noted that "attrition of enemy personnel is not a completely adequate criterion of effectiveness of ground operations even when linked to the ability and will of the enemy to replace them."[59] In short, there were too many variables to measure Cedar Fall's impact on the war effort as a whole.

Westmoreland, though, hoped to maintain some sense of momentum and in late February launched Operation Junction City. Over 25 US and ARVN battalions swept into Tay Ninh province in War Zone C to locate the elusive Central Office for South Vietnam (COSVN) headquarters and destroy NLF forces and base areas. Similar to the Iron Triangle, the war zone long had been a haven for insurgents who enjoyed relatively easy access to nearby Cambodia and the sanctuaries within. Westmoreland believed that if he could drive out the communists, the allies might establish their own base areas from which to conduct follow-on operations against any returning communists.[60] These sizable military offensives, however, were planned as the opening rounds of a much longer campaign. Following the MACV commander's longstanding concept, Junction City aimed not only to attrite enemy forces but to "provide a shield for revolutionary development in the area."[61] More than 35,000 allied troops took part in the largest operation of the war to dismantle the enemy's political-military infrastructure in War Zone C and thus afford pacification a chance to thrive.

Of note, Operation Fairfax occurred simultaneously with Junction City. The joint US-ARVN mission on the outskirts of Saigon focused on civic action during the day and extensive patrolling at night. Westmoreland hoped that by operating at night the allies would disturb community life in Gia Dinh province as little as possible while harassing NLF insurgents when they were most active. The MACV commander also intended that the "double force" nature of the operation—for every American unit engaged in Fairfax, an ARVN unit took part—would allow the South Vietnamese to assume responsibility for Gia Dinh's security when US troops withdrew.[62] At first, Fairfax appeared effective.

The allies secured and reopened roadways, established outposts, and assisted local police in arresting suspected insurgents. As the operation continued into 1967, however, Westmoreland worried that the "extended integration" of US and South Vietnamese forces was becoming counterproductive. Despite the creation of a Combined Intelligence Center (CIC) and a Combined Civic Action Coordination Center (CACC), it seemed as if the local forces were content to let the Americans take charge. As Lieutenant General Ngo Quang Truong recalled, the "permanent danger was that the ARVN had become psychologically and materially too dependent on Americans." Thus, while Westmoreland was heartened by an improving security situation around Saigon, he equally was disappointed with the "buddy" concept on which Fairfax rested.[63]

Perhaps unsurprisingly, the results in War Zone C proved similarly ambiguous. As in both Fairfax and Cedar Falls, the numbers of enemy casualties—2,728 killed—and captured equipment during Junction City indicated a successful mission. The statistics, however, failed to acknowledge the impermanence of these search and destroy missions. As the MACV Command History conceded, "Major operations, such as Cedar Falls and Junction City, required that several units be massed to obtain the requisite 25 to 30 battalions, but competing requirements for the available forces did not permit sustained operations of such magnitude."[64] Brigadier General Bernard W. Rogers, the 1st Infantry's assistant division commander, further highlighted the problems of many MACV operations. "One of the discouraging features of both Cedar Falls and Junction City was the fact that we had insufficient forces, either U.S. or South Vietnamese, to permit us to continue to operate in the Iron Triangle and War Zone C and thereby prevent the Viet Cong from returning. In neither instance were we able to stay around, and it was not long before there was evidence of the enemy's return."[65]

If US tactical operations delivered only ephemeral results, the military contest in the countryside also forced an unprecedented demographic shift to urban areas. The physical destruction of war quite literally transformed rural Vietnamese society. By mid-1968, South Vietnam's urban areas experienced a population increase of roughly 1,500,000, most of these refugees dislocated from their ancestral homes. This exodus clearly undermined the larger goals of nation building. Some senior American officials wondered aloud if depopulation of the countryside, awful as it was, deprived the enemy of a sea within which to swim and facilitated the government's control over its people. Westmoreland himself was among those considering the possibilities of what Harvard political scientist Samuel Huntington called "forced draft urbanization and modernization."[66]

Back in early January, less than a month before the 1968 Tet offensive, the MACV commander penned a memorandum titled "The Refugee Problem." "Frustrated with the high costs and slow progress of pacification," Westmoreland discussed the insurgency's doggedness in maintaining its control over the civilian population. Perhaps drying up the "water" of villagers would cause the "fish" of the National Liberation Front to wither and die. As the general saw it, in what can best be described as a think piece (this was not a signed directive), only two options were available: "either the communists and their political control must be driven from the populated areas and security provided to keep them out, or the people must be relocated into areas that will facilitate security and prevent communist control apparatus from re-entering the community." While Westmoreland preferred the first option, he expressed concern that the "time consuming" process was showing itself to be costly in terms of both resources and manpower. The second option, though, could be "carried out relatively quickly and is not as expensive in security troops as the first course of action."[67] Once more, the element of time entered into Westmoreland's calculations. If the Saigon government was finding it difficult to motivate and mobilize the rural population, and Americans at home increasingly were questioning the war's progress, conceivably a relocation of that population to urban areas might facilitate a more rapid dismantling of the NLF political and military infrastructure.

The costs, however, of any such approach were obviously high. Draining the sea was far from a peaceful endeavor. As one Hiep Duc villager recounted, the people "resented the GVN when it shelled the village day and night even when there were no liberation troops in the village." American journalist Frances Fitzgerald, reporting on the worsening conditions in Saigon, found "gigantic sewers" and "lakes full of stagnant filth." (Already by 1966, Saigon's infant mortality rate exceeded 35 percent.)[68] Moreover, Senator Edward Kennedy, serving as chairman of the Senate Judiciary Subcommittee on Refugees, blasted the disintegration of South Vietnam's rural society caused by American military operations. "No great nation can long claim to have won freedom and democracy for another people," Kennedy proclaimed in late 1967, "if, in the process, the destruction of their land and way of life was the hallmark of the effort."[69]

Commanders like those in the 25th Infantry Division, as well as senior leaders like Westmoreland, realized the local population's role in contesting NLF influence within South Vietnam. Even doctrine admitted as such. "The local population within the area of operations may exert considerable influence upon the operational environment," the army's principal field manual declared. "Its attitude, action and capabilities may facilitate or hinder military operations."[70] The battlefield thus extended far beyond the confines of tactical engagement areas. While the 25th Infantry Division based its area security mission on sensible counterinsurgency concepts, the ideological and political aspects of the war complicated the efforts of foreign troops seeking to connect a people to its government. Fighting a war among the people necessarily meant disruption, dislocation, and destruction. Westmoreland unmistakably understood this from the start. As he wrote to the Joint Chiefs in August 1965, "We are keenly aware of the problem associated with noncombatant casualties caused by US troops." To establish a shield behind which pacification could prosper, though, required those same "US troops to be involved repeatedly in populated areas, much as we would like to avoid it."[71] Unfortunately for American soldiers fighting among the hamlets and villages of South Vietnam, no lines demarcated the boundaries between the enemy and the population.

Commander's Prerogative

The experiences of the 25th Infantry Division stood in stark contrast with those of the 1st Cavalry Division in the Central Highlands, the 9th Infantry Division in the Mekong Delta, or even the US Marines in the northern provinces of South Vietnam. MACV's commander presided over a war best described as a mosaic in which "each situation required different military tactics and a different mixture of military and political *dau tranh* [struggle]."[72] Thus, it should be no surprise that techniques varied widely between units. Yet tactics fluctuated within units as well, modified by commanders who approached the political-military problem based on their individual ideas and initiatives. Personnel replacement policies promoted these variations. In the 4th Infantry Division, for instance, four different commanders led the unit between September 1966 and November 1968. Only once during this time period did a commander lead the division for a full year. Operating mostly in the II Corps Tactical Zone—one detached brigade served in War Zone C with the 25th Division—the 4th Infantry spent much of its time concentrated on the border between Cambodia and South Vietnam. Despite the division's constant focus on North Vietnamese units infiltrating across the border, Westmoreland permitted each commander to approach his unique tactical problems as he best saw fit.[73]

Troop increases in 1966 allowed MACV's commander to send the 4th Infantry into Pleiku without weakening his defense of the coast. As Westmoreland recalled, because "the North Vietnamese seemed determined to continue to fight for the Highlands," he had to defend against the enemy maintaining an offensive posture in so crucial a region. In fact, Hanoi regarded the Central Highlands as a "theater of extreme strategic importance."[74] If Westmoreland had to focus his attention on the more populated coastal region, he could not ignore the enemy threat near Pleiku. Arriving in August, the 4th Infantry went straight to work in torrential rains and fog carving out an operating base along the western frontier. Major General Arthur S. Collins, the division commander, received simple guidance from his boss, Lieutenant General Stanley R. "Swede" Larsen. The I Field Force commander recommended Collins " 'hit the enemy early' and keep him off balance by launching spoiling attacks." With six NVA maneuver regiments, plus numerous logistical bases, in the Central Highlands sector, the 4th Infantry Division would have its hands full wresting the initiative away from the enemy.[75]

Collins retained a relatively free hand in fulfilling Larsen's direction to keep the 1st and 10th PAVN Divisions off balance. Part of this latitude stemmed from the decentralized nature of the conflict. In a mosaic war, neither Westmoreland nor his successor Abrams felt comfortable dictating tactical methods to their division commanders. The high personnel turnover rate also helped explain the varying ways in which unit leaders approached their task. Hoping to avoid mistakes from World War II and Korea, where most soldiers served on the front lines without any chance of rotation, the US Army instituted a policy of 12-month tours. (The Marines, "in their unavoidable way of making the worst out of a bad situation," served 13-month tours, "adding one for bad luck.")[76] Critics lambasted the policy, particularly the decision to set battalion and company command billets at six months. Not only did short tours undermine the ability of soldiers to develop a deeper awareness of the political-social character of the war, but officers focused on career advancement or "ticket punching" saw little incentive in investing themselves in a war that would continue long after they left command. Westmoreland generally supported the rotation policy in part because he thought leaders with firsthand knowledge of combat would make better staff officers once they unavoidably left command.[77]

In the "Ivy" Division, 4th Infantry commanders following Collins approached the tactical problem based on their own accounting of the situation. William R. Peers, who took command in January 1967, held a deep respect for the enemy and appreciated the advantages the Cambodian sanctuaries offered the NVA. "They were effective," the UCLA graduate recalled. "If we really cracked these guys, they could get back across the border—that was the one thing they had. But as far as being soldiers was concerned, they would hang in there."[78] Peers, who later in the war would preside over the commission investigating the My Lai massacre, saw his mission as threefold: eliminating North Vietnamese and NLF main force units in Pleiku province, improving the effectiveness of the ARVN, and assisting in pacification. The division accordingly thrust itself into accomplishing a multitude of tasks. Not only did 4th Infantry soldiers seek out and destroy enemy forces, but they also conducted reconnaissance along the Cambodian border, destroyed enemy base camps and supply installations, supported revolutionary development and refugee resettlement programs, and trained local ARVN units. Throughout Peers worried about the security of his own forces. As he warned in August 1967, "Overnight the enemy can position and support a large force to initiate an attack on a smaller US unit operating within ten kilometers of the border."[79] Collins may have received fairly simple guidance on keeping the enemy off balance, but Peers viewed his mission as multifaceted and one that posed significant danger to his division.

Peers's replacement, Charles P. Stone, took command of the 4th Infantry in January 1968. Educated at City University of New York with World War II service in North Africa and Sicily, Stone retained the principal mission of blocking enemy infiltration across the Cambodian border and conducting spoiling attacks to force the NVA from gaining the local initiative. Yet in studying after action reports before taking command, Stone believed that the "concept of search and destroy operations was not a valid one." The new commander did away with indiscriminate harassment and interdiction fires and eschewed the use of body counts. Stone, however, held his adversary in much lower regard than Peers. A dishonest press had led Americans to believe the enemy was "ten feet tall." "The truth of the matter," Stone opined, "is that the enemy we face in Vietnam has not succeeded in accomplishing any of his major goals and has instead been forced on numerous occasions to abandon his efforts, all of which is a measure of our military success in Vietnam."[80] Writing in the aftermath of Tet, Stone blamed journalists for misrepresenting what he deemed a successful defensive against a countrywide offensive. Throughout his tenure, the division

Figure 4.2 THE DARK SIDE OF "POPULATION SECURITY". A member of the 7th Cavalry, 1st Cavalry Division destroys a Vietnamese hut with a flame thrower during Operation Thayer II, 5 December 1966. (RG 111-CV, NARA, 401)

commander spoke of his soldiers in glowing terms—"the finest fighting machine in the history of the US Army"—and believed that "three years of experience have enabled us to develop tried and true methods of employing this machine to maximum effectiveness."[81] It seems doubtful that any commander spouting such fulsome praise could evaluate objectively either his unit or the war's progress.

In spite of his supposed disdain for body counts, Stone spoke often on the firepower and mobility advantages his division enjoyed over its enemy. This assumed tactical dominance led him to develop a four-phased methodology in employing the 4th Infantry against NVA and PLAF main force units: reconnaissance, find, fix, and destroy. If Stone seemed mesmerized by delivering massive firepower on the battlefield, the division's support of civic action programs complicated the narrative that the US Army in Vietnam saw its role as simply killing the enemy. Both of Stone's predecessors saw the value of integrating civic action activities into more traditional missions of defeating enemy forces in Pleiku province. Under Collins, the division "adopted" the Highland Junior Military Academy while incorporating medical aid and water resource improvement programs into its daily missions. (The unit even initiated a pilot project to improve the health and breeding of the local livestock.) Medical teams filtered out through the villages and hamlets, not only to provide family care but to train volunteer nurses as well. As one "lessons learned" report noted, the "main effort was geared to 'nation-building' projects" designed to support the GVN revolutionary development program. Division leaders hoped that an appreciative population would demonstrate their thanks by providing valuable intelligence on the enemy's network, a popular assumption in contemporary counterinsurgency doctrine.[82] That this theory too often failed in practice says volumes about the true strengths of an NLF political infrastructure deeply entrenched within the rural population.

Back in February 1967, Peers, still in command of the 4th Infantry, took the division's civic action mission a step further with the inauguration of the "Good Neighbor" program. Peers considered that a friendly population advanced his mission of providing local security, regardless of the division's proximity to the Cambodian border and the threat posed by NVA main force units operating in his area. To support the initiative, the general ordered that each battalion and separate company field a 10-man civic action team to work full-time with local Upland Peoples, known as Montagnards. The program rested on a simple belief: "Killing the Viet Cong, alone, can't achieve the goal of defeating the enemy. The concept of nation building ties together the military, political, economic, social and educational programs which aim to liberate the people from Viet Cong control."[83] Problematically, few if any of the soldiers assigned to the Good Neighbor program had any experience with civic action. Worse, with nearly 70 hamlets falling within a 10 kilometer radius of the division base camp, the program competed for both resources and attention with more traditional combat operations. NLF cadre quickly took notice and adjusted their tactics. Insurgents threatened to cut off villagers' heads if they worked with the Americans and abducted several chiefs for collaborating with US soldiers. Further complicating the process of building ties between the people and the GVN, ethnic Vietnamese long had viewed Upland Peoples with fear and hostility. It seems doubtful any American approach could have bridged such a wide cultural divide.[84]

While the Good Neighbor initiative endured into Stone's tenure as division commander, the program highlighted how different American military leaders experimented with new ideas in Vietnam. Such experimentation required a great deal of information to be transferred between outgoing and incoming commanders who rotated on a regular cycle. Experience, however, proved much more difficult to convey, especially in a "people's war" where local relationships governed the political struggle. Critics who condemned the rotation policy, arguing that US forces "remained essentially an army of amateurs," thus hit upon an important point. Personnel continuity mattered in such a complex war as Vietnam.[85] Given the breadth of Westmoreland's strategy, the US Army required a level of maturation, if not finesse, made nearly impossible by the 12-month tour policy. The perceptive journalist Ward Just noted that Americans too often had to improvise given so many uncertainties: "if there was no agreement on precisely what the situation was, there could be no agreement on what steps to take to deal with it."[86] Thus, while the army in Vietnam experimented with fresh initiatives, a lack of continuity among its officers and soldiers attenuated the implementation of Westmoreland's plans. How commanders passed hard-won knowledge to their successors every six to twelve months had an enormous impact on MACV strategy.

Further complicating the transference of wartime learning, commanders rarely fought on a static battlefield. The political and military sands shifted more rapidly than any personnel rotation policy. For instance, General Peers, who instituted the Good Neighbor program in February 1967, found himself immersed in more conventional operations by November. In what would become the opening rounds for the 1968 Tet offensive, NVA and NLF forces had launched a series of "limited uprisings" in October near the Cambodian frontier.[87] Peers's intelligence staff soon determined that the entire 1st North Vietnamese Army Division was preparing for an assault near Dak To. Meanwhile, NLF main force units unleashed diversionary attacks against such targets as Kontum City. On 3 November, the 4th Infantry Division made its first significant contact with the NVA and for the remainder of the month became consumed in a bloody struggle for the borderlands. In all, over 370 Americans were killed in battle. Estimates of enemy losses ranged between 1,000 and 1,600 dead. Peers may have understood the importance of civic action and gaining support from the local population, but communist plans to draw the Americans into battle along the frontier before

Tet had forced upon him a change in emphasis.[88] It seems likely that General
Stone, who took command of the 4th Infantry less than one month after the
battles at Dak To, placed a greater emphasis on firepower and maneuver because
of the high losses so recently incurred by the Ivy Division.

The relatively abrupt change in the 4th Infantry's focus, from civic action to
conventional combat, illustrates how the volatility of an uncertain environment
wreaked havoc on the implementation of Westmoreland's strategy. Not only
did MACV have to react to a flexible enemy, but to the varying temperaments
of their own commanders as well. As one senior officer remarked, "Some were
sensitive to community relations and the political, economic, social, psychological impact of military operations on attainment of US objectives whereas
others, less sensitive, failed to recognize that military operations could negate
progress in winning support of the people."[89] Not all American commanders
were narrow-minded brawlers, just as not all were enlightened social engineers.
In such a multifaceted war, Westmoreland had to rely on a wide array of army
officers to realize his plans. Given this complexity, it should be unsurprising that
many soldiers believed they were receiving mixed messages from their commanders. A trooper in the 4th Infantry under Peers must have wondered if his
main focus was aiding the population or killing the enemy. In a series of company
actions that ran the gamut from civic action to combat operations, the seemingly
fractured implementation of MACV strategy surely appeared bewildering to any
young soldier immersed in a culture and landscape so far from home.[90]

Learning, Language, and the Limits of Strategy

The confusing nature of the war undoubtedly complicated how different units
and their commanders executed Westmoreland's plans. Yet claims that the
army in Vietnam failed to adapt to changing circumstances ring false when one
examines how MACV approached the daily tasks of combating both a conventional and unconventional and a political and military threat inside South
Vietnam. In reality, all division commanders made tactical revisions to support
Westmoreland's broad strategic concepts. US Army officers not only learned
about their dynamic environment but adjusted their behavior in hopes of being
more effective against a tough, resourceful enemy. This learning process occurred
across the spectrum of US operations in Vietnam. As early as February 1966,
only a few short months after the Ia Drang battle, MACV reported that search
and destroy operations "continued to dominate friendly actions as GVN and
Free World forces pushed deeply into VC territory in an effort to deny the enemy
the security of his base areas, destroy his logistical support, fragment and disrupt
his operations, and entrap and destroy his forces." This same report, however,

stressed the importance of revolutionary development programs, psychological operations, and civic action. Already US Army units were conducting combined operations with their ARVN counterparts, coordinating intelligence initiatives and population security missions. The overriding aim of all these programs remained restoring governmental control to areas dominated by the NLF.[91]

Quite simply, the US Army had learned in Vietnam. The problem for Westmoreland remained one of translating strategic concepts into effective methods at the tactical level of war that made sense to those implementing his strategy. Soldiers might adapt to their environment and still find it difficult to translate battlefield success into political progress. Even harder was understanding what progress looked like in the context of South Vietnam's murky social and political environs. Here soldiers faced no easy task. One army captain recalled that it "dawned on me about three or four months in Vietnam that we can kill all we want. But this is like stirring an anthill with a stick."[92] Clearly success rested on more than just killing the enemy. Yet few soldiers could relate the act of killing to the larger goals of breaking Hanoi's will and helping maintain an independent, noncommunist government in South Vietnam. As one historian has reasoned, "Attrition, in theory, was a means towards the end of eroding the enemy's will. But to the men on the spot, killing appeared to be the end in itself."[93] Westmoreland, it seems, can rightly be faulted for failing to articulate more clearly how the tactics of combat operations or civic action advanced his strategic aims. In a war without front lines, soldiers too often lacked clearly stated objectives. The complexity of a highly politicized civil war, one in which the United States forcefully had inserted itself, made this communication breakdown all the more damaging to US strategic objectives.

It should be no surprise that different commanders interpreted Westmoreland's broad—some critics have argued "vague"—strategic and operational concepts differently. With little cohesion among commanders operating in a dispersed environment, few senior leaders agreed on the direction of the war effort. As one general officer asked, "what is the proper role of U.S. troops?" Westmoreland realized the problem of explaining the war to both his own soldiers and Americans following the war at home. In remarks to a group of correspondents in late 1966, the MACV commander noted that the "situation is so complex that it is very difficult to understand, even if one is on the scene."[94] Of course, the lack of tangible progress engendered domestic frustration with the war's conduct but to blame Westmoreland for squandering four years of public support appears highly overblown. It is doubtful that any US commander could have unraveled the knotty problem of South Vietnamese independence in less than four years. If Westmoreland failed as a strategic communicator—and evidence suggests that he did—he at least attempted to articulate through words like "attrition" that American forces were involved in a lengthy conflict that involved more than just killing enemy forces. To be fair, the general deserves criticism for being unable to convey more clearly his understanding of the war to his army, to his South Vietnamese allies, and to the American public at home. It was a fundamental deficiency for someone in his position. In outlining a comprehensive if not complicated strategic plan, Westmoreland unintentionally had caused confusion among his ranks.[95]

Westmoreland's experiences as MACV commander thus suggest the vital role strategic articulation plays in implementing multifaceted war plans, especially in complex conflicts where the political struggle extends far beyond the range of rifle fire. To many Americans, Vietnam was "simply confusing." We should take care, however, in arguing that Westmoreland's failures in fully articulating his strategy to operational commanders—and to the American home front— meant that he did not understand the role of public opinion and perception. Time and again the MACV commander stressed the need to inform the public about US policy. Throughout his time in Saigon he worried about making sense of the war. In a 1966 directive on revolutionary development, Westmoreland was distressed that the American people misunderstood the true nature of the war. "It is a matter of continuing concern," he wrote his commanders in October, "that the difficult task of 'Nation Building' fails to receive the public attention that is accorded to combat actions in Vietnam."[96] Maxwell Taylor, a special consultant to the president in 1966, concurred with Westmoreland's assessment. As Taylor recalled, the "magnitude of the nonmilitary programs never got through to the American public because of the difficulty in interesting the press in anything but the violent aspects of the conflict."[97] While blaming the media for a lost war became a favorite postwar pastime for many retired military officers, MACV nevertheless faced significant obstacles in elucidating such a complicated war to a wide array of interested parties—soldiers in the field, politicians in Washington, and Americans at home.

The decentralized implementation of Westmoreland's broad strategy not only led to problems with communication but also afforded critics an opportunity to make counterfactual assertions that a change in tactics would have produced better strategic results. The "if only" arguments are many: if only Westmoreland had focused more on counterinsurgency; if only MACV had spent less time on search and destroy missions and more time securing the population; if only Westmoreland had better understood the importance of civic action and pacification; if only the general had not fought a war of "attrition." Such flawed arguments overlook the various missions US Army units actually performed during their time in Vietnam. All army divisions, as well as the Marine Corps, experimented with new tactics and attempted to improve their effectiveness in a political-military environment. Senior commanders adjusted their methods based on the enemy threat peculiar to their areas of responsibility.

They reacted as best they could to NVA units posing a conventional challenge, as in the Central Highlands, and to NLF insurgents posing a political challenge, as in Hau Nghia province. Reviewing how units operated on a daily basis tears down the misguided belief that Westmoreland presided over an army doing little more than killing the enemy. Simply changing tactics would not have led the army to victory in Vietnam. Tactical success does not necessarily equate to strategic success.

In fact, one of the key difficulties Westmoreland and the entire US Army faced in Vietnam centered on the problem of translating tactical success into strategic progress. Only on rare occasions could units achieve results that promoted MACV's larger aims. This had less to do with tactical competence and more to do with the political context of Vietnam. Despite an increase in US activity beginning in 1965, the South Vietnamese government never made significant strides in building a viable nation that embodied the desires of a diverse urban and rural population. Westmoreland's forces could provide a semblance of security but never a sense of political community. The enemy retained its control over the population—granted, uneven control as the war progressed—in large part because they never relinquished the political initiative.[98] American forces made easy targets for those wishing to paint the war as a sacred one for nationalism and independence. In the end, the Saigon government, consistently painted by Hanoi as a "puppet" regime of the United States, never found a better, more compelling idea around which the population could rally. Thus, as South Vietnamese leaders struggled to create their own version of a sovereign nation, the sustaining force of American military power undercut their claims of independence. In the process, South Vietnam, and with it American grand strategy for Southeast Asia, became a contradiction. Westmoreland might stem enemy offensives and offer the population physical security inside South Vietnam, but those actions could not build an independent nation capable of resisting communist influence in the Cold War era.

An Army and Adaptation

If the US Army's tactics offered no panacea to the strategic conundrum within South Vietnam, they did illustrate commanders' willingness to follow doctrinal prescriptions and experiment with techniques and methods to meet the specific situation at hand. Field manuals styled counterinsurgency warfare as a "contest of imagination, ingenuity, and improvisation by opposing commanders."[99] Nowhere was this truer than on the battlefields of Vietnam. Far from dictating subordinate commanders to conduct search and destroy operations, Westmoreland allowed his officers wide latitude in choosing how best to confront the enemy's political-military threat. Given the mosaic nature of the war, such an approach made eminent sense. While postwar commentaries, usually by junior officers, castigated battalion and brigade commanders for overt micromanagement, most leaders at division and corps levels believed MACV's supervision of the war was "about right." Westmoreland, in fact, based his command philosophy on the precept that "all operations of friendly forces would be conducted through centralized direction, but decentralized execution." The general realized early on that he could not dictate tactical methods in a dispersed environment where methods employed in one area might be irrelevant or even counterproductive in another. This approach, however, came with the risk of strategic ambiguity. Lacking clear territorial objectives, Westmoreland struggled, unsuccessfully it would seem, to define the type of war in which Americans were engaging.[100]

Though "attrition" became convenient (and inaccurate) shorthand to remedy the problem of strategic articulation, learning processes within MACV demonstrate the shortcomings of arguments claiming the US Army in Vietnam remained wedded to arcane conventional methods of warfare. Nearly all units operating in South Vietnam moved through an organizational learning cycle, analyzing their weaknesses and adjusting their tactical methods to their distinctive locales. Moreover, MACV made a conscious effort to transmit "lessons learned" throughout the theater. Official publications conveyed "information, evaluation, and recommendations on combat operations" to unit commanders throughout the country. In the 173rd Airborne Brigade, for instance, Brigadier General Ellis W. Williamson issued weekly Commander's Combat Notes with the intent to "continue those things that were proven to be good and to avoid repeating our mistakes."[101] Bulletins like Williamson's made the rounds through nearly every American unit in South Vietnam. Thus, to argue that the US Army failed in Vietnam because it chose not to learn about or adapt to its unconventional environment, neglects the learning process embraced by all divisions under Westmoreland's command. However uncomfortable a truth, it is possible to learn and still lose.

American soldiers may have found the battlefields of South Vietnam bewildering, yet evidence suggests the army as a whole genuinely strove to implement all of MACV's wide-ranging strategic tasks. Had Westmoreland demanded nothing more than the physical attrition of enemy forces, one might expect to find different divisions fighting in similar fashion across the breadth of Vietnam. Such was not the case. Commanders applied broad principles according to variations in the terrain, the enemy threat, and the local population. If continuity could be found within the US Army, observers perceived instead a common inability to link tactical success to something larger. Correspondent Malcolm Browne, for example, noticed that "as the years wore on, each American blow was like a sledgehammer landing on a floating cork. Somehow the cork refused

Figure 4.3 THE SOLDIER's Load; SP4 Harold K. Collins, a radio operator in the 2nd Brigade, 25th Infantry Division, takes a break while on a sweep through rice paddies during Operation Kolekole. (RG 111-CV, NARA, 369)

to stay down."[102] The will of Hanoi's leaders, shaken by American military operations in Vietnam, remained frustratingly unbroken. Yet not only on the fields of battle did Westmoreland and his senior commanders at MACV discover first-hand the limits of US power abroad. In the thousands of villages and hamlets inside South Vietnam, Americans quickly learned the depths of local resistance to outside influence.

5

The Parallel War

In the weeks leading to the November 1965 battles in the Ia Drang Valley, an obviously displeased Westmoreland sent a terse message to Chairman of the Joint Chiefs of Staff Earle "Bus" Wheeler. The general, responding to claims that MACV had failed to establish procedures for nonmilitary programs, insisted that "civic action has had my personal attention since I have been in command." Westmoreland wanted to make it clear that "practical policies have been established in this important field" and that numerous units "have taken a great interest in civic action and have done an excellent job."[1]

The MACV commander's message, more than a personal defense against unsubstantiated reports, hinted at deeper debates over American strategy inside South Vietnam. Critics long have claimed that Westmoreland cared little for anything but killing enemy soldiers, one even alleging that he "personally was determined to remain uninvolved" in supporting the nonmilitary aspects of pacification. Historical evidence, however, presents quite a different picture. Throughout his term, pacification remained an integral part of Westmoreland's strategy.[2] This truth should not be surprising. Most all contemporaries spoke of the "highly interdependent parts" of the "regular" war and pacification, a program that MACV defined as "the military, political, economic, and social process of establishing or re-establishing local government responsive to and involving the participation of the people." While many civilian and military leaders dubbed it the "other war," at least some in the US mission found such a portrayal unsatisfactory. Ambassador Ellsworth Bunker remarked in June 1967 that he disliked the term. "To me this is all one war."[3] While Creighton Abrams later would capitalize on Bunker's depiction, the idea of stressing pacification in Vietnam was hardly a new idea. Throughout the late 1950s and early 1960s, most all Americans involved in directing the war effort appreciated, both in theory and in practice, the importance of the countryside's political and social struggles.[4]

Even MACV's definition of pacification underscored the wide-ranging nature of a process intended to link the rural population to the central government in

Saigon. More than just military operations mattered in this type of war. In fact, the MACV commander saw internal security as a means to a larger political end. To Westmoreland, pacification included "the provision of sustained and credible territorial security and the genuine, voluntary involvement of the people as well as the initiation of self-sustaining and expanding economic and social activity."[5] While such an approach made theoretical sense, faulty assumptions undermined the application of this crucial MACV program. Few Americans asked what might happen if the population refused to give its voluntary support to the government after allied forces had offered them security. How could Americans best balance destructive military operations with the construction of a viable economic or political infrastructure? What if local security forces could not penetrate the National Liberation Front's political network? Could foreign forces even hope to foster popular participation in local governance? While these vital questions too often went unanswered, MACV valued—even if it did not fully understand—the political and social context of the villages in which American troops were operating. Thanks to experience gained in a decade of advice and support in-country, US Army officers and soldiers sought to integrate the military and political struggle into a logical whole. As Westmoreland saw the problem, population security would lead to political stability which in turn would establish a foundation for achieving his mission of supporting an independent, noncommunist South Vietnam.[6]

A fuller reassessment of MACV strategy suggests the "other war" was in fact what Eric Bergerud has called a "parallel war," a series of diverse programs fully incorporated into Westmoreland's concept of operations. Though the general never believed it to be the "decisive element" of the war—he saw the North Vietnamese Army as being largely unaffected by allied civic action plans—pacification remained "the ultimate goal of both the Americans and the South Vietnamese government."[7] Throughout the war, Westmoreland attempted to link battlefield successes into something larger, seeking ways for military victories to advance and support the process of pacification and nation building. These views gained general consensus within the US mission and among the Americans' allies. In an October 1966 meeting with top US officials, General Nguyen Van Thieu, soon to be the South Vietnamese president, argued pacification was "of particular importance since the Viet Cong will not accept peace as opposed to war until they see manifestation of results in the pacification field."[8] The Americans, however, struggled to fuse military operations into a successful nation building program—parallel lines never intersect—and failed in helping the GVN convince the rural population that the Saigon government best represented their needs and aspirations. Pacification may have been a constant consideration for Westmoreland, but as an "ultimate goal" it proved well beyond the reach of the US mission in South Vietnam.

"Rings of Steel"

As might be expected, South Vietnamese leaders realized for themselves that the insurgent threat in the late 1950s and early 1960s required more than just a military approach. Initial GVN pacification efforts promised governmental reforms to initiate improvements in education, health care, and local governance. Diem's anti-communist campaign, however, preoccupied the president's inner circle even as the Ngo brothers sought ways to initiate a social transformation among the rural population. Reform efforts soon languished in the countryside. Following Diem's death, the Saigon government announced its *Chien Thang* ("Will to Victory") National Pacification Plan in March 1964. The strategy aimed to integrate economic, social, and governmental programs using a "spreading oil spot" concept to restore security and encourage development in contested and insecure areas.[9] Supported by American advisors, the program drew heavily from the British experience in Malaya. The successful campaign against the Malayan Communist Party in the 1950s seemingly offered a model for successful counterrevolutionary warfare, especially in the wake of the French defeat in Indochina. British specialists, such as Sir Robert Thompson, argued forcefully for "a proper balance between the military and civil effort, with complete coordination in all fields." While the *Chien Thang* plan faltered due to governmental instability and a lack of coordination among South Vietnamese agencies, it nonetheless established a foundation for future efforts in synchronizing political and military functions.[10]

In supporting *Chien Thang*, many American advisors found historical analogies like Malaya alluring. The British experience not only made apparent sense in the context of Vietnam, but also validated US Army counterinsurgency doctrine which counseled commanders that "police operations, civic action, and combat operations against the guerrilla force" should all be "conducted concurrently."[11] Implementation in the field, however, proved much more difficult. The increasing American commitment in Vietnam brought confusion over who was responsible for the growing number of military and civilian agencies operating within the war-torn country: MACV, the Agency for International Development (USAID), the United States Information Agency (USIA), and the CIA. As one army colonel noted, "everybody is wandering around without any clear-cut direction and management." Thus, while doctrine spoke of "clear and hold" operations as the "most effective" in preventing the enemy "from establishing permanent bases," the South Vietnamese and their American counterparts found it nearly impossible to coordinate the multiple military and civilian activities involved in pacification. Just the "hold" phase alone included innumerable tasks. Commanders had to facilitate government control over the population, develop a local capacity for area security, establish a political apparatus, and develop a reliable network of informants. Both historical precedence and army doctrine clearly advocated joint effort in South Vietnam. Still, questions over who led which aspect of the pacification program persisted at all levels.[12]

Despite their realization that the NLF held the political advantage among the rural population, many American officers still conceived of pacification through the lens of area security. One officer operating in the province just outside of Saigon in mid-1964 noted that the "pacification operation in Long An is essentially the employment of military force to provide security for the re-establishment of hamlets."[13] While the officer went on to highlight the importance of socioeconomic development and rural construction programs, he expressed concern that these plans were failing because the government had been incapable of offering security to the population. That July, MACV published a directive on how to measure progress in pacification and population and area control. The decree outlined responsibilities for collecting data to assess momentum in the village war and, like contemporary doctrine, outlined a number of diverse criteria—training local defense forces, electing hamlet committees, and setting up an effective communications system. Yet the directive clearly

Figure 5.1 STALKING THE VIETCONG. Members of the 7th Cavalry Regiment, 1st Cavalry Division, examine papers of a National Liberation Front insurgent during Operation Masher near Bong Son, 25 January 1966. (RG 111-CV, NARA, 377)

leaned toward military measures. In pacified hamlets, government forces had discovered and eliminated the NLF infrastructure, had established a defense network against the Vietcong, and had built obstacles and fortifications. Secure areas were those in which the National Liberation Front no longer found refuge. Only in these areas could a government presence flourish. Or so MACV believed.[14]

This conviction in security preceding development permeated the army's officer corps and influenced the evolution of South Vietnamese pacification plans. While doctrine suggested nonmilitary and military programs transpire concurrently, Americans clearly favored a sequential approach in which social and political affairs flourished in a safe environment. (Notably, the "security first approach" went hand-in-hand with the notions propounded by Walt Rostow, who, according to Edward Miller, argued that "nonmilitary activities would be ineffective unless and until a secure military environment had been established.")[15] Westmoreland came to a similar conclusion soon after taking command. The general, worried about NLF progress around the capital in the summer of 1964, put his weight behind a broad proposal from Ambassador Lodge to secure the national complex and surrounding provinces. With support from Rusk and McNamara, the *Hop Tac* program, "a coordinated political-military pacification effort radiating outward from Saigon," launched in September. American officials anticipated that pacification would spread like concentric "rings of steel" from the capital and provide a secure base from which to reach farther into the countryside.[16] Their aspirations quickly faded. As one US official quipped, "*Hop Tac* is the Vietnamese word for 'cooperation', which turned out to be just what *Hop Tac* lacked." Westmoreland summed up the problem in two words: "political instability." Vietnamese agencies bickered over command authority, allocation of resources, and the readiness of ARVN to implement the program. (Saigon leaders, for their part, regarded the American plan as an imposition by foreign overseers.) Unsurprisingly, progress in pacifying key areas around Saigon was hard to discern. Twisting the logic of US counterinsurgency doctrine, *Hop Tac* revealed the difficulties of achieving security in a politically unstable environment.[17]

The American-inspired pacification plan also called into question the generally held belief that local militia forces held the key for isolating the insurgent from the population. Contemporaries agreed the "militia should be the backbone of self-defence." As one South Vietnamese general argued, the "local character of the territorial forces made them particularly fit for the maintenance of security and pacification tasks."[18] Yet the *Hop Tac* program underlined the problems within South Vietnam's regional forces and popular forces (RF/PF), known to most Americans as "Ruff-Puffs." These units suffered from poor leadership as the most promising officers joined the ranks of the ARVN. Serving locally, the

RF/PF too often found themselves at the mercy of corrupt government officials who stole money out of operating funds and did little to help modernize outdated weapons and equipment. Moreover, working close to home placed many troops in the uncomfortable position of having to choose between defending their outposts or their families. National Liberation Front forces quickly identified the inherent weaknesses in the local defense apparatus and deliberately targeted local defense units. While American officers, Westmoreland included, believed that local militia were best suited to deal with the insurgent threat inside South Vietnamese villages, the RF/PF simply lacked the means to compete successfully against the NLF.[19] For the remainder of the war, MACV would struggle to implement effective training programs for local security and police forces. The results were mixed at best.

While the regional and popular forces' uneven capabilities bedeviled early MACV pacification plans, Westmoreland and senior US officials also contended with the problem of gaining voluntary support from the civilian population. Forced relocation of families, as required in Diem's earlier strategic hamlet program, fostered resentment among peasants who believed the government was displacing them from their spiritual homes. Many of these relocated civilians soon joined the ranks of NLF sympathizers. For American intelligence officers already at a cultural and linguistic disadvantage, any increased rapport with the Front portended serious troubles with the pacification effort. As one MACV report divulged, the "ability to properly identify personnel of the VC infrastructure is a problem of considerable magnitude. This step is of necessity the initial one in the elimination of the infrastructure, which in itself is the key to pacification and revolutionary development in the countryside."[20] Additionally, displacement of the population—either from government programs or from the ravages of war—oftentimes only compounded the underlying problem of Saigon being out of step with the realities of rural life. MACV officials worried that the inability to keep the "villager in the village" was undermining pacification. As one officer admitted in 1967, "the village society of today is rapidly disintegrating [and] this disintegration is prejudicial to our war aims."[21]

The cracks in village society already were apparent to most Americans by late 1964. Though the Saigon government had approved a National Pacification Plan in February, officers expressed concern that little headway was being made in the countryside. An American advisor in Long An province estimated that the government controlled only 20 percent of the land and population by mid-year. The officer worried that Saigon had assigned insufficient military forces to the all-important "clear and hold" mission and that local defense troops were failing to control the flow of information to the NLF. At MACV, the chief operations officer found his ARVN counterparts in I Corps uncertain of whether coastal areas were in fact being pacified. No system yet existed to measure the effectiveness of nonmilitary programs.[22] Westmoreland, still the deputy MACV commander that spring, had recognized the need for vast improvements in the pacification field. He believed the South Vietnamese should focus their efforts on the extension of control rather than on "'safaris' which started from a secure area, swept a contested area, and returned to base. In short, the philosophy and concepts of the National Pacification Plan needed translating into operational techniques."[23] By late 1964, however, the military situation seemed increasingly hopeless. Westmoreland feared that the introduction of North Vietnamese regulars not only would tip the balance of the war irretrievably in favor of Hanoi but serve as the catalyst to topple the Saigon government. If the allies had any chance of pacifying the countryside, the Americans ultimately would have to take charge.

Institutionalizing Change for Pacification

This belief in the need for a guiding American hand in pacification only grew as US combat forces deployed to South Vietnam in 1965. With no indications that the NLF political infrastructure had been damaged over the previous year, senior American officials called for an increased "emphasis on the primary civilian, political and social aspect of the rural reconstruction effort."[24] Westmorland concurred. Far from rejecting pacification, the MACV commander pursued it simultaneously with the ground war. Never did he embrace one aspect of the war at the rejection of another. Calls that Westmoreland should have embraced a "counterinsurgency strategy" thus fall flat. Early on the general understood both the importance and difficulties of linking the local population to the central government in Saigon. This was no easy task. As Westmoreland recalled, "Unhappiness and perplexity pervaded the whole country, contributing to a lack of cohesiveness. The people viewed Saigon as a 'French' city, a symbol of colonialism; that had a powerful psychological effect. Many people were not emotionally supportive of a government with a colonial image."[25] While Westmoreland realized the need for a unified approach to ensure the survival of a noncommunist government in South Vietnam, any pacification plan he advanced was destined to rest on an unstable foundation.

Perhaps unavoidably, the American approach started fitfully. Mismanagement beset rural construction efforts as the assorted US agencies disputed command relationships and access to limited resources. By early 1966 Washington officials no longer could ignore the inadequacy of governmental coordination in Vietnam. (Westmoreland, of course, had his hands full keeping NVA units at bay in the Central Highlands.) At the February Honolulu Conference, President Johnson met with South Vietnamese leaders to discuss the lagging pacification effort. The secretary of defense concurrently offered a grim assessment, noting that pacification was a "basic disappointment." McNamara concluded that "part of the problem undoubtedly lies in bad management on the American as well as the GVN side."[26] This pressure from civilian leadership proved an important, perhaps essential, element of organizational change in the US mission. The president's interest in what increasingly was being called the "other war" left both civilian and military war managers little choice in embracing the task of organizing for pacification support. Westmoreland, who had attended the conference, returned to Saigon and dutifully began placing additional command emphasis on pacification and revolutionary development.[27]

In truth, many uniformed officers already had come to similar conclusions as Johnson and McNamara. As early as December 1965, a senior MACV officer agreed with Westmoreland that "an effective Rural Construction Program is essential to the success of our mission." Nor were US Army officers ignorant of the problems in implementing such programs. The March 1966 PROVN report, for example, charged that "interagency competition" within the US mission was a major obstacle hindering the achievement of American objectives.[28] Westmoreland followed suit, stressing revolutionary development and civic action programs and noting in his strategic guidance for 1967 that the pacification effort should "properly dovetail the military and civil programs." In his concept of the war, successes on the battlefield against enemy main force units would permit pacification to flourish in the countryside. (Contemporary doctrine supported such an approach.) Even officers returning from South Vietnam were advocating a balanced approach to military strategy. One lieutenant colonel, writing his student essay at the Army War College in mid-1966, highlighted the need for an "integrated strategy" that synchronized the various military, economic, social, psychological, and political aspects of the war in Vietnam.[29]

This confluence of external and internal stimuli for organizational change provoked a reluctant US Embassy in Saigon to create the Office of Civil Operations (OCO) in November 1966. Though embassy officials feared that OCO would lead to a military takeover of civilian programs—Westmoreland supported MACV serving as the "single manager" for pacification—the new office quickly improved supervision of the pacification effort's civil side.[30] OCO unified interagency direction and created a pacification chain of command from Saigon to the countryside's districts and provinces. Senior officials working on pacification, from the CIA to USAID, now worked together in a central location, facilitating planning and coordination. The office consisted of six program divisions run by nearly 1,000 American civilians operating on a budget of $128 million. OCO now managed refugee programs, revolutionary development cadre training, psychological operations, and public safety planning. The military side of pacification, however, remained outside of OCO's purlieus. Thus, while the office served as the first full step toward a new pacification organization, the "other war" remained separated from those military operations being conducted by MACV. Less than six months later, American officials, citing a visible lack of improvement in the field, dismantled OCO and incorporated it into a new organization with a greatly expanded authority.[31]

CORDS in Charge

Despite its size, the Office of Civil Operations did not have the resources to implement the programs for which it provided oversight. Nevertheless, Westmoreland fully backed the program. MACV established an operational staff section, the J-33, to coordinate with OCO on revolutionary development support matters and designated one of its brightest officers, Brigadier General William Knowlton, to head the directorate. The American response, however, failed to advance larger US aims. Westmoreland's strategic concept for 1967, which as in past years considered more than just attrition of enemy forces, left OCO increasingly unable to cope with the coordination of civil and military efforts. Westmoreland recalled that as "the American military effort expanded, so did the programs managed by AID, CIA, and USIA, so that in time all agencies were competing for resources and scarce South Vietnamese manpower."[32] The problem simply was too large and complex for OCO to handle alone. Furthermore, both the British experience in Malaya and the more recent trends inside South Vietnam seemed to corroborate American claims that population security necessarily preceded pacification of the countryside. If OCO did not have the resources or capabilities to attain that security, it became clear that only one component of the US mission in Vietnam did have such means.[33]

On 9 May 1967, President Johnson charged MACV with responsibility as the "single manager" of pacification in South Vietnam. The president appointed Robert W. Komer, a longtime CIA analyst and National Security Council staff member, as Westmoreland's deputy for pacification. As Johnson declared, this "new organizational arrangement represents an unprecedented melding of civil and military responsibilities to meet the overriding requirements of Viet Nam."[34] Holding ambassadorial rank and nicknamed the "Blowtorch," Komer assumed control of the newly created Office of Civil Operations and Revolutionary Development Support (CORDS) and reported directly to Westmoreland. The new CORDS chief served neither as an advisor nor coordinator but rather held broad authority to manage the American pacification effort. Every program relating to pacification, whether civil or military, now fell under the supervision of Komer and his office. The integration of CORDS into MACV was one of the boldest restructurings of a wartime American military headquarters in the twentieth century. As Westmoreland recalled, it was an "unusual arrangement, a civilian heading a military staff section with a general as his deputy, and a similar pattern of organization was to follow down the chain of command." Thus, the president's "single manager" concept guided reorganization at every level of the US effort in South Vietnam.[35]

Unlike its predecessor, CORDS uniquely incorporated civilians into the military chain of command. The former OCO staff director, a civilian, headed the CORDS office in MACV while a brigadier general served as his deputy. (Komer even received authority for civilians to write performance evaluation reports on military personnel.) The main CORDS staff, operating alongside more traditional staff sections like intelligence and operations, oversaw a wide venue of programs. To make the transition easier, Komer maintained the six field program divisions established under the Office of Civil Operations. His reach over pacification programs, however, expanded greatly. "Personnel," Komer recalled, "were drawn from all the military services, and from State, AID, CIA, USIA, and the White House."[36] CORDS assumed responsibility for coordinating rural development programs, conducting village and hamlet administrative training, and overseeing agricultural affairs and public works projects. The integrated,

Figure 5.2 THE POPULATION AS THE KEY? PFC John Crean checks the identification card of a Vietnamese civilian while on duty with the 9th Cavalry, 1st Cavalry Division, Binh Dinh, 22 July 1967. (RG 1110CV, NARA, 391)

interagency office handled research and development planning, wrote MACV policy directives on pacification, and advised military commanders on civic action programs. Komer even assumed the job of training and equipping South Vietnamese regional and popular forces to provide local security for pacification programs.[37]

It was here, at the local level, that Komer sought to address the fundamental problems of pacification support through reorganization. The new ambassador assigned each of MACV's corps headquarters a deputy for CORDS, usually a civilian, who outranked the corps commander's chief of staff. Similarly, Komer appointed an advisor to each of South Vietnam's 44 provinces. Illustrating the collaborative approach of CORDS, 25 provincial advisors were military personnel, the other 19 civilian. These province teams reported directly to the corps deputies while coordinating local military operations with the entire array of pacification programs.[38] The sheer breadth of pacification requirements, however, strained the capacity of Americans in the field. In short, reorganization could accomplish only so much. One American colonel, advising a South Vietnamese infantry division, noted the extent of effort required by pacification. Once units had established security, they then had to "determine the people's needs, act as a link between the higher governmental agencies and the people, see that the people's needs were met, inform the people, organize hamlet self-government, assist the people in agricultural and economic development, establish intelligence nets, detect and eliminate the Viet Cong infrastructure, and eventually restore the legitimate government in the hamlet."[39] Establishing a "single manager" for pacification surely made sense. Coordinating the vast number of programs under that manager proved extraordinarily more difficult.

Still, the chief contribution of CORDS was to pull pacification's numerous activities under one centralized command. At its peak, CORDS employed roughly 5,500 officials to support its wide range of programs. Historical precedent in Malaya and external pressure to reform certainly encouraged the reorganization process. So too, however, did the support of Westmoreland. The MACV commander enthusiastically endorsed an arrangement that made few distinctions between civilian and military officials and backed Komer's ambitions of enlarging the role CORDS played in local population security. As Westmoreland recalled, "Who headed the program at each level depended upon the best man available, not whether he was military or civilian."[40] MACV's commander committed himself to facilitating the implementation of CORDS rather than serving as an obstacle. Thus, if CORDS represented the single most important managerial innovation during the Vietnam War, Westmoreland's support played a decisive role in the organization's inception and subsistence.[41]

Innovations in organizational design, however, did not lead automatically to innovations in strategic thought or problem solving. CORDS streamlined the process of pacification for MACV but Westmoreland's strategy still required resolving a wide range of military, political, economic, and social problems. Too often in South Vietnam, American military operations still worked at cross purposes with pacification. Success in one area did not equate to advances in other areas. Even the metrics for progress assessing population security and pacification efforts proved inadequate, if not inimical, to other efforts under Westmorland's purview. As seen later, American units rarely used data from the Hamlet Evaluation System to inform combat operations. Moreover, as MACV's 1967 Combined Campaign Plan noted, the "ultimate responsibility for population security in the RD [revolutionary development] plan rested with the RVN."[42] The US mission in Saigon may have reformed the American side of pacification but its South Vietnamese allies, those ultimately responsible for pacification's success, never made comparable revisions. At most, CORDS had solved only half of the problem.

In truth, CORDS never came to grips with the underlying difficulties of the war inside South Vietnam. If Americans profitably looked to the past for perspectives on integrating civil-military operations in unconventional warfare, they concomitantly underrated the failures of past counterinsurgents like the French in solving intractable problems within South Vietnamese society. Both civil and military leaders assumed that American military power could be wielded successfully to attain the Johnson administration's larger foreign policy objectives. In the process, they too often undervalued the challenges posed by a weak Saigon government. Those involved in pacification recognized the lack of flexibility among their allies, the widespread corruption in both the army and government, and the shortage of initiative and leadership within the South Vietnamese camp. Nonetheless, the CORDs restructuring effort, as significant as it was, never confronted directly these "fundamental constraints on effective administration."[43]

While the American pacification effort inside South Vietnam ultimately failed to break the enemy's political infrastructure, the creation of CORDS demonstrated Westmoreland's willingness to make significant organizational changes to support the larger mission as outlined by the Johnson administration. It equally revealed that American war managers realized success depended on more than just killing the enemy. As Komer recalled, "Pulling together civilian and military efforts ... led to greater recognition that the war was as much political as military and that adequate interface was essential."[44] Outside political pressure unquestionably served as an important stimulus for change. Key figures in MACV headquarters, however, were indispensable in advancing the transformation in organizational structure. For military officers often prone to act conservatively in a time of war, this willingness to embrace change should not be dismissed lightly. And yet despite this conversion to a

unified civil-military staff, CORDS eventually proved inadequate to further-
ing American war aims. Nowhere was this more evident than in the rural villages of South Vietnam.

Pacification in Action

By the beginning of 1967, American ground forces had been operating in South
Vietnam for nearly 18 months. Though frustrating times for US soldiers—the
enemy continued to prove both elusive and resilient—senior MACV leaders at
least could take comfort that they had averted disaster by sustaining the Saigon
government and its armed forces. Westmoreland accordingly adjusted the focus
of US battalions. In 1967, 60 percent of American units focused on offensive
operations against main force units, while 40 percent spent their time on operations related to pacification and local security. (Taking into account all allied battalions, the ratio reversed with 60 percent focused on pacification, security, and
operations against the NLF infrastructure.) In Hau Nghia province, the US 25th
Infantry Division dutifully altered its own approach to combat, one already pre-
disposed to area security missions in the relatively populous area outside Saigon.
The division's leadership reported in early 1967 that one of the "key features of
the '67 Combined Campaign Plan is the reorientation of missions so that ARVN
support of the provincial '67 RD plans and programs...is given vastly greater
importance than in previous years."[45] As Westmoreland neared full incorporation of the pacification effort into his headquarters, he already had initiated plans
to coordinate political, economic, and social developments within his military
strategy. MACV was pushing forward with nation building.[46]

For units like the 25th Infantry Division, though, providing local security
remained *the* precondition for successful nation building. Given the complexity
of the overall pacification task, this emphasis demonstrated the inherent contradictions in counterinsurgency doctrine. Senior army officers insisted that the
"central problem is, has been, and will continue to be security."[47] Yet achieving
this security tended to preempt other missions required by pacification. The
CORDS provincial reports for Hau Nghia listed a wide array of tasks for the
Americans and their South Vietnamese allies: resettling refugees, creating cen-
sus reports, improving the national police, stimulating the local economy, and
overseeing election activities. The security situation, however, remained at the
center of Americans' attention. CORDS officials worried about road security,
rice harvest security, and the personal security of provincial officials.[48] The government's lack of political authority helped generate these concerns. Villagers
with little regard for the Saigon government saw the National Liberation Front
as a legitimate alternative to the American-sponsored regime and provided the

Figure 5.3 AN IMAGE OF THE GENTLE WARRIOR. SSG Hugh L. Maple, 2nd Brigade, 1st Infantry Division, plays with a Vietnamese child while waiting in the chow line to receive a meal, 10 November 1967. (RG 111-CV, NARA, 293)

NLF political infrastructure with sustenance and sanctuary. Protection, if not collaboration, from the population allowed the Front to strike effectively against pacification programs aimed at altering the political balance in favor of Saigon. The parallel war thus became a vicious cycle of physical insecurity feeding political instability which in turn furthered the NLF's military struggle.

Americans in Hau Nghia, and throughout South Vietnam, appreciated the importance of the Front's political infrastructure. Even informal local alliances led to better intelligence which allowed the NLF to discriminate in their use of violence. These advantages impeded MACV's pacification plans. A March 1966 report concluded that in the three phases of pacification operations—clearing, securing, and development—the "first criterion has seldom been met" even though the government had declared many areas "pacified."[49] One year later, journalist David Halberstam found a similar state of affairs. After a visit to Vietnam, the Pulitzer-winning correspondent offered a pessimistic assessment of the political struggle. "The Americans here talk a good deal about rooting out the Vietcong infrastructure, the invisible shadow government which is the Communist key to local success. Yet it is frankly admitted that the infrastructure has barely been touched." Halberstam added that "while the enemy has lost bodies, it has not lost its apparatus, which is a very important distinction." MACV understood this distinction. So too did the NLF. In fact, Front cadres concentrated their political organization where the government was weakest: in the rural villages and hamlets throughout the countryside.[50]

If local conditions were crucial to understanding the progress of pacification, they also defined the relationship between peasants, revolutionary forces, and governmental agencies. The obstacles to influencing this triangular struggle ran high for MACV. Officers identified the objective of "winning the population's cooperation and denying the enemy their sympathy" but rarely could shape local attitudes already favoring NLF propaganda messages. Americans, as David Elliott rightly notes, "were in the final analysis outsiders who could not have a lasting impact on the villages or compensate for the deficiencies of the local administration."[51] Few advisors in CORDS had the cultural background or language skills to even define what constituted legitimacy in the eyes of South Vietnamese peasants. Without this foundation, attempts at controlling the population exposed the fundamental weaknesses not only of the Saigon government but of the overall American effort as well. How could US troops "control" the population if it could not even understand the people among whom they fought? How could CORDS personnel break the bonds between rural peasants and the NLF if the two groups had been collaborating long before the Americans arrived in South Vietnam? In the final analysis, the United States had invested enormously in the fallacious assumption that it could transform local circumstances in a foreign country.[52]

These questions, so critical to the ultimate outcome of the war, remained unresolved during Westmoreland's tenure at MACV. (Americans never fully answered them by war's end.) Enhanced tactics and organizational structures might lead to improved results in population security but not necessarily in pacification, at least as defined by MACV. After visiting South Vietnam, a US congressman ascertained one of the underlying problems with the village war in provinces like Hau Nghia. The concept of pacification, he maintained, was "based on the dubious premise that Government control results in political loyalty."[53] In a large sense, Americans in Vietnam made a fatal miscalculation. Hypotheses that the population would respect the social contract in which they turned against the insurgency after receiving services and security from the government proved false. Population control did not lead to political stability. Of course, government forces and their US allies never truly achieved control of the countryside because they failed to construct and maintain the links between the rural village and Saigon. This left Westmoreland, and the army he led, unable to resolve a basic question about military strategy inside South Vietnam. Were the Americans there to provide security or help build a nation? Most US Army officers believed the former their primary tactical purpose yet acknowledged the latter as essential for achieving the more enduring grand strategic objectives in Southeast Asia.[54]

Further complicating the implementation of pacification, control also inferred a police function, the lines of which became blurred with more conventional military operations. No doubt officers felt they were moving outside the traditional boundaries of warfighting as they melded "police action" concepts into their tactical plans. The Phoenix program, for instance, deliberately aimed to disrupt, if not dismantle, the Front's political infrastructure. Officially formed on 20 December 1967, Phoenix represented MACV's appreciation that military operations alone would not win the war. As one officer argued, "If you eliminated the local VC, you could eliminate the need to use bombs and gunships around the villages, which hurt the villagers far more than the pacification troops ever could."[55] Americans worked hand-in-hand with local police and paramilitary forces with the aim of acquiring enough intelligence to identify and neutralize the NLF's clandestine government. Yet as in other areas of the pacification program, the results of Phoenix were mixed. Westmoreland's chief intelligence officer recalled after the war that Phoenix "never really penetrated the VC underground, the VC infrastructure." US and Vietnamese forces only reluctantly shared intelligence, while Front forces adjusted to the new offensive by resorting to coercion to obtain supplies and new recruits. Though such an approach tended to alienate local villagers, the South Vietnamese too often failed to exploit these NLF missteps. As Westmoreland lamented afterward, "the problem was convincing the Vietnamese that they had to do the job, not us."[56]

While Westmoreland believed the Vietnamese best suited to local security and police functions—as explored in the following chapter—he equally saw the internment, rehabilitation, and reintegration of former insurgents as a GVN responsibility. Indeed, Saigon had initiated the Chieu Hoi (Open Arms) program in 1963 to "subvert the morale of enemy cadre and troops and call upon them to leave their ranks and rally to the national cause." Between its inception and early 1966, nearly 30,000 "ralliers" or Hoi Chanhs "returned to the path of right" and came under the Chieu Hoi program. MACV grasped the potential of returnees supporting counterinsurgency operations and authorized US units to hire Hoi Chanhs.[57] Soon ralliers were serving as scouts, helping locate enemy assembly areas and routes of movement, and assisting in search operations. GVN officials, however, offered only tepid support to the program. As one American noted, some South Vietnamese leaders thought "the only good Viet Cong is a dead Viet Cong and that there is little need therefore for psychological warfare and the injection of any political elements into the struggle." With little incentive to see Chieu Hoi succeed, local government officials failed to keep track of former ralliers. Worse, the NLF threatened the families of those who did defect. A 1967 MACV report noted with an air of frustration that while the Open Arms initiative "was promising, it bogged down because of GVN indifference."[58]

Discouraged Americans likely underestimated the social turmoil provoked by programs such as Chieu Hoi. Disabled veterans, for instance, protested their government was colluding with the enemy. Moreover, the social landscape was crumbling under the weight of constant war. By the end of 1967, CORDS carried over 810,000 South Vietnamese on their rolls as refugees. Most of these came from rural areas. By mid-June 1968, in the aftermath of the countrywide Tet offensives, the number skyrocketed to almost 1.5 million. According to US estimates, nearly one of out every 11 South Vietnamese was a refugee.[59] MACV believed thousands more to be homeless. While officials in CORDS believed their task "was to get the political process going again in the villages and hamlets," such aspirations made little sense in a society as dislocated as South Vietnam. American observers long had bemoaned the inexperience of village officials who seemed ill equipped to deal with both the NLF threat and the GVN's bureaucratic structure of government. One American social worker, complaining of the red tape, said "This is the first refugee program I have ever worked with where a refugee had to have a properly stamped paper proving he was an official refugee." Critics meanwhile derided US officials who argued that the movement of displaced people into areas controlled by the government served as "an indicator of progress in pacification."[60] The dialectic between security and nation building remained unresolved.

Measuring progress in a war without fronts actually plagued MACV officials throughout the war. A 1962 symposium sponsored by Rand spent an entire morning on the question: "When and how do you know that you are winning a counterguerrilla war?"[61] Westmoreland and his staff continued to wrestle with the problem after the introduction of US ground troops. In mid-1966, McNamara requested an improved method for measuring the progress of nonmilitary programs and the following year MACV instituted the Hamlet Evaluation System. The HES graded hamlets in both security and development areas, assessing NLF military activities, local defense force capabilities, and progress in health, education, and welfare. Over 220 US district advisors reported their findings on a monthly basis. With roughly 13,000 hamlets, the statistical data generated by HES soon overwhelmed MACV's staff; the system alone generated a monthly average of 90,000 pages.[62] Despite its apparent comprehensiveness, the evaluation scheme suffered from "data turbulence" according to one Department of Defense report. HES did not evaluate populations outside of rural hamlets—some 3.5 million people—and much of the data could be obtained only from the Vietnamese. Furthermore, CORDS advisors found it impossible to visit all of their hamlets in a given month, and even when they did visit, much of what they saw was filtered through an American lens unfamiliar with the intricacies of Vietnamese society. Thus, few US officials could discern any observable "output" from MACV's many nonmilitary programs. One officer believed the reporting system's shortcomings "a chronic difficulty" which plagued all American advisors.[63]

For those implementing pacification across a war-torn countryside, these problems with the HES illuminated larger frustrations with building a viable South Vietnam. Young soldiers particularly had a difficult time reconciling the war's contradictions. One fumed, "Westmoreland used to make me crazy with all that bullshit about winning the hearts and minds of the people." Another seethed with anger in describing his unit's mission to American correspondent Michael Herr. "Shit, last three patrols I was on we had fucking *orders* not to return fire going through the villages, that's what a fucked-up war it's gettin' to be anymore.... I mean if we can't shoot these people, what the fuck are we doing here?"[64] Such attitudes clearly undermined Westmoreland's strategic goals, even if they were not expressive of the larger US Army in Vietnam. Surely they did little to convince fence-sitters within the population to throw their support behind the government's cause. This political *attentisme* further discouraged CORDS advisors who believed they needed the villagers' cooperation to help stabilize governmental structures in the countryside. MACV, in short, was making little headway in building bridges between the rural peasant and the Saigon government.[65]

Illustrating Americans' discontent with pacification, one US senior advisor sent his "uninhibited thoughts" to Ambassador Komer in mid-1967. Titled "Frustration Points in the Vietnamese and Free World Military System as noted by RF/PF Advisors," Colonel H. W. Lange's report laid bare the largely intractable problems of the village war in Vietnam. Lange noted an "apparent lack of a common US goal at the working level" made worse by the "inherent barriers" between US and Vietnamese officials. The artillery officer complained that abbreviated duty tours combined with inadequate language training undermined advisors' ability to train local regional and popular forces. "The lack of institutional memory, the short tour in Vietnam so that an individual often does not learn more than a part of his job, the shuffling of individuals between jobs so that (in the case of RF/PF) the person never understands any of the problems, all contribute to slow progress." Lange went on to criticize the lack of logistical and transportation support US advisors received from MACV, remarking that these matters had been handled by "scrounging" and "hitch-hiking."[66] It was a brutally honest report. Yet Lange's remarks likely did not catch Komer off guard. The CORDS chief was well aware of the innumerable challenges posed by pacification and many of his own reports to Westmoreland and President Johnson hit upon similar themes.

These "frustration points" highlighted the larger countrywide difficulties MACV faced in coordinating the oftentimes opposing missions of military operations and pacification. The elements of the parallel war in fact tended to work against one another. The destruction caused by military engagements undermined the construction aims of pacification planners.[67] Contemporary officers plainly recognized this dilemma and sought ways to mitigate the impact dismantling the NLF's revolutionary organization had on building a viable counterrevolutionary substitute. Westmoreland, however, could not ignore destruction of enemy main force units at the expense of pacification and nation building. A 1969 special study group formed by the National Security Council endorsed this conclusion. Their report confirmed that "significant gains in pacification had not occurred until *after* 'the allies were able to gain the upper hand in the main force war, destroying, dispersing, and pushing back the enemy main force units.' "[68] Without question, the allies' attempts at destroying the enemy worked at cross purposes with civil activities and revolutionary development. Westmoreland arguably deserves criticism for failing to better combine these two efforts, yet evidence simply does not support those who condemn the general for ignoring pacification because of some parochial commitment to attrition warfare.[69] The conflict's intricacies demanded more from Westmoreland than merely choosing between attrition and pacification. At no point did this become clearer than during the 1968 Tet offensive.

Tet, Pacification, and a Stalemated War

By mid-1967, nearly all sides involved in the Vietnam War acknowledged the struggle had sputtered to a military and political deadlock. Leaders in Hanoi, Saigon, and Washington all debated the meaning of the impasse, some favoring continued escalation, others promoting a negotiated settlement to prevent further bloodshed.[70] In the American headquarters at Tan Son Nhut Air Base, Westmoreland continued to focus on integrating CORDS into MACV's larger military strategy. That August the general laid out his expectations for the role South Vietnamese units should play in relation to CORDS. Westmoreland wanted his senior division advisors to better train ARVN battalions to support provincial pacification and security programs, long a pillar in his strategic concept. The general also placed an emphasis on "insuring operations against main forces are coordinated with pacification activities to provide optimum concerted effort against the enemy." While US Army units had sustained civic action programs by driving enemy units away from population centers, the inability to dislocate the NLF infrastructure continued to bother Westmoreland. Just as problematic, the North Vietnamese retained their capability to infiltrate most all of the supplies needed to sustain both the NLF and the NVA operating inside South Vietnam.[71] Progress seemed excruciatingly slow.

This sense of stalemate sat heavily with American leaders in the summer of 1967. While some officers argued that the tactical successes of Westmoreland's strategy had kept the enemy off balance, MACV acceded that the war was far from over. "The enemy has demonstrated a willingness to accept the situation as it exists," noted the 1967 command history, "and continues to attack, harass, and terrorize in many areas of the countryside. The VC infrastructure persists as a significant influence over portions of the population."[72] Honest appraisals such as this one concerned senior Johnson administration officials who worried that the lack of tangible progress was weakening domestic support for an increasingly expensive war. Dissenters already were making their voices heard in the United States. The president, though, continued to sound resolute in public and trumpeted the fact that the allies had prevented further advancement by the NLF in the countryside. Hanoi, punished by the bombing campaign and stressed by the war's costs, was straining to remain in the game. Still, critics progressively used the word "stalemate" to describe a war that appeared to have no end.[73]

Debates over the war's state raged just as forcefully in Hanoi, if not more so than in Washington. Politburo leaders, still disputing the best response to US intervention and escalation, speculated whether the northern population and southern revolutionaries could sustain the current stalemate. After a lengthy quarrel with rival Vo Nguyen Giap, First Secretary Le Duan won over Hanoi's leaders, convincing them that only a military offensive, not negotiations, would break the deadlock. A "decisive victory" on the battlefield, Le Duan argued, would force the United States to realize it no longer could achieve its aims in Southeast Asia.[74] Having sidelined Giap, the first secretary began planning a general offensive across all of South Vietnam. This offensive would spark a general uprising in the cities and "liberate" southerners from the corrupt Saigon regime. Deliberations between Le Duan's faction and its detractors hampered military planning throughout the fall of 1967; in fact, so contentious had the political debate over strategy become that an "alleged infiltration among saboteurs" resulted in purges and arrests of countless cabinet ministers and high-ranking Politburo officers. Moreover, the desire to maintain the element of surprise left local and regional commanders in the south just over two weeks to prepare for the largest campaign of the war to date. Le Duan might have won the contest over military strategy, but the road to Tet had taken its toll on Hanoi's leaders.[75]

On the American side, Westmoreland struggled to gain a clear picture of what was progressing inside the enemy camp. Convinced that Hanoi had altered its strategy, by late 1967 MACV's commander believed that "the enemy decided that prolongation of his past policies for conducting the war would lead to his defeat, and that he would have to make a major effort to reverse the downward trend." Changes on the battlefield seemed to confirm Westmoreland's views. In the final quarter of the year, North Vietnamese forces mounted a rising number of offensives along South Vietnam's borders. MACV also observed increases in guerrilla attacks, subversion, and terrorism against the allied pacification program.[76] The "border battles," however, most concerned Westmoreland. Defense analysts surmised that Hanoi was seeking "to lure US forces to the periphery of Vietnam in order to disperse them and draw them away from populated areas." The vacuum left by American units moving outward clearly worried MACV—many US officers felt the move exposed the already fragile regional and popular forces—but Westmoreland felt he had little choice but to confront the enemy threat. As he wrote Chairman Wheeler on 10 December, "If we do not violently contest every attempt to get NVA units into SVN, we permit him to expand his system of bases in-country. He is in a better position to support the local forces and the guerrillas in the vital battle for the people. Conversely, the main forces are in a better position to levy taxes on the people, to get their rice and to prove to the people, visibly, that the NVA is very much alive in SVN."[77]

The massing of troops near places like Dak To and Khe Sanh thus signified both a change to the enemy's strategy and an additional challenge to the allies' pacification programs. Already concerned over South Vietnam's porous borders, Westmoreland equally saw an opportunity to interdict major infiltration routes and provoke a large-scale confrontation where he could exploit his firepower advantages without the risk of damaging the population. When the NVA massed troops around Khe Sanh in September 1967 and then launched an offensive there in late January 1968, Westmoreland took the bait. The Joint Chiefs concurred with MACV's stand. Not only did Khe Sanh anchor the western defenses along the demilitarized zone, but "its abandonment would bring enemy forces into areas contiguous to the heavily populated and important coastal area." Moreover, such a loss "would constitute a major propaganda victory for the enemy which would seriously affect Vietnamese and US morale."[78] Memories of the French loss at Dien Bien Phu in 1954 likely added to MACV's decision to defend Khe Sanh. In part, these border battles also reinforced a widely held belief that the North Vietnamese simply did not have the capacity for a countrywide offensive. Westmoreland believed Hanoi had shifted its strategic aims but possessed only limited means to achieve them. Confidently, he speculated that attrition had taken its toll. The military stalemate thus confirmed MACV's presumptions that the NVA was capable only of a spectacular yet limited strike.[79]

Despite the anxiousness over an impending enemy attack, Westmoreland nonetheless hoped that MACV would more effectively integrate pacification into the war effort in 1968. While planning had improved under CORDS, implementation still "was not conducted as a unified effort." Westmoreland consequently laid out a nine-step action program to improve pacification for 1968. The goals were ambitious. MACV planned for extensive use of "civil/ military pacification teams" to supplement revolutionary development, aimed to increase GVN involvement, and hoped to give local officials "a greater sense of personal commitment to the pacification progress."[80] Le Duan's success in championing the general offensive-general uprising, however, derailed Westmoreland's plans. Given the number of intelligence reports generated by both MACV and the CIA, it seems doubtful the coming Tet offensive surprised the Americans from a strategic standpoint. A MACV cable in late January, for example, reported the enemy exhibiting "a very unusual sense of energy" and advised that Hanoi was planning "a coordinated offensive designed to seize and hold key objectives in the northern two provinces." Clearly, the Americans had miscalculated both the precise timing and scope of Tet. (Even the president had failed to mention the possibility of an enemy attack in his State of the Union message only a few weeks earlier.) As Westmoreland recalled, he and his officers knew Hanoi was poised to strike but viewed the possibility of countrywide offensive as "unlikely."[81]

That offensive engulfed South Vietnam in the final days of January 1968. Roughly 84,000 NLF insurgents and NVA regulars launched coordinated attacks across the country, sending shock waves across both Vietnamese and American societies. The *Philadelphia Inquirer* howled that the "cozy assumption that the South Vietnamese government has been winning the confidence of the people has been virtually exploded by the daring Vietcong attacks." Le Duan's general offensive hit Saigon, South Vietnam's six largest cities, and 36 of 44 provincial capitals, as well as numerous smaller villages and hamlets. NLF sapper teams even broke into the US embassy compound in Saigon and damaged ships in Cam Ranh Bay.[82] Without the passive acceptance of, if not outright assistance from, large segments of the rural population, it seems doubtful Le Duan's plan would have met with such initial success. Yet the intended general uprising never followed the offensive. Between the end of January and 31 March, NLF and NVA losses topped 50,000, roughly 60 percent of the forces committed to battle. (One MACV report stated this "resulted in favorable operational statistics for the quarter.") Despite their abetment in Tet, most civilians continued their wait and see attitude. Worse, the Front's infrastructure suffered horrendous casualties and arguably never fully recovered the influence it enjoyed over the population before Tet. Indeed, Westmoreland cabled Pacific Command only days after the attacks began that the destruction of NLF units "presents us with an opportunity to inflict the same disastrous defeats on his NVA troops as we have on his VC forces."[83]

While militarily sensible, Westmoreland's notion of "opportunity" misjudged how Tet had jolted Americans' confidence in the Johnson administration's management of the war. Nor did the MACV commander's public comments impart confidence among those questioning how the enemy could so effectively launch a countrywide offensive. In an interview with Associated Press general manager Wes Gallagher, Westmoreland indicated all was well. "Basically, I see no requirement to change our strategy. Friendly forces still must find, fix, fight, and destroy the enemy, and concurrently provide the necessary security for the population."[84] Privately, however, Westmoreland advocated a fresh look at strategy for the war in Vietnam. Tet proved the enemy had "concluded that a protracted war was not in his long-range interest" and therefore had decided "to adopt an alternate strategy to bring the war to an early conclusion."[85] With indications from Admiral Sharp that Washington might "relax the military ceiling," Westmoreland envisaged "a new approach to the war that would take timely advantage of the enemy's apparent weakness; for whereas our setback on the battlefield was temporary, the situation for him as it developed during February indicated that the enemy's setbacks were, for him, traumatic."[86]

Washington politics, however, quickly interceded with the strategic possibilities envisioned by Westmoreland. On both 3 and 8 February, the MACV chief cabled Wheeler noting the first priority should be to accelerate the modernization of South Vietnam's armed forces to offset weaknesses "resulting from casualties and Tet desertions."[87] In fact, Westmoreland's focus during the first week of February was less on asking for additional US troops and more on bolstering the RVNAF. Wheeler, though, saw the enemy's countrywide offensive as a unique opportunity to pressure the president into mobilizing the military's strategic reserves, a step Johnson had been unwilling to take since the first deployment of US ground troops to Vietnam. In a series of personal backchannel messages, the JCS chairman prodded Westmoreland to ask for additional troops and equipment. Wheeler even suggested that MACV request Washington dispatch the 82nd Airborne Division and additional marine units to ensure the South Vietnamese army did not "falter here and there." The chairman, in short, was using the uncertainty caused by Tet to make the case for bolstering the United States' global military posture.[88]

Responding to signals from both Pacific Command and the Pentagon, Westmoreland, on 12 February, cabled Sharp and Wheeler. "If the enemy had changed his strategy, we must change ours," the general stated in his most forceful language to date. Not only did MACV's commander want to recover lost ground but now requested reinforcements to place maximum pressure on what he could only assume was a weakened enemy. Certainly, the post-Tet period created urgent needs in emergency refugee care, reopening key roadways, and restoring a sense of normalcy in Saigon and other cities. Yet if allowed to exploit the opportunity of an enemy who had sustained such heavy losses, Westmoreland believed he "could materially shorten the war."[89] In order to bring the issue to a head, Wheeler traveled to Saigon and developed with MACV a series of "force package requirements" to meet both global and local concerns. The first increment of 108,000 troops would be sent to Vietnam by 1 May 1968, while the second and third increments of 42,000 and 55,000 would be kept in strategic reserve. Westmoreland later recalled that it was his intention "not to make a specific request for troop deployment. It was instead a field commander's input to consideration of mobilizing resources to meet any contingency or to pursue an alternate strategy."[90]

The change in strategy never occurred. On 10 March the *New York Times* reported that Westmoreland personally was requesting 206,000 additional troops. Dissenters within the Johnson administration questioned why MACV needed more resources if the enemy suffered a military defeat in Tet. If the United States escalated, would not Hanoi do the same? Other advisors doubted the political will necessary to support Westmoreland's proposals for ground action in Cambodia or Laos. Vietnam, as one Johnson official quipped, seemed a "bottomless pit." Thus, while MACV argued that additional troops would help exploit the enemy's weakened position, critics claimed the infusion of more combat power simply would raise the level of violence.[91] Already the refugee crisis was overwhelming the South Vietnamese government. MACV recognized the "Tet aftermath resulted in a power vacuum in rural areas; a vacuum the enemy quickly recognized and is attempting to fill." While the allies had damaged the Front in early 1968, NLF cadre still found ways to extend their influence over rural areas. Ambassador Komer admitted the regression in pacification. At a mid-May commander's conference, the CORDS chief cited statistics indicating considerable setbacks in the countryside. "In terms of hamlets," Komer reported, "we lost 38% of our Tet holdings; we now have a functioning GVN controlled administration in but 4500 of 12,500 hamlets. In population, our losses from the secure category amounted to 2.7 million people."[92] For a strategy founded on population security, Komer's numbers were troubling.

While Westmoreland was proposing a change in military strategy and the president turned deeply pessimistic over the war's outlook, the CORDS staff scrambled to revise MACV's pacification plans. In February, US officials pressed Saigon to launch "Operation Recovery." The program sought to demonstrate the government's commitment to the rural population by focusing on "civil recovery activities" such as reviving the economy and upgrading local security. Countering enemy main forces units mattered, but so too did revitalizing MACV's nonmilitary agenda. As Komer noted, "There must be a parallel pacification offensive if we are to attain our goal of winning over the people."[93] The people, however, saw only a government and its American sponsors unable to prevent the enemy's offensive. How, they asked, could one of the world's greatest powers allow such an attack to happen? With thousands of Vietnamese stranded from their homes, confidence in the Saigon government eroded. One American correspondent reported that it was "impossible to avoid recognizing the great fear among the people."[94] Senior US officials might proclaim Tet a military victory, but the pacification program had suffered tremendously.

In fact, Tet, more than any other battle in the Vietnam War, exposed the fragility of MACV's pacification program. While some American officers blamed "an intensely hostile press" for "playing up the destruction" Tet caused, few disagreed that rural development had screeched to a halt in early 1968. One pessimistic Defense Department analysis concluded that "the enemy's current offensive appears to have killed the (pacification) program once and for all."[95] Though MACV magnified its efforts on pacification once the allies regained their footing after Tet, Westmoreland spent his final months in Vietnam simply trying to regain lost ground. That one offensive could undermine years of effort in building bridges between the rural population and the central government suggested the limits of American power when it came to nation building. Try as CORDS officials might, they never could fabricate a political society loyal to officials in Saigon. Too many civilians refused to honor the social contract advertised in counterinsurgency doctrine. Offering security and economic development in return for their voluntary support of the government made little impression upon rural peasants who doubted that Saigon could provide either. Even after Tet, Americans conceded that the National Liberation Front held the "psychological advantage in the countryside because they have an organization which permits their power to appear ubiquitous."[96] The best Westmoreland could achieve was a political and military stalemate.

Pacification, Population, and Political Change

The ultimate failure of pacification, at least in how MACV defined the term, resulted less from American missteps than the inability of Saigon's leaders to fashion a political community. US pacification plans evolved as the war progressed and remained a vital part of American strategy in South Vietnam. True, most senior officials believed revolutionary development could be carried out only from a position of strength. As Ambassador Komer remarked in late 1967, "Without continuous local security to keep the VC away from the farmer, the rest of pacification can't even get underway." A US Army advisor in Quang Ngai province agreed. "Without security there is nothing."[97] This focus on the population's safety, while well intentioned and promoted by counterinsurgency doctrine, never settled the underlying issue of poor leadership across the spectrum of South Vietnamese government. Tet may have weakened the National Liberation Front but GVN leaders at the district and provincial levels never persuaded the rural population that they should throw their full weight behind the Thieu government. No doubt the destruction and social dislocation caused by military operations made the GVN's task more difficult. Pacification was a violent process. At the village level, however, many peasants refused their allegiance to the Saigon government. Major General Nguyen Duc Thang, South Vietnam's minister for Rural Pacification, realized the dilemma. "Many people no longer like the Vietcong," he offered in early 1967, "but this does not mean they like us. We must not make the old mistakes and try to force people to cooperate. We must convince them."[98]

In reality, both the US and South Vietnamese armies struggled when applying coercive measures to separate the insurgency from the population. Military force could not compel political loyalty, especially foreign military force. MACV recognized this limitation and consistently emphasized nonmilitary programs aimed at building bonds between people and government. Yet American soldiers could penetrate South Vietnamese society only so far. Cultural ignorance, while unintentional, surely impeded Westmoreland's task of gaining the population's support. As Komer recalled after the war, "Our pacification advisory efforts suffered, like most other US efforts in Vietnam, from inadequate appreciation of the realities of Vietnamese social structure, behavior patterns, and motivations."[99] The social conditions which fostered the revolutionary movement too often remained outside of many Americans' view. Some officers, Westmoreland included, appreciated the war's disruptive nature and its impact on traditional patterns of life. In the end, however, involvement in pacification told Americans very little about the political revolution, the Vietnamese struggle for national identity, or the social transformations already at work long before the arrival of US combat troops. Pacification highlighted the basic inability of an outside force to build positive and permanent links between a foreign government and its people.[100]

Despite US and GVN efforts and adaption, the American-sponsored pacification program also demonstrated the resiliency of the NLF organization and political movement. At the end of Westmoreland's tour as MACV commander, the Front's political infrastructure remained a formidable, if depleted, presence in the countryside. An October 1968 report stated blandly that the Front "is still very much with us." South Vietnamese peasants continued to fear NLF terrorism and retributions for collaborating with the Americans. The Front created new "Liberation Committees" to reinvigorate the political struggle among southern villages. As MACV reported, in spite of "the myriad problems besetting the Viet Cong Infrastructure (VCI), it continues to show itself capable of exerting a varying degree of control over large segments of the population and of translating this control into relatively effective support for the VC military effort."[101] After years of opposing the US-backed pacification effort, the National Liberation Front retained its vital support role to Hanoi's war effort. This limited ability of American military might to achieve political ends further revealed itself in the thorny problem of training the South Vietnamese armed forces for a war of both conventional and unconventional threats.

6

Training an Uncertain Army

Historians long have criticized Westmoreland for his supposed inattention to the South Vietnamese armed forces. If only, they contend, MACV had placed more emphasis on and resources toward the betterment of ARVN troops the war might have turned out differently. As in other areas of traditional Vietnam War narratives, such arguments rest on scant evidence. From the beginning, the training of South Vietnamese armed forces stood as a pillar of American strategy in Vietnam. As early as June 1954, US advisors were drawing up plans for assisting the GVN military establishment, recognizing that a government backed by a strong, stable army offered the best—perhaps only—prospect for containing communism in Indochina.[1] Westmoreland equally stressed the crucial role of training an indigenous army for national defense. Even before the 1965 battles along the Ia Drang, the general emphasized to his commanders that "We are faced with waging a war on a cooperative basis in a sovereign country in which we are guests." Westmoreland admitted that relationships with the Vietnamese no doubt would be "awkward and on occasion frustrating." Still, the MACV commander realized that the South Vietnamese armed forces were the "backbone to the resistance of a communist takeover in SVN."[2]

Thus, while the US Army learned to fight a different kind of war in Southeast Asia it also strove to improve the force structure, capabilities, and even morale of the South Vietnamese armed forces. This was no easy task. As correspondent Ward Just noted, the "'government,' if such it could be called, was a hopelessly confused and confusing apparatus." Just, in fact, believed there were three distinct governments in South Vietnam (four if one included the Americans): the permanent civil service, the generals in Saigon, and the army's corps commanders operating in the countryside.[3] Rarely did these branches work well together. Frequent changes of government and tensions within and between GVN ministries undercut Americans' ability to make progress in vital programs like rural reconstruction. In truth, political chaos in Saigon enfeebled both pacification and military training programs. US advisors additionally struggled to persuade their Vietnamese counterparts who sometimes disregarded advice and declined assistance. This left American officers at all levels balancing a delicate combination of incentives, pleas, and threats to gain leverage over the Republic of Vietnam Armed Forces (RVNAF), all while fighting a dual war against NLF insurgents and NVA regulars.[4]

If the US advisory effort highlighted the limited capacity of Americans to steer the South Vietnamese military machine, the disparity between various defense forces further complicated MACV's training programs. South Vietnam's security relied on a wide array of organizations: the ARVN, the Civil Guard, the Self-Defense Corps, and the Regional Forces/Popular Forces (RF/PF) to name but a few. Without question, the Americans found ways to affect the training and equipment of these diverse forces. US advisors throughout South Vietnam resolved jurisdictional areas of conflict, balanced local security missions with larger offensive operations, and traversed the political landscape of the ARVN officer corps. Yet the absence of a combined command—what Robert Komer called a "lack of any interallied conflict management"—left Westmoreland with little control over the South Vietnamese defense establishment.[5] MACV's commander did enjoy close relations with his ARVN counterparts, eventually concluding that informal influence over his allies offered the best chance for managing the war effort as a whole. The general, however, never could solve the innate problems of a local army wracked by political vice, corruption, and war weariness. The path toward building an ARVN capable on its own of defending the South Vietnam nation led only so far.[6]

An Army for What End?

The creation of the US Military Assistance Advisory Group (MAAG) in 1950 suggested early in the Cold War that Southeast Asia's stability entailed American intervention. While limited at first to supporting the French war against the Viet Minh, the US security assistance program expanded in the wake of the 1954 Geneva Accords. American funding for South Vietnam increased exponentially as President Diem proclaimed a national policy of compulsory military service. From the very beginning, US advisors in MAAG advocated steps toward political reform.[7] Diem, however, concentrated on eliminating domestic threats posed by hostile and armed religious sects like the Cao Dai and Hao Hao. While American officers cringed at the idea of placing the South Vietnamese army's training on the back burner, Diem believed he had no choice but to consolidate his personal power in such a chaotic, if not dangerous, political environment. Not only was the president eager to eliminate his political rivals, he also pressed for the immediate withdrawal of remaining French forces in South Vietnam.

American officers, with little background in Vietnamese culture or language, slowly began to realize that Saigon leaders could, and often did, ignore their advice.[8]

While MAAG advisors prodded Diem to undertake political reforms, they immersed themselves in the more immediate problems of military force structure. The Army of the Republic of Vietnam (ARVN), which Diem formally established in December 1955, was reorganized from the Vietnamese National Army. Right away debate swirled over how the ARVN should be structured and where its focus should lie. While some senior officials pressed for a conventional force able to resist an external invasion from North Vietnam, others supported a military organization trained in the art of counterinsurgency to deal with internal subversion. MAAG chief Lieutenant General John W. O'Daniel straddled the debate.[9] The former 3rd Infantry Division commander in World War II desired a South Vietnamese army that could subdue both threats and recommended a force level of more than 150,000 men. While the Korean experience weighed heavily on the minds of many US officers, advisors in MAAG realized internal security ranked high among ARVN's principal missions. In short, Americans were not blind to the fact that South Vietnam faced two very distinct threats. All of O'Daniel's successors shared the MAAG chief's preference for an army capable of simultaneously fighting guerrillas and main force units. These two missions, however, required different organizations, skills, and equipment. As such, O'Daniel advocated training mobile field divisions on the US Army model and territorial units that could provide local security to the rural population.[10]

The Americans hoped these territorial forces would free the ARVN from static population security missions to concentrate on the enemy's main force threat. To confront the insurgency, MAAG officers lent their support to the Civil Guard and Self-Defense Corps. Civil Guard forces—what one American likened to a "mobilized national guard"—were assigned to province chiefs and organized to conduct patrols throughout the rural districts. The Self-Defense Corps, on the other hand, served as a part-time militia force that rarely did more than protect local villages from NLF subversion. While these provincial military forces numbered roughly 86,000 men by 1959, several factors undermined their effectiveness. Poorly equipped and ill-trained, the militia seldom attained the competency of most Vietcong units. One US report found that some of the Self-Defense Corps had been "equipped only with primitive weapons such as clubs and spears."[11] President Diem, however, found little incentive to outfit forces under provincial control that might later be used against him in a coup d'état. Tensions between local militia units and the ARVN further damaged resistance efforts. Since Diem saw the Civil Guard, a sort of hybrid police and military force, as a frontline defense force against communist operatives in the countryside, ARVN soldiers and paramilitary locals often viewed each other

with suspicion. American officers did their best to placate these political hostilities and instead focus on preparing South Vietnam's armed forces to confront
the dual NLF-NVA threat. They achieved only middling results. Still, the financing and training of the Civil Guard and Self-Defense Corps mission suggest that
the American advisory effort was concerned about more than just making the
ARVN look like the US Army.[12]

The US advisory group's training programs, in fact, demonstrated a willingness to consider more than just conventional warfare. MAAG helped organize a
Revolutionary Development center at Vung Tau on the southern coast to train
paramilitary forces and furnished ARVN forces with McGarr's treatise "Tactics
& Techniques of Counter-Insurgent Operations." The center taught small-unit
tactics, how to arrange for medical service, and how to obtain and transport
supplies from the provincial capital. By Westmoreland's tenure, MACV's training directorate was helping revise curricula for over 650 various courses. One
American officer believed local education programs excited district and village
officials and strengthened the pacification effort. "The program of instruction,"
Colonel John H. Cushman wrote, "was a composite of civil and military subjects.
For example, members of the pacification group would be taught 'Organization
of Hamlet Government' in the morning, 'Conduct of Ambush' in the afternoon."[13] While local training made sense for a war fought largely among the rural
population, US advisors struggled against numerous obstacles. Military schools
could not fill the severe shortage of company grade officers, and leadership problems continued to weaken all elements of South Vietnam's armed forces. The
demands of combat equally stymied attempts at maintaining an effective training program. With a focus on combating the NLF security threat in the villages,
political education fell to the wayside leaving many South Vietnamese defense
forces uncertain of their cause.[14]

By 1960, US advisors faced an uncertain future with their allies. The ARVN,
having completed its transition to American equipment, comprised seven divisions organized into three separate corps. With only 875 US military personnel
in Vietnam at the end of Eisenhower's presidency, overworked advisors could
provide assistance no lower than the regimental level. (By the end of 1963, the
number had skyrocketed to more than 16,000 Americans in country.) MAAG
officers reported the ARVN well short of its authorized 150,000 force level, a
cause for concern given the National Liberation Front's increased commitment
to the military struggle.[15] Still, the Americans realized the dual nature of the
threat to South Vietnam. Of the ARVN's seven infantry divisions, two concentrated on defending the northern border and demilitarized zone while the other
five maintained internal security. As US advisors sought to balance these diverse,
if not competing missions, they held little real influence over militia forces. Not
until 1964 did control of the Civil Guard and Self-Defense Corps move from

the interior minister to the defense minister. This awkward command structure complicated efforts at creating a unified strategy to deal with the growing threat to South Vietnam's stability and security. To Americans, President Diem's leadership style confused the matter further. As Ambassador Elbridge Durbrow complained to the State Department in February 1960, Diem was "moving in all directions at once" without any plan to meet the "deteriorating internal situation."[16]

If the Americans in MAAG and their South Vietnamese counterparts failed to agree upon a specific strategy in 1960, the Joint Chiefs of Staff at least gained approval to implement their "Counterinsurgency Plan" in February 1961. Senior officers admitted that the insurgency in South Vietnam had "developed far beyond the capacity of police control." The Joint Chiefs also were aware of "allegations that the United States is overtraining the Vietnamese Army for a Korea-type war with little or nothing being done to meet the terrorist problem in Vietnam."[17] Their plan suggested otherwise. The Chiefs assumed the NLF insurgency posed the greatest threat to South Vietnam's existence and defined the challenge in broad terms. Of the plan's four major tasks, only one related to security; the other undertakings included political, economic, and psychological measures. Without question, military operations remained at the core of the JCS plan. So too did South Vietnam's armed forces. In fact, given the Americans' advisory role, the RVNAF served as the principal agent for combating the growing insurgency throughout the country. Yet much work remained in preparing local forces for their counterinsurgency role. The plan's concept of operations defined as essential "the requirement to overcome inherent weaknesses in the current RVNAF force structure which contributes directly to the present deterioration in the morale, state of training, and combat effectiveness of the RVNAF." Even with 75 percent of the ARVN committed to pacification missions, Americans worried the "guerrilla problem" had become too serious for the Vietnamese to handle.[18]

Given these concerns over South Vietnam's capacity to meet the insurgent threat, the Counterinsurgency Plan set the foundation of military strategy for the remaining US advisory period. Offensive military operations of course ranked high among advisors' interests. Most US Army officers believed the ARVN could not take a defensive stance if it was to uproot and defeat National Liberation Front forces. (Here, the army's doctrinal emphasis on aggressiveness in counterinsurgency operations clearly shone through.) These same officers, however, viewed the struggle as multidimensional. Peter M. Dawkins, a West Point Rhodes Scholar and Heisman Trophy winner who served as an advisor in South Vietnam, listed "seven major categories of action" for province and district advisors. While Dawkins placed security and combat affairs first, he also included police affairs, civilian medical services, and community development among the catalogue of tasks required by American officers.[19] Securing organizational reforms to better implement these functions certainly eluded US advisors. Province officials often rejected advice from outsiders and it seems doubtful that foreigners could provide effective counsel on village development when they hardly understood the nuances of social relationships in rural Vietnam. Moreover, MAAG officers had to consider how these programs might aggravate local peasants rather than win their support for the government in Saigon.[20]

By 1962, nearly all US officers in South Vietnam realized that success or failure in the counterinsurgency mission depended on ARVN effectiveness. As they placed emphasis on training centers, they equally sought ways to better coordinate military and civilian activities and to synchronize US and South Vietnamese programs. While MACV later would introduce combined operations to offset inadequate ARVN training, American advisors labored to keep their allies in the forefront of the war. As General McGarr wrote President Kennedy in February, "in providing the GVN the tools to do the job," the United States "must not offer so much that they forget that the job of saving the country is theirs—only they can do it."[21] The MAAG chief's warning made sense, yet as the NLF made headway in the countryside, pressure for Americans to staunch the bleeding increased proportionately. Without a unified strategic concept being developed in Saigon, Americans naturally began inserting themselves into all levels of South Vietnamese military planning and resourcing. The political instability rising out of Diem's assassination in 1963 only spurred US advisors to greater involvement. So while officers like Maxwell Taylor warned of becoming the "primary doer" in South Vietnam, advisors on the ground felt the deteriorating situation demanded they take greater control. The impact on their allies was unsurprising. As General Cao Van Vien later observed, we "depended so heavily on the Americans for almost everything that it was difficult to get our opinions taken into account."[22]

In one sense, US Army advisors increasingly viewed the ARVN only as a tool to combat the internal security threat and prepare for an external invasion from the north. Few considered the deeper relationships between the army and a nation still trying to gain willing support from its population. The overall weakness of the South Vietnamese armed forces, though, justified the focus on military training. From 1960 to 1964, US advisors contended not only against a committed enemy but also with a seemingly apathetic Saigon government and an ARVN officer corps that lacked effective, confident leadership. The focus on the military struggle also made sense to them from a counterinsurgency perspective. A popular treatise of the day argued that "Military defeat of the guerrilla forces, widely and persuasively publicized, is among the strongest ways of convincing people that support of the guerrillas is unwise."[23] Of course, as in so many other aspects of the American mission in South Vietnam, the advisory effort could only accomplish so much. Martin J. Dockery, who served with an ARVN infantry battalion in the Mekong Delta, noted the limits of American influence before Westmoreland took command of MACV in mid-1964. "It was never possible that advisors alone," Dockery recalled, "could change the ARVN into an effective fighting force with enough energy and aggressiveness to defeat the Viet Cong." Nevertheless, the American effort depended almost wholly on these advisors.[24]

When an NLF main force battalion rebuffed ARVN forces at Ap Bac in January 1963, US advisors believed they had tangible proof of South Vietnamese ineptitude. Converging on a suspected Vietcong position, the ARVN 7th Division buckled under enemy fire. Only after nightfall, and the deliberate withdrawal of NLF forces, did the 7th Division secure Ap Bac. US advisors fumed at the missed opportunity to destroy the enemy. Lieutenant Colonel John Paul Vann called the battle a "miserable damn performance." Another advisor went further: "Time after time I have seen the same Vietnamese officers and troops make the same mistakes in virtually the same rice paddy."[25] American journalists, some already questioning the efficacy of the Saigon government and its armed forces, viewed Ap Bac in equally critical terms. David Halberstam, for instance, highlighted his concerns the following year: "To us and the American military advisers involved, Ap Bac epitomized all the deficiencies of the system: lack of aggressiveness, hesitancy about taking casualties, lack of battlefield leadership, a nonexistent chain of command."[26] Without question, assessing ARVN performance based solely on Ap Bac painted an inaccurate picture. The battle, however, seemed representative of larger trends. At year's end, a Defense Intelligence Agency report warned that the "government has apparently been unable to materially reduce the strength of the Viet Cong in spite of the increased number of RVN offensive operations."[27]

By 1964, as Westmoreland took command of MACV, most all Americans agreed that they had "gone about as far forward in influencing the planning and execution of operations as the advisory concept [would] permit." Despite years of advice and support, the Saigon government remained on the verge of collapse. In a large sense, the Americans had failed at the gargantuan task of training South Vietnam's armed forces for defending against both internal and external threats while simultaneously promoting political stability and nation building efforts. With no change to the grand strategic objective of maintaining an independent, noncommunist South Vietnam, Westmoreland had no recourse but to ask for greater US involvement. The results were predictable. As correspondent James Reston quipped, "When Uncle Sam moves in, somebody has to move over."[28] The exigencies of a faltering Saigon regime had eclipsed the US advisory mission. Westmoreland's challenge thus became one of escalating the war in Vietnam without marginalizing the government and its armed forces.

Americans' assessment of a "growing lack of confidence among the GVN leadership—political and military" and the uncertain role of the populace in the "ultimate success of the counterinsurgency" campaign made such a challenge all the more difficult. By the time Westmoreland presided over the introduction of US ground combat troops into Vietnam, the war already had undermined the trust between allies. Neither side appeared well situated for coalition warfare.[29]

Advising the South Vietnamese

"The Americans came in like bulldozers," remembered Bui Diem, a South Vietnamese official who watched the US escalation with both wonderment and trepidation. By mid-1965, few would disagree the war "was now indisputably an American enterprise."[30] Westmoreland, though, assigned the RVNAF two important objectives: defeating the insurgent forces inside South Vietnam and extending governmental control throughout the country. These missions fit neatly into the MACV commander's overall strategic concept, at least on paper. Though Westmoreland intended for the ARVN to focus on the insurgent threat, the "growing enemy strength in units of battalion size or larger" forced ARVN units to "abandon their pacification assignments, their relatively static defense of the population, in order to oppose the big units." As the general recalled, "Ignore the big units and you courted disaster."[31] Here, the enemy threat influenced the very role of the South Vietnamese armed forces. Unable to ignore the main force units, Westmoreland assigned the population security mission to territorial militia. Yet, as seen, the Civil Guard and Self-Defense Corps suffered from poor leadership, manpower shortages, and inadequate training. Their successors, the Regional and Popular Forces, struggled with similar problems. Senior MACV officers later would argue that only the Vietnamese could "handle the counterinsurgency job," but the local defense forces fought at a clear disadvantage when compared to the National Liberation Front.[32]

The territorial forces' lack of skill does not mean Westmoreland discounted the role played by either the ARVN or the militia. MACV never viewed the South Vietnamese as an inferior, bit-part player in the larger war. More accurately, Westmoreland intended for all allied forces—American, Australian, South Korean, and South Vietnamese alike—to mutually reinforce one another against the combined NVA-NLF threat. "All factors considered," the general wrote in August 1965, "we should continue to strive for RVNAF participation in operations from the outset."[33] For Westmoreland, local forces could best contribute to the war effort by pursuing pacification as their primary task. Accepting that pacification was *not* a secondary mission in MACV's strategic concept, the role of these local defense forces takes on a new light. Westmoreland believed that "US forces are more aggressive, have a greater capability and will inevitably find themselves involved in many of the tougher fights but by no means all of them." The general, though, considered the militia better suited for securing operations after US and ARVN units had cleared contested areas. Even before Ia Drang, Westmoreland intended "to make a major effort to fill in behind US and ARVN forces in areas to be pacified with regional and popular forces and pacification cadre."[34] Rather than marginalizing the territorial militia, MACV planned for the South Vietnamese to accomplish pacification behind a shield provided by US combat troops.[35]

This mutually supporting concept derived not from contempt for the ARVN or territorial forces but from doctrine that emphasized that the "primary responsibility for conducting counterinsurgency operations must rest with the local government." Americans saw pacification and revolutionary development as missions best accomplished by their South Vietnamese allies. The US Army even defined "civic action" as the "use of preponderantly indigenous military forces on projects useful to the local population at all levels," whether it be education, training, or economic development.[36] Westmoreland agreed. As he wrote the Joint Chiefs in June 1965, "US troops, by virtue of their ethnic background, are not as effective as RVNAF troops in a pacification role. When deployed in highly populated areas, US troops must be used with discrimination." Of course, the MACV commander, along with most senior US officials including the CIA station chief in Saigon, also appreciated the state of South Vietnam's armed forces. The advisory period had ended with an indigenous army incapable of simultaneously defeating the main force threat, overpowering the insurgency, and expanding government control in the countryside.[37] The challenge for Westmoreland lay in integrating US troops into a cohesive strategy that played to the advantages of both American and South Vietnamese forces. In short, both the "bully boys" and "termites" posed unique challenges to the defense of South Vietnam.

The widely held belief that US forces should focus on the task of "semi-conventional combat operations" and the ARVN on "the more complex political-military one of pacification" surely influenced Westmoreland's thinking on US-GVN relations.[38] Yet claims that he neglected the South Vietnamese (and pacification) miss the point of how local defense forces fit within MACV's larger military strategy. Critics like Lewis Sorley excoriate Westmoreland for failing to equip ARVN units with the new assault rifle, the M16, which placed the allies on surer ground against their AK47-equipped enemy. As early as December 1965, however, MACV's commander requested the new weapons, both for American and South Vietnamese troops. (Army Vice Chief of Staff Creighton Abrams struggled to meet these demands and even the US 1st Infantry Division deployed to Vietnam with the older, yet still effective, M14 rifle.)[39] Such accusations of neglect assume Westmoreland controlled armament procurement schedules—he did not—and that a better-equipped ARVN would have developed more quickly in terms of leadership and professional aptitude. The war, though, never turned simply on tactical acumen. In reality, the deficiencies of the South Vietnamese forces had little do with the type of rifle they carried—the NLF, for instance, only began to receive substantial quantities of the Soviet AK47 in late 1964. Rather, Americans in Vietnam were finding it difficult to resolve the social and cultural problems of an army trying to defend a political entity not seen as legitimate in the eyes of the population.[40]

Progress in securing the population, though, depended on local defense units like the regional forces and popular forces (RF/PF). Officers in MACV well understood this point and the relationships between revolutionary development and the destruction of the NLF infrastructure. As one report noted, the "RD program can grow only as fast as our side can provide the RF/PF troops to secure and pacify the new areas we have seized from the enemy."[41] Sound in concept, problems in linking the diverse missions of territorial forces with those of ARVN bedeviled American advisors. In many cases local hamlet militia fought off enemy attacks while waiting in vain for regional force or ARVN reinforcements to appear. Perhaps unsurprisingly, morale within these local units plummeted. In fact, the "Ruff-Puffs" suffered the highest casualties of any South Vietnamese defense force during the entire war. One US Department of Defense report estimated the RF/PFs bore 55 to 66 percent of South Vietnam's military deaths, a cold reminder of the deadly village war that engulfed the country throughout much of the 1960s. These statistics, however, do not substantiate allegations of Westmoreland's disregard for local defense forces. Rather, they demonstrate the deadly efficiency of a political-military infrastructure that long had preceded American entry into the war.[42]

In reality, MACV understood the need to bolster local, regional, and regular forces throughout South Vietnam. The command sponsored numerous programs to improve RF/PF and ARVN effectiveness such as district level intelligence centers for striking at the NLF and refresher courses for training ARVN battalions. In 1967 Westmoreland backed yet another organizational change within MACV, creating Mobile Advisory Teams to explicitly advise the regional and popular forces. These small elements, usually no more than five Americans, lived daily with their allied units and served as a focal point for organizing security inside rural villages and districts. One former advisor recalled that these "small teams operated with relative independence and were often out of sight of everyone save for their villagers and the enemy around them."[43] The "mobile" concept envisioned Americans staying with their counterparts until they were trained well enough for the advisors to move on to another unit and start the process over again. In practice, many teams never moved because of the RF/PF's severe training deficiencies or because the needs of the immediate area trumped calls for relocation. In these situations, Americans working in such close proximity with Vietnamese soldiers gained a new appreciation for the plight of local peasants. One advisor found that he "learned to empathize with them and see some of their actions in view of a nearly continuous war the previous thirty years."[44]

While programs like the Mobile Advisory Teams helped change some Americans' attitudes toward their beleaguered allies, the demands of the larger advisory program tended to overwhelm most soldiers. An advisor was all at once a military trainer, a political representative, a counselor and administrator, and a funnel through which US funds and support flowed. These advisors oversaw operations aimed to weaken the NLF political infrastructure, taught English in schools, and expedited refugee relief. All the while, the Americans lacked the language capabilities to truly understand their Vietnamese partners. The one-year rotation did little to build lasting relationships so necessary for an effective counterinsurgency campaign.[45] John H. Cushman, a senior advisor who served three tours in Vietnam, identified well the problems of the local commander who had been fighting the Vietcong for years and now was forced to serve with an American overseer. "He's got all these problems on his mind, all these troops he has to take care of. He's not even sure he's going to survive the next day. And here comes this new adviser, some captain fresh out of advisory school. Doesn't know how to live in the rice paddies. Gets diarrhea the first week he's there." Unacquainted with Vietnamese culture, politics, and social norms, Americans tried—too often unsuccessfully—to find meaning in a hostile and alien world. To Cushman it was a "very interesting situation: an adviser who's got to learn from his counterpart."[46]

In part, the failures of the advisory mission rested with Westmoreland. His all-embracing strategy simply overtaxed those in the field. In attempting to focus on more than just ARVN and its ability to help defeat enemy main force units, the MACV commander broadly stressed "the effectiveness of National Police, Revolutionary Development Cadre, land reforms, corruption, RF/PF effectiveness and the general ineptitude of Government administrators from hamlet to Saigon level." As Westmoreland put it, "I feel we must look at the whole problem and attack the deficiencies on all fronts."[47] While laudable, such an approach proved unfeasible. Most US advisors were too impatient in implementing development programs and never solved the problem of finding qualified South Vietnamese leaders at all levels within the armed forces. Just as challenging, local commanders found their initiative stifled by US Army officers and worried about their diminished authority and prestige when serving alongside their more powerful allies. Lacking "leverage" over their counterparts, American officers fared even worse in their relations with the rural population. One Vietnamese official, speaking on revolutionary development, noted that the "people in the countryside are indifferent to the program and go along only for cement, roofing, wheat flour, rice, and other gifts from the generous Americans." Westmoreland might have seen the war from a holistic perspective, but implementing his strategy through uncertain allies frustrated the general's otherwise well-conceived plans.[48]

It seems plausible that no strategy, however thorough, could have overcome the cultural divide between Americans and South Vietnamese during Westmoreland's time in MACV. In a war without fronts, nearly all US soldiers remained suspicious of the local population. Thomas Giltner, a platoon leader in the 25th Infantry Division, found this outlook the "hallmark of the war: You could never tell who was the enemy and who was not. Therefore, you treated everybody with suspicion and mistrust." One 1966 "Lessons Learned" report even urged "Do not trust children at any time. They may be VC agents."[49] With soldiers already inclined to view the Vietnamese as inferior people, American attitudes shifted from skepticism to hostility. Soldiers found the locals "treacherous" and "dirty rats" who farmed during the day and served with the VC at night. "Some of us hated them," one veteran recalled, "Everybody was a zip, gook, or animal.... You couldn't trust them."[50] These attitudes, all too common for Americans dropped into the middle of a foreign civil war, illustrated the limitations of soldiers serving as cultural ambassadors in Vietnam. While many American advisors made lasting friendships with their Vietnamese counterparts, the depth of cultural wariness on both sides proved insurmountable for the advisory effort to make durable gains in building an effective South Vietnamese defense establishment.[51]

In the end, Westmoreland and the US Army in Vietnam never succeeded in matching the dual threat posed by the North Vietnamese Army and the National Liberation Front. The allies could ignore neither menace. When ARVN commanders spread out their forces to provide local security, these smaller formations became vulnerable to enemy main force units. When they attempted to parry the thrusts of enemy battalions and regiments, an exposed population risked infiltration and attack from NLF insurgents. Westmoreland intended for the Americans to fend off the "bully boys" while the South Vietnamese handled the "termites," but neither the ARVN nor the territorial forces matured enough to carry out their demanding assignments. The enemy's increased political and military activities in the early 1960s simply kept the GVN defense forces off balance. Providing the ARVN with better rifles hardly would have solved the intractable problems of leadership, morale, and military professionalism. Try as the Americans might to resolve these fundamental issues, the influence they wielded over their South Vietnamese allies went only so far.[52]

"Wanted: South Vietnam Army Heroes"

In the summer of 1967, the US Public Affairs Office in Vietnam embarked upon an "image-building campaign" aimed at the American press, and through it the American home front, to promote South Vietnam's armed forces. "We need more ARVN heroes," exclaimed Barry Zorthian. As the US public relations point-man in Vietnam, Zorthian worried about growing impressions that the South Vietnamese were doing little to defend their own country. His speech to a group of public relations officers in Saigon left a clear message: highlight the performance of the US allies to sustain support for the war at home.[53] Without question, journalists had emphasized the American side of the war since the introduction of US ground combat troops in 1965. Yet Zorthian's entreaty highlighted larger issues with the performance of South Vietnam's armed forces. Was American support (and salesmanship) enough to compensate for the long-standing deficiencies of an indigenous army? Social stratification and class discrimination, for example, had beset the local defense establishment since at least the French-Indochina War. Could American troops overcome these deep-seated social problems within diverse organizations like the ARVN and the regional and popular forces? In retrospect, it seems doubtful. Such a question, however, implies that what happened outside the strict confines of MACV's training programs determined the ultimate ability of the RVNAF to successfully defend South Vietnam on its own.[54]

Frustrated Americans were quick to malign the ARVN—and Vietnamese in general—for their perceived inability to overcome the NLF insurgency. Generals and privates alike believed the "basic motivation of the ARVN seldom equaled the motivation of the VC and NVA."[55] Yet the South Vietnamese army had been under the tutelage of a committed US advisory effort since the Geneva Accords in 1954. Were not the Americans themselves somewhat to blame? In part, the ARVN exemplified at least some aspects of the American approach to war such as reliance on technology and firepower to aggressively close with the enemy. Rather than look inward at deficiencies in their training programs or, more important, social factors contributing to the ARVN's shaky performance, many US officers instead tended to focus on their allies' failures. Americans were quick to point out the high numbers of desertions and battlefield weapons losses, the percentage of Vietnamese soldiers "missing in action," and the seemingly irresolvable problem of army leadership.[56] At the unit level, US soldiers excoriated their unsteady allies. As one vented, "I was really angry with Vietnamese men. I started hating ARVNs because they were so unreliable and a couple times in ambushes the ARVNs disappeared. I hated Vietnamese men." Marine General Victor Krulak even proposed that the RVNAF "had little stomach" for the task of defeating the insurgency and providing day-to-day protection for the people.[57] While such opinions hardly reflected all Americans in Vietnam, they were prevalent enough to help erode the trust so crucial for coalition warfare.

If some of the ARVN's problems emanated from the US advisory effort, others derived from the very expansion of the South Vietnamese armed forces. Between 1964 and 1966 alone, the RVNAF increased over 50 percent, from 390,000 to 620,000. (The troop expansion's financial burden to the GVN hardly helped the overall war effort.) One MACV report noted the resultant problems: "shortages of equipment, lack of training, shortages of housing, over-strength units, and finally and most importantly, serious shortages of qualified officers and NCOs."[58] This quantitative growth posed special problems for Westmoreland, whose strategy of pacifying the countryside rested with South Vietnamese units. Moreover, the shortages within ARVN's officer corps left the MACV commander with a sizable leadership challenge of his own. As Westmoreland recalled, "It was like trying to push a piece of cooked spaghetti. We had contradictory objectives: get results, but we could not do that without assuming command, and if we did that, we would build no senior South Vietnamese leadership. Some Vietnamese leaders would have been happy to lean on us just as they had done with the French, but in that case we would never have been able to leave."[59]

Westmoreland and his staff understood clearly the problems posed by an ARVN officer corps obsessed with "politics, corruption and nepotism." Yet here, it seems, US Army leaders placed too much faith in their ability to solve South Vietnam's internal political and social ills. At a conference in late 1966, Westmoreland told his senior subordinate commanders that in order "for ARVN to be successful, a re-education process is necessary from the generals on down.... The attitude of the soldiers toward the people is frequently poor.... We must do all we can to change this."[60] Such comments no doubt made sense. Proper relationships with the local population formed a central theme in counterinsurgency doctrine. Regardless of whether his ARVN general allies were receptive or not to this type of advice, Westmoreland overvalued his ability to make such sweeping changes among the South Vietnamese army's officer ranks. It seems unlikely Americans truly could "re-educate" their allies in any meaningful way. The decade-long advisory period before Westmoreland's arrival in Saigon alone suggested the limits of influence within the US training and education program. By mid-1967, little had changed. "The single most perplexing problem facing the United States in Vietnam today," one advisor said, "is the Vietnamese army—how to get it to carry its share of the load."[61]

The ARVN, of course, had been carrying a heavy load for years. Most senior officers had served in the French-Indochina War and the unending conflict had taken its toll. As William DePuy aptly remarked, "The war went on forever and you can't be brave every day, every week, and every month, every year for ten years."[62] The demoralization afflicting some ARVN units appears more under-standable when viewed from this long war perspective. Rank-and-file soldiers, many from the poorest social class, simply lacked the means to both care for their families and defend their nation. One US advisor articulated the burdens suffered by underpaid and poorly led local units. "The Gov. just doesn't look after their soldiers well enough to keep them happy. All soldiers' housing is ter-rible, dependents are not thought of in the least—they have no provisions for getting pay home when the husband is off on a big operation, maybe for over a month."[63] In such a setting, ARVN soldiers regularly deserted to take care of their families. Rash American officers too quickly derided their allies for com-plaining about "quality of life" issues instead of concentrating on fighting com-munists. Here, the disparity between allies did little to foster effective working relationships. ARVN captain Tram Buu described Americans as if from another world. "But look at the US soldier: he is well-paid, well-fed, well-supported, gets good housing, doesn't have to worry about the safety of his wife and family while he's away, gets R&R trips and sometimes a trip home, and he can leave for good in one year."[64]

While the ARVN grappled with desertions, pay and promotion inequi-ties, and disruptive draft policies, a lack of ideological training more deeply impaired South Vietnamese soldiers. The National Liberation Front, and their Viet Minh predecessors, long had emphasized the role of proselytiz-ing as part of the political struggle. Defeating imperial oppressors to achieve true Vietnamese independence resonated throughout the ranks of both the NLF and NVA. Saigon, however, lacked an equally powerful political vision. As South Vietnamese writer Ngo Quynh recalled, his country never moved beyond being the "the bastard child of French colonialism and American anti-communism.... We had no idea why we were fighting other than to rid the nation of Communists."[65] Westmoreland's senior officers might grumble over ARVN's "lack of motivation," yet they seem to have missed a key element in understanding the political element of the war. Nation building efforts were doomed to failure if the army and the population from which it sprang con-tinued to hold diverse notions of the nation itself. The inability of the South Vietnamese state to mobilize large numbers of people around a single idea only exacerbated these problems. MACV surely valued the political struggle in efforts aimed at both nation building and countering the NLF insurgency. Westmoreland spoke of its role often. Nevertheless, he and his officers could not impose the *idea* of South Vietnamese nationhood on a populace that ques-tioned the legitimacy of the Saigon government. No military training could overcome deficiencies in political purpose.[66]

These disadvantages in the political struggle revealed themselves in the countryside, where weak linkages between Saigon and the rural population further undercut the counterinsurgency effort. Communist propaganda successfully labeled the ARVN "the puppet army, the primary tool of the enemy regime." Far from seeing them as liberators fending off a rebellious enemy, civilians viewed ARVN soldiers as little more than armed extensions of the Saigon government. American advisors worried that a lack of political identification with the GVN and an inability to participate in governance left the population "infected with the same political causative factors for insurgency as they were prior to 1954."[67] The South Vietnamese army's reluctance to participate in civic action and pacification further frustrated Westmoreland, whose military strategy depended in part on winning over the rural population. Even as late as 1967, the MACV commander was discussing with General Cao Van Vien the problems of ARVN troops "taking food from the people and thereby antagonizing them." Such actions clearly made efforts at controlling, even securing, the population difficult. Yet the government's inability to rule the countryside posed deeper problems. No pacification plan could succeed if the NLF forces remained closer to the population than South Vietnam's own army.[68]

ARVN injustices undoubtedly influenced rural peasants' tendencies to support the NLF. Civilians resented being treated like they were the enemy. One villager explained that "when the ARVN came, everyone was frightened.... The soldiers are free to beat anybody, kill anybody." Another peasant added, "Every time the Army came they made more friends for the V.C." When asked why the people did not support the Saigon government, one civilian responded, "because the ARVN ... often burns the villagers' houses and rapes the women."[69] Such acts, though hardly representative of all ARVN soldiers, undermined American plans in South Vietnam. Westmoreland did his best to limit these transgressions but in his advisory role could do little more than point out the offenses and appeal for improved behavior. (Of course, the American armed forces' own record on this score was hardly unblemished.) The MACV commander could not accomplish what South Vietnam needed most—the creation of an army instilled with the ideals and notions of a young nation that regarded itself as something more than just a legacy of French colonialism. A sense of nationalism could not be built on anti-communism alone. In this sense, the South Vietnamese army would never amount to more than its host government. As journalist Frances Fitzgerald explained in rather patronizing terms, "the ARVN was more like a collection of individuals, all of whom happened to be carrying weapons." Surely, the Vietnamese armed forces were fighting for more than just themselves. Still, for Westmoreland, who ultimately intended to hand over the war effort fully to his allies, such depictions painted a gloomy picture for the future of South Vietnam.[70]

The Trials of Vietnamization

Five days after the inauguration of Richard M. Nixon on 20 January 1969, the president's National Security Council met to discuss the possibility of small reductions in the US force presence inside South Vietnam. By March, Nixon's senior leaders concluded the time was ripe for "de-Americanizing" the war. Secretary of Defense Melvin Laird, however, believed an alternate "term like 'Vietnamizing'...put the emphasis on the right issues."[71] While the phrase "Vietnamization" expressed Nixon's goal of entrusting responsibility for the war effort entirely to Saigon, the concept was hardly novel. In fact, helping the South Vietnamese armed forces attain self-sufficiency had served as a pillar of the US advisory effort since the late 1950s. MAAG Chief Samuel T. Williams told the Senate Foreign Relations Committee in July 1959 that he wanted the Vietnamese to "learn what we are trying to teach...so we can get out and go home." By 1963, the new MACV commander, Paul Harkins, forwarded a plan to the Joint Chiefs which proposed the Saigon government would be capable of defending itself within the next three years. The optimistic Harkins believed he could have US advisors out of Vietnam by the end of 1965.[72]

Few Americans in 1965, of course, believed the RVNAF capable of defending the war torn-country on its own. In fact, US Army officers in Saigon pointed to the ARVN's erratic performance as rationale for American escalation. By mid-1966, the state of South Vietnam's military drew the attention of top officials in Washington. In May, the chairman of the Joint Chiefs of Staff expressed to Westmoreland his concerns over American casualties exceeding those of Vietnamese forces. Wheeler pointedly explained that this "fact is taken by the American people as proof positive of assertions continuously made by those in opposition to our Vietnamese policy that United States forces are fighting the war against VC/NVA forces while the South Vietnamese, whose freedom and country are at stake, squabble pettily among themselves to achieve political advantage."[73] Unfair accusations like this troubled Westmoreland who viewed firsthand the sacrifices being made by ARVN soldiers. The MACV commander grasped his allies' limitations yet realized that "ARVN's structure and capabilities have been moulded by the necessity for its employment against major conventional enemy forces as well as guerrillas." If US forces had any hope of leaving Vietnam, the South Vietnamese had to combat both threats successfully. Westmoreland and his staff were under no illusions about the difficulty in achieving this goal.[74]

Despite his concerns, the general remained committed to using ARVN forces as the primary tool for supporting revolutionary development. The 1967 combined campaign plan included an "action program" to expand and improve

RVNAF support for pacification and included training plans for all components of the South Vietnamese armed forces. To preside over these numerous tasks, Westmoreland assigned his new deputy, Creighton Abrams, to supervise the advisory and support effort. MACV's chief intended Abrams to "spend 85 percent of his time with the Vietnamese and Free World troops and their affairs while I would reverse my emphasis."[75] Westmoreland's deputy worked closely with ARVN field commanders throughout 1967, prodding, cajoling, encouraging. In October, Abrams led a study to improve the combat effectiveness of the regional and popular forces resulting in what Westmoreland called "a massive improvement program that addressed all aspects of administration, logistical support, and tactical operations of territorial units." Abrams put his shoulder into the mighty task of addressing RVNAF weaknesses and subsequently developed a profound respect for his allies. Westmoreland too understood the importance of his deputy's mission, noting that "the morale, welfare, a patriotic sentiment of RVNAF personnel and their dependents has been singled out for special attention."[76]

With Abrams's efforts, MACV's training program appeared to gain ground in 1967. By September, the command reported 53 ARVN infantry battalions, 219 RF companies, and 755 PF platoons were "in position performing missions in direct support of RD." This emphasis on revolutionary development accorded well with Westmoreland's campaign plan. Late that summer, the general believed he was glimpsing "the emergence of an effective Vietnamese ground force."[77] Yet problems remained just under the surface. In the fall, MACV reported the overall pacification effort "behind schedule" thanks to materiel shortages, NLF terrorism and harassment, and continued leadership problems within the ARVN's ranks. Saigon officials also discovered the regular army had 20,000 "phantom troops" on its rosters who did not in fact exist.[78] The ARVN's role in pacification further unraveled when the enemy began its border attacks in preparation for the upcoming Tet offensive. To meet the new threat in the I Corps tactical zone, Westmoreland diverted US forces, and with them some ARVN units, to defend the country's outlying areas and maintain South Vietnam's territorial integrity. With this redeployment of troops, MACV admitted "it was questionable whether the military forces were adequate to support an aggressive pacification effort." In short, the ARVN was being pulled in two different directions.[79]

Still, the Tet battles in January and February 1968 suggested, to some at least, that the South Vietnamese armed forces had improved over the previous year. The countrywide offensive certainly rattled the allies but the ARVN performed admirably given the unprecedented scale of the assault. Westmoreland immediately surveyed his senior advisors to report on their counterparts' performance. The results were encouraging. Of the "149 ARVN maneuver battalions, 42 had performed exceptionally well during the attack, while only eight were rated poor in performance. Not a single ARVN unit defected to the enemy. In some cases,

RVNAF units carried out effective counterattacks even though outnumbered."[80] Westmoreland, no doubt searching for a silver lining in the aftermath of such a traumatic event, heaped praise on his allies. At President Johnson's ranch in May, the general applauded the South Vietnamese who had "fought bravely and well. The aggressive spirit displayed by the ARVN during and after the Tet offensive," Westmoreland cheered, "is by far the greatest I have observed in my almost four and a half years in South Vietnam."[81] Perhaps Tet could be viewed as the first test case in which the ARVN had demonstrated its ability to embrace the lessons from their American advisors.

So it seemed in the spring of 1968. From all quarters, US officials paid tribute to their allies. MACV's commander believed the Tet offensive "had the effect of a 'Pearl Harbor.'" As he later explained, "the South Vietnamese government was intact and stronger; the armed forces were larger, more effective, and confident; the people had rejected the idea of a general uprising; and enemy forces, particularly those of the Viet Cong, were much weaker." Ambassador Ellsworth Bunker agreed. Months later, Bunker argued that Tet "had *constructive* effects in giving the Vietnamese confidence—more confidence—in themselves."[87] Advisors in the field equally viewed Tet in positive terms, noting that the offensive demonstrated the loyalty of the population and the resolve of the armed forces. The greatest impact, nevertheless, occurred at the political level. Officials in Saigon might praise the RVNAF, but an impatient American public questioned how Tet could happen in the first place. Furthermore, if the allies had succeeded in crippling the insurgency, why did US forces need to remain? The president concluded the time for true Vietnamization had come. While sending only limited reinforcements to Westmoreland after Tet, Johnson funneled resources toward modernizing the South Vietnamese armed forces. As Robert Komer recalled, "Tet made Vietnamization feasible."[83]

As with so many aspects of the Vietnam War, troubles lingered just under the veneer of progress. In February, Secretary of Defense Robert McNamara, soon to depart for the World Bank, expressed apprehension over "the stability of the political structure in Vietnam and a lack of motivation by the ARVN and the PF and RF."[84] The volatility caused by Tet most affected the allies' pacification campaign where regional and popular forces struggled to blunt the enemy's offensive. In some areas, gains painstakingly achieved over the last two years had been wiped away in a matter of days and weeks. Major General William Peers, the acting I Field Force commander that spring, observed a troubling phenomenon in the attack's wake. "The people's confidence in the GVN to protect them had been greatly reduced as the VC propaganda, prior to the Tet offensive, indicated the cities would be attacked and entered, and the VC did exactly what they had promised." While Peers discerned a renewed sense of "national purpose," the country-wide attack had damaged Saigon's prestige.[85] American officers, however, blamed a biased media for sensationalizing the campaign's negative aspects. One army colonel seethed with disgust over the "irresponsible journalism.... Press canards and distortion of facts and US achievements are unprecedented in US military annals."[86] Nonetheless, Tet revealed to many observers the fragility of the ARVN's territorial security mission and perhaps the larger war effort as a whole.

If General Peers correctly identified a new unity of effort among the South Vietnamese, President Nguyen Van Thieu's call for a general mobilization in mid-June 1968 caused new problems for the GVN. The decision to draft 18- and 19-year-olds placed additional strains on a population increasingly exhausted from war. With the army already lacking qualified officers, the mobilization further aggravated the shortages in ARVN leadership. Combat losses during Tet only made matters worse. While Westmoreland supported the recruitment effort, and even encouraged recalling older reservists to active service, Hanoi responded by sending an additional 80,000 to 90,000 replacements into South Vietnam.[87] In a large sense, the stalemate simply continued at a higher level. Weary ARVN soldiers responded through high desertion rates. By November 1968, the gross rate of desertions (which made no allowances for returnees) exceeded 15 percent. One survey found that 80 percent of deserters had less than six months of service. As the official Joint Chiefs of Staff history recorded, the reasons for desertion were as familiar as they were numerous: "fear and confusion on the part of servicemen, concern for the welfare of dependents, excessive periods of exposure to combat, inadequate pay, expectation of an imminent peace settlement, and laxity of enforcement of punitive measures."[88] For all MACV's focus on building and strengthening a local defense establishment, the RVNAF could not overcome its internal weaknesses.

The advisory effort under Westmoreland thus illustrated the Americans' inability to solve the chronic ails of an indigenous army. False arguments that MACV narrowly focused on training ARVN for conventional operations additionally mask the deeper issues confronting South Vietnam's army. Westmoreland and his staff understood that "Vietnamization" could succeed only if the ARVN was capable of countering a cross-border invasion from the north *and* dealing with southern insurgency which had been decimated but not defeated after Tet. The long advisory years, however, had built a local army dependent on US aid and support. One American lieutenant colonel working with the ARVN 22nd Division noticed how these dependencies left the South Vietnamese at a significant moral and psychological disadvantage when compared to the enemy. "Continued massive combat support and a perpetual advisory presence erodes the national pride of our allies. A crippling dichotomy sets in: They are afraid to do without us, and, at the same time, are ashamed of receiving so much."[89] The decision against a joint command, in which the RVNAF would have served under American officers, ultimately stemmed from this paradox. Still, the armed forces' problems derived less from problems in organization than in leadership.

Throughout Westmoreland's tour, political sponsorship often trumped military merit for promotion in ARVN's officer corps.[90] No amount of organizational restructuring under MACV's watchful eye would have altered the unpleasant fact that the South Vietnamese armed forces had been incapable of promoting on their own a lasting bond between the government and its people.

By mid-1968, most Americans retained only slight confidence in the ARVN's capacity to sustain the war effort unaided. One American officer thought it "impossible to write a timetable for any plan to put South Vietnamese into combat jobs the U.S. is now doing."[91] Statements like this suggested that Westmoreland had failed in his ultimate mission of helping build a stable, noncommunist South Vietnam. Certainly, both he and his subordinate commanders were responsible in part for this failure. Melvin Zais, a senior MACV commander, descriptively criticized the US advisory effort for assuming too much of the wartime burden. "We must be working ourselves out of a job, but we're not. We're not coaching a team; we're like five college football players who have come down to coach a high school team and have inserted ourselves into the lineup."[92] Westmoreland, though, faced a near impossible dilemma. Without acting, South Vietnam risked political and military defeat. By playing a vital role in his ally's survival, Westmoreland alternatively slowed RVNAF's development into a force capable of handling a complex threat from within and beyond its nation's borders. In a long war of "attrition," neither the United States nor South Vietnam benefited from this delay. It seems doubtful, though, that Westmoreland could have accelerated the pace of ARVN's training and modernization. As much progress as it had made between 1964 and 1968, the South Vietnamese army had matured as far and as fast as the political and social environment would allow.

The Failures of Army and Nation Building

Theodore H. White arrived in Chungking, China, in the spring of 1939. The American political journalist and historian landed from the Yangtze River into a province spoiled by civil war, where for years nationalist forces had been struggling to gain the upper hand against communist revolutionaries. The war with Japan, begun in earnest in 1937, not only placed the civil war on hold but complicated both sides' political aims. As nationalist leader Chiang Kai-shek noted of his longstanding enemy, "The Japanese are a disease of the skin. The Communists are a disease of the heart."[93] White seemed impressed by his fellow countrymen working in the US advisory system yet found that few "Americans understood [the] other 'government' of China, which began where the Americanized Chinese officials reached the limit of authority." Perhaps what most affected White, however, was the violence. Soon after the journalist's arrival, the Japanese bombed Chungking, killing thousands. The senseless killing had an "immediate and primordial" impact on his political thinking. As White recalled, "What I learned was that people accept government only if the government accepts its first duty—which is to protect them."[94]

White's experiences in Chungking mirrored the tenuous relationship that had developed nearly three decades later between South Vietnam's army, its people, and the central government in Saigon. Despite its efforts, MACV could not strengthen the fragile links which held together the larger anti-communist war effort. Nor could American troops force the local population to willingly support the Saigon regime. Contemporary observers realized that "lasting solutions must be worked out by the Vietnamese themselves and cannot be imposed from outside."[95] Yet officers like Westmoreland also accepted that without outside intervention, Hanoi's victory appeared unavoidable. As in Chungking, the South Vietnamese government lacked the capacity to protect its people. Was this failure Westmoreland's fault? Given the host country's "staggering array of internal problems," it seems unfair to blame one general for all of South Vietnam's ills. MACV alone could not facilitate political settlement to a civil war that long preceded American involvement. As two Southeast Asia experts wrote while Westmoreland was still in command, the South "must be able to engage in political activity under conditions in which the American presence is not dominant and the conduct of military operations is not the overriding consideration."[96] Through the first half of 1968, such conditions simply did not exist.

MACV's agenda for the RVNAF—and with it, the larger allied strategy—lacked a viable program to rival the National Liberation Front's political and ideological training. Senior officers, though, did speak of using NLF methods to establish a "grass roots indoctrination program" for better communicating with the South Vietnamese people. Yet gaining the loyalty and confidence of the rural population eluded the Saigon government.[97] MACV well understood the implications. As William DePuy reported in February 1965, "unless we devise a system whereby we can go into the minds of every member of the RVNAF and eventually through them and other public officials into the minds of all the effective leadership in this country, and lead them into a conviction that the government can and must win for good and logical reasons, we will have no chance in the long run of seeing any return on our very expensive investment."[98] DePuy's comments, so early in the American war, signified MACV's awareness of a crucial gap in its approach to the political-military conflict in Vietnam. Perhaps his observations also illustrated a certain naïveté to US strategy. No American system ever could get into the minds of a Vietnamese people culturally attuned to question, if not resist, foreign influence in internal political affairs.

Figure 6.1 A DISLOCATED POPULATION. Vietnamese civilians evacuate their homes as members of Co A, 30th Ranger Battalion move in on Vietcong insurgents during the Lunar New Year holidays, 31 January 1968. (RG 111-CV, NARA, 529)

Critics of the US mission have suggested that the "political situation in South Vietnam itself should have prompted more realistic contingency plans against failure of the Vietnamese," if nothing else to provide the Johnson administration with options other than precipitous withdrawal. Without question, Westmoreland offered few if any alternatives when it came to assisting the ARVN, in part because he believed his command was doing all it could to stabilize the military situation and afford their allies time to mature.[99] Given the president's commitment to a noncommunist South Vietnam, Westmoreland had few choices. In the end, he could bring only so much pressure to bear on a sovereign government and its defense establishment. The divides of culture, of language, of understanding simply were too wide to bridge. Advisors, furthermore, could not command. While going it alone was a "perpetual temptation," Americans realized ultimate success rested on the effectiveness of the established government. The incapacity of the South Vietnamese polity and armed forces to fulfill their assigned missions within Westmoreland's larger military strategy thus demonstrates the limitations of what a foreign force can achieve when advising indigenous armies. Despite its power, the US mission in Vietnam could not simultaneously create an army, build a nation, and fight a war.[100]

Conclusion

When Strategy May Not Matter

On 3 July 1968, Major General Kenneth Wickham swore in William C. Westmoreland as the United States Army's twenty-fifth chief of staff. The promotion—some viewed the move as proof of a senior officer being "kicked upstairs"—was bittersweet for Westmoreland. The general no doubt coveted the army's top leadership position yet was leaving behind a messy, unfinished war. Less than a month before departing Saigon, Westmoreland noted at a press conference that it was "unrealistic to expect a quick and early defeat of the Hanoi-led enemy."[1] At best, he was bequeathing to his successor, Creighton Abrams, a stalemate. Yet beneath headlines appraising the failures of Tet and an exposed credibility gap, some journalists took pause to review Westmoreland's accomplishments. Journalist Peter Braestrup, himself a veteran of the Korean War, felt Abrams had "shrewdly profited by circumstances and his predecessor's mixed experience." The new army chief had handed down "an apparently weakened foe, a vast logistics network to give U.S. forces mobility and firepower, and a growing South Vietnamese Army which, to the private surprise of its own leaders, had held up rather well at Tet."[2]

Observers yearning to find "sharp contrast" between Westmoreland and Abrams soon overshadowed those highlighting the continuity between the two MACV commanders. After four years of war that led only to stalemate, Abrams's appointment offered hope that a new general with an improved strategic concept would turn the war effort around. This "better war" thesis, however, remains problematic. A 1970 MACV report admitted that "the basic concept and objectives of pacification, to defeat the VC/NVA and to provide the people with economic and social benefits, have changed little since the first comprehensive GVN plan was first published in 1964."[3] A review of Abrams's command messages equally finds language similar to that used by Westmoreland. As soon as he took charge of MACV, Abrams spoke of providing security to the population, conducting cordon and search operations, and targeting enemy base areas. The new commander even directed the 25th ARVN Division to conduct a "multi-battalion size operation in Hau Nghia province."[4] Abrams undeniably shifted emphasis given the changed environment in Tet's aftermath. Suffering setbacks in mid-1968, the enemy suspended its main force operations thus allowing MACV to place greater weight on pacification. Abrams also bolstered the ARVN training program, realizing that the president no longer would authorize reinforcements from the United States. Yet even here one finds little substantial change. As Ronald Spector has noted, "no new mechanism had been introduced to ensure that the South Vietnamese armed forces would be reformed and improved to the point where they could take over the major burden of the war."[5]

In a large sense, then, the standard history of the Vietnam War is flawed. Critics who maintain that the campaign in the south "was the product of a conventional military that understood the war chiefly in terms of killing the enemy, not fighting an insurgency" reduce the American experience to the point of distortion.[6] Perhaps ironically, officers at the time predicted this line of criticism. One senior officer, writing a "post-mortem" for Westmoreland in late 1968, believed "MACV strategy will be the target of a great deal of criticism. Since the enemy never won any major military battles, critics . . . will of necessity have to concentrate on the psychological, civic action, CORDS type of activities designed to gain broad popular support of the peasantry. They will say MACV neglected this area, concentrated on military operations, built up their own forces and relegated to a secondary role the build-up of ARVN and the strengthening of the image of the Saigon government."[7] The evaluation could not have been more prescient. So too was the advice of Brigadier General Willard Holbrook Jr., who had warned Westmoreland as he assumed command not to be "made a scapegoat for a situation for which there may be no solution." In the flawed narrative of the Vietnam War, a scapegoat is exactly what Westmoreland has become.[8]

A reexamination of the Westmoreland years suggests that the MACV commander in fact developed a comprehensive military strategy consistent with the president's larger political objectives. Matching available means to strategic ends, Westmoreland devised an operational plan that accorded well with the complex realities of the Vietnamese revolutionary war. In implementing this plan, many US Army officers and soldiers in Vietnam, far from being wedded to conventional concepts, did learn and adapt during a near decade-long conflict. Army units and their commanders approached the problems of a hybrid war with varied and at times innovative responses to the political and military problems across the breadth of a war-torn country. In short, the forces Westmoreland commanded understood they were not refighting World War II. One officer, as an example, believed it "extremely difficult to divorce the political, economic, the psychological, and the military, because they are all so intermeshed." Another commander gave his brigade the nickname " 'Diplomats and Warriors' to emphasize the two-fold nature of our mission."[9] Still another senior officer felt the objective in limited wars like Vietnam was "not destruction of [the] enemy's military machine but, rather, neutralization of his political and military influence among the people." Though a gripping tale, the story of Westmoreland and the army losing in Vietnam because of a foolhardy devotion to conventional operations and a zealous pursuit of high body counts is quite simply fiction.[10]

What failed in Vietnam was not merely a strategy of "attrition" but something much more complex. Arguably, historians of the war have predetermined the supposed success or failure of Westmoreland's strategy by framing their language in terms that are too narrow. In the process, they have misappropriated the past for presumed use in the future. If attrition failed in Vietnam, then the critical "lesson" for those prosecuting war is to avoid strategies that rely on similarly ill-advised concepts.[11] The catch, however, is that a careful reading of Westmoreland's approach fails to support such reductionist suppositions. The ramifications of this hypothesis are worth considering beyond the tropes and clichés of a lost war in Southeast Asia. Talented American generals can develop and implement a comprehensive political-military strategy and still lose a war. In fact, the Vietnam experience suggests that strategy can be perfectly rational, in line with political restraints and available resources, and still fail. Good strategy, in short, does not guarantee success. Westmoreland's own strategy was one that recognized American limitations. Perhaps the crucial point worth considering is that strategy itself may also be fraught with limitations.

In the end, the possibility exists that the war in Vietnam was not fully about the US Armed Forces, the possibility that the war's outcome resulted from circumstances beyond the influence of American military power. American historians, however, long have wished their readers to believe that the United States lost in Vietnam because of its own strategic missteps.[12] Such arguments grant little agency to either Hanoi's leaders or the southern insurgency. Given the international context of decolonization and rising Third World nationalism in the turbulent Cold War era, it seems plausible that American presidents from Eisenhower to Nixon devised their grand strategic objectives with the acknowledgment that short wars of annihilation might no longer be as feasible as in the past. Yet if Hanoi, Saigon, and Washington, DC, all conceived of the struggle as a protracted war of attrition, then such a conflict better suited the military weak but politically strong. In the process, too many Americans, placing their faith in the utility of force, underestimated the enemy's determination. Too many Americans misjudged Ho Chi Minh, who declared in 1966: "The war may still last ten, twenty years, or longer. Hanoi, Haiphong, and other cities and enterprises may be destroyed, but the Vietnamese people will not be intimidated! Nothing is more precious than independence and freedom." Even if this notion of communists being prepared to fight on forever was mainly propaganda, Ho's comments illustrated a key point about strategy in Vietnam. What the enemy did mattered.[13]

The Other Side of the Hill

Vietnam War histories that begin from the faulty premise that American actions alone determined victory or defeat overlook the reciprocal nature of warfare. As General George Pickett quipped when explaining why the Confederates lost at Gettysburg, "I think the Union Army had something to do with it." Simply put, war is about interaction.[14] During the American phase of the Vietnam War, Hanoi's leaders went to great lengths debating and adapting their strategy and tactical methods to offset the entry of US combat troops. At various times throughout the war, the communists also struggled with problems of morale and legitimacy in both the north and the south, even if they did hold significant advantages over their southern adversaries.

Thus, as Westmoreland adjusted to the changing environment between 1964 and 1968, so too did Le Duan, Truong Chinh, and Vo Nguyen Giap. These strategic alterations encompassed more than just military means. In the wake of US entry, for instance, COSVN launched a "wide-ranging political campaign throughout the armed forces and the civilian population to develop to the highest possible level our revolutionary heroism, to build resolve to fight and defeat the Americans, and to maintain firm confidence in our final victory." Defining the struggle as a "sacred war" to liberate the south and defend the north held long-term strategic implications, for both sides. By refusing to characterize its war in limited military terms, especially after the United States' entrance, Hanoi complicated the strategic equation for American analysts. Victory or defeat would not turn simply on the military successes of US forces.[15]

To borrow B. H. Liddell Hart's expression, observing "the other side of the hill" reveals a heated debate over strategic options and the proper balance between political and military means. If American strategy was negotiated between Washington and Saigon, in a large sense it also was negotiated between the Hanoi Politburo and the southern National Liberation Front. As Lien-Hang Nguyen recently has demonstrated, North Vietnamese strategists juggled "multiple, at times conflicting, factors to maintain a critical balance in [their] internal and external policies—a fragile balance crucial to waging a successful revolutionary struggle within the wider Cold War."[16] Throughout Westmoreland's term, Hanoi leaders disputed the best route to victory and Vietnamese unification, arguing over the need for large-scale military offensives, the risks entailed in negotiations, and the relationship with their Chinese and Soviet benefactors. Only with considerable reluctance did they turn to the military option. American strategists thus had to ponder how three separate entities—the Saigon government, the Hanoi Politburo, and the NLF—all constructed their own goals and definitions of what victory meant. These differences of opinion within both enemy and allied camps made MACV's own strategic response all the more difficult. How wartime participants coped with US intervention influenced not only decision making in Hanoi and Saigon, but in Washington, DC, and Tan Son Nhut as well.[17]

For leaders in Hanoi, experience suggested that only through a protracted war could a small Southeast Asian country hope to defeat a superpower like the United States. The "people's war" against the French demonstrated to generals like Vo Nguyen Giap that "strategy must be the *strategy of a long-term war.*" Giap's counsel failed to convince all Politburo members, especially those like Le Duan who championed a military solution to the problem of national reunification. Still, Le Duan sought to combine any large-scale military offensive with a political uprising in the cities. At no time did Hanoi leaders rely simply on armed force to achieve their ultimate goals.[18] Senior American officers did not miss this crucial point. In his July 1968 debriefing report, Lieutenant General Fred C. Weyand noted how "experience taught that there was no single element of the enemy's organization that, if attacked alone, would cause the collapse of his force structure or the reduction of his will to resist." Weyand realized, as did many MACV officers, that the enemy's political arm adhered to a supporting military arm at nearly every level of war. Thus, in reacting to Hanoi's holistic approach, Americans were forced to put pressure on the "entire enemy system." As Weyand reported, "we have found that the decimation of the enemy's main ground forces may not have an immediate nor direct impact on the central objective, namely, the control and security of the populated areas."[19] If the enemy developed a comprehensive political-military strategy, MACV would have to reply in kind.

Perhaps, in the process of focusing their lens narrowly on American actions, too many historians have failed to consider how Westmoreland, by necessity, had to create a reactive strategy, at least in the early years of 1964 and 1965. The problem of wresting initiative from the enemy troubled MACV from the beginning. Westmoreland worried constantly over the enemy's ability to set the pace of fighting. He recalled later that "this whole war has been a matter of action and reaction."[20] By stressing "maximum flexibility in their own military and political planning," however, Hanoi leaders never relinquished the upper hand. In 1966, as an example, MACV was still reacting to the combined NVA-NLF threat, thus forcing many senior officers in the American headquarters to think in tactical terms rather than in strategic ones. Furthermore, the enemy's ability to make corresponding strategic changes to each level of US escalation complicated MACV planning. The results proved frustrating. Westmoreland's chief of staff, William B. Rosson, saw US strategy as being "largely reactive and fluid in nature as opposed to providing stable, long-term guidance."[21]

Rosson's depiction of an irresolute military strategy illuminates one of Westmoreland's chief problems during the Vietnam War—matching the flexibility of an enemy well versed in revolutionary warfare. Americans certainly appreciated the obstacles in front of them. As early as April 1966, CIA analyst George A. Carver Jr. commented on the enemy's talents in learning from past failures. "Throughout their almost four decades of unremitting struggle for political power, the Vietnamese Communists have demonstrated great skill in coping with new problems and great tactical flexibility in pursuing unwavering strategic objectives." Other analysts correctly observed "a series of threat variations consisting of mixes of tactics fitted to local situations."[22] Thus through decades of political struggle, flexibility and pragmatism became hallmarks of the revolutionary leaders' approach to war. (Of course, like Americans, Hanoi's leaders made missteps as well.) As wartime circumstances changed, the balance between the political and military struggle changed. Astounded by Hanoi's expert handling of the war, US Army officers and defense analysts afterward portrayed North Vietnamese strategy as "so invincible that 'there is no known proven counter strategy.'"[23] Had American blood and treasure been sacrificed for a war that simply could not have been won? Was it possible that no matter what strategy Westmoreland devised, the United States would never achieve its goals in South Vietnam?

Faith in US military power abroad during the 1960s often eclipsed such unpleasant questions on the possibility of an "unwinnable war." Still, most American officials directing the war effort well understood the role politics played within Hanoi's strategy. Rather than ignoring the implications of communist revolutionary warfare, many US Army officers turned to the writings of Mao Tse-tung or Vo Nguyen Giap searching for insights on protracted wars of national liberation. What they found likely caused concern. If Americans were supposed to be fighting "limited wars" in the age of nuclear weapons, their enemies seemed far less constrained. "The application of this strategy of long-term resistance," Giap declared, "required a whole system of education, a whole ideological struggle among the people and Party members, a gigantic effort of organisation in both military and economic fields, extraordinary sacrifices and heroism from the army as well as from the people, at the front as well as in the rear."[24] Westmoreland and his officers had no way of knowing the contentious strategic debate within Hanoi's Politburo, yet they plainly realized the totality of effort required for communist victory. If President Johnson doubted the resolve of "a piddling piss-ant little country," MACV itself never questioned the enemy's capacity to bring all military, political, social, and economic elements of power to bear in the struggle for national independence.[25]

Officials in the US mission equally appreciated the capacity of enemy forces to adapt their tactical methods in the face of overwhelming firepower. The introduction of American ground troops forced the enemy to reevaluate not only its strategy but also its battlefield techniques. Journalist Peter Arnett, writing in early 1967, related how the communists were "moving main forces into hidden redoubts and jungle sanctuaries" while placing increased "emphasis on guerrilla warfare in the populated regions."[26] American military successes, along with Westmoreland's increasing emphasis on pacification, no doubt helped stimulate these changes. Such tactical adjustments allowed Hanoi to control its loss rates and keep casualties within acceptable margins. More important, effectively countering US offensives precluded Westmoreland from reaching any "crossover point" in which MACV was killing more enemy than Hanoi was able to put into the field. As one postwar report concluded, the enemy had "seized, early, the political-military initiative and seldom relinquished it."[27]

Ultimately, any candid discussion of American strategy during the Vietnam War must accept the premise that the United States could not dictate events simply because it desired to do so. One cannot evaluate fully Westmoreland's strategy without considering Le Duan's strategy. One cannot explain the basis for American defeat in Vietnam without contemplating the reasons for North Vietnam's victory. The key point, in Hew Strachan's words, is that war deals with "reactive elements, not...with fixed values." War always has been a form of human intercourse.[28] Westmoreland's war was no different—a protracted struggle in which both sides sought to frustrate their enemy's designs, cripple their will, and force them to quit. Hanoi's eventual victory says just as much about Vietnamese strategy as it does American.[29]

Moving Beyond an "Unwinnable War"

The question of an inevitable American defeat in Vietnam continues to elicit sharp debate among veterans and scholars alike, despite the notion being both unproven and unproveable. Even before Westmoreland's departure from Saigon, critics spoke of "illusory progress" and a "futile" military strategy. In February 1968, Senator Robert F. Kennedy proclaimed, "It is time to face the reality that a military victory is not in sight, and that it probably will never come."[30] One month later Under Secretary of the Air Force Townsend Hoopes wrote the Secretary of Defense on the "infeasibility of military victory in Vietnam." Even US Army officers found that civic action programs combined with combat operations had "failed to generate the broad popular support desired." General Bruce Palmer Jr. later judged that there "was no way we could win that war."[31] Surely contemporary critiques reflected the pessimism of a nation shocked by the 1968 Tet offensive, but the condemnations also suggested that Vietnam was a problem for which there may not have been a military solution. Given the political constraints under which he operated, Westmoreland had developed an all-embracing, even sound, military strategy yet that strategy was not, in itself, sufficient for victory.

This is not to argue that Westmoreland made no mistakes while commanding MACV. Like all generals commanding in war, he built a record of both accomplishments and missteps. Nor in implementing strategy was the US Army's performance in Vietnam beyond reproach. Soldiers' actions frequently caused vast destruction that drove rural Vietnamese into the NLF camp.[32] Perhaps more important, too many US leaders, both military and civilian, lacked the patience required for the "long pull." Practical Americans thought mostly in the present while the problems of Vietnam proved much more expansive in terms of space and time. The history of a village, for instance, mattered just as much to Vietnamese families as did the present or the future. Frustrated Americans quickly disparaged their allies over the differing conceptions of time. As one analyst observed, "the Vietnamese seem to lack a sense of urgency, and do not display any enthusiasm for their tasks or even a desire to 'get things done.'" This impatience mattered greatly when compared to the North Vietnamese who saw it as their sacred duty to fight against an American war of aggression for their independence and freedom.[33]

In truth, Hanoi never viewed Vietnam as two distinct, independent countries. As Colonel Quach Hai Luong recalled, "All our strategies were based on this basic premise: that Vietnam is one country, unfortunately and artificially divided in two."[34] Westmoreland's own strategy never overcame this fundamental weaknesses—what many Vietnamese believed to be the artificiality of the GVN. No army, foreign or indigenous, could save a government that was not representative of the population at large. Americans in the 1960s realized the problems posed by the lack of a unified political community in South Vietnam. Officers listed countless problems with the GVN: a stratified bureaucracy, a limited number of trained administrators, the existence of petty and grand corruption, to name but a few. Political scientists, denouncing "a polity that has been governed on the basis of limiting power rather than expanding it," suggested the need for a "profound change in the kind of government and administration that now exists in the countryside and urban areas."[35] Though its invocations of an anticommunist form of Vietnamese national identity did not always fall on deaf ears, the Saigon government's prospects for gaining popular support, at least to many Americans, seemed dim indeed. These American leaders realized that their counterparts lacked a widely accepted political and social vision—a detriment to any counterinsurgency campaign—but deemed the international stakes too high when debating the costs of involvement in this revolutionary war.[36] Besides, interventionists argued, American military power would compensate for the lack of political constancy in South Vietnam.

Westmoreland's failure in attaining the president's grand strategic objectives exposed the impracticality of such long-held assumptions. In the 1950s, the image of South Vietnam, as a nation, remained unclear. Under President Ngo

Dinh Diem, a national identity began to take hold yet the lengthy process of post-colonial revolution left the Saigon government ill-equipped to see through the Ngo brothers' vision of social and political transformation.[37] Thus, the contest over nation building was still playing out when the NLF made its bid for political power. On the eve of Westmoreland's appointment as MACV commander in 1964, South Vietnam, in the words of journalist Hanson Baldwin, was "more a loose amalgam of village, tribal and factional loyalties and rivalries." One year later, as the Johnson administration debated escalation, Maxwell Taylor found similar weaknesses in the war-torn country's political foundation. "SVN has never been a nation in spirit," Taylor observed (perhaps unfairly), "and, until recently, has never had a government which the people could regard as their own. Even now their instinct is to consider any government as intrinsically their enemy."[38] Given these problems in developing a strong political community, Saigon's leaders—and their American sponsors—faced overwhelming odds in mobilizing the population against a committed insurgency. It seems unlikely that any form of US military support could compensate for the inherent weaknesses of a manufactured national government, even if it did possess a distinct political ethos from the north. The GVN was more than just dysfunctional. To many southern Vietnamese, it was a fabrication that never manifested itself into a truly national political culture. Thus, the contest over legitimacy with the Viet Minh and their communist successors stood at the very heart of efforts to build the capacity of an effective GVN apparatus. Americans quite simply could not answer these fundamental questions on Vietnamese identity and nationalism.[39]

Despite realizing the limitations of their host government, US leaders chose to intervene. Faith in their ability to transform another country via military, political, social, and economic programs infected nearly all civilian and military leaders involved with strategic planning for Vietnam. Former National Security Council member Michael V. Forrestal believed the United States had overestimated the capability of Saigon's leaders to run simultaneously an effective government and counterinsurgency campaign. "And I suppose, worst of all," Forrestal recalled, "the worst mistake and the one which there's least defense to, is that we vastly overestimated the United States' ability as a government, as a machine, to handle the affairs of a small country twelve thousand miles away."[40] Thus, at the grand strategic level, US policymakers had miscalculated the ways in which military and other means could achieve political ends. Any strategy, therefore, at any level, devised by the Americans was likely to be deficient. In the process, policymakers failed to consider the possibility that when interceding in foreign revolutionary wars, even great powers like the United States might not be able to leverage their influence. As Vietnamese scholar Douglas Pike emphasized after the war, "The question is, how far can foreigners, outsiders, go in a country in winning political struggle?"[41]

These missteps in grand strategy, while not a focus of this work, held far-reaching implications for Westmoreland's military strategy. Such errors should not obscure the fact that MACV equally, and unsurprisingly, made mistakes. No army's performance in war is flawless. Military methods under Westmoreland periodically undermined larger political goals. Equally important, MACV's commander may not have always appreciated the full ethical implications of military operations that caused the forced relocation of hundreds of thousands of Vietnamese. As one critic wrote in 1966, "Our strategy in Vietnam is rather like trying to weed a garden with a bulldozer. We occasionally dig up some weeds, but we dig up most of the turf, too."[42] On the grounds of both ethics and efficiency, Westmoreland certainly was aware of the downsides of forcibly relocating entire communities. Still, the creation of free-fire zones and the transformation of civilians into refugees remain practices, authorized by the MACV commander and his subordinates, well worth evaluation and criticism.

Westmoreland also faced challenges in modifying the army's approach to war in general. General Weyand believed the US Army's "strong and natural tendency" to concentrate on enemy main force units lessened pressure on the remainder of the enemy's force structure.[43] Not all officers and soldiers in MACV embraced the importance of the southern insurgency. One lieutenant colonel saw sharp differences between the NLF and the North Vietnamese Army. "I consider the VC nothing but goddamn highway robbers and bandits. You know, the types that'll try to nickel and dime your asses to death. So I didn't have any respect for those bastards." Such appraisals did little to further Westmoreland's counterinsurgency campaign. Nor did Americans' conviction that governmental control—however one defined such an imprecise term—led automatically to political loyalty.[44]

While American military and civilian leaders disagreed at times over how military force should be used, few questioned, especially in the war's early years, that the US mission could solve South Vietnam's problems and uphold the larger policy of containment. The exertions required in nation building gave some observers pause for sure. Historian and wartime critic Barbara Tuchman later asked "What nation ever has been built from the outside?"[45] As the Johnson administration moved the nation to war, however, most all Americans believed they could control events in Southeast Asia. Diplomats and warriors would cure the "political and social sickness" in South Vietnam. MACV's commander might speak of a long war of attrition, but decent, industrious Americans, heeding the call of a slain president to bear any burden, ultimately would fulfill this noble cause. Whether it be hubris or naïveté, the reluctance to consider the limitations of US power abroad held lasting ramifications for American military strategy in South Vietnam. David Halberstam, for instance, felt that Westmoreland's greatest failing was believing he could accomplish the great task before him. The general was not alone. Throughout most of Westmoreland's tenure, Americans believed—truly believed—that local successes would lead to political promise.[46]

This distortion of the US armed forces' capabilities, especially in the aftermath of the 1965 Ia Drang battle, unquestionably influenced how MACV assessed the implementation of its military strategy. Writing in 1970, former Green Beret Brian M. Jenkins believed four years of experience had not altered military leaders' conception of warfare. "In Vietnam, instead of a series of large scale conventional battles, we have fought myriad little battles, but many still believe that the side that loses the most men must lose the war." Jenkins agreed that "winning hearts and minds" had entered the professional lexicon but such notions were "considered incidental."[47] Indeed, many of MACV's staff officers and commanders remained optimistic about the war's future in the summer of 1968. One senior officer, in a July interview, claimed that "we have never been in a better position militarily than we are at the present time."[48] This narrow focus on the enemy's casualties during the Tet offensives suggested that not all of Westmoreland's subordinates viewed the war in a comprehensive manner. Yet to dismiss the army's performance as entirely flawed reduces its wartime experiences to the point of oversimplification. Not all US Army officers disagreed with Westmoreland's contention that "the pacification effort and the main force war were essentially inseparable." Not all soldiers engaged solely in a military conflict.[49]

Most commanders and their units likely saw counterinsurgency as a technique that treated the symptoms instead of the root causes of South Vietnam's social-political problems. Few questioned the assumption that once the population was secured, political stability would follow. The doctrinal prescriptions of the army's counterinsurgency manuals, however, proved indecisive at the strategic level. Westmoreland had been unable to resolve deeper issues within South Vietnam's political community, but not because of a narrow focus on attrition. Rather, the United States and the Saigon government offered no persuasive alternative to the National Liberation Front. The NLF's message on political, social, and economic change resonated with the rural population in a way not easily replicated by a foreign force and its "puppet" regime.[50] General William DePuy well outlined how American strategy "foundered on the political track." To the former 1st Infantry Division commander, the US effort ultimately rested on "the comparative national political strength of the South Vietnamese government and the North Vietnamese regime." Against the bottom line, DePuy argued, "we never quite induced the growth of a strong independent government of South Vietnam. It was a shaky structure girded and propped by a pervasive American presence."[51]

That presence, alone, could not solve the multifaceted problems of such a complex war. Thus, the war's outcome cannot be explained alone by identifying independent factors that influenced its conduct. For instance, a lack of coordination between MACV, the ARVN, and other US agencies like the CIA tells only part of the story. So do historical narratives that blame Westmoreland for a faulty strategy narrowly focused on attrition.[52] More accurately, the war revealed that military force has its limitations. Inside South Vietnam, neither Westmoreland nor the army he led could build a nation while simultaneously winning a war. The foundation on which they waged a struggle involving both construction of an effective government and destruction of a committed enemy proved too fragile. If Westmoreland deserves blame, it seems best placed on his reluctance to consider that the US Army in Vietnam could achieve only so much. As Secretary of Defense Robert McNamara fittingly recalled years later, "We failed then—as we have since—to recognize the limitations of modern, high-technology military equipment, forces, and doctrine in confronting unconventional, highly motivated people's movements."[53] In spite of a sound military strategy, American forces, given Cold War limitations and the unique setting of Vietnam, could not affect the war's final result in a time period and in costs acceptable to the American public and its political leadership.

Generalship and Strategy in Vietnam

The US Army's failures in Vietnam continue to offer valuable perspectives on the development and implementation of military strategy and its relationship to US foreign policy. Few conflicts in the Cold War era presented the United States with such complex challenges. American military leaders, Westmoreland included, appreciated these difficulties. As DePuy professed, "Everybody recognized that there were several levels of war going on simultaneously, all the way from the very quiet, subversive political war and war of terror down in the hamlets and villages, all the way up to the main forces and everything in between."[54] Yet understanding a problem and solving a problem are two separate matters. Far from cliché, this point seems crucial for understanding the role of generalship in modern wars like Vietnam. Without question, the choices commanders make influence the conduct and course of armed conflict. Long past, however, are the days when heroic leaders determine victory or defeat through their actions alone. As Eliot Cohen and John Gooch have argued, "modern war—like modern life—is a complex business. The commander no longer has a free hand to do whatever he likes."[55]

Perhaps such an assertion matters most when assessing generalship and strategy in the Vietnam War. No American general could dictate the myriad

political, social, economic, and military circumstances on which the war's outcome depended. To believe otherwise is hubristic speculation. A more productive path leads to an examination of generalship as part of a larger whole. Jon
Sumida has noted that "strategic outcomes are the product of a broad range of
happenings from the tactical level to the strategic, which, moreover, affect each
other."[56] In short, war is an interconnected whole of which generalship and strategy are only attendant parts. Thus, critics who blame the MACV commander
alone for a failed war oversimplify the past. Even correspondent Neil Sheehan,
himself no fan of Westmoreland, surmised in 1966 that "Success depends on a
number of circumstances that could be radically altered by the instability that
has marked the Vietnamese war."[57] Beyond question, understanding American
actions in South Vietnam between 1964 and 1968 requires an appreciation of
Westmoreland's strategy, his leadership, and his conduct as a general. Yet isolating one man from the balance of a complex, modern war promotes the role
of commander to exaggerated heights. No wartime general is an independent
variable.[58]

A key question remains—how much was William Westmoreland responsible
for the American failure in Vietnam? Conceivably, a good deal less than previous historians have claimed. False arguments about a futile strategy of attrition
have relied on imprecise language which fails to consider how Westmoreland
realized the war's outcome depended on more than just military might. A part of
MACV's strategy has been mistaken for the whole.

Arguably, the political viability of South Vietnam offers clues for leveling
judgment against MACV's commander. In late 1966, the Office of National
Security Studies at Ann Arbor, Michigan, prepared a paper on indicators of
political success in South Vietnam. The project team admitted that "measuring
political success is a very difficult task even under the best of conditions." Still,
the group had proposed four alternate concepts for evaluation: success in terms
of nation building, government stability, effectiveness, and popular support. All
of the four models contained flaws and the research team questioned how US
forces could influence local political processes. For instance, the group doubted
Americans could affect "the development of South Vietnam from a traditional
society to an independent, responsible, viable, modern nation."[59] And yet this
was exactly Westmoreland's task.

In fact, the general's concept of operations well supported larger American
policy goals. The inability of Westmorland to impose his own president's will
on Saigon political leaders, of his incapacity to persuade the South Vietnamese
people to accept their government, says less about US military strategy in
Vietnam than it does about American grand strategy in the Cold War era.
Nonetheless, even a potentially unwinnable war imposes on the commander the
imperative of assessing the applicability of military force to the nation's political

objectives. To designate a war as unwinnable does not absolve the commander of responsibility.[60]

Yet an overemphasis on the general, of looking at the commander as the locus of strategy, is to misconstrue the very definition of strategy. The primacy of the individual has its limits just as the utility of force has its limits. Westmoreland was part of a larger political-military struggle, even if he was an influential element of American participation in that struggle. The search for blame, long an affliction of Vietnam War scholarship, unfortunately has clouded our judgment of Westmoreland's generalship and of the strategy which he devised for a long war.[61] That American goals proved unattainable does not undermine the thesis that MACV's strategy was sound. The war's outcome cannot be explained merely by arguing that an unsophisticated general chose poorly when it came to military strategy.[62] Far from being "notably stupid," Westmoreland understood the broader context of a revolutionary struggle far from home. In wartime correspondent David Halberstam's estimation, he "did not seem like a man who enjoyed killing, there was no stench of death around him, he seemed more like what you would want a citizen army to produce in a great democracy, an intelligent, reasonable, dedicated man."[63]

Perhaps it is time to reevaluate American strategy in Vietnam, to consider the limitations of what US military force was able to achieve overseas in the 1960s. Perhaps it is worth considering the possibility that a flawed grand strategy cannot always be rescued by a well-conceived military strategy. Perhaps it is time to stop blaming one general for a failed strategy and examine the American experience not based *only* on the war's outcome. Perhaps the time has come to envisage Westmoreland not as a bad general, but rather as a good general fighting a bad war.

NOTES

Preface

1. Ulysses S. Grant wrote in July 1865 that peace in the Civil War only could have been achieved once "the military power of the rebellion was entirely broken.... I therefore determined ... to hammer continuously against the armed force of the enemy and his resources, until by mere attrition, if in no other way, there should be nothing left to him but an equal submission with the loyal section of our common country to the constitution and laws of the land." Grant to E. M. Stanton, 22 July 1865, *The War of the Rebellion: A Compilation of the Official Records of the Union and Confederate Armies*, Series I, Vol. 36, Part I (Washington, DC: US Government Printing Office, 1891), 12–13.
2. Indicative of this line of historical argumentation is Christian G. Appy's contention that "Attrition was the central American strategy; search and destroy was the principle tactic; and the enemy body count was the primary measure of progress." *Working-Class War: American Combat Soldiers and Vietnam* (Chapel Hill: University of North Carolina Press, 1993), 153. For other traditional narratives on a strategy of attrition, see Guenter Lewy, *America in Vietnam* (New York: Oxford University Press, 1978), 46; George C. Herring, *America's Longest War: The United States and Vietnam, 1950–1975*, 4th ed. (New York: McGraw-Hill, 1979, 2002), 179; and Robert D. Schulzinger, *A Time for War: The United States and Vietnam, 1941–1975* (New York: Oxford University Press, 1997), 182.
3. As an example, see Samuel Hynes, *The Soldiers' Tale: Bearing Witness to Modern War* (New York: Penguin Press, 1997), 188. For an overview of criticisms, see Douglas Kinnard, *The War Managers: American Generals Reflect on Vietnam* (Hanover, NH: University Press of New England, 1977; New York: Da Capo Press, 1991), 42–44. Phillip B. Davidson, MACV's chief intelligence officer from 1967 to 1969, argued that "Westmoreland's strategy for 1965 to 1967 has been erroneously oversimplified." *Secrets of the Vietnam War* (Novato, CA: Presidio Press, 1990), 138.
4. My sincere thanks to Roger Spiller for helping me revise my views on the topic of assessing strategy through more than just outcomes.
5. "The Guardians at the Gate," *Time*, 7 January 1966, 15.
6. "The Guardians at the Gate," 19.
7. Quoted in Renata Adler, *Reckless Disregard: Westmoreland v. CBS et al.; Sharon v. Time* (New York: Alfred A. Knopf, 1986), 5. On the subsequent trial, see also Bob Berwin and Sydney Shaw, *Vietnam on Trial: Westmoreland vs. CBS* (New York: Atheneum, 1987).
8. For an overview of revisionist versus orthodox interpretations, see Gary R. Hess, *Vietnam: Explaining America's Lost War* (Malden, MA: Blackwell, 2009), 13–19.
9. Jon Tetsuro Sumida, *Decoding Clausewitz: A New Approach to On War* (Lawrence: University Press of Kansas, 2008), 189.

10. Johnson quoted in USMACV Command History, 1967, Office of Secy, Joint Staff, Mil. Hist. Branch, Entry MACJ03, Box 5, RG 472, NARA, 307. Broadening the war in William Conrad Gibbons, *The U.S. Government and the Vietnam War: Executive and Legislative Roles and Relationships, Part IV: July 1965–January 1968* (Washington, DC: US Government Printing Office, 1994), 49. Limits in Westmoreland to Wheeler, 30 October 1967, Policy/ Strategy 21–31 Oct 67 Folder, Box 6, Paul L. Miles Papers, MHI, p. 4; and Orrin Schwab, *A Clash of Cultures: Civil-Military Relations during the Vietnam War* (Westport, CT: Praeger Security International, 2006), 63. Alexander S. Cochran Jr. argues that a "precise strategy was never developed in Washington largely because the president sought flexibility." In John Schlight, ed., *The Second Indochina War: Proceedings of a Symposium Held at Airlie, Virginia, 7–9 November 1984* (Washington, DC: Center of Military History, 1986), 78.

11. Ideally, Westmoreland would have been a contributor or collaborator in the framing of grand strategic guidance. Evidence suggests, however, that Westmoreland only attempted to follow administration guidance, trying to keep pace as grand strategy evolved. McNamara to Johnson, 20 July 1965, in *Vietnam and America: A Documented History*, ed. Marvin E. Gettleman, Jane Franklin, Marilyn Young, and H. Bruce Franklin (New York: Grove Press, 1985), 283, and William Conrad Gibbons, *The U.S. Government and the Vietnam War: Executive and Legislative Roles and Relationships, Part III: January–July 1965* (Princeton, NJ: Princeton University Press, 1989), 231. On civilian supremacy, see James McAllister, "Who Lost Vietnam? Soldiers, Civilians, and U.S. Military Strategy in Vietnam," *International Security*, Vol. 35, No. 3 (Winter 2010/11): 100; Peter D. Feaver, *Armed Servants: Agency, Oversight, and Civil-Military Relations* (Cambridge, MA: Harvard University Press, 2003), 60; and Blair Clark, "Westmoreland Appraised," *Harper's* (November 1970): 101.

12. John Lewis Gaddis, *Strategies of Containment: A Critical Appraisal of Postwar American National Security Policy* (New York: Oxford University Press, 1982), 23. See also David L. Anderson, ed., *The Columbia History of the Vietnam War* (New York: Columbia University Press, 2011), 81; and Yitzhak Klein, "A Theory of Strategic Culture," *Comparative Strategy*, Vol. 10, No. 1 (January 1991): 9. US objectives in Gareth Porter, ed., *Vietnam: A History in Documents*, ed. Gareth Porter (New York: New American Library, 1981), 273.

13. Westmoreland quoted in Gibbons, *The U.S. Government and the Vietnam War*, Part IV, 530. Military and political victory in Denis W. Brogan, "Naïveté versus Reality in Vietnam," in *Who We Are*, ed. Robert Manning and Michael Janeway (Boston: Little, Brown, 1969), 60. On enemy will, see MACV Monthly Evaluation Report, August 1966, MHI, p. 3.

14. Gil Merom argues that "democracies fail in small wars because they find it extremely difficult to escalate the level of violence and brutality to that which can secure victory." *How Democracies Lose Small Wars: State, Society, and the Failures of France in Algeria, Israel in Lebanon, and the United States in Vietnam* (New York: Cambridge University Press, 2003), 15.

15. Bruce Palmer Jr., *The 25-Year War: America's Military Role in Vietnam* (Lexington: University Press of Kentucky, 1984), 42. Edward J. Drea contends that "Westmoreland's dilemma was how to correct a mismatch between the U.S. troops he had and the troops he needed to do his job." *McNamara, Clifford, and the Burdens of Vietnam, 1965–1969* (Washington, DC: Historical Office of the Secretary of Defense, 2011), 113.

16. MACV Commander's Conference, 21 May 1967, Box 5, Paul L. Miles Papers, MHI, 10. On linking resources to objectives, see C. Dale Walton, *The Myth of Inevitable US Defeat in Vietnam* (London: Frank Cass, 2002), 56; and Robert Shaplen, *The Road from War: Vietnam 1965–1970* (New York: Harper and Row, 1970), 140.

17. This is the unconvincing, overly reductive thesis of Lewis Sorley's *Westmoreland: The General Who Lost Vietnam* (Boston: Houghton Mifflin Harcourt, 2011). As noted in the introduction, some recent, penetrating scholarship has advanced beyond crude interpretations like Sorley's.

18. James Reston, "We May Win the War but Lose the People," *New York Times*, 12 September 1965. Kinnard makes a similar argument regarding the enemy's will on 40.

Introduction

1. Maxwell D. Taylor, *Swords and Plowshares* (New York: W.W. Norton, 1972), 315. On Taylor's critique of the New Look program, see pp. 169–177. Westmoreland's time as SGS is outlined

in Ernest B. Furgurson, *Westmoreland: The Inevitable General* (Boston: Little, Brown, 1968), 232–242.

2. Maxwell D. Taylor, *The Uncertain Trumpet* (New York: Harper & Brothers, 1960), 31. On strategic planning, see Kenneth W. Condit, *The Joint Chiefs of Staff and National Policy, 1955–1956* (Washington, DC: Historical Office, Joint Staff, 1992), 39–40. On developments inside the US Army at this time, see Jonathan M. House, *A Military History of the Cold War, 1944–1962* (Norman: University of Oklahoma Press, 2012), 225–229. House argues the "resulting ferment about doctrine and organization caused more confusion than improvement," p. 229.

3. William C. Westmoreland, *A Soldier Reports* (Garden City, NY: Doubleday, 1976), 34.

4. On Pentomic divisions, see Robert T. Davis II, *The Challenge of Adaptation: The US Army in the Aftermath of Conflict, 1953–2000* (Fort Leavenworth, KS: Combat Studies Institute Press, 2008), 25–28; organic nuclear capability in Leonard Rapport and Arthur Northwood Jr., *Rendezvous with Destiny: A History of the 101st Airborne Division* (Greenville, TX: 101st Airborne Division Association, 1965), 782.

5. Westmoreland, *A Soldier Reports*, 36. Dave Derence, "Recondo Training in the 101st Airborne Division," *Airborne Quarterly* (August 1959): 6–8. Recondo stood for "reconnaissance" and "doughboy." The training was especially useful for junior noncommissioned officers who underwent a shorter version of Ranger School that they otherwise would not have experienced. My thanks to John O'Brien at Fort Campbell for sharing this useful article with me.

6. John F. Kennedy, Remarks at West Point to the Graduating Class of the US Military Academy, 6 June 1962; full text found at *The American Presidency Project*, http://www.presidency.ucsb.edu/ws/index.php?pid=8695.

7. Lance Betros, *Carved from Granite: West Point since 1902* (College Station: Texas A&M University Press, 2012), 141, 230. Westmoreland, *A Soldier Reports*, 46. Furgurson, *Westmoreland*, 274.

8. Paul L. Miles, "Westmoreland and the Making of Strategy in the Vietnam War: A Reconsideration" (lecture, Virginia Military Institute, Lexington, VA, 18 April 2007).

9. J. C. Wylie, *Military Strategy: A General Theory of Power Control* (New Brunswick, NJ: Rutgers University Press, 1967), 13. On the origins of the word "strategy," see Beatrice Heuser, *The Evolution of Strategy: Thinking War from Antiquity to the Present* (New York: Cambridge University Press, 2010), 4; and Bernard Brodie, "Strategy," in *International Encyclopedia of the Social Sciences*, Vol. 15, ed. David L. Sills (New York: Macmillan/Free Press, 1968), 281.

10. On strategy as both a theory and a behavior, see Colin S. Gray, *Fighting Talk: Forty Maxims on War, Peace, and Strategy* (Westport, CT: Praeger Security International, 2007), 48; and David J. Lonsdale, "Strategy" in David Jordan, James D. Kiras, et al., *Understanding Modern Warfare* (New York: Cambridge University Press, 2008), 24. Hew Strachan discusses the evolution of the word over time in "The Lost Meaning of Strategy," *Survival*, Vol. 47, No. 3 (Autumn 2005): 34–35.

11. Carl von Clausewitz, *On War*, ed. and trans. Michael Howard and Peter Paret (New York: Alfred A. Knopf Everyman's Library, 1976, 1993), 207. On the role of tactical success, see p. 165 and Hew Strachan, *Clausewitz's On War: A Biography* (New York: Atlantic Monthly Press, 2007), 117.

12. Clausewitz, *On War*, 208, 238. On strategic interplay, see Azar Gat, *A History of Military Thought: From the Enlightenment to the Cold War* (New York: Oxford University Press, 2001), 222.

13. For an overview of war's interdependent variables, see Heuser, *The Evolution of Strategy*, 18–19. On principles and rules, see Williamson Murray and Mark Grimsley, "Introduction: On Strategy," in *The Making of Strategy: Rulers, States, and War*, ed. Williamson Murray, Macgregor Knox, and Alvin Bernstein (New York: Cambridge University Press, 1994), 1. It is worth noting that Harry G. Summers Jr. used Clausewitz as a framework to critique American strategy in Vietnam. *On Strategy: A Critical Appraisal of the Vietnam War* (Novato, CA: Presidio, 1982).

14. B. H. Liddell Hart, *Strategy*, 2nd rev. ed. (New York: Frederick A. Praeger, 1957), 335. See also Michael Howard, "The Classical Strategists," in *Problems of Modern Strategy*, ed. Alastair

Buchan (New York: Praeger, 1970), 47; and Paul Kennedy, *Grand Strategies in War and Peace* (New Haven, CT: Yale University Press, 1991), 4.

15. Liddell Hart, *Strategy*, 333–336. See also Gat, *A History of Military Thought*, 677–679, 685. Writing in the midst of World War II, Edward Mead Earle, editor of *Makers of Modern Strategy*, elaborated on the meaning of grand strategy. "But as war and society have become more complicated," Earle observed, "strategy has of necessity required increasing consideration of nonmilitary factors, economic, psychological, moral, political and technological." He then offered his own definition of strategy as the "art of controlling and utilizing the resources of a nation—or a coalition of nations—including its armed forces, to the end that its vital interests shall be effectively promoted and secured against enemies, actual, potential, or merely presumed." Introduction to *Makers of Modern Strategy: Military Thought from Machiavelli to Hitler* (Princeton, NJ: Princeton University Press, 1943), viii.

16. Colin S. Gray, *The Strategy Bridge: Theory for Practice* (New York: Oxford University Press, 2010), 7; Colin S. Gray, *Modern Strategy* (New York: Oxford University Press, 1999), 17. On the relationships within strategy, see also Lonsdale in Jordan, Kiras, et al., *Understanding Modern Warfare*, 22.

17. Gray, *The Strategy Bridge*, 29.

18. Matthew B. Ridgway, *The Korean War* (Garden City, NY: Doubleday, 1967; reprint, New York: Da Capo Press, 1986), 232. It is important to note that civilian leaders felt the same as Ridgway. Secretary of Defense Robert S. McNamara recalled that "Military strategy must be a derivative of foreign policy." Robert McNamara, interview by Walt W. Rostow, 8 January 1975, LBJL, I-10.

19. Michael Howard, *The Mediterranean Strategy in the Second World War* (New York: Frederick A. Praeger, 1968), 2. On improvisation, see Brian M. Linn, "The American Way of War Revisited," *Journal of Military History*, Vol. 66, No. 2 (April 2002): 503; and David A. Garvin, *Learning in Action: A Guide to Putting the Learning Organization to Work* (Boston: Harvard Business School Press, 2000), xi.

20. Daniel J. Hughes, *Moltke on the Art of War: Selected Writings* (Novato, CA: Presidio, 1993), 47. For a more modern characterization, see Thomas C. Schelling, *The Strategy of Conflict* (Cambridge, MA: Harvard University Press, 1960), 160.

21. Hughes, *Moltke*, 46. On learning, see Richard Duncan Downie, *Learning from Conflict: The U.S. Military in Vietnam, El Salvador, and the Drug War* (Westport, CT: Praeger, 1998), 2; and Harold R. Winton and David R. Mets, eds., *The Challenge of Change: Military Institutions and New Realities, 1918–1941* (Lincoln: University of Nebraska Press, 2000), xii. Dennis J. Vetock argues that "US Army self examination in the Vietnam conflict surpassed all previous efforts to collect, evaluate, and apply operational experiences." *Lessons Learned: A History of US Army Lesson Learning* (Carlisle Barracks, PA: US Army Military History Institute, 1988), 104.

22. Liddell Hart, *Strategy*, 335–336. On grand strategy relationships, see Edward N. Luttwak, "The Impact of Vietnam on Strategic Thinking in the United States," in *Vietnam: Four American Perspectives*, ed. Patrick J. Hearden (West Lafayette, IN: Purdue University Press, 1990), 63. See also John M. Collins, *Grand Strategy: Principles and Practices* (Annapolis, MD: Naval Institute Press, 1973), 14; Gray, *Fighting Talk*, 82; and Paul Kennedy, *Grand Strategies in War and Peace* (New Haven, CT: Yale University Press, 1991), 5.

23. Kennan quoted in John Lewis Gaddis, *George F. Kennan: An American Life* (New York: Penguin Press, 2011), 591. For a similar critique, see James M. Gavin, "Vietnam Policy—Testimony at the Committee Hearings," *Congressional Digest*, Vol. 45, No. 4 (April 1966): 107.

24. Barry R. Posen, *The Sources of Military Doctrine: France, Britain, and Germany between the World Wars* (Ithaca, NY: Cornell University Press, 1984), 13; Bernard Brodie, *War and Politics* (New York: Macmillan, 1973), 2; Collins, *Grand Strategy*, 14.

25. Department of the Army, *Field Manual 100-5, Field Service Regulations—Operations* (Washington, DC: February 1962), 3. On the role of JCS, the NSC, and Congress, see Lawrence J. Korb, *The Joint Chiefs of Staff: The First Twenty-five Years* (Bloomington: Indiana University Press, 1976), 7.

26. *Field Manual 100-5*, 4.

27. Department of the Army, *Army Regulations 320-5, Dictionary of United States Army Terms* (Washington, DC: January 1961), 538.

28. Westmoreland, *A Soldier Reports*, 91. On defining military strategy, see Archer Jones, *Elements of Military Strategy: An Historical Approach* (Westport, CT: Praeger, 1996), xiii, 199; and Morton H. Halperin, *Contemporary Military Strategy* (Boston: Little, Brown, 1967), 33.

29. Full Montgomery quotation in John Nagl, *Learning to Eat Soup with a Knife: Counterinsurgency Lessons from Malaya and Vietnam* (Chicago: University of Chicago Press, 2002), 87; purpose and plan in Wylie, *Military Strategy*, 14–15.

30. McNamara to Johnson, 20 July 1965, *FRUS, 1964–1968*, III: 172. Problems of defining victory in Larry Cable, *Unholy Grail: The US and the Wars in Vietnam, 1965–8* (London: Routledge, 1991), 25; and Robert Mandel, *The Meaning of Military Victory* (Boulder, CO: Lynne Rienner, 2006), 5.

31. For recent scholarship which presents a more balanced picture of Westmoreland and the US Army in Vietnam, see Graham A. Cosmas, *MACV: The Joint Command in the Years of Escalation, 1962–1967* (Washington, DC: Center of Military History, 2006); Andrew J. Birtle, "PROVN, Westmoreland, and the Historians: A Reappraisal," *Journal of Military History*, Vol. 72, No. 4 (October 2008); and John Prados, *Vietnam: The History of an Unwinnable War, 1945–1975* (Lawrence: University Press of Kansas, 2009). On the hold of the conventional narrative, see Max Boot, *Invisible Armies: An Epic History of Guerrilla Warfare from Ancient Times to Present* (New York: Liveright, 2013). As an example, Boot argues: "On the basis of his limited experience, Westmoreland had a one-word solution to the insurgency: 'Firepower,'" 418.

32. Vietcong literally meant Communist Traitor to the Vietnamese Nation. Guenter Lewy, *America in Vietnam* (New York: Oxford University Press, 1978), 52. Stanley Karnow, *Vietnam: A History* (New York: Viking Press, 1983), 18. On organizational culture, see Yitzhak Klein, "A Theory of Strategic Culture," *Comparative Strategy*, Vol. 10, No. 1 (January 1991): 5; and Jeffrey S. Lantis, "Strategic Culture: From Clausewitz to Constructivism," in *Strategic Culture and Weapons of Mass Destruction: Culturally Based Insights into Comparative National Security Policymaking*, ed. Jeannie L. Johnson, Kerry M. Kartchner, and Jeffrey A. Larsen (New York: Palgrave Macmillan, 2009), 35.

33. On culture and organizational choice, see Theo Farrell, "Culture and Military Power," *Review of International Studies*, Vol. 24, No. 3 (July 1998): 410; strategy as problem solving in J. Boone Bartholomees Jr., *U.S. Army War College Guide to National Security Policy and Strategy* (Carlisle, PA: Strategic Studies Institute, 2006), 80; as a process, see Heuser, *The Evolution of Strategy*, 17.

34. This point taken from Brian Linn, exchange with author, 23 June 2011.

35. On the limits of cultural explanations, see Peter H. Wilson, "Defining Military Culture," *Journal of Military History*, Vol. 72 (January 2008): 21; and Elizabeth Kier, "Culture and Military Doctrine: France between the Wars," *International Security*, Vol. 19, No. 4 (Spring 1995): 71. On learning from experience, see Léon de Caluwé and Hans Vermaak, *Learning to Change: A Guide for Organization Change Agents* (Thousand Oaks, CA: Sage, 2003), 267.

36. Peter Braestrup, *Big Story: How the American Press and Television Reported and Interpreted the Crisis of Tet 1968 in Vietnam and Washington*, Vol. 1 (Boulder, CO: Westview Press, 1977), 23. On the war's complexity, see Douglas Pike, "Conduct of the War: Strategic Factors, 1965–1968," in *The Second Indochina War: Proceedings of a Symposium Held at Airlie, Virginia, 7-9 November 1984*, ed. John Schlight (Washington, DC: Center of Military History, 1986), 101; and Historical Division, Joint Chiefs of Staff, "The Joint Chiefs of Staff and the War in Vietnam, 1960–1968," Part I (hereafter cited as JCS History) JCSHO, 4–5. On observing historical events more accurately, see Jon Tetsuro Sumida, *Decoding Clausewitz: A New Approach to On War* (Lawrence: University Press of Kansas, 2008), 48.

37. This is not to argue that success or failure is insignificant in an assessment of any strategy. Of course, it is. Taylor, quoted in Robert W. Komer, *Bureaucracy at War: U.S. Performance in the Vietnam Conflict* (Boulder, CO: Westview Press, 1986), 10. On difficulties translating power into policy, see Henry A. Kissinger, *Nuclear Weapons and Foreign Policy* (New York: Harper & Brothers, 1957), 7. Carter Malkasian argues "there is no set framework for success in a war of attrition." *A History of Modern Wars of Attrition* (Westport, CT: Praeger, 2002), 9.

38. William S. Turley, *The Second Indochina War: A Concise Political and Military History*, 2nd ed. (Lanham, MD: Rowman and Littlefield, 2009), 99.

39. Hew Strachan, "Attrition," in *The Oxford Companion to Military History*, ed. Richard Holmes (New York: Oxford University Press, 2001), 105. On Delbrück, see Gordon A. Craig, "Delbrück: The Military Historian," in *Makers of Modern Strategy: From Machiavelli to the Nuclear Age*, ed. Peter Paret (Princeton, NJ: Princeton University Press, 1986), 341–342; and William C. Martel, *Victory in War: Foundations of Modern Strategy*, rev. ed. (New York: Cambridge University Press, 2011), 95–96. In relation to Vietnam, see John Prados, "American Strategy in Vietnam," in *The Columbia History of the Vietnam War*, ed. David L. Anderson (New York: Columbia University Press, 2011), 248.

40. Ward S. Just, "Notes on a Losing War," *Atlantic*, Vol. 223, No. 1 (January 1969): 41. On absence of strategy, see Dave Richard Palmer, *Summons of the Trumpet: U.S.-Vietnam in Perspective* (San Rafael, CA: Presidio Press, 1978), 117; and H. R. McMaster, *Dereliction of Duty: Lyndon Johnson, Robert McNamara, the Joint Chiefs of Staff, and the Lies that Led to Vietnam* (New York: Harper Perennial, 1997), 333. On critiques of attrition, see Malkasian, *A History*, 7 and Jones, *Elements of Military Strategy*, 209.

41. Kent Roberts Greenfield, *American Strategy in World War II: A Reconsideration* (Malabar, FL: Krieger, 1963, 1982), 32. Russell F. Weigley, *The American Way of War: A History of United States Military Strategy and Policy* (New York: Macmillan, 1973), 334. Louis Morton, "Germany First: The Basic Concept of Allied Strategy in World War II," in *Command Decisions*, ed. Kent Roberts Greenfield (Washington, DC: Center of Military History, 2000), 43. On how the World War II experience influenced Vietnam-era officers, see Harry G. Summers, "The United States Army Institutional Response to Vietnam," in *Proceedings of the 1982 International Military History Symposium*, ed. Charles R. Shrader (Washington, DC: US Army Center of Military History, 1984), MHI holdings, p. 296.

42. Lodge quoted in William Conrad Gibbons, *The U.S. Government and the Vietnam War: Executive and Legislative Roles and Relationships, Part IV: July 1965–January 1968* (Washington, DC: US Government Printing Office, 1994), 451. Westmoreland quoted in ibid., 452.

43. Brodie in Sills, *International Encyclopedia of the Social Sciences*, 286. Problems with annihilation strategy in McNamara interview, 8 January 1975, LBJL, I-27; and Scott S. Gartner and Marissa E. Myers, "Body Counts and 'Success' in the Vietnam and Korean Wars," *Journal of Interdisciplinary History*, Vol. 25, No. 3 (Winter, 1995): 382.

44. Charles M. Fergusson, "Strategic Thinking and Strategic Studies: Prerequisites for Sound Strategy," US Army War College Student Thesis, 8 March 1963, MHI, 6. Control in Jordan, Kiras, et al., *Understanding Modern Warfare*, 26, quoting J. C Wylie. On an expanded definition of strategy, see Edward N. Luttwak, *Strategy: The Logic of War and Peace* (Cambridge, MA: Belknap Press of Harvard University Press, 1987), 240.

45. On compartmentalization, see Charles A. Stevenson, *Warriors and Politicians: US Civil-Military Relations under Stress* (London: Routledge, 2006), 57. On war's complexity, see George C. Herring, *LBJ and Vietnam: A Different Kind of War* (Austin: University of Texas Press, 1994), 36–37.

46. W. C. Westmoreland, interview by Paul L. Miles, 10 April 1971, Box 1, Paul L. Miles Papers, MHI, 17. Colin S. Gray argues that friction is so damaging at the strategic level because of the need to "accommodate, integrate, and direct all of the activities that constitute war." *Explorations in Strategy* (Westport, CT: Greenwood Press, 1996), 11. On the air-ground war debate, see Willard J. Webb, "The Single Manager for Air in Vietnam," *Joint Forces Quarterly* (Winter 1993–94): 88–98; and Ian Horwood, *Interservice Rivalry and Airpower in the Vietnam War* (Fort Leavenworth, KS: Combat Studies Institute Press, 2006).

47. Phillip B. Davidson, *Vietnam at War: The History: 1946–1975* (Novato, CA: Presidio, 1988), 354.

48. Westmoreland quoted in Peter M. Dawkins, "The United States Army and the 'Other' War in Vietnam: A Study of the Complexity of Implementing Organizational Change" (Ph.D. diss., Princeton University, 1979), 231. Westmoreland laid out his multiple tasks in U.S. Grant Sharp and William C. Westmoreland, *Report on the War in Vietnam* (Washington, DC: US Government Printing Office, 1969), 113.

49. Summers, *On Strategy*, 86, 91. Jeffrey Record argues that Summers "ignored South Vietnam's abject political and military incapacity to deal with the internal insurgent threat." *Beating Goliath: Why Insurgencies Win* (Washington, DC: Potomac Books, 2007), 125.

50. Davidson, *Vietnam at War*, 320. Italics in original. On disagreements over the war's nature and threats, see Wilbur H. Morrison, *The Elephant and the Tiger: The Full Story of the Vietnam War* (New York: Hippocrene Books, 1990), 41; and G. C. Reinhardt, *Guerrilla-Combat, Strategy and Deterrence in Southeast Asia* (Santa Monica, CA: The RAND Corporation, 1964), 6.

51. James W. Johnson and Charles Anello, "Measurement of Pacification Progress in Vietnam," Research Analysis Corporation Technical Paper, September 1968, CMH Library, 8. Lewis Sorley never mentions pacification or CORDS in *Westmoreland*.

52. US Army Special Warfare School, *Counterinsurgency Planning Guide, Special Text Number 31-176* (Fort Bragg, NC: Department of Counterinsurgency, May 1964), 21; linkages between pacification and territorial security in R.W. Komer, "Impact of Pacification on Insurgency in Vietnam," August 1970, Folder 5, Box 15, Douglas Pike Collection: Unit 01-Assessment and Strategy, TTUVA, 5–6; and USMACV, Guide for Province and District Advisors, 1 February 1968, Historian's Files, CMH, pp. 2–4, 2–6.

53. Embassy Telegram, 7 March 1965, *FRUS*, 1964–1968, II: 409. Communist political activity in Jeffrey Race, "How They Won," *Asian Survey*, Vol. 10, No. 8 (August 1970): 637.

54. Gibbons, IV, 15. McGeorge Bundy wrote to the president in early 1966 that "Westmoreland has never neglected the critically important task of persistent effort to strengthen the forces of the GVN." *FRUS*, 1964–1968, IV: 233.

55. Gibbons, IV, 45. Westmoreland's conferrals with Vien in Cosmas, *MACV*, 350. On weaknesses in ARVN, see Westmoreland to JCS, 7 June 1965, *FRUS*, 1964–1968, II: 734.

56. Robert Shaplen, *The Road from War: Vietnam 1965–1970* (New York: Harper and Row, 1970), 139. Hanson Baldwin, "Vietnam War Evaluation Being Made for Johnson," *New York Times*, 15 November 1967.

57. Address by LTG Frederick L. Weyand to the National Guard Association of the United States, 10 October 1968, Officials, Weyand, Frederick L., Folder #73, Westmoreland Personal Papers, Box 3, RG 319, NARA. On war as a synthesis, see Gabriel Kolko, *Anatomy of a War: Vietnam, the United States, and the Modern Historical Experience* (New York: Pantheon Books, 1985), 176; and Douglas Kinnard, *The War Managers: American Generals Reflect on Vietnam* (Hanover, NH: University Press of New England, 1977; New York: Da Capo Press, 1991), 56.

58. Jeffrey Record, for instance, argues Westmoreland "displayed an utter obliviousness to the political nature of the war," while Bill Bundy thought the general "a blunt instrument," Record, 121. Bundy in David Halberstam, *The Best and the Brightest* (New York: Random House, 1969), 549.

59. George C. Herring, "American Strategy in Vietnam: The Postwar Debate," *Military Affairs* Vol. 46, No. 2 (April 1982): 61. John Nagl argues, with little evidence except that the United States lost the war, that "the army had neither the knowledge nor the desire to change its orientation away from conventional war." *Learning to Eat Soup with a Knife*, 126.

Chapter 1

1. It is, of course, possible to speak of a common set of shared beliefs that were present in the US Army during the 1950s and 1960s. There existed a common commitment to national security, a common way of thinking, and a common set of practices handed down from generation to generation that were not necessarily amenable to revolutionary changes of direction. Still, as in any exclusive community, there were members who were more flexible of mind and behavior. Roger Spiller, comments to author, 14 January 2103. For arguments the US Army was incapable of fighting unconventional wars well, see Jeffrey Record, "How America's Own Military Performance in Vietnam Aided and Abetted the 'North's' Victory," in *Why the North Won the Vietnam War*, ed. Marc Jason Gilbert (New York: Palgrave, 2002), 123; Andrew F. Krepinevich Jr., *The Army and Vietnam* (Baltimore: Johns Hopkins University Press, 1986),

5; and Anthony T. Bouscaren, ed., *All Quiet on the Eastern Front: The Death of South Vietnam* (Old Greenwich, CT: Devin-Adair, 1977), 13.

2. James E. King, "Deterrence and Limited War," *Army*, Vol. 8, No. 1 (August 1957): 23. On army leaders recognizing that "military methods to defeat... insurgency were insufficient," see Boyd L. Dastrup, *The US Army Command and General Staff College: A Centennial History* (Manhattan, KS: Sunflower University Press, 1982), 112.

3. John J. McCuen, *The Art of Counter-Revolutionary War* (Harrisburg, PA: Stackpole Books, 1966), 27. On war being different than in World War II, see Walter E. Kretchik, *U.S. Army Doctrine: From the American Revolution to the War on Terror* (Lawrence: University Press of Kansas, 2011), 187.

4. Walter Darnell Jacobs, "This Matter of Counterinsurgency," *Military Review*, Vol. 44, No. 10 (October 1964): 80. Armed liberation strategy in Director, CIA memorandum, 29 November 1963, *FRUS, 1961–1963*, IV: 642. Writings in Henry G. Gole, *General William E. DePuy: Preparing the Army for Modern War* (Lexington: University Press of Kentucky, 2008), 139.

5. Carl M. Guezlo, "The Communist Long War," *Military Review*, Vol. 40, No. 9 (December 1960): 15. See also Walter D. Jacobs, "Mao Tse-tung as a Guerrilla—A Second Look," in *Modern Guerrilla Warfare: Fighting Communist Guerrilla Movements, 1941–1961*, ed. Franklin Mark Osanka (New York: Free Press of Glencoe, 1962), 166. On the Maoist model, see William J. Duiker, "Ho Chi Minh and the Strategy of People's War," in *The First Vietnam War: Colonial Conflict and Cold War Crisis*, ed. Mark Atwood Lawrence and Fredrik Logevall (Cambridge, MA: Harvard University Press, 2007), 153.

6. Charles Wolf Jr., *Insurgency and Counterinsurgency: New Myths and Old Realities* (Santa Monica, CA: Rand Corporation, 1965), 1. On officers being open-minded and progressive, see Samuel P. Huntington, *The Soldier and the State: The Theory and Politics of Civil-Military Relations* (Cambridge, MA: Belknap Press of Harvard University Press, 1957; repr., 1985), 71.

7. As an example, see Colonel Virgil Ney, "Guerrilla Warfare and Modern Strategy," in *Modern Guerrilla Warfare: Fighting Communist Guerrilla Movements, 1941–1961*, ed. Franklin Mark Osanka (New York: Free Press of Glencoe, 1962), 25–38.

8. Kennan in John Lewis Gaddis, *Strategies of Containment: A Critical Appraisal of Postwar American National Security Policy* (New York: Oxford University Press, 1982), 49. NSC paper in *The Pentagon Papers: The Defense Department History of United States Decisionmaking in Vietnam* [Senator Gravel, ed.], 5 vols. (Boston: Beacon Press, 1971–1972), I: 185. George C. Herring, *From Colony to Superpower: U.S. Foreign Relations since 1776* (New York: Oxford University Press, 2008), 600–601. Lloyd Gardner, "The Last Casualty? Richard Nixon and the End of the Vietnam War, 1969–75," in *A Companion to the Vietnam War*, ed. Marilyn B. Young and Robert Buzzanco (Malden, MA: Blackwell, 2002), 230.

9. US power in David L. Anderson, ed., *The Columbia History of the Vietnam War* (New York: Columbia University Press, 2011), 23. Ideology in Stuart Kinross, *Clausewitz and America: Strategic Thought and Practice from Vietnam to Iraq* (London: Routledge, 2008), 25; and Kenneth E. Boulding, *Conflict and Defense: A General Theory* (New York: Harper Torchbooks, 1963), 282.

10. Department of the Army, Field Manual 100–5, *Field Service Regulations Operations*, February 1962, 5.

11. Quoted in Herring, *From Colony to Superpower*, 596. Change in Robert B. Asprey, *War in the Shadows: The Guerrilla in History* (Garden City, NY: Doubleday, 1975), 671. On decolonization and the World Wars, see Odd Arne Westad, *The Global Cold War: Third World Interventions and the Making of Our Times* (New York: Cambridge University Press, 2007), 79, 86. Power vacuum in Melvyn P. Leffler, *For the Soul of Mankind: The United States, the Soviet Union, and the Cold War* (New York: Hill and Wang, 2007), 144.

12. Nathan Leites and Charles Wolf Jr., *Rebellion and Authority: An Analytic Essay on Insurgent Conflicts* (Chicago: Markham, 1970), 32. On global insurrections, see Jeremy Black, *War and the World: Military Power and the Fate of Continents, 1450–2000* (New Haven, CT: Yale University Press, 1998), 270. Michael H. Hunt discusses the relationship between European defense against the Soviet Union and decolonization in *Lyndon Johnson's War: America's Cold War Crusade in Vietnam, 1945–1968* (New York: Hill and Wang, 1996), 7.

13. Truman quoted in Herring, *From Colony to Superpower,* 615. On the Truman Doctrine, see John Lewis Gaddis, *The Cold War: A New History* (New York: Penguin Press, 2005), 30–32.

14. On NSC-68, see Gaddis, *Strategies of Containment,* 89–106. On serving the army's institutional agenda, see David T. Fautua, "The 'Long Pull' Army: NSC 68, the Korean War, and the Creation of the Cold War U.S. Army," *Journal of Military History,* Vol. 61 (January 1997): 96.

15. Kennan in John Lewis Gaddis, *George F. Kennan: An American Life* (New York: Penguin Press, 2011), 256–257. International communist movement in Gaddis, *Strategies of Containment,* 239. On Indochina, see Leslie H. Gelb with Richard K. Betts, *The Irony of Vietnam: The System Worked* (Washington, DC: Brookings Institution, 1979), 44.

16. Fish in the sea in Roger Hilsman, "Two American Counterstrategies to Guerrilla Warfare: The Case of Vietnam," in *China's Policies in Asia and America's Alternative,* ed. Tang Tsou (Chicago: University of Chicago Press, 1968), 271. See also Roger Hilsman, *To Move a Nation: The Politics of Foreign Policy in the Administration of John F. Kennedy* (Garden City, NY: Doubleday, 1964, 1967), 413–414. Mao's writings and men over machines in Arthur Waldron and Edward O'Dowd, "Mao Revisited," in *Mao Tse-tung on Guerrilla Warfare,* trans. Samuel B. Griffith II (Baltimore: Nautical & Aviation Publishing, 1992), 19. Specific strategy in Edward L. Dreyer, *China at War, 1901–1949* (London: Longman, 1995), 350. Communist expansion in Henry Kissinger, *Diplomacy* (New York: Simon and Schuster, 1994), 623.

17. Albert G. Wing Jr., "The Contributions of Mao Tse-tung to Military Thought on Guerrilla Warfare," 8 March 1963, Student Thesis, US Army War College, MHI, 60.

18. Matthew B. Ridgway, *The Korean War* (Garden City, NY: Doubleday, 1967; reprint, New York: Da Capo Press, 1986), 232. On the relationship between Korea and Indochina, see Robert D. Schulzinger, *A Time for War: The United States and Vietnam, 1941–1975* (New York: Oxford University Press, 1997), 45; Westad, *The Global Cold War,* 180; and Lloyd C. Gardner, *Approaching Vietnam: From World War II through Dienbienphu, 1941–1954* (New York: W.W. Norton, 1988), 115. Russell Weigley argued that "for all its frustrations the Korean War gave a new sense of purpose to the Army, and made possible a sort of Army renaissance." *History of the United States Army* (New York: Macmillan, 1967), 525.

19. G. C. Reinhardt, "Guerrilla-Combat, Strategy and Deterrence in Southeast Asia," January 1964, Rand Corporation Report, MHI General Holdings, p. 15. On army officers understanding the problems of "local" wars, see Fautua, "The 'Long Pull' Army," 99. Adrian R. Lewis argues that these "limited wars went against the American culture of war." *The American Culture of War: The History of U.S. Military Force from World War II to Operation Iraqi Freedom* (New York: Routledge, 2007), 20.

20. Maxwell D. Taylor, *The Uncertain Trumpet* (New York: Harper and Brothers, 1960), 5. On soldiers agreeing with scholarly criticism of the New Look, see G. A. Lincoln and Amos A. Jordan Jr., "Limited War and the Scholars," *Military Review* Vol. 37, No. 10 (January 1958): 50–60. On budget concerns, see Herring, *From Colony to Superpower,* 659. Reticence to use ground troops in Kinross, *Clausewitz and America,* 51.

21. Robert E. Osgood, *Limited War: The Challenge to American Security* (Chicago: University of Chicago Press, 1957), 1. See also William C. Martel, *Victory in War: Foundations of Modern Strategy,* rev. ed. (New York: Cambridge University Press, 2011), 132–133. Concerns on relying too heavily on technology in A. J. Bacevich, *The Pentomic Era: The U.S. Army between Korea and Vietnam* (Washington, DC: National Defense University Press, 1986), 53. On New Look and criticisms, see Morton C. Halperin, *Contemporary Military Strategy* (Boston: Little, Brown, 1967), 46–50.

22. Henry A. Kissinger, *Nuclear Weapons and Foreign Policy* (New York: Harper and Brothers, 1957), 140. See also Colin S. Gray, "National Style in Strategy: The American Example," *International Security,* Vol. 6, No. 2 (Fall 1981): 34–35; and Russell F. Weigley, *The American Way of War: A History of United States Military Strategy and Policy* (New York: Macmillan, 1973), 414.

23. Khrushchev quoted in Leffler, *For the Soul of Mankind,* 195. On US experiences in Greece and the Philippines, see Douglas S. Blaufarb, *The Counterinsurgency Era: U.S. Doctrine and Performance, 1950 to Present* (New York: Free Press, 1977), 22–24. Percentage of advisors in Andrew J. Birtle, *U.S. Army Counterinsurgency and Contingency Operations Doctrine, 1942–1976* (Washington, DC: Center of Military History, 2006), 23.

24. Edward R. Wainhouse, "Guerrilla War in Greece, 1946–49: A Case Study," *Military Review*, Vol. 37, No. 3 (June 1957): 25. See also Anastase Balcos, "Guerrilla Warfare," *Military Review*, Vol. 37, No. 12 (March 1958): 49–54. On absence of blinders, see Bacevich, *The Pentomic Era*, 60.

25. On attrition in Korea, see Carter Malkasian, "Toward a Better Understanding of Attrition: The Korean and Vietnam Wars," *Journal of Military History*, Vol. 68, No. 3 (July 2004): 918, 927; and Scott S. Gartner and Marissa E. Myers, "Body Counts and 'Success' in the Vietnam and Korean Wars," *Journal of Interdisciplinary History*, Vol. 25, No. 3 (Winter, 1995): 393. On limited wars being protracted, see Christopher M. Gacek, *The Logic of Force: The Dilemma of Limited War in American Foreign Policy* (New York: Columbia University Press, 1994), 136.

26. Kissinger, *Nuclear Weapons*, 168. Weigley, *History of the United States Army*, 417. Jeffrey Record argues that under limited war theory, "Force was to be employed primarily not to destroy, but rather to communicate resolve, to signal determination to use more force if necessary." *The Wrong War: Why We Lost in Vietnam* (Annapolis, MD: Naval Institute Press, 1998), 42–43.

27. Robert K. Cunningham, "The Nature of War," *Military Review*, Vol. 39, No. 8 (November 1959): 48. On sociopolitical struggle, see Michael Howard, *The Causes of War*, 2nd ed. (Cambridge, MA: Harvard University Press, 1984), 109. Need to adapt in McCuen, *The Art of Counter-Revolutionary War*, 78.

28. "Spectrum of conflict" in Robert Duncan Downie, *Learning from Conflict: The U.S. Military in Vietnam, El Salvador, and the Drug War* (Westport, CT: Praeger, 1998), 53. Historical examples in Richard Betts, "Misadventure Revisited," in *Vietnam as History: Ten Years after the Paris Peace Accords*, ed. Peter Braestrup (Washington, DC: University Press of America, 1984), 7.

29. Taylor quoted in Gacek, *The Logic of Force*, 135–136. On Kennedy and flexible response, see Lawrence Freedman, *Kennedy's Wars: Berlin, Cuba, Laos, and Vietnam* (New York: Oxford University Press, 2000), 287.

30. Robert McNamara, "The Third Challenge," in *Special Warfare U.S. Army* (Washington, DC: U.S. Department of the Army, Office of the Chief of Information, 1962), 13. FM100-5 in Kretchik, *U.S. Army Doctrine*, 180–181.

31. Army Regulation 320-5 quoted in George B. Jordan, "A Case Study of Communist Guerrilla Warfare, and Its Implications, in Southeast Asia," 8 May 1962, Student Thesis, US Army War College, MHI, p. 17. See also Edward N. Luttwak, *Strategy: The Logic of War and Peace* (Cambridge, MA: Belknap Press of Harvard University Press, 1987), 240. On resistance to counterinsurgency, see Krepinevich, *The Army and Vietnam*, 36. Daniel C. Hallin argues that Americans were aware "that the conflict in Vietnam had a political dimension which made it different from, say, the Korean War." *The "Uncensored War": The Media and Vietnam* (New York: Oxford University Press, 1986), 54.

32. Field Manual 100-5, 4.

33. Dave R. Palmer, *Summons of the Trumpet: U.S.-Vietnam in Perspective* (San Rafael, CA: Presidio Press, 1978), 24. Deborah D. Avant, *Political Institutions and Military Change: Lessons from Peripheral Wars* (Ithaca, NY: Cornell University Press, 1994), 49. John Nagl, *Learning to Eat Soup with a Knife: Counterinsurgency Lessons from Malaya and Vietnam* (Chicago: University of Chicago Press, 2002), 126.

34. On interchangeable terms, see James Eliot Cross, *Conflict in the Shadows: The Nature and Politics of Guerrilla War* (Garden City, NY: Doubleday, 1963), 3.

35. Department of the Army, Field Manual 31-15, *Operations against Irregular Forces*, May 1961, 4. On growing interest in counterinsurgency, see Blaufarb, *The Counterinsurgency Era*, 50–51. On preference for military considerations, see David G. Marr, "The Rise and Fall of 'Counterinsurgency': 1961–1964," in *The Pentagon Papers*, Vol. V, 203.

36. FM 100-5 quoted in Larry E. Cable, *Conflict of Myths: The Development of American Counterinsurgency Doctrine and the Vietnam War* (New York: New York University Press, 1986), 119. On growing interest in counterinsurgency, see Blaufarb, *The Counterinsurgency Era*, 50–51.

37. Robert L. Gallucci, *Neither Peace nor Honor: The Politics of American Military Policy in Viet-Nam* (Baltimore, MD: Johns Hopkins University Press, 1975), 15.

38. Kennedy quoted in Arthur M. Schlesinger, *Robert Kennedy and His Times* (Boston: Houghton Mifflin, 1978), 463. Roger Hilsman, interview I, 15 May 1969, LBJL, 17. On the president's views, see Birtle, *U.S. Army Counterinsurgency,* 223 and Duiker, *The Communist Road to Power,* 217

39. Kennedy in Schlesinger, *Robert Kennedy and His Times,* 463. On tensions between security and reform, see Cable, *Conflict of Myths,* 192, and Blaufarb, *The Counterinsurgency Era,* 61.

40. Cable, *Conflict of Myths,* 113. Birtle, *U.S. Army Counterinsurgency,* 134–135.

41. The United States Army Special Warfare School, *Counterinsurgency Planning Guide, Special Text Number 31-176* (Fort Bragg, NC: US Army Special Warfare School, May 1964), viii. See also Kretchik, *U.S. Army Doctrine,* 183.

42. FM 31-15, 18-19. See also Downie, *Learning from Conflict,* 54–55; and Wolf, *Insurgency and Counterinsurgency,* 11.

43. Jonathan F. Ladd, "Some Reflections on Counterinsurgency," *Military Review,* Vol. 44, No. 10 (October 1964): 73.

44. Department of the Army, Field Manual 31-16, *Counterguerrilla Operations,* March 1967, 11.

45. Department of the Army, Field Manual 31-16, *Counterguerrilla Operations,* February 1963, 94, 97. See also Austin Long, *Doctrine of Eternal Recurrence: The U.S. Military and Counterinsurgency Doctrine, 1960–1970 and 2003–2006* (Santa Monica, CA: Rand Corporation, 2008), 7–8.

46. Field Manual 31-16, 1963, 2. Confusing terminology in John Shy and Thomas W. Collier, "Revolutionary War," in *Makers of Modern Strategy: From Machiavelli to the Nuclear Age,* ed. Peter Paret (Princeton, NJ: Princeton University Press, 1986), 817. Austin Long, however, argues that written doctrine had only a "modest effect on the actual conduct" of counterinsurgency operations. Long, *Doctrine of Eternal Recurrence,*1.

47. David Galula, *Counterinsurgency Warfare: Theory and Practice* (New York: Frederick A. Praeger, 1964, 2005), 88. Field Manual 31-16, 1967, 29. On aggressiveness, see Cable, *Conflict of Myths,* 123; and Birtle, *U.S. Army Counterinsurgency,* 137. General Earle Wheeler, chairman, the Joint Chiefs of Staff, noted in 1965 that "If we can secure the military situation, it seems likely that we can get some kind of stable government." Quoted in Lloyd C. Gardner, "Lyndon Johnson and the Bombing of Vietnam: Politics and Military Choices," in Anderson, *The Columbia History,* 177.

48. Lemnitzer quoted in Hilsman, "Two American Counterstrategies," 273. "Something special" in Roger Hilsman, "The New Communist Tactic," *Military Review,* Vol. 42, No. 4 (April 1962): 14. See also John S. Pustay, *Counterinsurgency Warfare* (New York: Free Press, 1965), 84.

49. R. C. H. Miers, "Both Sides of the Guerrilla Hill," *Army,* Vol. 12, No. 8 (March 62): 48. For a counterview, see John E. Beebe, "Beating the Guerrilla," *Military Review,* Vol. 35, No. 9 (December 1955): 18.

50. Operations Report—Lessons Learned 4-67—"Observations of a Battalion Commander," 7 June 1967, CMH Library, 2.

51. Department of the Army, Field Manual 31-73, *Advisor Handbook for Counterinsurgency,* April 1965, 10. In a popular work of the day, Peter Paret and John Shy argued that "Tactical victories are of little value if they compromise the strategic objective." *Guerrillas in the 1960's* (New York: Frederick A. Praeger, 1962), 5.

52. Sanders in Wray R. Johnson, *Vietnam and American Doctrine for Small Wars* (Bangkok: White Lotus Press, 2001), 36. On CONARC, see Birtle, *U.S. Army Counterinsurgency,* 259.

53. Johnson quoted in Ann Marlowe, *David Galula: His Life and Intellectual Context* (Carlisle, PA: Strategic Studies Institute, 2010), 14.

54. Officer and Palmer quoted in Brian M. Linn, *The Echo of Battle: The Army's Way of War* (Cambridge, MA: Harvard University Press, 2007), 182–183. Bruce Palmer Jr., *The 25-Year War: America's Military Role in Vietnam* (Lexington: University Press of Kentucky, 1984), 2.

55. William P. Yarborough, "Counterinsurgency: The U.S. Role—Past, Present, and Future," in *Guerrilla Warfare and Counterinsurgency,* ed. Richard H. Shultz Jr., Robert L. Pfaltzgraff Jr., Uri Ra'anan, William J. Olson, and Igor Lukes (Lexington, MA: Lexington Books, 1989), 106.

56. Kenneth W. Kennedy, "Civic Action as a Cold War Weapon," 14 May 1962, Student Thesis, US Army War College, MHI, 9. Albert G. Wing Jr., "The Contributions of Mao Tse-tung

to Military Thought on Guerrilla Warfare," 29 May 1963, Student Thesis, US Army War College, MHI, pp. 65–66.

57. Robert M. Montague Jr., "Pacification: The Overall Strategy in South Vietnam," Student Essay, US Army War College, 22 April 1966, Box 1, Robert M. Montague Papers, MHI, p. 5. Carl W. Schaad, "The Strategic Hamlet Program in Vietnam: The Role of the People in Counterinsurgency Warfare," 25 May 1964, Student Thesis, US Army War College, MHI, p. 77. Jordan, MHI, 32.

58. Allen B. Jennings, ed., "Readings in Counterinsurgency" (West Point, NY: USMA Department of Social Sciences, 1962), 91–94. See also Birtle, *U.S. Army Counterinsurgency*, 261.

59. Report of Counterinsurgency Committee, 19 June 1963, Training Operations Files— Counterinsurgency Committee, WPSC, 3. Department of Tactics, "Counterinsurgency: First Class Fundamentals," 1964, WPSC, 26.

60. Ron Milam, *Not a Gentleman's War: An Inside View of Junior Officers in the Vietnam War* (Chapel Hill: University of North Carolina Press, 2009), 31, 38. Yarborough, "Counterinsurgency," 104.

61. William M. Hartness, "Social and Behavioral Sciences in Counterinsurgency," *Military Review*, Vol. 46, No. 1 (January 1966): 9.

62. Krepinevich, *The Army and Vietnam*, 51.

63. Headquarters, US Army in Vietnam, Battlefield Reports: A Summary of Lessons Learned, 30 August 1965, NARA, p. I-12. Case studies in James W. Dunn, "Province Advisers in Vietnam, 1962–1965," in *Lessons from an Unconventional War: Reassessing U.S. Strategies for Future Conflicts*, ed. Richard A. Hunt and Richard H. Shultz Jr. (New York: Pergamon Press, 1982), 7. "Increased Emphasis—Counterinsurgency and Unconventional Warfare Instruction," *Armor*, Vol. 73, No. 1 (January–February 1964): 58.

64. Milam, *Not a Gentleman's War*, 67. Christian G. Appy, *Working-Class War: American Combat Soldiers and Vietnam* (Chapel Hill: University of North Carolina Press, 1993), 113.

65. The Joint Chiefs of Staff, Office of Special Assistant for Counterinsurgency & Special Activities, "Partial Bibliography on Counterinsurgency and Related Matters," 19 March 1962, author's possession. "Guerrilla Warfare," *Military Review*, Vol. 42, No. 5 (May 1962): 73–82.

66. Andrew R. Molnar, *Undergrounds in Insurgent, Revolutionary, and Resistance Warfare* (Washington, DC: American University, 1963), viii–x. G. C. Hickey, *The American Military Advisor and His Foreign Counterpart: The Case of Vietnam* (Santa Monica, CA: Rand Corporation, 1965), 67–70.

67. Roger Trinquier, *Modern Warfare: A French View of Counterinsurgency* (Westport, CT: Praeger Security, 1964, 2006), 5. See also Peter Paret, *French Revolutionary Warfare from Indochina to Algeria: The Analysis of a Political and Military Doctrine* (New York: Frederick A. Praeger, 1964), 30–31.

68. Lionel C. McGarr, interview by Mr. McDonald and Mr. von Luttichau, n.d., VNIT Folder 1106, CMH, p. 58. Course topics in Program of Instruction, Command and General Staff Officer Course, 7 August 1964, Special Collections, CARL, p. See also Birtle, *U.S. Army Counterinsurgency*, 313.

69. Quoted in Dastrup, *The US Army Command*, 110.

70. Decker quoted in Birtle, *U.S. Army Counterinsurgency*, 226. On Soviet threat, see Gary R. Hess, *Vietnam and the United States: Origins and Legacy of War* (New York: Twayne, 1990), 34, and Linn, *The Echo of Battle*, 181.

71. Hugo W. Heffelfinger, "Mao Tse-tung and Guerrilla Warfare," 7 May 1962, Student Thesis, US Army War College, MHI, 46. Organizational biases in Morton H. Halperin, Priscilla A. Clapp, and Arnold Canter, *Bureaucratic Politics and Foreign Policy*, 2nd ed. (Washington, DC: Brookings Institution Press, 2006), 32–33, and Avant, *Political Institutions*, 35. On conflicting trends, see Robert A. Doughty, *The Evolution of US Army Tactical Doctrine, 1946–1976* (Fort Leavenworth, KS: Combat Studies Institute, 1979), 47.

72. Jordan, MHI, 1. On influence of service journals, see Bacevich, *The Pentomic Era*, 5.

73. Wing, MHI, 61. Blaufarb, *The Counterinsurgency Era*, 49.

74. William C. Westmoreland, *A Soldier Reports* (Garden City, NY: Doubleday, 1976), 65. See also Johnson, *Vietnam and American Doctrine for Small Wars*, 54.

75. Robert B. Rigg, "Red Parallel: The Tactics of Ho and Mao," in *Modern Guerrilla Warfare: Fighting Communist Guerrilla Movements, 1941–1961*, ed. Franklin Mark Osanka (New York: Free Press of Glencoe, 1962), 268. See also Robert S. McNamara, James G. Blight, Robert K. Brigham, et al., *Argument without End: In Search of Answers to the Vietnam Tragedy* (New York: Public Affairs, 1999), 174; and Timothy J. Lomperis, *The War Everyone Lost—and Won: America's Intervention in Viet Nam's Twin Struggles* (Washington, DC: CQ Press, 1993), 141. For a scholarly treatment, see Chen Jian, *Mao's China and the Cold War* (Chapel Hill: University of North Carolina Press, 2001), 206–207.

76. Uldarico S. Baclagon, *Lessons from the Huk Campaign in the Philippines* (Manila: M. Colcol, 1960), 230–239. Robert Ross Smith, "The Hukbalahap Insurgency," *Military Review*, Vol. 45, No. 6 (June 1965): 35–42. On Magsaysay, see Birtle, *U.S. Army Counterinsurgency*, 62–65.

77. Edward Geary Lansdale, *In the Midst of Wars: An American's Mission to Southeast Asia* (New York: Harper and Row, 1972), 71. Boyd T. Bashore, "Dual Strategy for Limited War," *Military Review*, Vol. 40, No. 2 (May 1960): 60.

78. Osgood, *Limited War*, 223. See also Robert Buzzanco, *Masters of War: Military Dissent and Politics in the Vietnam Era* (Cambridge: Cambridge University Press, 1996), 28; and Donald W. Hamilton, *The Art of Insurgency: American Military Policy and the Failure of Strategy in Southeast Asia* (Westport, CT: Praeger, 1998), 97. On ignoring the French, see W. Scott Thompson and Donaldson D. Frizzell, eds., *The Lessons of Vietnam* (New York: Crane, Russak, 1977), 36–37; and Thomas C. Thayer, *War without Fronts: The American Experience in Vietnam* (Boulder, CO: Westview Press, 1985), 17–18.

79. Charles P. Biggio, "Let's Learn from the French," *Military Review*, Vol. 46, No. 10 (October 1966): 28, 29. As early as 1957, *Military Review* published articles from French officers on their experiences in Indochina. See Captain André Souyris, "An Effective Counterguerrilla Procedure," *Military Review*, Vol. 36, No. 12 (March 1957): 86–90. Of note, the Central Party in Hanoi directed a project in 1963 "to review and summarize lessons learned in both the armed struggle and the building of the people's armed forces during the resistance war against the French." *Victory in Vietnam: The Official History of the People's Army of Vietnam, 1954–1975*, trans. Merle L. Pribbenow (Lawrence: University Press of Kansas, 2002), 102.

80. Paret, *French Revolutionary Warfare*, 4, 30–32. Walter Laqueur, *Guerrilla: A Historical and Critical Case Study* (Boulder, CO: Westview Press, 1976, 1984), 374–375.

81. George A. Kelly, "Revolutionary War and Psychological Action," *Military Review*, Vol. 40, No. 7 (October 1960): 4. Constantin Melnik, *Insurgency and Counterinsurgency in Algeria* (Santa Monica, CA: Rand Corporation, 1964). On relationship between Algeria and Vietnam, see David L. Schalk, *War and the Ivory Tower: Algeria and Vietnam* (New York: Oxford University Press, 1991).

82. Donn A. Starry, "La Guerre Révolutionnaire," *Military Review*, Vol. 47, No. 2 (February 1967): 70. A recent study argues that French theory made sense in principle, yet failed when implemented in the field. See Grégor Mathias, *Galula in Algeria: Counterinsurgency Practice versus Theory*, trans. Neal Durando (Santa Barbara, CA: Praeger, 2011).

83. Richard L. Clutterbuck, "Communist Defeat in Malaya: A Case Study," *Military Review*, Vol. 43, No. 9 (September 1963): 63–78. Kenneth Darling, "British Counterinsurgency Experience: A Kermit Roosevelt Lecture," *Military Review*, Vol. 45, No. 1 (January 1965): 7. See also Sir Robert Thompson, *Defeating Communist Insurgency: The Lessons of Malaya and Vietnam* (New York: Frederick A. Praeger, 1966), 51–58, for a list of his basic principles of counterinsurgency. Thompson would become a leading critic of the American war in Vietnam.

84. Bernard B. Fall, *The Two Viet-Nams: A Political and Military Analysis* (New York: Frederick A. Praeger, 1963), 339. F. B. Schoomaker, "The Apparent Similarities and Significant Differences between the Vietnamese and the Malayan Insurgencies," 19 January 1966, US Army War College Student Paper, Folder 6, Box 132, Series II Official Papers, Harold K. Johnson Collection, MHI, 3.

85. Josiah A. Wallace, "Principles of War in Counterinsurgency," *Military Review*, Vol. 46, No. 12 (December 1966): 76. See also Edward F. Downey Jr., "Theory of Guerrilla Warfare,"

Military Review, Vol. 39, No. 2 (May 1959): 45–55; and John B. Bellinger Jr., "Civilian Role in Antiguerrilla Warfare," *Military Review*, Vol. 41, No. 9 (September 1961): 92.

86. Major Bill Bricker in *Infantry in Vietnam*, ed. Albert N. Garland (Nashville, TN: Battery Press, 1967, 1982), 39. The original article appeared in the July–August 1966 issue of *Infantry*.

87. Harry F. Walterhouse, "Civic Action: A Counter and Cure for Insurgency," *Military Review* Vol. 42, No. 8 (August 1962): 47–48. William F. Long, "Counterinsurgency: Some Antecedents for Success," *Military Review*, Vol. 43, No. 10 (October 1963): 91. Hilsman, "The New Communist Tactic," 19.

88. Hoyt R. Livingston and Francis M. Watson Jr., "Civic Action: Purpose and Pitfalls," *Military Review*, Vol. 47, No. 12 (December 1967): 22. Robert L. Burke, "Military Civic Action," *Military Review*, Vol. 44, No. 10 (October 1964): 63.

89. Samuel W. Smithers Jr., "Combat Units in Revolutionary Development," *Military Review*, Vol. 47, No. 10 (October 1967): 38. See also Lewis Sorley, "The Quiet War: Revolutionary Development," *Military Review*, Vol. 47, No. 11 (November 1967): 13–19. In an interesting aside, Sorley refused to discuss this topic in his biography on Westmoreland despite the author's personal experiences in the G3 Revolutionary Development Branch in MACV.

90. Robert S. McNamara, *The Essence of Security: Reflections in Office* (New York: Harper and Row, 1968), 149. James M. Carter, *Inventing Vietnam: The United States and State Building, 1964–1968* (New York: Cambridge University Press, 2008), 31. On military security tasks in revolutionary development, see Michael D. Healy, "Revolutionary Development—Pacification: An Offensive Strategy in Vietnam," 13 November 1967, Student Essay, US Army War College, MHI, 14–16.

91. On the global threat of communism, see Osgood, *Limited War*, 4; Downie, *Learning from Conflict* 51; and Marilyn B. Young, *The Vietnam Wars, 1945–1990* (New York: HarperCollins, 1991), 77. Officers' views in George B. Jordan, "Objectives and Methods of Communist Guerrilla Warfare," *Military Review*, Vol. 39, No. 10 (January 1960): 51; and Franklin A. Lindsay, "Unconventional Warfare," *Military Review*, Vol. 42, No. 6 (June 1962): 62.

92. Blaufarb, *The Counterinsurgency Era*, 66–67. For an alternative view, in which officers ignored such prescriptions, see Cincinnatus, *Self-Destruction: The Disintegration and Decay of the United States Army during the Vietnam Era* (New York: W.W. Norton, 1981), 37–38.

93. Johnson quoted in Maurice E. Jessup, "The Validity of the Civic Action Concept," 24 January 1968, US Army War College Student Paper, MHI, p. 3. On organizational culture, see Isabel Hull, *Absolute Destruction: Military Culture and the Practices of War in Imperial Germany* (Ithaca, NY: Cornell University Press, 2005), 94. Emphasizing military action in Marr, 203.

94. Wayne E. Lee, ed., *Warfare and Culture in World History* (New York: New York University Press, 2011), 3. Patrick Porter, *Military Orientalism: Eastern War through Western Eyes* (New York: Columbia University Press, 2009), 18, 81. See also Stephen Peter Rosen, "Military Effectiveness: Why Society Matters," *International Security*, Vol. 19, No. 4 (Spring 1995): 11–14.

95. For such arguments, see Loren Baritz, *Backfire: A History of How American Culture Led Us into Vietnam and Made Us Fight the Way We Did* (Baltimore, MD: Johns Hopkins University Press, 1985), 51; and Record, *The Wrong War*, 92. W. Warner Burke argues that "Change in mission and strategy means that the organization's culture must be modified if success of the overall change effort is to be realized." *Organization Change: Theory and Practice* (Thousand Oaks, CA: Sage, 2002), 13.

96. As an example, a former commandant of the US Army War College argued that "war preparation is only half of the art and science of war. In Vietnam it appeared that our failings were in the other half of that equation—the conduct of war proper." MG Jack N. Merritt in foreword to Harry G. Summers Jr., *On Strategy: A Critical Appraisal of the Vietnam War* (Novato, CA: Presidio, 1982), xii.

Chapter 2

1. Paper prepared by Johnson, *FRUS*, 1961–1963, I: 151. On gradual involvement, see Gary R. Hess, *Vietnam: Explaining America's Lost War* (Malden, MA: Blackwell, 2009), 50; and see

Leslie H. Gelb with Richard K. Betts, *The Irony of Vietnam: The System Worked* (Washington, DC: Brookings Institution, 1979), 25.

2. Daniel C. Hallin, *The "Uncensored War" The Media and Vietnam* (New York: Oxford University Press, 1986), 35. For a counterargument, in which the army did not change its orientation, see Richard Lock-Pullan, *US Intervention Policy and Army Innovation: From Vietnam to Iraq* (London: Routledge, 2006), 31. Fredrik Logevall articulates well the tensions within early American policymaking when viewing events inside Vietnam as more than just military developments. See *Embers of War: The Fall of an Empire and the Making of America's Vietnam* (New York: Random House, 2012), 575, 646, 680.

3. NSC policy statement, 16 January 1954, in *The Pentagon Papers: The Defense Department History of United States Decisionmaking in Vietnam* [Senator Gravel, ed., 5 vols.] (Boston: Beacon Press, 1971–1972), Vol. I, 435. For similar ideas through consecutive administrations, see Donald W. Hamilton, *The Art of Insurgency: American Military Policy and the Failure of Strategy in Southeast Asia* (Westport, CT: Praeger, 1998), 101; John M. Newman, "The Kennedy-Johnson Transition: The Case for Policy Reversal," in *Vietnam: The Early Decisions*, ed. Lloyd C. Gardner and Ted Gittinger (Austin: University of Texas Press, 1997), 161; and Harry McPherson, *A Political Education: A Washington Memoir* (Boston: Houghton Mifflin, 1988), 388. For an overview of Johnson's policy, see "Text of Secretary McNamara's Address on United States Policy in South Vietnam," *New York Times*, 27 March 1964.

4. George B. Jordan, "A Case Study of Communist Guerrilla Warfare, and Its Implications, in Southeast Asia," 8 May 1962, Student Thesis, US Army War College, MHI, p. 18. Robert C. Dennison Jr., "The Importance of South Vietnam," 5 February 1962, Student Thesis, US Army War College, MHI, p. 43. F. B. Schoomaker, "The Apparent Similarities and Significant Differences between the Vietnamese and the Malayan Insurgencies," 19 January 1966, US Army War College Student Paper, Folder 6, Box 132, Series II Official Papers, Harold K. Johnson Collection, MHI, p. 10.

5. Kennedy quoted in Henry Kissinger, *Diplomacy* (New York: Simon and Schuster, 1994), 848. "Outline of Counterinsurgency Operations" in *FRUS, 1961–1963*, II: 17–21.

6. Douglas Pike quoted in *Strange Ground: Americans in Vietnam, 1945–1975, an Oral History*, ed. Harry Maurer (New York: Henry Holt, 1989), 93. Robert D. Schulzinger, *A Time for War: The United States and Vietnam, 1941–1975* (New York: Oxford University Press, 1997), 5. Stanley Karnow, *Vietnam: A History* (New York: Viking Press, 1983), 99.

7. David L. Anderson, *The Columbia Guide to the Vietnam War* (New York: Columbia University Press, 2002), 7. David L. Anderson, ed., *The Columbia History of the Vietnam War* (New York: Columbia University Press, 2011), 11–12. Mark Atwood Lawrence, *The Vietnam War: A Concise International History* (New York: Oxford University Press, 2008), 9–10. Edward G. Miller, comments to author, 27 August 2013.

8. Anderson, *The Columbia Guide to the Vietnam War*, 10–11. Karnow, *Vietnam*, 107. Frances FitzGerald, *Fire in the Lake: The Vietnamese and the Americans in Vietnam* (Boston: Little, Brown, 1972), 14. Ellen J. Hammer, *The Struggle for Indochina, 1940–1955* (Stanford, CA: Stanford University Press, 1954), 54–55. Edward G. Miller, comments to author, 27 August 2013.

9. John H. and Mae H. Esterline, *"How the Dominoes Fell": Southeast Asia in Perspective* (Lanham, MD: Hamilton Press, 1986), 22–25. Mark Philip Bradley, *Vietnam at War* (New York: Oxford University Press, 2009), 15. Anthony James Joes, *The War for South Viet Nam, 1954–1975*, rev. ed. (Westport, CT: Praeger, 2001), 4–5. William J. Duiker, *The Communist Road to Power*, 2nd ed. (Boulder, CO: Westview Press, 1996), 5, 34.

10. Neil L. Jamieson, *Understanding Vietnam* (Berkeley: University of California Press, 1993), 98–99. Michael H. Hunt, ed., *A Vietnam War Reader: A Documentary History from American and Vietnamese Perspectives* (Chapel Hill: University of North Carolina Press, 2010), 3. Anderson, *The Columbia Guide to the Vietnam War*, 12–13. Esterline, *"How the Dominoes Fell,"* 26–27. There were, however, plenty of other Vietnamese responses to colonialism, some of which were quite critical of French policies and practices, but which advocated reform and cultural transformation rather than armed rebellion. Edward G. Miller, comments to author, 27 August 2013.

11. William J. Duiker, "Victory by Other Means: The Foreign Policy of the Democratic Republic of Vietnam," in *Why the North Won the Vietnam War*, ed. Marc Jason Gilbert (New York: Palgrave, 2002), 49. Bradley, *Vietnam at War*, 32–33. Duiker, *The Communist Road to Power*, 44, 71.

12. FitzGerald, *Fire in the Lake*, 63. Timothy J. Lomperis, *The War Everyone Lost—and Won: America's Intervention in Viet Nam's Twin Struggles* (Washington, DC: CQ Press, 1993), 15. This process, however, was far from peaceful. As Neil Jamieson reminds us, "Administratively, politically, and militarily Vietnam was a chaotic nightmare in the summer of 1945. At least a million people starved to death." *Understanding Vietnam*, 191.

13. Hammer, *The Struggle for Indochina*, 97. Joes, *The War for South Viet Nam*, 14–15, James M. Carter, *Inventing Vietnam: The United States and State Building, 1964–1968* (New York: Cambridge University Press, 2008), 25. Bernard B. Fall, *The Two Viet-Nams: A Political and Military Analysis* (New York: Frederick A. Praeger, 1963), 63.

14. Quoted in *The Pentagon Papers*, I, 50. On DRV independence, see Esterline, *"How the Dominoes Fell,"* 29. Bradley, *Vietnam at War*, 33–39. Hundreds of thousands at the independence rally in Logevall, *Embers of War*, 96.

15. Marshall quoted in *The Pentagon Papers*, I, 50. See also Schulzinger, *A Time for War*, 33; and Mark Atwood Lawrence, *Assuming the Burden: Europe and the American Commitment to War in Vietnam* (Berkeley: University of California Press, 2005), 92–93. Another motivation for increased US support of the French effort in Vietnam was to get France's agreement to the rearming of Germany against the Soviet threat.

16. Giap quoted in John M. Gates, "People's War in Vietnam," *Journal of Military History*, Vol. 54, No. 3 (July 1990): 329. Bernard Fall, *Street without Joy* (Mechanicsburg, PA: Stackpole Books, 1994), 15, 46. Edgar O'Ballance, *The Indo-China War, 1945–1954: A Study in Guerrilla Warfare* (London: Faber and Faber, 1964), 80. Duiker, *The Communist Road to Power*, 154. On the use of "people's war," see William J. Duiker, "Ho Chi Minh and the Strategy of People's War," in *The First Vietnam War: Colonial Conflict and Cold War Crisis*, ed. Mark Atwood Lawrence and Fredrik Logevall (Cambridge, MA: Harvard University Press, 2007), 160–162.

17. Ho Chi Minh quoted in War Experiences Recapitulation Committee of the High-Level Military Institute, *The Anti-U.S. Resistance War for National Salvation 1954–1975: Military Events* (Hanoi: People's Army Publishing House, 1980), 4. Walter Laqueur, *Guerrilla: A Historical and Critical Case Study* (Boulder. CO: Westview Press, 1976, 1984), 266. Marilyn B. Young, *The Vietnam Wars, 1945–1990* (New York: HarperCollins, 1991), 35.

18. George A. Carver, "The Faceless Viet Cong," *Foreign Affairs*, Vol. 44, No. 3 (April 1966): 357. War Experiences Recapitulation Committee, 3. On US military intervention, see Luu Doan Huynh in Robert S. McNamara, James G. Blight, Robert K. Brigham, et al., *Argument without End: In Search of Answers to the Vietnam Tragedy* (New York: Public Affairs, 1999), 83. On Geneva, see Hunt, *A Vietnam War Reader*, 29; Anthony Short, *The Origins of the Vietnam War* (London: Longman, 1989), 153–181; and Chen Jian, "China and the Indochina Settlement at the Geneva Conference of 1954," in *The First Vietnam War: Colonial Conflict and Cold War Crisis*, ed. Mark Atwood Lawrence and Fredrik Logevall (Cambridge, MA: Harvard University Press, 2007), 240–262. William J. Duiker rightfully notes that Vietnam had been "divided into two temporary regroupment zones." *Sacred War: Nationalism and Revolution in a Divided Vietnam* (Boston: McGraw-Hill, 1995), 137.

19. Rufus Phillips quoted in Christian G. Appy, *Patriots: The Vietnam War Remembered from All Sides* (New York: Viking, 2003), 51. Ellen J. Hammer, *The Struggle for Indochina, 1940–1955* (Stanford, CA: Stanford University Press, 1954, 1966), 346–347.

20. Gary R. Hess, *Vietnam and the United States: Origins and Legacy of War* (New York: Twayne, 1990), 52, 172–173. George C. Herring, *America's Longest War: The United States and Vietnam, 1950–1975*, 4th ed. (New York: McGraw-Hill, 1979, 2002), 29. Andrew J. Rotter, "Chronicle of a War Foretold: The United States and Vietnam, 1945–1954," in *The First Vietnam War: Colonial Conflict and Cold War Crisis*, ed. Mark Atwood Lawrence and Fredrik Logevall (Cambridge, MA: Harvard University Press, 2007), 301. Lawrence, *The Vietnam War*, 36. Logevall, *Embers of War*, 575. On the impact of the 1955 battle of Saigon, see

Edward Miller, *Misalliance: Ngo Dinh Diem, the United States, and the Fate of South Vietnam* (Cambridge, MA: Harvard University Press, 2013), 124–125.

21. Frederick Nolting, *From Trust to Tragedy: The Political Memoirs of Frederick Nolting, Kennedy's Ambassador to Diem's Vietnam* (New York: Praeger, 1988), 30–31. Anderson, *The Columbia History of the Vietnam War*, 31. Lloyd C. Gardner, *Approaching Vietnam: From World War II through Dienbienphu, 1941–1954* (New York: W.W. Norton, 1988), 342. At the time, General J. Lawton Collins found Diem "unready to assert the type of leadership that can unify this country and give it a chance of competing with the hard, effective, unified control of Ho Chi Minh." In Barbara W. Tuchman, *The March of Folly: From Troy to Vietnam* (New York: Alfred A. Knopf, 1984), 275. On Diem's life and impact to US policy, see Seth Jacobs, *Cold War Mandarin: Ngo Dinh Diem and the Origins of America's War in Vietnam, 1950–1963* (Lanham, MD: Rowman and Littlefield, 2006).

22. Karnow, *Vietnam*, 199. Richard Betts, "Misadventure Revisited," in *Vietnam as History: Ten Years after the Paris Peace Accords*, ed. Peter Braestrup (Washington, DC: University Press of America, 1984), 7. Herring, *America's Longest War*, 80–81. Communist Strategy as Reflected in Lao Dong Party and COSVN Resolutions, Folder 26, Box 7, Douglas Pike Collection: Unit 06—Democtratic Republic of Vietnam, TTUVA, 1.

23. Ang Cheng Guan, *The Vietnam War from the Other Side: The Vietnamese Communists' Perspective* (New York: Routledge Curzon, 2002), 41–43. Robert K. Brigham, *Guerrilla Diplomacy: The NLF's Foreign Relations and the Viet Nam War* (Ithaca, NY: Cornell University Press, 1999), 10. David Halberstam, *The Making of a Quagmire: America and Vietnam during the Kennedy Era* (New York: Alfred A. Knopf, 1964, 1988), 32. War Experiences Recapitulation Committee, 14. On inheriting Viet Minh infrastructure, see Schoomaker, MHI, 14.

24. Vo Nguyen Giap, *People's War, People's Army: The Viet Công Insurrection Manual for Underdeveloped Countries* (New York: Frederick A. Praeger, 1962), 27. Richard A. Hunt, *Pacification: The American Struggle for Vietnam's Hearts and Minds* (Boulder, CO: Westview Press, 1995), 6.

25. Huong Van Ba quoted in David Chanoff and Doan Van Toai, *"Vietnam": A Portrait of Its People at War* (London: I.B. Tauris, 1986), 155. On this point, see also *Victory in Vietnam: The Official History of the People's Army of Vietnam, 1954–1975*, trans. Merle L. Pribbenow (Lawrence: University Press of Kansas, 2002), 85. James Walker Trullinger Jr., *Village at War: An Account of Revolution in Vietnam* (New York: Longman, 1980), 99. Gabriel Kolko, *Anatomy of a War: Vietnam, the United States, and the Modern Historical Experience* (New York: Pantheon Books, 1985), 155. It is important to note, however, that while some Vietnamese had such a hatred, and others came to acquire one, many Vietnamese had rather more complex feelings about the United States and Americans.

26. McPherson, *A Political Education*, 388. See also Larry Berman, *Planning a Tragedy: The Americanization of the War in Vietnam* (New York: W.W. Norton, 1982), 30, and Michael Lind, *Vietnam: The Necessary War* (New York: Free Press, 1999), 34. Odd Arne Westad argues that "the American view of South Vietnam's role in Communist thinking within Southeast Asia was largely correct." *The Global Cold War: Third World Interventions and the Making of Our Times* (New York: Cambridge University Press, 2007), 180.

27. JSPC quoted in Robert Buzzanco, *Masters of War: Military Dissent and Politics in the Vietnam Era* (Cambridge: Cambridge University Press, 1996), 35. Schulzinger, *A Time for War*, 97. Michael H. Hunt, *Lyndon Johnson's War: America's Cold War Crusade in Vietnam, 1945–1968* (New York: Hill and Wang, 1996), 11.

28. Chester Cooper quoted in Appy, *Patriots*, 84. On formation of MAAG, see George S. Eckhardt, *Vietnam Studies: Command and Control, 1950–1969* (Washington, DC: US Government Printing Office, 1974, 2004), 7–14.

29. Recent freedom quotation from John L. Erickson, "Impact of the United States Military Assistance Advisory Group in Vietnam," 10 February 1961, Student Thesis, US Army War College, MHI, p. 17. Most senior ARVN officers, however, were trained under the French. Many were nationalists, but their feelings about the French were rather more complex and ambiguous than Erickson's statement allows. One might ask, as an example, if it was at least possible that the ARVN officers just thought that American advice was wrong. Laurence

J. Legere to Thomas Thayer, 10 November 1971, Folder 90, MACV Info & Reports Working Group, Thayer Papers, CMH, p. 3. The BDM Corporation, "A Study of Strategic Lessons Learned in Vietnam," Vol. II, South Vietnam, MHI General Holdings, 5–7.

30. Briefing Charts, Personal Use of Lt. General S.T. Williams, 31 May 1957, Conversations with President Diem Folder, Box 3, Samuel T. Williams Papers, MHI, 5–6. Dong Van Khuyen, "The RVNAF," in *The Vietnam War: An Assessment by South Vietnam's Generals*, ed. Lewis Sorley (Lubbock: Texas Tech University Press, 2010), 5–7. Andrew Wiest, "The 'Other' Vietnam War," in *America and the Vietnam War: Re-examining the Culture and History of a Generation*, ed. Andrew Wiest, Mary Kathryn Barbier, and Glenn Robins (New York: Routledge, 2010), 57–58. Eckhardt, *Vietnam Studies*, 19. Short, *The Origins of the Vietnam War*, 213.

31. Williams Briefing Charts, MHI, 10. Alexander S. Cochran Jr., "American Planning for Ground Combat in Vietnam: 1952–1965," *Parameters*, Vol. 14, No. 2 (Summer 1984): 64–65. Eric M. Bergerud, *The Dynamics of Defeat: The Vietnam War in Hau Nghia Province* (Boulder, CO: Westview Press, 1991), 34. Buzzanco, *Masters of War*, 65. One GVN official, however, noted that even "a well trained, well equipped Vietnamese army and a relatively large administration cannot effectively fight Communist political subversion because the leaders of the regime consistently refuse to stamp out the roots of corruption and inefficiency." Nguyen Thai, *Is South Vietnam Viable?* (Manila, Philippines: Carmelo and Bauermann, 1962), xi.

32. Paper Prepared by the Chief of the Military Assistance Advisory Group in Vietnam, 28 December 1955, *FRUS, 1955–1957*, I: 608. Mark Moyar, *Triumph Forsaken: The Vietnam War, 1954–1965* (Cambridge: Cambridge University Press, 2006), 68–69. Bergerud, *The Dynamics of Defeat*, 24. For a counterargument, see Deborah D. Avant, *Political Institutions and Military Change: Lessons from Peripheral Wars* (Ithaca, NY: Cornell University Press, 1994), 52–53; and Thomas E. Ricks, *The Generals: American Military Command from World War II to Today* (New York: Penguin Press, 2012), 224–226.

33. S. T. Williams, "Noted on Anti-guerrilla Operations," 17 March 1960, Historian's Files, CMH, p. 4. Thomas L. Ahern Jr., *Vietnam Declassified: The CIA and Counterinsurgency* (Lexington: University Press of Kentucky, 2010), 35. Williams ultimately sought to develop a program that would "work the American military advisory group out of a job in Vietnam." "The Joint Chiefs of Staff and the War in Vietnam, 1960–1968," Part I, JCSHO, 1–9.

34. "Chaotic" in JCS 1992/412 quoted in Buzzanco, *Masters of War*, 48. On Williams being open to Vietnamese concerns, see Edward G. Lansdale, *In the Midst of Wars: An American's Mission to Southeast Asia* (New York: Harper and Row, 1972), 338–339. Moyar, *Triumph Forsaken*, 70–71. Carter, *Inventing Vietnam*, 88.

35. Robert W. Komer, *Bureaucracy at War: U.S. Performance in the Vietnam Conflict* (Boulder, CO: Westview Press, 1986), 47. Mark Lawrence argues that the complexity of the war eluded American policymakers who were "prone to see the conflict simply as a result of Northern aggression against the South." *The Vietnam War*, 65.

36. Truong Nhu Tang with David Chanoff and Doan Van Toai, *A Vietcong Memoir: An Inside Account of the Vietnam War and Its Aftermath* (New York: Harcourt Brace Jovanovich, 1985), 65. Law, 10–59 in Duiker, *The Communist Road to Power*, 203. Pacification in Lansdale, *In the Midst of Wars,* 228. On ARVN, see Jacobs, *Cold War Mandarin*, 112; and Andrew Wiest, *Vietnam's Forgotten Army: Heroism and Betrayal in the ARVN* (New York: New York University Press, 2008), 25.

37. Ellen J. Hammer, "Progress Report on Southern Viet Nam," *Pacific Affairs*, Vol. 30, No. 3 (September 1957): 225. Report by the Vice President, *FRUS, 1961–1963*, I: 155. See also Roger Hilsman in *Vietnam: A History in Documents*, ed. Gareth Porter (New York: New American Library, 1981), 233–235.

38. As quoted in Neil Sheehan, "Crisis in Vietnam: Antecedents of the Struggle," *New York Times*, 27 April 1964. See also Bernard B. Fall, "South Viet-Nam's Internal Problems," *Pacific Affairs*, Vol. 31, No. 3 (September 1958): 257. William Duiker, "Waging Revolutionary War: The Evolution of Hanoi's Strategy in the South, 1959–1965," in *The Vietnam War: Vietnamese and American Perspectives*, ed. Jayne S. Werner and Luu Doan Huynh (Armonk, NY: M.E. Sharpe, 1993), 26.

39. Memorandum, Edward G. Lansdale, " 'Pacification' in Vietnam," 16 July 1958, US Strategy, Vietnam, 1955–1964, Historian's Files, CMH, p. 2. On latent sympathies, see Bernard B. Fall, "Indochina: The Last Year of the War, Communist Organization and Tactics," *Military Review*, Vol. 36, No. 7 (October 1956): 7.

40. Christopher K. Ives, *US Special Forces and Counterinsurgency in Vietnam: Military Innovation and Institutional Failure, 1961–1963* (London: Routledge, 2007), 81. On McGarr's views on counterinsurgency programs, see *FRUS, 1961–1963*, I: 61–63. Of note, McNamara inquired about the use of helicopters in "counter-guerrilla operations," for which McGarr believed there was a role.

41. Lionel C. McGarr, interview by Mr. McDonald and Mr. von Luttichau, n.d., VNIT Folder 1106, CMH, 5, 8. *The Pentagon Papers*, II: 434–435. Hamilton, *The Art of Insurgency*, 140.

42. McGarr interview, CMH, 6. MAAG-Vietnam, "Tactics & Techniques of Counter-Insurgent Operations," 10 February 1962, Historian's Files, CMH, 2. Lionel C. McGarr to Nguyen Donh Thuan, 28 October 1960, Folder 14, Box 2, Douglas Pike Collection: Unit 01— Assessment and Strategy, TTUVA. William Rosenau, *US Internal Security Assistance to South Vietnam: Insurgency, Subversion and Public Order* (London: Routledge, 2005), 104–105.

43. Headquarters of the Commander in Chief Pacific, "Counter-Insurgency Operations in South Vietnam and Laos," 27 April 1960, 1960–61 Counterinsurgency Plan, Historian's Files, CMH, 4, 6, 8. Jack Schulimson, *The Joint Chiefs of Staff and the War in Vietnam, 1960–1968*, Part I (Washington, DC: Office of Joint History, 2011), 25–26. JCS History, Part I, JCSHO, 4-5-4-6. *The Pentagon Papers*, II: 138.

44. JCSM 704–61 quoted in Buzzanco, *Masters of War*, 103.

45. JCS History, Part I, JCSHO, 1–21. Basic Counterinsurgency Plan for Viet-Nam, 4 January 1961, *FRUS, 1961–1963*, I: 1–3. Douglas S. Blaufarb argues that US plans "did seek to incorporate the necessary nonmilitary elements into a complex combined effort and in that respect was in line with the developing doctrine of the counterinsurgency theorists in Washington." `

46. MAGAG-CH 1473, 10 September 1961, Folder 2, Box 2, Douglas Pike Collection: Unit 01—Assessment and Strategy, TTUVA. Douglas Pike, interview I by Ted Gittinger, 4 June 1981, LBJL, p. 7. *The Pentagon Papers*, II: 23–25. The BDM Corporation, "A Study of Strategic Lessons Learned in Vietnam," Vol. V, Planning the War, MHI General Holdings, pp. 5–20.

47. Quoted in Brigham, *Guerrilla Diplomacy*, 12. Nguyen Vu Tung, "Coping with the United States: Hanoi's Search for an Effective Strategy," in *The Vietnam War*, ed. Peter Lowe (New York: St. Martin's Press, 1998), 40. On NLF structure, see Douglas Pike, *Viet Cong: The Organization and Techniques of the National Liberation Front of South Vietnam* (Cambridge, MA: MIT Press, 1966).

48. Vann quoted in David W.P. Elliott, *The Vietnamese War: Revolution and Social Change in the Mekong Delta, 1930–1975*, concise ed. (Armonk, NY: M.E. Sharpe, 2007), 176. George W. Allen, *None So Blind: A Personal Account of the Intelligence Failure in Vietnam* (Chicago: Ivan R. Dee, 2001), 138. On McGarr's relationship with Diem, see Lawrence Freedman, *Kennedy's Wars: Berlin, Cuba, Laos, and Vietnam* (New York: Oxford University Press, 2000), 338.

49. McGarr interview, CMH, 41. US military personnel numbers confirmed by Andrew Birtle, CMH, email to author, 16 April 2013. Most Americans in Vietnam in 1962 were not advisers at all. Rather they were aviation, communications, logistics, and other support personnel. Problems still persisted throughout 1962. See Rufus Phillips, "A Report on Counter-Insurgency in Vietnam," 31 August 1962, Folder 4, Box 1, Earl R. Rhine Collection, TTUVA.

50. Taylor quoted in Buzzanco, *Masters of War*, 109. Felt to McGarr, 8 February 1962, *FRUS, 1961–1963*, II: 111–112. Eckhardt, Vietnam Studies, 28. Graham A. Cosmas, *MACV: The Joint Command in the Years of Escalation, 1962–1967* (Washington, DC: Center of Military History, 2006), 35–36. Harkins background in Paul D. Harkins, interview by Mr. McDonald and Mr. von Luttichau, 9 November 1970, VNIT Folder 1105, CMH and *Time*, 11 May 1962, 19.

51. Lacking curiosity in Neil Sheehan, *A Bright Shining Lie: John Paul Vann and America in Vietnam* (New York: Random House, 1988), 285. Central principle in Roger Hilsman, *To*

Move a Nation: The Politics of Foreign Policy in the Administration of John F. Kennedy (Garden City, NY: Doubleday, 1967), 578. On problems with mission organization, see W. C. Westmoreland, interview by Major Paul L. Miles, 10 April 1971, Box 1, Paul L. Miles, Papers, MHI, 1.

52. Paul D. Harkins, interview by Ted Gittinger, 10 November 1981, LBJL, I-13. On Hanoi's strategic concerns at this time, see Nguyen Vu Tung in Lowe, *The Vietnam War*, 43, and John Prados, *The Blood Road: The Ho Chi Minh Trail and the Vietnam War* (New York: John Wiley, 1999), 45. The Joint Chiefs, in a top secret memorandum, had authorized MACV to conduct small cross border operations into Laos for "intelligence missions only." JCS Memorandum to MACV, Operation Delta, 20 May 1964, Historians Background Material Files, Box 3, RG472, NARA.

53. Denis Warner, "Fighting the Viet Cong," *Army*, Vol. 12, No. 2 (September 1961): 20. JCS History, Part I, JCSHO, 4–1. Diem's fears in Wilbur H. Morrison, *The Elephant and the Tiger: The Full Story of the Vietnam War* (New York: Hippocrene Books, 1990), 69, and George McTurnan Kahin and John Wilson Lewis, *The United States in Vietnam*, rev. ed. (New York: Dial Press, 1967, 1969), 131.

54. National Campaign Plan, Phase II, 22 June 1963, Part I, Historian's Background Material Files, 206–02, Box 1, RG 472, NARA, p. 6. Freedman offers a negative view of Harkins on p. 357. David Kaiser, *American Tragedy: Kennedy, Johnson, and the Origins of the Vietnam War* (London: Belknap Press of Harvard University Press, 2000), 152, 162–164.

55. JCS History, Part I, JCSHO, 4–24. National Campaign Plan, Phase II, 22 June 1963, NARA, 2–3. Schulimson, *The Joint Chiefs of Staff*, 269–270. A. J. Langguth, *Our Vietnam: The War, 1954–1975* (New York: Simon and Schuster, 2000), 191. See also Hilsman, "A Strategic Concept for South Vietnam," in *FRUS, 1961–1963*, II: 73, 78–79.

56. John Michael Dunn, interview by Ted Gittinger, 25 July 1984, LBJL, I-12. CIA report, 11 January 1963, *FRUS, 1961–1963*, III: 19–21. "Three M's" in Sheehan, *A Bright Shining Lie*, 288.

57. Roger Hilsman, 19 December 1962, *FRUS, 1961–1963*, II: 789–792. Harkins also expressed concern over ARVN, noting that many politically minded officers "didn't want to have too many casualties." Harkins, interview, CMH, 17. US economic aid in Milton C. Taylor, "South Viet-Nam: Lavish Aid, Limited Progress," *Pacific Affairs*, Vol. 34, No. 3 (Autumn 1961): 245.

58. Command History, United States Military Assistance Command, 1964, Entry MACJ03, Box 1, RG 472, NARA, 55. *The Pentagon Papers*, II: 714. Order of battle in Allen, *None So Blind*, 135–136. Harkins's issues with ARVN in Moyar, *Triumph Forsaken*, 165–166.

59. Problems with indicators in CINCPAC-COMUSMACV Conference Agenda Items, 30 October 1963, Historian's Background Material Files, Box 16, RG 472, NARA. The problem would remain unresolved at the end of Harkins's tenure. See NARA 9–6. On strengthening Diem's popular support, see JCS History, Part I, JCSHO, 2–8.

60. On the influence of French counterinsurgency theory on the Ngo brothers' view of the strategic hamlet program, see Miller, *Misalliance*, 232–233. Miller also argues, persuasively, that the Ngos "were adamant that the program was not merely a military strategy…strategic hamlets were supposed to catalyze a host of changes within South Vietnamese rural society," 234.

61. Ted Serong quoted in Anne Blair, *There to the Bitter End: Ted Serong in Vietnam* (Crows Nest, Australia: Allen and Unwin, 2001), 35. US Embassy Telegram, 19 December 1962, *FRUS, 1961–1963*, II: 788.

62. Bernard B. Fall, *Viet-Nam Witness: 1953–66* (New York: Frederick A. Praeger, 1966), 198. The BDM Corporation, "A Study of Strategic Lessons Learned in Vietnam," Vol. V, Planning the War, MHI General Holdings, pp. 5–17. Larry H. Addington, *America's War in Vietnam: A Short Narrative History* (Bloomington: Indiana University Press, 2000), 63.

63. Carl W. Schaad, "The Strategic Hamlet Program in Vietnam: The Role of the People in Counterinsurgency Warfare," 6 March 1964, Student Thesis, US Army War College, MHI, p. 79. Hunt, *Lyndon Johnson's War*, 36. Walter Laqueur, *Guerrilla Warfare: A Historical & Critical Case Study* (New Brunswick, NJ: Transaction, 1998, 2006), 271. One US advisor noted in mid-1964 that "large numbers of the population will not be decisively influenced by the government since they are outside the hamlet and beyond the scope of the present plan."

Earl J. Young, Long An Province Policy Review, 31 July 1964, Box 4, Robert M. Montague
Papers, MHI, p. 6.
64. MACV "Summary of Highlights" quoted in Edwin E. Moise, "JFK and the Myth of
Withdrawal," in *A Companion to the Vietnam War*, ed. Marilyn B. Young and Robert Buzzanco
(Malden, MA: Blackwell, 2002), 166. NARA 9–3. *The Pentagon Papers*, II, 164. GVN problems in Maurer, *Strange Ground*, 97.
65. Harkins to Diem, 23 February 1963, *FRUS*, 1961–1963, III: 118. See also Harkins to Diem,
15 May 1963, *FRUS*, 1961–1963, III: 296–299. Allen, *None So Blind*, 143. Moyar, *Triumph
Forsaken*, 204. Michael D. Pearlman, *Warmaking and American Democracy: The Struggle
over Military Strategy, 1700 to Present* (Lawrence: University Press of Kansas, 1999), 341.
Subordinate criticisms in Blair, *There to the Bitter End*, 43, 71.
66. Diem quoted in Lloyd C. Gardner, *Pay Any Price: Lyndon Johnson and the Wars for Vietnam*
(Chicago: Ivan R. Dee, 1995), 75. Francis X. Winters, *The Year of the Hare: America in
Vietnam, January 25, 1963—February 15, 1964* (Athens: University of Georgia Press, 1997),
59. Schulzinger, *A Time for War*, 125.
67. Lodge quoted in Legere to Thayer, CMH, 9. Harkins to Felt, 19 September 1963, *FRUS*,
1961–1963, IV: 266–267.
68. C. A. Youngdale, "Viet Cong Strategy and Tactics during 1964," 15 March 1965, MHI,
3. Command History, USMACV, 1964, NARA, 64. Bradley, *Vietnam at War*, 104. Tang, *A
Vietcong Memoir*, 91.
69. Lawrence E. Grinter, "Bargaining between Saigon and Washington: Dilemmas of Linkage
Politics during War," *Orbis*, Vol. 18, No. 3 (Fall 1974): 852. Winters, *The Year of the Hare*, 205.
Deputy Chief of US Mission William C. Trueheart believed the Americans did not have "any
particular strategic conception of how to deal with the problem of the VC" after Diem's coup.
Interview by Ted Gittinger, 2 March 1982, LBJL, p. I-59.
70. NSAM 273 in JCS History, Part I, JCSHO, 8–14. See also Lawrence S. Kaplan, Ronald D.
Landa, and Edward J. Drea, *The McNamara Ascendancy, 1961–1965* (Washington, DC: Office
of the Secretary of Defense Historical Office, 2006), 499. On post-coup problems, see *FRUS*,
1961–1963, IV: 628–629; Edward G. Lansdale, "Viet Nam: Do We Understand Revolution?"
Foreign Affairs, Vol. 43, No. 1 (October 1964): 82; and Elliott, *The Vietnamese War*, 194.
71. McNamara in *The Vietnam War: A History in Documents*, ed. Marilyn B. Young, John
J. Fitzgerald, and A. Tom Grunfeld (New York: Oxford University Press, 2002), 67.
Westmoreland, interview, MHI, 15. William C. Westmoreland, *"Vietnam in Perspective,"* ed.
Patrick J. Hearden (West Lafayette, IN: Purdue University Press, 1990), 41.
72. Cosmas, *MACV,*122. David Halberstam, *The Best and the Brightest* (New York: Random
House, 1969), 405.
73. Peter Grose, "Harkins Optimistic on War in Vietnam," *New York Times*, 19 June 1964. See
also Peter Grose, "Harkins Leaves Saigon Command," *New York Times*, 21 June 1964. On
officer dissent with Harkins, see Buzzanco, *Masters of War* 137–138.
74. William C. Westmoreland, *A Soldier Reports* (Garden City, NY: Doubleday, 1976), 74. On
the state of affairs in early 1964, see Scott Sigmund Gartner, *Strategic Assessment in War* (New
Haven, CT: Yale University Press, 1997), 119.
75. Westmoreland quoted in Cosmas, *MACV*, 159; and Michael Charlton and Anthony
Moncrieff, *Many Reasons Why: The American Involvement in Vietnam* (New York: Hill and
Wang, 1978), 155. Westmoreland's operations officer, William E. DePuy, concurred that "no
one is in power, and that explains much of the trouble we are having." In Henry G. Gole,
General William E. DePuy: Preparing the Army for Modern War (Lexington: University Press
of Kentucky, 2008), 150.
76. There are three biographies of Westmoreland. Ernest B. Furgurson's *Westmoreland: The
Inevitable General* (Boston: Little, Brown, 1968) is overly sympathetic, while Lewis Sorley's
Westmoreland: The General Who Lost Vietnam (Boston: Houghton Mifflin Harcourt, 2011)
is little more than a veiled attempt at character assassination. The best work remains Samuel
Zaffiri, *Westmoreland: A Biography of General William C. Westmoreland* (New York: William
Morrow, 1994). For a shorter biographical sketch, see Halberstam, *The Best and the Brightest*,
553–567.

77. Bruce Palmer Jr., *The 25-Year War: America's Military Role in Vietnam* (Lexington: University Press of Kentucky, 1984), 40.

78. Westmoreland to Lucien W. Pye, 1 June 1962, WPSC. David A. Duffy, "A Reflection of the Army: West Point and Counterinsurgency, 1962–1968," LD720 Research Paper, United States Military Academy Tactical Officer Education Program, 1995, WPSC.

79. Stilwell in Duffy, "A Reflection of the Army." "Patron Saint" in Andrew J. Birtle, "In Pursuit of the Great White Whale: Lewis Sorley's *Westmoreland: The General Who Lost Vietnam*," *Army History*, (Summer 2012): 28. On Galula, see Ann Marlowe, "Forgotten Founder: The French Colonel Who Wrote the Book(s) on Counterinsurgency," *Weekly Standard*, 19 October 2009.

80. William C. Westmoreland, interview by Martin L. Ganderson, 1982, Box 1, Senior Officer Oral History Program, William C. Westmoreland Papers, MHI, 142. Westmoreland in *Time*, 19 February 1965, 20. On Malaya not being relevant to Vietnam, see Fall, *Viet-Nam Witness*, 272, and John Ellis, *A Short History of Guerrilla Warfare* (New York: St. Martin's Press, 1976), 179.

81. Yarborough quoted in Buzzanco, *Masters of War*, 162. Dave Richard Palmer, *Summons of the Trumpet: U.S.-Vietnam in Perspective* (San Rafael, CA: Presidio Press, 1978), 54–55. Westmoreland seemed to take Yarborough's advice to heart. At a conference in late 1964, the general noted that "in the Viet Cong organization throughout the country, political and military functions are closely integrated. Every VC political headquarters down to the village level includes a military or paramilitary component, and every VC military unit has its political staff element or member." Vietnam Situation Report to SEATO Plan 4 Conference, 16 September 1964, Box 44, Speeches (1944–1969), WPUSC.

82. Westmoreland, *A Soldier Reports*, 82. U.S. Grant Sharp and William C. Westmoreland, *Report on the War in Vietnam* (Washington, DC: USGovernment Printing Office, 1969), 105.

83. Paper by Ambassador Taylor, *FRUS, 1964–1968*, I: 949, 951. Maxwell D. Taylor, *Swords and Plowshares* (New York: W.W. Norton, 1972), 326. D. W. Beveridge, "The Ground War in Vietnam, a Strategy of Tactics: US Operational Concepts under Westmoreland," *Defence Force Journal*, No. 76 (May/June 1989): 36. Halberstam, *The Best and the Brightest*, 544. Schulzinger, *A Time for War*, 163.

84. George Donelson Moss, *Vietnam: An American Ordeal*, 5th ed. (Upper Saddle River, NJ: Pearson Prentice Hill, 1990, 2006), 170. On Tonkin, see Herring, *America's Longest War*, 141–147. Edwin E. Moïse, *Tonkin Gulf and the Escalation of the Vietnam War* (Chapel Hill: University of North Carolina Press, 1996) remains the best monograph on the subject.

85. Robert S. McNamara, interview by Walt W. Rostow, 8 January 1975, LBJL, I-30. Trip report quoted in *The Pentagon Papers*, II: 313. See also JCS History, Part I, JCSHO, 9-12–9-16 and Herbert Y. Schandler, *America in Vietnam: The War That Couldn't Be Won* (Lanham, MD: Rowman and Littlefield, 2009), 46. On links between Tonkin and escalation, see Hallin, *The "Uncensored War,"* 80. Marilyn B. Young argues that withdrawal from Vietnam would have "exposed American impotence." *The Vietnam Wars, 1945–1990* (New York: HarperCollins, 1991), 135.

86. Wheeler to Westmoreland, 16 October 1964, Folder 2, Box 1, Series I Official Correspondence, W. C. Westmoreland Collection, MHI, 5. Gordon M. Goldstein, *Lessons in Disaster: McGeorge Bundy and the Path to War in Vietnam* (New York: Times Books, 2008), 132. Kaiser, *American Tragedy*, 347.

87. Command History, 1965, Headquarters, USMACV, Secretary of Joint Staff (MACJ03), Entry MACJ03, Military History Branch, Box 2, RG 472, NARA, 2. Sharp and Westmoreland, *Report*, 97. Berman, *Planning a Tragedy*, 34.

88. Westmoreland to Taylor and Felt, 25 June 1964, Folder 14, Box 3, Douglas Pike Collection: Unit 01—Assessment and Strategy, TTUVA. Ronnie L. Brownlee and William J. Mullen III, *Changing an Army: An Oral History of General William E. DePuy, USA Retired*, 1986, Box 1, William E. DePuy Papers, MHI, 121. Command History, USMACV, 1964, NARA, 124. Cosmas, *MACV*, 140.

89. Westmoreland to Taylor, 6 September 1964, *FRUS, 1964–1968*, I: 736–741. R. Michael Pearce, *Evolution of a Vietnamese Village—Part I: The Present, after Eight Months of Pacification* (Santa Monica, CA: Rand, 1965), vii.

90. Westmoreland to Wheeler, 17 October 1964, *FRUS, 1964–1968*, I: 838. See also in H. R. McMaster, *Dereliction of Duty: Lyndon Johnson, Robert McNamara, the Joint Chiefs of Staff, and the Lies that Led to Vietnam* (New York: Harper Perennial, 1997), 165–166. Taylor, *Swords and Plowshares*, 333–334.

91. William Conrad Gibbons, *The U.S. Government and the Vietnam War: Executive and Legislative Roles and Relationships, Part III: January–July 1965* (Princeton, NJ: Princeton University Press, 1989), 60–61. Phillip B. Davidson, *Vietnam at War: The History: 1946–1975* (Novato, CA: Presidio, 1988), 302–303.

92. Headquarters, USMACV, Monthly Evaluation Report, March 1965, MHI, 2. John Prados, *The Hidden History of the Vietnam War* (Chicago: Ivan R. Dee, 1995), 104. John Prados, *Vietnam: The History of an Unwinnable War, 1945–1975* (Lawrence: University Press of Kansas, 2009), 151. James Carter makes the important point that the "kind of infrastructure being put in place was explicitly military and did not aid in the development of an independent southern state." *Inventing Vietnam*, 202.

93. Bundy quoted in Gibbons, *The U.S. Government and the Vietnam War*, 118. On Rolling Thunder, see Joseph R. Cerami, "Presidential Decisionmaking and Vietnam: Lessons for Strategists," *Parameters*, Vol. 26, No. 4 (Winter 1996–97): 67–69 and *The Pentagon Papers*, III, 391. A. J. Langguth notes the Bundy brothers argued that "the crumbling of the South Vietnamese government was not a signal to cut U.S. losses and get out but rather as proof that America must bomb the implacable North to strengthen the will of the corrupt South." *Our Vietnam*, 341.

94. Westmoreland quoted in Berman, *Planning a Tragedy*, 71. Sharp to Wheeler, 6 March 1965, *FRUS, 1964–1968*, II: 407. On "fire brigade" approach see *Outlook in Vietnam*, Folder 7, Box 8, Douglas Pike Collection, Unit 02: Military Operations, TTUVA, 12; Sharp and Westmoreland, *Report*, 114; and Zaffiri, *Westmoreland*, 131.

95. On the introduction of Marines, see Embassy in Vietnam to the Joint Chiefs of Staff, 22 February 1965, *FRUS, 1964–1968*, II: 347–349; and *The Pentagon Papers*, III, 389. Base security strategy in William B. Rosson, "Four Periods of American Involvement in Vietnam: Development and Implementation of Policy, Strategy and Programs, Described and Analyzed on the Basis of Experience at Progressively Senior Levels" (Ph.D. diss., University of Oxford, 1979), 189.

96. Victor H. Krulak, *First to Fight: An Inside View of the U.S. Marine Corps* (Annapolis, MD: Naval Institute Press, 1984), 182–183.

97. Westmoreland quoted in *The Pentagon Papers*, III: 467. See also Westmoreland, *A Soldier Reports*, 169. On ARVN assessments, see JCS History, Part II, JCSHO, 19–6, and Halberstam, *The Best and the Brightest*, 582. On troop requests, see Gibbons, *The U.S. Government and the Vietnam War*, 356–357; Moss, *Vietnam*, 187; Andrew F. Krepinevich, "Vietnam: Evaluating the Ground War, 1965–1968," in *An American Dilemma: Vietnam, 1964–1973*, ed. Dennis E. Showalter and John G. Albert (Chicago: Imprint Publications, 1993), 91. Westmoreland believed at least some of the 44 battalions could come from allied nations, specifically a division of troops from the Republic of Korea.

98. Berman, *Planning a Tragedy*, 80. Lloyd Gardner, "America's War in Vietnam: The End of Exceptionalism?" in *The Legacy: The Vietnam War in the American Imagination*, ed. D. Michael Shafer (Boston: Beacon Press, 1990), 22. Porter, *Vietnam*, 307. Westmoreland did not believe, however, that either Hanoi or the NLF's leadership would alter its intentions with the deployment of additional US forces. Westmoreland to Wheeler and Sharp, 30 June 1965, US Strategy, Vietnam, 1965–75, Historian's Files, CMH, p. 30.

99. Johnson in Melvyn P. Leffler, *For the Soul of Mankind: The United States, the Soviet Union, and the Cold War* (New York: Hill and Wang, 2007), 220. See also Doris Kearns, *Lyndon Johnson and the American Dream* (New York: Harper and Row, 1976), 252, and Schandler, *America in Vietnam*, 47. For a contemporary argument against US troop commitment, see George Kennan in *Major Problems in the History of the Vietnam War*, 2nd ed., ed. Robert J. McMahon (Lexington, MA: D.C. Heath, 1995), 246–248.

100. Alsop quoted in Command History, USMACV, 1965, NARA, 24. Eliot A. Cohen, *Supreme Command: Soldiers, Statesmen, and Leadership in Wartime* (New York: Free Press, 2002), 180.

101. Bundy in Gibbons, *The U.S. Government and the Vietnam War,* 48. Command History, USMACV, 1965, NARA, 1. MACV Concept of Operations in the Republic of Vietnam, 30 August 1965, US Strategy, Vietnam, 1965-75, Historian's Files, CMH, 1. On problems of prestige, see Bernard Brodie, *War and Politics* (New York: Macmillan, 1973), 160–161.

102. Ball quoted in Porter, *Vietnam,* 312–313, and Gardner, *Pay and Price,* 147. Brian VanDeMark, *Into the Quagmire: Lyndon Johnson and the Escalation of the Vietnam War* (New York: Oxford University Press, 1991), 89. On options, see Robert S. McNamara, *In Retrospect: The Tragedy and Lessons of Vietnam* (New York: Times Books, 1995), 71.

103. Quoted in Cosmas, *MACV,* 238. In the 24 June message, Westmoreland noted that the struggle had become a "war of attrition," a point that is examined fully in Chapter 3.

Chapter 3

1. NSAM 288 in William Conrad Gibbons, *The U.S. Government and the Vietnam War: Executive and Legislative Roles and Relationships, Part IV: July 1965–January 1968* (Washington, DC: US Government Printing Office, 1994), 45. "The Joint Chiefs of Staff and the War in Vietnam, 1960–1968" (hereafter cited as JCS History), Part I, JCSHO, 14–26. William C. Westmoreland recalled that the objective "remained essentially the same throughout American involvement." *A Soldier Reports* (Garden City, NY: Doubleday, 1976), 69. Jeffrey Record, however, argues that even before Tet in 1968 "defeat avoidance" was the chief US aim. *The Wrong War: Why We Lost in Vietnam* (Annapolis, MD: Naval Institute Press, 1998), 4.

2. Johnson quoted in David Kaiser, *American Tragedy: Kennedy, Johnson, and the Origins of the Vietnam War* (Cambridge, MA: Belknap Press of Harvard University Press, 2000), 424. See also Lyndon Baines Johnson, *The Vantage Point: Perspectives on the Presidency, 1963–1969* (New York: Holt, Rinehart and Winston, 1971), 132.

3. Robert S. McNamara, *In Retrospect: The Tragedy and Lessons of Vietnam* (New York: Times Books, 1995), 203. On failure to develop strategy, see George C. Herring, *LBJ and Vietnam: A Different Kind of War* (Austin: University of Texas Press, 1994), 22; Jeffrey J. Clarke, *Advice and Support: The Final Years, 1965–1973* (Washington, DC: Center of Military History, 1988), 106; and JCS History, Part II, JCSHO, 23–1.

4. McNamara to Johnson, 20 July 1965, in *Vietnam: A History in Documents,* ed. Gareth Porter (New York: New American Library, 1981), 317–320.

5. Johnson, *The Vantage Point,* 241. Stephen Peter Rosen argues that Johnson's advisors "knew limited war theory and defense economics, but not military strategy." In "Vietnam and the American Theory of Limited War," *International Security,* Vol. 7, No. 2 (Autumn, 1982): 99.

6. Peter M. Dawkins, "The United States Army and the 'Other' War in Vietnam: A Study of the Complexity of Implementing Organizational Change" (Ph.D. diss., Princeton University, 1979), 30. DePuy in *Strange Ground: Americans in Vietnam, 1945–1975, an Oral History,* ed. Harry Maurer (New York: Henry Holt, 1989), 451. Harry G. Summers Jr., *On Strategy: A Critical Appraisal of the Vietnam War* (Novato, CA: Presidio, 1982), 101.

7. George Donelson Moss, *Vietnam: An American Ordeal,* 5th ed. (Upper Saddle River, NJ: Pearson Prentice Hall, 1990, 2006), 191. Fredrik Logevall, *The Origins of the Vietnam War* (Harlow, England: Longman, 2001), 87. Lawrence Freedman, "Vietnam and the Disillusioned Strategist," *International Affairs,* Vol. 72, No. 1 (January 1996): 136. For an example of contemporary criticism, see CIA officer Harold P. Ford in Gibbons, *The U.S. Government and the Vietnam War,* IV, 21. The relationship between commander in chief and his or her role in devising and managing military strategy can be a contentious topic. The best work on this subject is Eliot A. Cohen, *Supreme Command: Soldiers, Statesmen, and Leadership in Wartime* (New York: Free Press, 2002).

8. Loren Baritz, *Backfire: A History of How American Culture Led Us into Vietnam and Made Us Fight the Way We Did* (Baltimore. MD: Johns Hopkins University Press, 1985), 159. Christopher M. Gacek argues that no one in the administration had "satisfactory answers to these questions: the connections between achieving real, military objectives and attaining American political goals were not delineated as they should have been." *The Logic of Force: The*

Dilemma of Limited War in American Foreign Policy (New York: Columbia University Press, 1994), 215.

9. Command History, United States Military Assistance Command, 1965, Entry MACJ03, Box 1, RG 472, NARA, 161.

10. "A Systems Analysis View of the Vietnam War: 1965–1972," Vol. 4—Allied Ground and Naval Operations, Geog. V. Vietnam-319.1, CMH, p. 51. On US strategy involving nonmilitary means, see Raymond Aron, "The Evolution of Modern Strategic Thought," in *Problems of Modern Strategy*, ed. Alastair Buchan (New York: Praeger, 1970), 27.

11. Senior Officer Debriefing Program Report of LTG Fred C. Weyand, 4 October 1968, MHI, 3. This phenomenon likely explains Larry E. Cable's critique, in which he argues that the "Americans lacked a clear focus as to what the operational center of gravity should be in South Vietnam." *Conflict of Myths: The Development of American Counterinsurgency Doctrine and the Vietnam War* (New York: New York University Press, 1986), 210.

12. Westmoreland quoted in Gibbons, *The U.S. Government and the Vietnam War*, IV, 15. Richard H. Immerman, "'A Time in the Tide of Men's Affairs': Lyndon Johnson and Vietnam," in *Lyndon Johnson Confronts the World: American Foreign Policy, 1963–1968*, ed. Warren I. Cohen and Nancy Bernkopf Tucker (New York: Cambridge University Press, 1994), 63. Rand analysts at the time argued the decisive factor "must be the strength and determination of the Vietnamese communists." In Mai Elliott, *Rand in Southeast Asia: A History of the Vietnam War Era* (Santa Monica, CA: Rand Corporation, 2010), 141.

13. U.S. Grant Sharp, *Strategy for Defeat: Vietnam in Retrospect* (San Rafael, CA: Presidio Press, 1978), 270. JCS in Gibbons, *The U.S. Government and the Vietnam War*, IV: 9. On China, see Carter Malkasian, "Toward a Better Understanding of Attrition: The Korean and Vietnam Wars," *Journal of Military History*, Vol. 68, No. 3 (July 2004): 929; and Larry Berman, "Waiting for Smoking Guns: Presidential Decision-making and the Vietnam War, 1965–1967," in *Vietnam as History: Ten Years after the Paris Peace Accords*, ed. Peter Braestrup (Washington, DC: University Press of America, 1984), 17. On strategic interaction, see Peter D. Feaver, *Armed Servants: Agency, Oversight, and Civil-Military Relations* (Cambridge, MA: Harvard University Press, 2003), 54.

14. Westmoreland quoted in Michael Charlton and Anthony Moncrieff, *Many Reasons Why: The American Involvement in Vietnam* (New York: Hill and Wang, 1978), 136. Thomas C. Schelling discussed the "threat of inadvertent war" as early as 1960. *The Strategy of Conflict* (Cambridge, MA: Harvard University Press, 1960), 188–190. F. Charles Parker IV argues that the "decision to limit the US commitment . . . left an army in combat whose only goal was to avoid defeat." *Vietnam: Strategy for a Stalemate* (New York: Paragon House, 1989), 3.

15. Lloyd C. Gardner, *Pay Any Price: Lyndon Johnson and the Wars for Vietnam* (Chicago: Ivan R. Dee, 1995), xv. Doris Kearns, *Lyndon Johnson and the American Dream* (New York: Harper and Row, 1976), 268. Harry McPherson, *A Political Education: A Washington Memoir* (Boston: Houghton Mifflin, 1988), 390. Christopher T. Fisher, "The Illusion of Progress: CORDS and the Crisis of Modernization in South Vietnam, 1965–1968," *Pacific Historical Review*, Vol. 75, No. 1 (February 2006): 28–31. On not risking escalation, see Brian VanDeMark, *Into the Quagmire: Lyndon Johnson and the Escalation of the Vietnam War* (New York: Oxford University Press, 1991), 48.

16. Parker, *Vietnam*, 79. For a counterargument, in which LBJ instructed the military to fight using a firepower-intensive strategy, see Jonathan D. Caverley, "The Myth of Military Myopia," *International Security*, Vol. 34, No. 3 (Winter 2009/10): 155.

17. Edward J. Drea, *McNamara, Clifford, and the Burdens of Vietnam, 1965–1969* (Washington, DC: Office of the Secretary of Defense Historical Office, 2011), 49. Michael H. Hunt, *Lyndon Johnson's War: America's Cold War Crusade in Vietnam, 1945–1968* (New York: Hill and Wang, 1996), 101. Of note, neither did the press question the wisdom of US presence in South Vietnam in the war's early years. See William M. Hammond, "The Press in Vietnam as Agent of Defeat: A Critical Examination," *Reviews in American History*, Vol. 17, No. 2 (June 1989): 318.

18. Ball quoted in *A Vietnam War Reader: A Documentary History from American and Vietnamese Perspectives*, ed. Michael H. Hunt (Chapel Hill: University of North Carolina Press, 2010), 78; and Larry Berman, *Planning a Tragedy: The Americanization of the War in Vietnam*

(New York: W.W. Norton, 1982), 109. See also David L. Di Leo, *George Ball, Vietnam, and the Rethinking of Containment* (Chapel Hill: University of North Carolina Press, 1991), 80, 82, 107. On serious consequences of withdrawal, see JCS History, Part I, JCSHO, 14–4.

19. Alain C. Enthoven and K. Wayne Smith, *How Much Is Enough? Shaping the Defense Program, 1961–1969* (New York: Harper and Row, 1971), 62. McNamara quoted in James M. Roherty, *Decisions of Robert S. McNamara: A Study of the Role of the Secretary of Defense* (Coral Gables, FL: University of Miami Press, 1970), 68. See also Michael T. Klare, *War without End: American Planning for the Next Vietnams* (New York: Alfred A. Knopf, 1972), 63; Gregory Palmer, *The McNamara Strategy and the Vietnam War: Program Budgeting in the Pentagon, 1960–1968* (Westport, CT: Greenwood Press, 1978), 5; and Morton H. Halperin, *Contemporary Military Strategy* (Boston: Little, Brown, 1967), 52–54.

20. George C. Herring, *"Cold Blood": LBJ's Conduct of Limited War in Vietnam*, The Harmon Memorial Lectures in Military History, No. 33 (Washington, DC: US Government Printing Office, 1990), 3. Herring argues that McNamara challenged the JCS only on the issue of bombing.

21. McNamara Memo on Vietnam Strategy, 26 June 1965, Folder 11, Box 04, Douglas Pike Collection: Unit 01—Assessment and Strategy, TTUVA. This memorandum was revised on 1 July before being sent to Johnson. See Gibbons, *The U.S. Government and the Vietnam War*, III: 330–331.

22. McNamara to Johnson, 20 July 1965, Recommendations of additional deployments to Vietnam, Folder 15, Box 02, Larry Berman Collection (Presidential Archives Research), TTUVA. Edgar F. Raines Jr. and David R. Campbell argue that McNamara defined his role as "questioning, suggesting alternatives, proposing objectives, and stimulating progress." *The Army and the Joint Chiefs of Staff: Evolution of Army Ideas on the Command, Control, and Coordination of the U.S. Armed Forces, 1942–1985* (Washington, DC: U.S. Army Center of Military History, 1986), 109. For McNamara's public views at this time, see Jack Raymond, "M'Namara Finds Situation Worse in Vietnam War," *New York Times*, 21 July 1965.

23. Legislation quoted in Raines and Campbell, *The Army and the Joint Chiefs of Staff*, 92. Wheeler quoted in Paul L. Miles to Westmoreland, 1 September 1971, Strategic Planning for RVN—June 1965, Historian's Files, US Strategy, Vietnam, 1965–1975, CMH, p. 2. On the limited JCS role, see Michael W. Davidson, "Senior Officers and Vietnam Policymaking," *Parameters*, Vol. 16, No. 1 (Spring 1986): 58. Andrew J. Goodpaster noted at the time that the "Chief's basic contribution" fundamentally was to "give advice." "The Role of the Joint Chiefs in the National Security Structure," in *Issues of National Security in the 1970's: Essays Presented to Colonel George A. Lincoln on His Sixtieth Birthday*, ed. Amos A. Jordan Jr. (New York: Frederick A. Praeger, 1967), 237.

24. "Memo for JCS, Trip Report, Vietnam, 8–12 Dec. 64," 21 December 1964, Historians Background Materials Files, Box 8, Memos & Misc. Studies, RG 472, NARA. Control in Lawrence J. Korb, *The Joint Chiefs of Staff: The First Twenty-Five Years* (Bloomington: Indiana University Press, 1976), 163. *The Pentagon Papers: The Defense Department History of United States Decisionmaking in Vietnam* [Senator Gravel, ed., 5 vols.] (Boston: Beacon Press, 1971–1972), Vol. III: 481. For a harsh critique of the JCS, see also H. R. McMaster, *Dereliction of Duty: Lyndon Johnson, Robert McNamara, the Joint Chiefs of Staff, and the Lies that Led to Vietnam* (New York: Harper Perennial, 1997), 328. Jack Schulimson argues though that the JCS was "quite aware that the making of military and defense policy was 'essentially a political process.'" In *The Joint Chiefs of Staff and the War in Vietnam, 1960–1968*, Part I (Washington, DC: Office of Joint History, 2011), 7.

25. On JCS views in 1965, see JCS History, Part I, JCSHO, 12-41–12-42. Joint Chiefs of Staff to McNamara, 27 August 1965, *FRUS*, 1964–1968, III: 356–363. Wheeler to Sharp and Westmoreland, 20 November 1965, Folder 7, Box 2, Official Correspondence, Series I, W. C. Westmoreland Collection, MHI. *The Pentagon Papers*, IV: 294–295.

26. On the JCS understanding the role of politics in military calculations, see Gardner, *Pay Any Price*, 117. Bruce Palmer Jr. argues the greatest failing of the JCS was that they did not tell the president that "the strategy being pursued most probably would fail and that the United States would be unable to achieve its objectives." *The 25-Year War: America's Military Role in Vietnam* (Lexington: University Press of Kentucky, 1984), 46.

27. Sharp, *Strategy for Defeat*, 92. See also Graham A. Cosmas, *MACV: The Joint Command in the Years of Escalation, 1962–1967* (Washington, DC: Center of Military History, 2006), 250. John Prados, *Vietnam: The History of an Unwinnable War, 1945–1975* (Lawrence: University Press of Kansas, 2009), 107. On the JCS and CINPAC recognizing the "inseparable political, economic, sociological, and military factors" of the war, see Command History, United States Military Assistance Command, 1965, Entry MACJ03, Box 1, RG 472, NARA, p. 339.

28. On compartmentalization, see Richard H. Shultz Jr., "The Great Divide: Strategy and Covert Action in Vietnam," *Joint Forces Quarterly*, No. 23 (Autumn–Winter 1999–2000): 94; and Peter M. Dunn, "The American Army: The Vietnam War, 1965–1973," in *Armed Forces and Modern Counter-Insurgency*, ed. Ian F.W. Beckett and John Pimlott (New York: St. Martin's Press, 1985), 82. Observations on the MACOV Study, Personal Correspondence, Box 2, 1969–1972, Donn A. Starry Papers, MHI, p. 3. In mid-1965, the JCS put together a study group, led by General Andrew Goodpaster, to study the strategic problem in Vietnam. See *FRUS*, 1964–1968, III: 181–187, for its concept and appraisal.

29. Volney Warner, email to author, 17 April 2012. On the less than enthusiastic attitude of the South Vietnamese on a combined command, see Ngo Quang Truong, "RVNAF and US Operational Cooperation and Coordination," in *The Vietnam War: An Assessment by South Vietnam's Generals*, ed. Lewis Sorley (Lubbock: Texas Tech University Press, 2010), 137.

30. William B. Rosson, "Four Periods of American Involvement in Vietnam: Development and Implementation of Policy, Strategy and Programs, Described and Analyzed on the Basis of Experience at Progressively Senior Levels" (Ph.D. diss., University of Oxford, 1979), 188. As an example, Westmoreland noted in March 1966 the difficulties of stemming the "inflationary trends within the GVN." General Westmoreland's Historical Briefing, 15 March 1966, Reel 6, Folder 4, 30 Jan–13 Mar 66, WCWP. Sharp blamed the secretary of defense for failing to approve an overall concept for fighting the war. *Strategy for Defeat*, 96.

31. Ho Chi Minh quoted in James P. Harrison, *The Endless War: Vietnam's Struggle for Independence* (New York: Columbia University Press, 1989), 153. On competing objectives, see War Experiences Recapitulation Committee of the High-Level Military Institute, *The Anti-U.S. Resistance War for National Salvation 1954–1975: Military Events* (Hanoi: People's Army Publishing House, 1980), 15.

32. The strategic debate is best outlined in Lien-Hang T. Nguyen, *Hanoi's War: An International History of the War for Peace in Vietnam* (Chapel Hill: University of North Carolina Press, 2012), 71. See also Nguyen Vu Tung, "Coping with the United States: Hanoi's Search for an Effective Strategy," in *The Vietnam War*, ed. Peter Lowe (New York: St. Martin's Press, 1998), 46–48; and Hanoi Assessment of Guerrilla War in South, November 1966, Folder 17, Box 06, Douglas Pike Collection: Unit 01-Assessment and Strategy, TTUVA. Resolution 12 in Communist Strategy as Reflected in Lao Dong Party and COSVN Resolutions, Folder 26, Box 07, Douglas Pike Collection: Unit 06-Democratic Republic of Vietnam, TTUVA, p. 3. Escalation in Jeffrey S. Milstein, *Dynamics of the Vietnam War: A Quantitative Analysis and Predictive Computer Simulation* (Columbus: Ohio State University Press, 1974), 49.

33. William E. DePuy, "Vietnam: What We Might Have Done and Why We Didn't Do It," *Army*, Vol. 36, No. 2 (February 1986): 23. See also Andrew J. Birtle, *U.S. Army Counterinsurgency and Contingency Operations Doctrine, 1942–1976* (Washington, DC: Center of Military History, 2006), 371. NLF legitimacy in Noam Chomsky, *Rethinking Camelot: JFK, the Vietnam War, and U.S. Political Culture* (Boston, MA: South End Press, 1993), 58. US buildup posing problems for Le Duan in William J. Duiker, *The Communist Road to Power*, 2nd ed. (Boulder, CO: Westview Press, 1981, 1996), 273.

34. Romie L. Brownlee and William J. Mullen III, *Changing an Army: An Oral History of General William E. DePuy, USA Retired* (Carlisle Barracks, PA: US Military History Institute, 1986), Box 1, William E. DePuy Papers, MHI, p. 135. On logistic situation in RVN, see Staff Study, Improvement of US Logistic System in RVN, 26 October 1964, 1964 Folder, Box 7, Frank Osmanski Papers, MHI; Command History, USMACV, 1965, NARA, 4.

35. Johnson quoted in Command History, USMACV, 1966, NARA, 338. On role of external assistance, see Jeffrey Record, *Beating Goliath: Why Insurgencies Win* (Washington,

DC: Potomac Books, 2007), 48. On LBJ's preoccupation with China, see Henry Kissinger, *Diplomacy* (New York: Simon and Schuster, 1994), 661.

36. James Reston, "The Undefinable War," *New York Times,* 26 August 1965.

37. Westmoreland, directive to US commanders, 17 September 1965, in Hunt, *A Vietnam War Reader,* 89. MACV Concept of Operations in the Republic of Vietnam, 30 August 1965, Historian's Files, US Strategy, Vietnam, 1965–1975, CMH, 10–4.

38. Lodge to State Department, 18 September 1965, *FRUS, 1964–1968,* III: 394. Of note, McGeorge Bundy sent a similar message to the president which outlined Westmoreland's concept. See *FRUS, 1964–1968,* III: 414–415. CINCPAC also appeared to mirror Westmoreland's views, noting that the "role of U.S. military forces in South Vietnam is to assist the people, the government and the armed forces of Vietnam win their war, and not to supplant them in any of the processes." Sharp to Wheeler and Westmoreland, 23 November 1965, Folder 8, Box 2, Official Correspondence, Series I, W. C. Westmoreland Collection, MHI.

39. Miles to Westmoreland, 1 September 1971, CMH, 9. Westmoreland was not the only officer to use the term "long pull." See J. Lawton Collins in *The First Vietnam War: Colonial Conflict and Cold War Crisis,* ed. Mark Atwood Lawrence and Fredrik Logevall (Cambridge, MA: Harvard University Press, 2007), 304. Pacification and the training of ARVN were to be "pursued throughout all three phases" of MACV's strategy. Westmoreland, *A Soldier Reports,* 176.

40. Robert B. Semple, "Westmoreland Finds Hanoi Firm in Its War Effort," *New York Times,* 15 August 1966.

41. Department of the Army, Field Manual 31–16, *Counterguerrilla Operations,* February 1963, 20. Westmoreland's views on an enclave strategy in *The Lessons of Vietnam,* ed. W. Scott Thompson and Donaldson D. Frizzell (New York: Crane, Russak, 1977), 59–60.

42. Guenter Lewy, *America in Vietnam* (New York: Oxford University Press, 1978), 52.

43. For example, Westmoreland noted in late 1966 that "We must certainly continue to attack and destroy the enemy's large units. It is equally important however that we devote great energies to the systematic destruction of the smaller units as well as the Viet Cong leadership in the hamlets and villages." Speech for Mobile Training Team Course, 8 December 1966, Box 44, Speeches (1944–1969), WPUSC.

44. Westmoreland to the Joint Chiefs of Staff, telegram, 7 June 1965, *FRUS, 1964–1968,* II: 733–734. See also Cosmas, *MACV,* 203, and Prados, *Vietnam,* 116.

45. Herbert Y. Schandler, *The Unmaking of a President: Lyndon Johnson and Vietnam* (Princeton, NJ: Princeton University Press, 1977), 27. Troop numbers in Robert D. Schulzinger, *A Time for War: The United States and Vietnam, 1941–1975* (New York: Oxford University Press, 1997), 183.

46. Westmoreland, *A Soldier Reports,* 175.

47. As quoted in *Victory in Vietnam: The Official History of the People's Army of Vietnam, 1954–1975,* trans. Merle L. Pribbenow (Lawrence: University Press of Kansas, 2002),154. For an overview of Hanoi's strategy, see David W. P. Elliott, "Hanoi's Strategy in the Second Indochina War," in *The Vietnam War: Vietnamese and American Perspectives,* ed. Jayne S. Werner and Luu Doan Huynh (Armonk, NY: M.E. Sharpe, 1993), 79–83; and William J. Duiker, *Sacred War: Nationalism and Revolution in a Divided Vietnam* (Boston: McGraw-Hill, 1995), 179–184.

48. Westmoreland, "Concept of Operations—Force Requirements and Deployments, South Vietnam," 14 June 1965, Folder 04, Box 02, Larry Berman Collection (Presidential Archives Research), TTUVA. On phases of Maoist revolutionary warfare, see Phillip B. Davidson, *Vietnam at War, the History: 1946–1975* (Novato, CA: Presidio Press, 1988), 320–321.

49. Westmoreland, *A Soldier Reports,* 175. Many historians, however, continue to argue that Westmoreland had a choice to make—"whether to fight a war of search and destroy or of counterinsurgency and pacification." As an example, see Randall B. Woods, *Shadow Warrior: William Egan Colby and the CIA* (New York: Basic Books, 2013), 258. The reality, as Westmoreland recognized, was that both problems had to be tackled simultaneously.

50. Westmoreland cable to Wheeler, 24 June 1965, Historian's Files, US Strategy, Vietnam, 1965–1975, CMH. Westmoreland describes a "war of attrition" in *A Soldier Reports*, 185.

51. Davidson, *Vietnam at War*, 354.

52. Survey data taken from Douglas Kinnard, *The War Managers: American Generals Reflect on Vietnam* (Hanover, NH: University Press of New England, 1977; DaCapo Press, 1991), 24–25.

53. U. S. Grant Sharp and William C. Westmoreland, *Report on the War in Vietnam* (Washington, DC: US Government Printing Office, 1969), 100. Command History, USMACV, 1965, NARA, 141–143; *The Pentagon Papers*, IV: 296. Leslie H. Gelb and Richard K. Betts note that the *Pentagon Papers* "analysts deduced a prognosis for victory by the end of 1967 in this plan. But the wording of the plan was imprecise about the terminal date…and Westmoreland maintained that he neither stated nor intended a prediction of victory for 1967." *The Irony of Vietnam: The System Worked* (Washington, DC: The Brookings Institution, 1979), 132.

54. Westmoreland to Collins, cable MAC 0117, 7 January 1966, Pacification Overview/Conclusions Folder, Historian's Files, CMH.

55. Cosmas, *MACV*, 140. Westmoreland later recalled that since the war took place "in large measure among the civilian population…it was essential from the first to do everything possible to avoid civilian casualties." In his memoirs, Westmoreland related his guidance on limiting violence against civilians and stressing the discriminate use of firepower. The general acknowledged, however, that "Rules, regulations, cards, even indoctrination quite obviously would not forestall all civilian casualties in such a war." *A Soldier Reports*, 347–348. For a counterargument in which civilian suffering was the norm and war crimes a natural outgrowth of US command policies, see Nick Turse, *Kill Anything That Moves: The Real American War in Vietnam* (New York: Metropolitan Books, 2013).

56. "The Plan for Vietnam," *Christian Science Monitor*, 27 June 1964. For an early critique on being too defensive minded, see Albert L. Fisher, "To Beat the Guerrillas at Their Own Game," *Military Review*, Vol. 43, No. 12 (December 1963): 81.

57. James M. Gavin, *Crisis Now* (New York: Random House, 1968), 62. On the JCS reaction to Gavin's 1966 criticisms, see FRUS, 1964–1968, IV: 198–201; and JCS History, Part II, JCSHO, 33-1–33-2.

58. Wheeler quoted in George C. Herring, *America's Longest War: The United States and Vietnam, 1950–1975*, 4th ed. (New York: McGraw-Hill, 2002), 163. Magnets in Sharp to Wheeler and Westmoreland, 31 October 1965, Folder 6, Box 2, Official Correspondence, Series I, W. C. Westmoreland Collection, MHI. Initiative in John S. Pustay, *Counterinsurgency Warfare* (New York: Free Press, 1965), 110. Westmoreland, *A Soldier Reports*, 156. It is important to note that military logic and a rational analysis of the enemy helped inform Westmoreland's dissatisfaction with an enclave approach. Offensive operations made sense if MACV held any chance of blunting NVA forces that were infiltrating into South Vietnam in 1965.

59. Joseph Alsop, "Vietnam Coastal Enclave Strategy Could Mean Many Dien Bien Phus," *Los Angeles Times*, 9 February 1966. See also Joseph G. Clemons Jr., "The Dilemma of the Vietnam Enclaves," 13 January 1967, Student Essay, US Army War College, MHI.

60. Krulak quoted in Gibbons, *The U.S. Government and the Vietnam War*, IV, 198. Krulak's criticisms undervalued the fact that Marine intelligence indicated in late 1967 that forty-three NVA and eighteen NLF battalions were operating in I Corps alone, not including the demilitarized zone. If Westmoreland could not ignore the enemy main force threat, neither could Krulak, despite his desires to do otherwise.

61. On CAP missions, see Victor H. Krulak, *First to Fight: An Inside View of the U.S. Marine Corps* (Annapolis, MD: Naval Institute Press, 1984), 191; Keith F. Kopets, "The Combined Action Program: Vietnam," *Military Review*, Vol. 82, No. 4 (July–August 2002): 79; and Robert L. Gallucci, *Neither Peace nor Honor: The Politics of American Military Policy in Viet-Nam* (Baltimore, MD: Johns Hopkins University Press, 1975), 119–120.

62. Walt to Westmoreland, 19 November 1965, Folder 7, Box 2, Official Correspondence, Series I, W. C. Westmoreland Collection, MHI. Walt noted in this memorandum that he "completely support[ed] the concept that when significant size VC units can be identified and located, they will be sought out and destroyed." Westmoreland, *A Soldier Reports*, 200. Walt

admitted after the war, "I don't think you could ignore the main force war." L. W. Walt, interview, 24 January 1969, LBJL, 4.

63. The Situation in I Corps, 15 November 1965, 1965 Folder, Box 4, William E. DePuy papers, MHI. For additional critiques, see Michael E. Peterson, *The Combined Action Platoons: The U.S. Marines' Other War in Vietnam* (Westport, CT: Praeger, 1989), 23; and Mark Moyar, *Phoenix and the Birds of Prey: Counterinsurgency and Counterterrorism in Vietnam* (Lincoln: University of Nebraska Press, 1997, 2007), 45.

64. F.J. West Jr., *The Village* (New York: Harper and Row, 1972), 11. On failure to "isolate" the battlefield, see Michael A. Hennessy, *Strategy in Vietnam: The Marines and Revolutionary Warfare in I Corps, 1965–1972* (Westport, CT: Praeger, 1997), 7.

65. William J. Ankley, "Civic Action—Marine or Army Style?" 11 January 1968, Student Essay, US Army War College, MHI, 13. For details on these similarities, see Guide for Province and District Advisors, 1 February 1968, Historian's Files, CMH.

66. West, *The Village*, 256. In his personal notes, Westmoreland worried that "the Marines were spreading over so much real estate that their offensive punch could become minimal; and, secondly, that they seemed to be thinking too much in terms of providing security for the countryside using their own troops rather than coordinating their efforts closely with the RVNAF." History Notes, 20 October 1965, Box 12, Military Papers, WPUSC.

67. Ho Chi Minh quoted in Chester L. Cooper, *The Lost Crusade: America in Vietnam* (New York: Dodd, Mead, 1970), 294. On US assumptions, see *The Pentagon Papers*, IV, 296. Westmoreland did realize that the enemy's strategy was "designed to continue a protracted war." Assessment of the Enemy Situation, 23 February 1967, Box 6, Paul L. Miles Papers, MHI.

68. Concept of Military Operations in SVN, 26 August 1966, Historian's Files, US Strategy, Vietnam, 1965–76, CMH. On Hanoi's loss of initiative, see George L. MacGarrigle, *Taking the Offensive: October 1966 to October 1967* (Washington, DC: Center of Military History, 1998), 18; Nguyen, *Hanoi's War*, 76–78; and Ang Cheng Guan, *The Vietnam War from the Other Side: The Vietnamese Communists' Perspective* (New York: Routledge Curzon, 2002), 110–111.

69. Westmoreland quoted in *The Pentagon Papers*, IV: 331. On linking military operations to RD, see Westmoreland to Wheeler, 30 October 1967, Box 6, Paul L. Miles Papers, MHI. That October, McNamara noted that "while American forces had succeeded in preventing a North Vietnamese military victory they had failed to translate their success into the 'end products' that counted." In Lewy, *America in Vietnam*, 77.

70. "Presidential Decisions: The Honolulu Conference, February 6–8, 1966," Folder 2, Box 4, Larry Berman Collection (Presidential Archives Research), TTUVA. John T. Wheeler, "Only a Fourth of South Viet Nam Is under Control of Saigon Regime," *Washington Star*, 25 January 1966.

71. "1966 Program to Increase the Effectiveness of Military Operations and Anticipated Results Thereof," 8 February 1966, Incl. 6, Folder 4, Reel 6, WCWP. See also *FRUS, 1964–1968*, IV: 216–219. Westmoreland took to heart the importance of rural construction. See MACV Commander's Conference, 20 February 1966, Counter VCI Folder, Historian's Files, CMH.

72. Charles Mohr, "U.S. Forces Frustrated in Political Aspects of Vietnamese War," *New York Times*, 29 June 1966. Spoiling attacks in Westmoreland to Sharp, 22 November 1966, Folder 6, Box 2, Official Correspondence, Series I, W. C. Westmoreland Collection, MHI; Concept of Military Operations, 26 August 1966, Box 6, Paul L. Miles Papers, MHI; and JCS History, Part II, JCSHO, 33–6. Davidson, *Vietnam at War*, 365.

73. On numerous metrics, see Gregory A. Daddis, *No Sure Victory: Measuring U.S. Army Effectiveness and Progress in the Vietnam War* (New York: Oxford University Press, 2011). On problems with spoiling attacks, see McNamara, *In Retrospect*, 237; and Larry Berman, *Lyndon Johnson's War: The Road to Stalemate in Vietnam* (New York: W.W. Norton, 1989), 13. Graham Cosmas argues persuasively that attrition "was in reality more an objective and measurement of progress than a concept that shaped the deployment and maneuver of forces at theater and corps level." *MACV*, 399.

74. Johnson quoted in Andrew J. Birtle, "PROVN, Westmoreland, and the Historians: A Reappraisal," *Journal of Military History*, Vol. 72, No. 4 (October 2008): 1216.

75. Deputy Chief of Staff for Military Operations, "A Program for the Pacification and Long-Term Development of South Vietnam (Department of the Army, March 1966), 1, 3. (Hereafter cited as PROVN.) See also Richard A. Hunt, *Pacification: The American Struggle for Vietnam's Hearts and Minds* (Boulder, CO: Westview Press, 1995), 75.

76. On no new ideas, see Austin Long, *Doctrine of Eternal Recurrence: The U.S. Military and Counterinsurgency Doctrine, 1960–1970 and 2003–2006* (Santa Monica, CA: Rand Corporation, 2008), 11. The debate over PROVN remains contentious. For the "missed opportunity" thesis, see Lewis Sorley, "To Change a War: General Harold K. Johnson and the PROVN Study," *Parameters*, Vol. 28, No. 1 (Spring 1998): 93–109. For a more persuasive, scholarly treatment see Birtle, "PROVN, Westmoreland, and the Historians: A Reappraisal," and Dale Andrade, "Westmoreland Was Right: Learning Wrong Lessons from the Vietnam War," *Small Wars & Insurgencies*, Vol. 19, No. 2 (June 2008): 145–181.

77. PROVN, 106. See also *The Pentagon Papers*, II: 577–578. Robert W. Komer recalled that "none of these studies were coordinated with the GVN." *Organization and Management of the "New Model" Pacification Program—1966–1969* (Santa Monica, CA: Rand, 1970), 32.

78. Volney Warner, email to author, 9 February 2012. PROVN implementation in Gibbons, *The U.S. Government and the Vietnam War*, IV: 212.

79. PROVN, 49, 54. MACV did set up a special subcommand called "Tiger Hound" which specifically concerned itself with infiltration routes from Laos. Tiger Hound had the authority to "devastate all eastern reaches of the Ho Chi Minh Trail in Laos, and to intercept all traffic before it gets into south Viet Nam." Telegram from Embassy in Laos to Department of State, 3 January 1966, *FRUS, 1964–1968*: XXVIII, Laos: Document 216. Operation Shining Brass, approved on 20 September 1965, also allowed for "penetrations by small, 10-man (later 11-man) teams including not more than 3 US personnel to a maximum depth of 20 kilometers west of the border for intelligence/reconnaissance patrols in the southern Laos panhandle." *FRUS, 1964–1968*: XXVIII, Laos: Document 270.

80. Command History, USMACV, 1966, NARA, 340. *FRUS, 1964–1968*, IV: 605. See also Cosmas, *MACV*, 400–401.

81. Concept of Military Operations in South Vietnam, 26 August 1966, Folder 3, Box 5, Larry Berman Collection (Presidential Archives Research), TTUVA. Westmoreland to Sharp, Strategy and Concept of Operations for 1967, Historian's Files, CMH.

82. MACV Staff, Blueprint for Vietnam, 1967, General Holdings, MHI, p. 1725. See also Command History, USMACV, 1966, NARA, 348, and Gibbons, *The U.S. Government and the Vietnam War*, IV, 405. On parallel wars concept, see Eric Bergerud, "The Village War in Vietnam, 1965–1973," in *The Columbia History of the Vietnam War*, ed. David L. Anderson (New York: Columbia University Press, 2011), 278.

83. White House Press Conference, 5 February 1966, Folder 9, Box 1, John Prados Collection, TTUVA. Command History, USMACV, 1967, NARA, 109. Westmoreland to Sharp and Wheeler, 17 February 1967, Historian's Files, CMH. See also Blueprint for Vietnam, MHI, 1721. A 7 July 1966 National Intelligence Estimate believed the total infiltration for 1966 would be between 55,000 and 75,000 enemy soldiers. *FRUS, 1964–1968*, IV: 489. ON COMUSMACV recommending expanded operations in Laos, see *FRUS, 1964–1968*: XXVIII, Laos: Document 308.

84. *Southeast Asia Analysis Report*, March 1967, MHI, 5. "How Big Is the Enemy?" *Chicago Tribune*, 23 December 1967. On problems of accurately assessing rates, see Command History, USMACV, 1965, NARA, 11. John Prados, *The Blood Road: The Ho Chi Minh Trail and the Vietnam War* (New York: John Wiley, 1999), 19. Charles Wolf Jr., *Insurgency and Counterinsurgency: New Myths and Old Realities* (Santa Monica, CA: Rand Corporation, 1965), 20.

85. Samuel A. Adams, interview by Ted Gittinger, 20 September 1984, LBJL, I-3. Thomas C. Thayer, *War without Fronts: The American Experience in Vietnam* (Boulder, CO: Westview Press, 1985), 28. Thomas C. Thayer, "How to Analyze a War without Fronts: Vietnam, 1965–72," *Journal of Defense Research, Series B: Tactical Warfare*, Vol. 7B, No. 3 (Fall 1975): 785. Duiker, *Sacred War*, 142.

86. James J. Wirtz, "Intelligence to Please? The Order of Battle Controversy during the Vietnam War," *Political Science Quarterly*, Vol. 106, No. 2 (Summer 1991): 256. On the debate from

the CIA perspective, see Sam Adams, "Vietnam Cover-Up: Playing War with Numbers," *Harper's*, Vol. 250, No. 1500 (May 1975): 41–73; and Sam Adams, *War of Numbers: An Intelligence Memoir* (South Royalton, VT: Steerforth Press, 1994).

87. Abrams to Wheeler, Sharp, and Westmoreland, 20 August 1967, Folder 3, Box 6, Official Correspondence, Series I, W. C. Westmoreland Collection, MHI. On numbers and political pressure, see Affidavit of David Halberstam, Folder 42, Box 1, Larry Berman Collection (Westmoreland vs. CBS), TTUVA, p. 19. On relation of infiltration to US bombing, see Milstein, *Dynamics of the Vietnam War*, 44.

88. Compromise in Wirtz, "Intelligence to Please?" 252. MACV reported the number as 282,000 in the summer of 1966. Charles Mohr, "Foe Put at 282,000 in South Vietnam," *New York Times*, 10 August 1966. On intelligence inadequacies, see R. W. Komer, *Bureaucracy Does Its Thing: Institutional Constraints on U.S.-GVN Performance in Vietnam* (Santa Monica, CA: Rand, 1972), 59.

89. "Vietnam: How Long a War?" *Los Angeles Times*, 10 August 1966. Pustay, *Counterinsurgency Warfare*, 86. On village war, see Bernard B. Fall, *Viet-Nam Witness: 1953–66* (New York: Frederick A. Praeger, 1966), 198.

90. 1st Cavalry troop Mark Smith quoted in Stanley Karnow, *Vietnam: A History* (New York: Viking Press, 1983), 468. On importance of RD, see Command History, USMACV, 1967, NARA, 323. Clearly MACV understood the role of villagers, many officers focusing their attention on the province level intelligence effort. See Colonel Arndt L. Mueller, Senior Officer Debriefing Reports, 15 July 1967, Box 12, RG 472, NARA, p. 3.

91. Bunker to Johnson, 21 June 1967, Folder 23, Box 1, Veteran Members of the 109th Quartermaster Company Collection, TTUVA. State Department criticisms in *The Pentagon Papers*, IV: 398.

92. Westmoreland to Wheeler, Sharp, 2 January 1967, *FRUS, 1964–1968*, V: 5. Casualty figures in Gerard J. DeGroot, *A Noble Cause? America and the Vietnam War* (Harlow, Essex: Longman, 2000), 157. Hanoi Politburo perspectives in Nguyen, *Hanoi's War*, 76–80. For a rather optimistic report from the JCS, see 14 October 1966 memorandum to the Secretary of Defense, Folder 10, Box 5, Larry Berman Collection (Presidential Archives Research), TTUVA. Still, the report noted that the Chiefs could not "predict with confidence that the war can be brought to an end in two years."

93. Charles F. Brower, IV, "Strategic Reassessment in Vietnam: The Westmoreland 'Alternate Strategy' of 1967–1968," *Naval War College Review*, Vol. 44, No. 2 (Spring 1991): 26–31. Special Communications, Westmoreland to Sharp, January 1967, Reel 8, Folder 12 History File, 13 Dec 66–26 Jan 67, WCWP. McNamara alternatively proposed building a fortified barrier line between Laos and South Vietnam. See Prados, *The Blood Road*, 213–214; and Thomas G. Mahnken, *Technology and the American Way of War* (New York: Columbia University Press, 2008), 107–113.

94. JCS to COMUSMACV, 14 December 1966, Reel 18, CSA Statements Folder, Oct–Dec 66, WCWP. It is important to note, these tasks were in order. On troop requests, see *FRUS, 1964–1968*, V: 253–255.

95. USMACV Quarterly Evaluation Report, December 1967, MHI, 4–5; and JCS History, Part III, JCSHO, 42-1–42-2. Rice denial operations in Rosson to Westmoreland, 9 October 1967, Folder 7, Box 6, Official Correspondence, Series I, W. C. Westmoreland Collection, MHI. On few alternatives, see Schandler, *The Unmaking of a President*, 62.

96. Enthoven quoted in Gibbons, *The U.S. Government and the Vietnam War*, IV, 627. "Westmoreland Reports No End of War in Sight," *New York Times*, 15 April 1967. Walter Lippman, "Today and Tomorrow: An Insoluble War?" *Washington Post*, 2 May 1967. Ward Just, "This War May Be Unwinnable," *Washington Post*, 4 June 1967. R. W. Apple Jr., "Vietnam: Signs of Stalemate," *New York Times*, 7 August 1967.

97. Westmoreland to Wheeler, Johnson, Sharp, 1 August 1967, Folder 29, Box 1, Veteran Members of the 109th Quartermaster Company Collection, TTUVA. Undersecretary of Defense Nicholas Katzenbach wrote the president in November that the "war can be lost in the United States." Memorandum to the President, 16 November 1967, Folder 19, Box 2, Veteran Members of the 109th Quartermaster Company Collection, TTUVA.

98. W.W. Rostow, *The Diffusion of Power: An Essay in Recent History* (New York: Macmillan, 1972), 512. On the relationship between the war effort and the home front, see Charles DeBenedetti with Charles Chatfield, *An American Ordeal: The Antiwar Movement of the Vietnam Era* (Syracuse: Syracuse University Press, 1990), 177; and David Maraniss, *They Marched into Sunlight: War and Peace, Vietnam and America October 1967* (New York: Simon and Schuster, 2003), 196.

99. Joint News Conference, 17 July 1967, Folder 10, Box 08, Douglas Pike Collection: Unit 01—Assessment and Strategy, TTUVA. Peter Grose, "War of Attrition Called Effective by Westmoreland," *New York Times*, 20 November 1967. See also Robert Mann, *A Grand Delusion: America's Descent into Vietnam* (New York: Basic Books, 2001), 548. On selling the war, see Berman, *Lyndon Johnson's War*, 84. Pressure on Westmoreland to report progress in Wheeler to Westmoreland, Johnson, 2 August 1967, Folder 1, Box 6, Official Correspondence, Series I, W. C. Westmoreland Collection, MHI; and Wheeler to Westmoreland, 31 October 1967, Folder 9, Box 6, Official Correspondence, Series I, W. C. Westmoreland Collection, MHI.

100. On credibility gap, see Gibbons, *The U.S. Government and the Vietnam War*, IV, 844. On Westmoreland's beliefs, see William C. Westmoreland, interview by Paul L. Miles, 7 January 1971, Box 1, Paul L. Miles Papers, MHI.

101. Harold K. Johnson, "Vietnam—Progress or Stalemate?" *Army Digest*, Vol. 22, No. 12 (December 1967): 6–7. Of note, the article ran under the byline "The Chief of Staff sets the record straight."

102. Gibbons, *The U.S. Government and the Vietnam War*, IV: 929. Blueprint for Vietnam, MHI, p. 1725. Willard Pearson, Post Mortem on Vietnam Strategy, 6 September 1968, Historian's Files, US Strategy, Vietnam, 1965–1975, CMH, 2.

103. Harold K. Johnson, Validity of Present Strategy of Operations in South Vietnam, 1 February 1968, Folder 3, Box 76, Series I, Official Correspondence, Harold K. Johnson Collection, MHI, p. 4. L. F. Chapman, Strategy for the Conduct of the War in SEASIA, 2 February 1968, Folder 3, Box 76, Series I, Official Correspondence, Harold K. Johnson Collection, MHI, p. 4. On non-military roles in the 1968 campaign plan, see Command History, USMACV, 1968, NARA, p. 21 and Westmoreland to Sharp, 10 December 1967, Reel 12, History File #26, 29 Nov–16 Dec 67, WCWP.

104. Quoted in Tom Wicker, "Vietcong's Attacks Shock Washington," *New York Times*, 2 February 1968.

105. Clark M. Clifford, "A Viet Nam Reappraisal," *Foreign Affairs*, Vol. 47, No. 4 (July 1969): 612. Hanoi's reaction to Tet in Nguyen, *Hanoi's War*, 112. On Clark, see also *FRUS*, 1964–1968, VI: 167 and Schandler, *The Unmaking of a President*, 241–255. Overestimating Hanoi's will in William E. DePuy, interview by Les Brownlee and Bill Mullen, 26 March 1979, Box 1, William E. DePuy Papers, MHI, 21.

106. Abrams and Wheeler meeting with the president, 26 March 1968, *FRUS*, 1964–1968, VI: 463.

107. Douglas Kinnard quoted in Christian G. Appy, *Patriots: The Vietnam War Remembered from All Sides* (New York: Viking, 2003), 322. Kinnard's point, however, is worth viewing with a critical eye. Certainly, the communists fought hard, but they did not fight equally hard everywhere all the time, and they were not capable of fighting hard forever, despite what their propaganda declared. Equally of note, statements like those from Kinnard became a convenient way for at least some senior army officers to avoid acknowledging their own strategic and tactical shortcomings during the war.

108. Taylor, 6 January 1965, *FRUS*, 1964–1968, II: 13. See also The BDM Corporation, "A Study of Strategic Lessons Learned in Vietnam," Volume II, South Vietnam, General Holdings, MHI, p. EX-2. For an alternative explanation that Westmoreland failed to consider the implications if Hanoi was not deterred, see Gordon M. Goldstein, *Lessons in Disaster: McGeorge Bundy and the Path to War in Vietnam* (New York: Times Books, 2008), 177.

109. Professor Eugenia C. Kiesling, United States Military Academy Department of History, aided in the development of this point on the poverty of strategic language. On various aspects of war, see Phillip Davidson, interview by Ted Gittinger, 30 March 1982, LBJL, I-75; and Larry H. Addington, *America's War in Vietnam: A Short Narrative History* (Bloomington: Indiana University Press, 2000), 172.

Chapter 4

1. Sharp to Wheeler, 22 September 1965, in William Conrad Gibbons, *The U.S. Government and the Vietnam War: Executive and Legislative Roles and Relationships, Part IV: July 1965–January 1968* (Washington, DC: US Government Printing Office, 1994), 75.

2. Westmoreland quoted in "Excerpts from Speeches by Ky and Westmoreland at Manila," *New York Times*, 25 October 1966.

3. Wesley R. Fischel, ed., *Vietnam: Anatomy of a Conflict* (Itasca, IL: F.E. Peacock,1968), 495. For similar critiques on the American use of firepower, see Robert A. Doughty, *The Evolution of US Army Tactical Doctrine, 1946–1976* (Fort Leavenworth, KS: Combat Studies Institute, 1979), 38; Guenter Lewy, *America in Vietnam* (New York: Oxford University Press, 1978), 46; and Robert L. Gallucci, *Neither Peace nor Honor: The Politics of American Military Policy in Viet-Nam* (Baltimore, MD: Johns Hopkins University Press, 1975), 116. Tactics permitting strategic success in Hew Strachan, *Clausewitz's On War: A Biography* (New York: Atlantic Monthly Press, 2007), 117. On interrelationships between tactics and strategy, see Colin S. Gray, *Modern Strategy* (New York: Oxford University Press, 1999), 38.

4. John Nagl, *Learning to Eat Soup with a Knife: Counterinsurgency Lessons from Malaya and Vietnam* (Chicago: University of Chicago Press, 2002), 176, 199, 201. Nagl resolved to shoehorn the American experience into a narrowly constructed social science model without thoroughly analyzing how the army conducted operations on a daily basis, instead preferring to argue, without much countervailing evidence, that army leaders chose not to learn in their new environment. Collins, "Concept for Operations," Arthur S. Collins Jr. Papers, Box 5, MHI, p. 3. Tactics as politics in Anthony James Joes, *Resisting Rebellion: The History and Politics of Counterinsurgency* (Lexington: University Press of Kentucky, 2004, 2006), 243.

5. Command History, United States Military Assistance Command, 1965, Entry MACJ03, Box 1, RG 472, NARA, 161. Shelby L. Stanton, *The Rise and Fall of an American Army: U.S. Ground Forces in Vietnam, 1965–1973* (Novato, CA: Presidio, 1985), 82.

6. MACV Directive 525-4, Tactics and Techniques for Employment of US Forces in the Republic of Vietnam, 17 September 1965, Vietnam Tactics & Techniques In Country Publications Folder, Historian's Files, CMH. Warren Wilkins, *Grab Their Belts to Fight Them: The Viet Cong's Big Unit War against the U.S., 1965–1966* (Annapolis, MD: Naval Institute Press, 2011), 138–139. For an opposing view, Loren Baritz argues "there was no strategy, the tactics were everything." *Backfire: A History of How American Culture Led Us into Vietnam and Made Us Fight the Way We Did* (Baltimore, MD: Johns Hopkins University Press, 1985), 277.

7. Ward Just, *To What End: Report from Vietnam* (Boston: Houghton Mifflin, 1968; New York: Public Affairs, 2000), 108. See also William J. Duiker, *The Communist Road to Power*, 2nd ed. (Boulder, CO: Westview Press, 1996), 210. On body counts, see Ron Milam, *Not a Gentleman's War: An Inside View of Junior Officers in the Vietnam War* (Chapel Hill: University of North Carolina Press, 2009), 97. Difficulties in adjusting in Bruce Palmer Jr., *The 25-Year War: America's Military Role in Vietnam* (Lexington: University Press of Kentucky, 1984), 156.

8. Process in W. Warner Burke, *Organization Change: Theory and Practice* (Thousand Oaks, CA: Sage, 2002), 14. Military operations in USMACV Guide for Province and District Advisors, 1 February 1968, CMH, 13–1. Micheal Clodfelter notes that "U.S. troops were forced to develop a wide variety of tactical approaches to the special problems of the war in Vietnam." *Vietnam in Military Statistics: A History of the Indochina Wars 1772–1991* (Jefferson, NC: McFarland, 1995), 77. Planning, of course, does not equal execution. Just because a higher level staff plans for a broad counterinsurgency campaign does not mean field units fully understand the plan or are willing to follow it.

9. Westmoreland quoted in "Victory Still Far Off, Says U.S. Viet Chief," *Chicago Tribune*, 25 November 1965. Tactical defined in Department of the Army, *Army Regulations 320-5, Dictionary of United States Army Terms* (Washington, DC: January 1961), 558.

10. Zeb B. Bradford, "US Tactics in Vietnam," *Military Review*, Vol. 52, No. 2 (February 1972): 85. Randall B. Woods argues otherwise, noting that Westmoreland's was "a rigid, unwieldy strategy that did not permit adaptation to varying local conditions…and failed to take into

account the complex political and cultural divisions in Vietnam." *Shadow Warrior: William Egan Colby and the CIA* (New York: Basic Books, 2013), 255.

11. Andrew F. Krepinevich Jr., *The Army and Vietnam* (Baltimore, MD: Johns Hopkins University Press, 1986), 169. For reviews, see Bob Buzzanco, *Political Science Quarterly*, Vol. 102, No. 1 (Spring, 1987): 148–149; and Ronald H. Spector, *International Security*, Vol. 11, No. 4 (Spring, 1987): 130–134.

12. For counterarguments on the constraining nature of culture, see Richard Lock-Pullan, *US Intervention Policy and Army Innovation: From Vietnam to Iraq* (London: Routledge, 2006), 8; and Adrian R. Lewis, *The American Culture of War: The History of U.S. Military Force from World War II to Operation Iraqi Freedom* (New York: Routledge, 2007), 8.

13. George Donelson Moss, *Vietnam: An American Ordeal*, 5th ed. (Upper Saddle River, NJ: Pearson Prentice Hill, 1990, 2006), 211. Robert B. Asprey, *War in the Shadows: The Guerrilla in History* (Garden City, NY: Doubleday, 1975), 1112. See also J. D. Coleman, ed., *Memoirs of the First Team: Vietnam, August 1965–December 1969* (Tokyo: Dia Nippon Printing, 1970).

14. Shelby L. Stanton, *Anatomy of a Division: The 1st Cav in Vietnam* (Novato, CA: Presidio, 1987), 45. Duiker, *The Communist Road to Power*, 259. Urged on by Army Vice Chief of Staff Creighton Abrams, the 1st Cav's division commander, Harry Kinnard, wanted to press into the panhandle of Laos to stop infiltration. Westmoreland had to explain that "such a plan was not in the cards in the foreseeable future because of complex political and other considerations." History Notes, 29 August 1965, Box 12, Military Papers, WPUSC.

15. Lodge to State, 26 August 1965, FRUS, 1964–1968, III: 346. MACV estimate in "MACV Concept of Operations in the Republic of Vietnam," 30 August 1965, Historian's Files, CMH, A-1. See also JCS History, JCSHO, 17–3.

16. Man quoted in Wilkins, *Grab Their Belts to Fight Them*, 92. See also Merle L. Pribbenow, "The Fog of War: The Vietnamese View of the Ia Drang Battle," *Military Review*, Vol. 81, No. 1 (January–February 2001): 93–97.

17. Robert Thompson, "Feet on the Ground," *Survival*, Vol. 8, No. 4 (April 1966): 117. J. D. Coleman, *Pleiku: The Dawn of Helicopter Warfare in Vietnam* (New York: St. Martin's Press, 1988), 93. On making the transition from a nuclear battlefield, see Thomas G. Mahnken, *Technology and the American Way of War* (New York: Columbia University Press, 2008), 89; John M. Carland, "How We Got There: Air Assault and the Emergence of the 1st Cavalry Division (Airmobile), 1950–1965," *The Land Warfare Papers*, No. 42 (May 2003); and John J. Tolson, *Airmobility, 1961–1971* (Washington, DC: US Government Printing Office, 1973).

18. Westmoreland to Wheeler, 18 August 1965, Box 5, Paul L. Miles Papers, MHI. Limiting civilian casualties in MACV Command History, 1965, NARA, 161; and Mark Moyar, *Phoenix and the Birds of Prey: Counterinsurgency and Counterterrorism in Vietnam* (Lincoln: University of Nebraska Press, 1997, 2007), 286.

19. History Notes, 6 October 1965, Box 12, Military Papers, WPUSC.

20. For a general history on this topic, see John Schlight, *The War in South Vietnam: The Years of the Offensive, 1965–1968* (Washington, DC: Office of Air Force History, 1988). See also Larry Cable, "The Operation Was a Success, but the Patient Died: The Air War in Vietnam, 1964–1969," in *An American Dilemma: Vietnam, 1964–1973*, ed. Dennis E. Showalter and John G. Albert (Chicago: Imprint, 1993), 109–158.

21. Villager in David Hunt, *Vietnam's Southern Revolution: From Peasant Insurrection to Total War* (Amherst: University of Massachusetts Press, 2008), 208. On linkages to population, see Matthew Adam Kocher, Thomas B. Pepinsky, and Stathis N. Kalyvas, "Aerial Bombing and Counterinsurgency in the Vietnam War," *American Journal of Political Science*, Vol. 55, No. 2 (April 2011): 201–218.

22. Jack P. Smith, "Death in the Ia Drang Valley," *Saturday Evening Post*, Vol. 240, No. 2 (28 January 1967): 83. William C. Westmoreland, *A Soldier Reports* (Garden City, NY: Doubleday, 1976), 190. On battle, see Harry G. Summers Jr., "The Bitter Triumph of Ia Drang," *American Heritage* (February–March 1984): 51–58; and Harold G. Moore and Joseph L. Galloway, *We Were Soldiers Once... and Young* (New York: HarperCollins, 1993).

23. Body counts in Gregory A. Daddis, *No Sure Victory: Measuring U.S. Army Effectiveness and Progress in the Vietnam War* (New York: Oxford University Press, 2011), 80. See also Harry W. O. Kinnard, "A Victory in the Ia Drang: The Triumph of a Concept," *Army*, Vol. 17, No. 9 (September 1967): 71–91.

24. Robert S. McNamara, *In Retrospect: The Tragedy and Lessons of Vietnam* (New York: Times Books, 1995), 222. Westmoreland quoted in "Westmoreland Surveys Action," *New York Times*, 20 November 1965. Gibbons, *The U.S. Government and the Vietnam War*, IV, 101–107.

25. McNamara quoted in Moore, *We Were Soldiers Once*, 400. On problems inside the 1st Cav, see Hanson W. Baldwin, "U.S. First Cavalry Is Sternly Tested," *New York Times*, 20 November 1965. Gerard J. DeGroot, *A Noble Cause? America and the Vietnam War* (Harlow, Essex: Longman, 2000), 148.

26. Grave doubts in Chester L. Cooper, *The Lost Crusade: America in Vietnam* (New York: Dodd, Mead, 1970), 288. Wilkins, *Grab Their Belts to Fight Them*, 116. On NLF/NVA tactics, see Michael Lee Lanning and Dan Cragg, *Inside the VC and the NVA: The Real Story of North Vietnam's Armed Forces* (New York: Fawcett Columbine, 1992), 173–179.

27. Operations Report, Lessons Learned, 3–66, The Pleiku Campaign, 10 May 1966, CMH Library, 224. A similar report noted the "inadequacy of conventional military concepts and principles…when applied to insurgency-type wars." The Army Land Warfare Lab at Aberdeen Proving Ground, "Mobility in Counterinsurgency Warfare," November 1966, Digital Archive Collection, USAAWCL. Guenter Lewy, "Some Political-Military Lessons of the Vietnam War," in *Assessing the Vietnam War: A Collection from the Journal of the U.S. Army War College*, ed. Lloyd J. Matthews and Dale E. Brown (Washington, DC: Pergamon-Brassey's International Defense Publishers, 1987), 148.

28. Westmoreland to Wheeler, 11 November 1965, Pacification Folder, Box 4, Paul L. Miles Papers, MHI. Operational Report—Lessons Learned, 1st Cavalry Division, 28 November 1966, Box 1, 1st Cavalry Division OR/LL, MACV Command Historian's Collection, MHI, 29–31.

29. COMUSMACV memorandum, "Increased Emphasis on Rural Construction," 8 December 1965, Correspondence, 1965–1966, Box 35, Jonathan O. Seaman Papers, MHI.

30. Operational Report—Lessons Learned, 1 May–31 July 1966, 1st Infantry Division, 15 August 1966, Box 1, 1st Infantry Division OR/LL, MACV Command Historian's Collection, MHI, 4. "A Summary of Lessons Learned," 30 June 1966, Vol. 2, USARV Battlefield Reports, Box 1, RG 472, NARA. Quarterly Command Report, 31 December 1965, 1st Infantry Division, Box 8, USARV Command History OR/LL, RG472, NARA, 13. James Scott Wheeler, *The Big Red One: America's Legendary 1st Infantry Division from World War I to Desert Storm* (Lawrence: University Press of Kansas, 2007), 419. John M. Carland, *Stemming the Tide: May 1965 to October 1966* (Washington, DC: Center of Military History, 2000), 68.

31. Operational Report—Lessons Learned, 1 January–30 April 1966, 1st Infantry Division, Box 1, 1st Infantry Division OR/LL, MACV Command Historian's Collection, MHI, 24. 1st Infantry Division OR/LL, 1 May–31 July 1966, In-Country Documents, 1st Infantry Division, Historian's Files, CMH. William E. DePuy, interview by Les Brownlee and Bill Mullen, 26 March 1979, Box 1, William E. DePuy Papers, MHI, 4

32. Commanders Notes, 27 March 1966, In-Country Documents, 1st Infantry Division, Historian's Files, CMH.

33. Commanders Notes, 27 March 1966. See also Wheeler, *The Big Red One*, 432. Westmoreland noted in his journal that DePuy "feels that military power is the overwhelming force in influencing the people of the hamlet to abandon the Viet Cong." General Westmoreland's Historical Briefing, 25 February 1967, Folder 13, History File, Reel 8, WCWP.

34. Malcolm W. Browne, *The New Face of War*, rev. ed. (Indianapolis: Bobbs-Merrill, 1968), 164–165. Albert N. Garland, ed., *Infantry in Vietnam: Small Unit Actions in the Early Days: 1965–66* (Nashville, TN: Battery Press, 1982), 69. On problems finding the enemy, see Department of the Army Pamphlet No. 350-15-9, *Training, Operations—Lessons Learned*, 1 April 1968, MHI, 32; and Anthony Harrigan, "Ground Warfare in Vietnam," *Military Review* Vol. 47, No. 4 (April 1967): 82.

35. Micheal Clodfelter, *Mad Minutes and Vietnam Months: A Soldier's Memoir* (Jefferson, NC: McFarland, 1988), 85. Soldier's helmet in Coleman, *Pleiku*, 102. "Met anywhere" in

Department of the Army Pamphlet No. 525-2, *Vietnam Primer: Lessons Learned*, 21 April 1967, MHI, 25.

36. Wheeler, *The Big Red One*, 425. Intelligence collection frustrations in Lessons Learned, 15 March 1966, 1st Infantry Division, Box 1, 1st Infantry Division OR/LL, MACV Command Historian's Collection, MHI; and James R. Ebert, *A Life in a Year: The American Infantryman in Vietnam, 1965–1972* (Novato, CA: Presidio, 1993), 178–179.

37. W. C. Westmoreland, Tactical Employment of US Forces and Defensive Action, 1966 Folder, Box 4, William E. DePuy Papers, MHI.

38. MACV Directive 525-3, Combat Operations Minimizing Non-Combatant Battle Casualties, 7 September 1965, MACV Directives, Command Historian Collection, MHI. See also Operational Report—Lessons Learned, 1 January–30 April 1966, 1st Infantry Division, MHI, p. 1; and Lessons Learned, 15 March 1966, 1st Infantry Division, MHI, 8.

39. John H. Hay Jr., *Tactical and Materiel Innovations* (Washington, DC: US Government Printing Office, 2002), 137–141.

40. 1st Infantry Division OR/LL ending 31 Oct 66, Box 8, USARV Command History OR/LL, RG472, NARA.

41. Operational Report—Lessons Learned, 1 January–30 April 1966, 1st Infantry Division, MHI, 5. Combat Operations Report, 1st Brigade, 1st Infantry Division, 28 March 1966, Folder 58, Box 01, William E. LeGro Collection, TTUVA. Operational Report—Lessons Learned, 1 May–31 July 1966, 1st Infantry Division, MHI.

42. Combat Operations Report, 1st Brigade, 1st Infantry Division, 28 March 1966, TTUVA, 16.

43. On Attleboro, see Romie L. Brownlee and William J. Mullen III, *Changing an Army: An Oral History of General William E. DePuy, USA Retired* (Carlisle Barracks, PA: US Military History Institute, 1986), Box 1, William E. DePuy Papers, MHI, ps. 144–146; Wheeler, *The Big Red One*, 440–450; and Spencer C. Tucker, *Vietnam* (Lexington: University Press of Kentucky, 1999), 131. On order of battle, see *Southeast Asia Analysis Report*, February 1967, MHI, 4.

44. 25th Division Pacification Operations in Hau Nghia Province, 7 August 1966, US 25th Division Pacification Folder, Historian's Files, CMH. Eric M. Bergerud, *Red Thunder, Tropic Lightning: The World of a Combat Division in Vietnam* (Boulder, CO: Westview Press, 1993), 221. Shelby L. Stanton, *Vietnam Order of Battle: A Complete Illustrated Reference to U.S. Army Combat and Support Forces in Vietnam, 1961–1973* (Mechanicsburg, PA: Stackpole Books, 2003), 81.

45. Soldier quoted in Bergerud, *Red Thunder, Tropic Lightning*, 31. Carland, *Stemming the Tide*, 338–339. Richard A. Hunt, *Pacification: The American Struggle for Vietnam's Hearts and Minds* (Boulder, CO: Westview Press, 1995), 49–50.

46. Westmoreland to Wheeler, 20 February 1966, Box 6, Paul L. Miles Papers, MHI.

47. Civil and Military Structure of South Vietnam Lesson Plan, "Counter VC Tips," 18 February 1966, In-Country Publications Folder, Historian's Files, CMH. Louis A. Wiesner, *Victims and Survivors: Displaced Persons and Other War Victims in Viet-Nam, 1954–1975* (Westport, CT: Greenwood Press, 1988), 72. Stanton, *The Rise and Fall of an American Army*, 98.

48. Weyand quoted in Carland, *Stemming the Tide*, 344. Fred C. Weyand, "Winning the People in Hau Nghia Province," *Army*, Vol. 17, No. 1 (January 1967): 53.

49. Westmoreland quoted in Jeffrey J. Clarke, *Advice and Support: The Final Years, 1965–1973* (Washington, DC: Center of Military History, 1988), 184. CLIP in Boyd T. Bashore, "Revolutionary Development Support in the Republic of Vietnam: Tropic Lightning Helping Hand and 'The Other War,'" 19 January 1968, Student Essay, US Army War College, MHI, 19–20.

50. Soldier quoted in Bergerud, *Red Thunder, Tropic Lightning*, 221.Hunt, *Pacification*, 50. On cultural misunderstandings, see Lt. Col. Erik G. Johnson, VNIT Folder 100, CMH, 8.

51. "A Program against the VC Infrastructure," 27 July 1967, Box 4, Richard M. Lee Papers, MHI, 2.

52. Soldier quoted in Bergerud, *Red Thunder, Tropic Lightning*, 222. On intelligence problems, see Larry Berman, *Lyndon Johnson's War: The Road to Stalemate in Vietnam* (New York: W.W. Norton, 1989), 14; Thomas L. Ahern Jr., *Vietnam Declassified: The CIA and Counterinsurgency* (Lexington: University Press of Kentucky, 2010), 258; and Austin Long, *The "Other War:"*

Lessons from Five Decades of RAND Counterinsurgency Research (Santa Monica, CA: Rand Corporation, 2006), 36.

53. Operational Report—Lessons Learned, 5 March 1968, Box 00, Folder 01, Bud Harton Collection, TTUVA. The division also acknowledged that major operations took forces away from civic action programs. See Operational Report for Quarterly Period Ending 30 April 1967, 25th Infantry Division OR/LL, Box 2, MACV Command Historian's Collection, MHI.

54. W. A. Knowlton to Thomas E. Griess, 12 February 1967, Vietnam Materials, Box 1, WPSC. Gabriel Kolko, *Anatomy of a War: Vietnam, the United States, and the Modern Historical Experience* (New York: Pantheon Books, 1985), 126. Sir Robert Thompson, *No Exit from Vietnam* (New York: David McKay, 1969), 32.

55. Rand Study in *Southeast Asia Analysis Report,* September 1967, MHI, 5. Role of NLF in MACV Command History, 1966, NARA, 194. Network of contacts in Frances FitzGerald, *Fire in the Lake: The Vietnamese and the Americans in Vietnam* (Boston: Little, Brown, 1972), 183.

56. COL Leonard Daems, VNIT, Folder 109A, CMH. MHI, 12-45. See also George M. Shuffer Jr., "Finish Them with Firepower," *Military Review,* Vol. 47, No. 12 (December 1967): 11–15.

57. 1LT James Simmen quoted in Bernard Edelman, ed., *Dear America: Letters Home from Vietnam* (New York: Pocket Books, 1986), 94–95. Johnson quoted in Doris Kearns, *Lyndon Johnson and the American Dream* (New York: Harper and Row, 1976), 252.

58. Phillip B. Davidson, *Vietnam at War: The History: 1946–1975* (Novato, CA: Presidio, 1988), 383. Samuel Zaffiri, *Westmoreland: A Biography of General William C. Westmoreland* (New York: William Morrow, 1994), 184–185. Westmoreland, *A Soldier Reports,* 248–251. Gibbons, *The U.S. Government and the Vietnam War,* IV, 540–545.

59. Systems Analysis View of the Vietnam War: 1965–1972, Vol. 4—Allied Ground and Naval Operations, File HRC, Geog V Vietnam 319.1, CMH, 135. 25th Infantry Division Combat Operations after Action Report, Operation Cedar Falls, 10 March 1967, Box 01, Folder 35, Ron Leonard Collection, TTUVA. Statistics in MACV Monthly Evaluation Report, January 1967, MHI, 3; and Bernard W. Rogers, *Cedar Falls-Junction City: A Turning Point* (Washington, DC: US Government Printing Office, 1974, 2004), 74. Engineers in Wheeler, *The Big Red One,* 455.

60. George L. MacGarrigle, *Taking the Offensive: October 1966 to October 1967* (Washington, DC: Center of Military History, 1998), 113–114. Stanton, *The Rise and Fall of an American Army,* 147.

61. MACV Monthly Evaluation Report, February 1967, MHI, 5. U.S. Grant Sharp and William C. Westmoreland, *Report on the War in Vietnam* (Washington, DC: US Government Printing Office, 1969), 133–134.

62. On Operation Fairfax, see MACV Command History, 1967, Part 1, Box 00, Folder 01, Bud Harton Collection, TTUVA, 383–384; MacGarrigle, *Taking the Offensive,* 155–162; and Stanton, *The Rise and Fall of an American Army,* 143–143. The Command History noted that "Cumulative enemy losses for Fairfax by the end of August 1967 included 957 VC killed and 247 weapons captured or destroyed." The NLF political infrastructure, however, remained intact.

63. Ngo Quang Truong, "RVNAF and US Operational Coordination and Cooperation," in *The Vietnam War: An Assessment by South Vietnam's Generals,* ed. Lewis Sorley (Lubbock: Texas Tech University Press, 2010), 162. On the Vietnamese "leaving everything to the Americans," see Eric M. Bergerud, *The Dynamics of Defeat: The Vietnam War in Hau Nghia Province* (Boulder, CO: Westview Press, 1991), 166. "Extended integration" in MacGarrigle, *Taking the Offensive,* 162.

64. MACV Command History, 1967, Part 1, Box 00, Folder 01, Bud Harton Collection, TTUVA, 144.

65. Rogers, *Cedar Falls-Junction City,* 158. On elusiveness, see also Robert Buzzanco, *Masters of War: Military Dissent and Politics in the Vietnam Era* (New York: Cambridge University Press, 1996), 279. Arguably, Junction City serves as a good example of just paying lip service to counterinsurgency. The operation was supposed to provide a "shield for revolutionary development" but there was no plan for American units to stay around to do that.

66. On relocation, see Samuel P. Huntington, "The Bases of Accommodation," *Foreign Affairs*, Vol. 46, No. 4 (July 1968): 649–650; Neil Sheehan, *A Bright Shining Lie: John Paul Vann and America in Vietnam* (New York: Random House, 1988), 621; David W. P. Elliott, *The Vietnamese War: Revolution and Social Change in the Mekong Delta, 1930–1975*, concise ed. (Armonk, NY: M.E. Sharpe, 2003, 2007), 227. James William Gibson notes that Robert Komer wanted to "step up refugee programs deliberately aimed at depriving the VC of a recruiting base." *The Perfect War: Technowar in Vietnam* (New York: Vintage Books, 1986), 228. Socioeconomic dislocation in Robert K. Brigham, "Vietnamese Society at War," in *The Columbia History of the Vietnam War*, ed. David L. Anderson (New York: Columbia University Press, 2011), 321; and George McTurnan Kahin and John Wilson Lewis, *The United States in Vietnam*, rev. ed. (New York: Dial Press, 1969), 239.

67. "The Refugee Problem," 4 January 1968, File 28, Folder 1, Box 15, Reel 12, WCWP. For a discussion of this memorandum, see Mai Elliott, *RAND in Southeast Asia: A History of the Vietnam War Era* (Santa Monica, CA: Rand, 2010), 300–301; Elliott, *The Vietnamese War*, 335–336; and Brigham, "Vietnamese Society at War," 324.

68. On Fitzgerald and the infant mortality rate, see Nick Turse, *Kill Anything That Moves: The Real American War in Vietnam* (New York: Metropolitan Books, 2013), 146. Turse's argument that the US ground forces in South Vietnam were remorseless killing machines wielding unlimited firepower undervalues senior leaders' attempts to limit violence and protect the civilian population throughout the war.

69. Kennedy quoted in Pamela A. Conn, "Losing Hearts and Minds: U.S. Pacification Efforts in Vietnam during the Johnson Years" (Ph.D. diss., University of Houston, 2001), 22. Villager in Hunt, *Vietnam's Southern Revolution*, 129.

70. Department of the Army, Field Manual 100-5, *Field Service Regulations Operations*, February 1962, 16–17.

71. Westmoreland to Wheeler, 18 August 1965, Folder 2, Box 18, Official Correspondence, Series 1, W. C. Westmoreland Collection, MHI. Ideological and political confrontation in Rupert Smith, *The Utility of Force: The Art of War in the Modern World* (New York: Alfred A. Knopf, 2007), 240. See also Peter M. Dawkins, "The United States Army and the 'Other' War in Vietnam: A Study of the Complexity of Implementing Organizational Change" (Ph.D. diss., Princeton University, 1979), 22.

72. Phillip B. Davidson, *Secrets of the Vietnam War* (Novato, CA: Presidio Press, 1990), 20.

73. Roster of 4th Infantry commanders in Stanton, *Vietnam Order of Battle*, 75. On techniques varying widely, see Gordon L. Rottman, "Tactics in a Different War: Adapting US Doctrine," in *Rolling Thunder in a Gentle Land: The Vietnam War Revisited*, ed. Andrew Wiest (New York: Osprey, 2006), 259.

74. Westmoreland, *A Soldier Reports*, 198. War Experiences Recapitulation Committee of the High-Level Military Institute, *The Anti-U.S. Resistance War for National Salvation 1954–1975: Military Events* (Hanoi: People's Army Publishing House, 1980), 62. On 4th Infantry initial deployments, see W. R. Peers, interview by James H. Breen and Charlie B. Moore, 13 April 1977, Senior Officers Debriefing Program, William R. Peers Papers, MHI, 37–38; and Stanton, *The Rise and Fall of an American Army*, 70.

75. Larsen quoted in MacGarrigle, *Taking the Offensive*, 67.

76. Philip D. Beidler, *Late Thoughts on an Old War: The Legacy of Vietnam* (Athens: University of Georgia Press, 2004), 14. Decentralized war from Francis West in *The Lessons of Vietnam*, ed. W. Scott Thompson and Donaldson D. Frizzell (New York: Crane, Russak, 1977), 81. On tour lengths, see Bradley D. Helton, "Revolving Door War: Former Commanders Reflect on the Impact of the Twelve-Month Tour upon their Companies in Vietnam" (Master's thesis, North Carolina State University, 2004).

77. Westmoreland, *A Soldier Reports*, 360. On critics, see David R. Holmes, "Some Tentative Thoughts after Indochina," *Military Review*, Vol. 42, No. 8 (August 1977): 85–86; Richard A. Gabriel and Paul L. Savage, *Crisis in Command: Mismanagement in the Army* (New York: Hill and Wang, 1978), 72, 137; and George C. Wilson, "Hard-Learned Lessons in a Military Laboratory" in *A Short History of the Vietnam War*, ed. Allan R. Millett (Bloomington: Indiana University Press, 1978), 64.

78. Senior Officer debriefing transcript, Box 12, William R. Peers Papers, MHI, 44.

79. Operations Report—Lessons Learned, 4th Infantry Division, 20 December 1967, Box 1, 4th Infantry Division OR/LL, MACV Command Historian's Collection, MHI, 44. Missions in Operations Report—Lessons Learned, 4th Infantry Division, 15 May 1967, Box 1, 4th Infantry Division OR/LL, MACV Command Historian's Collection, MHI, 6; and Operational Report—Lessons Learned for Quarterly Period Ending 31 January 1968, 7 March 1968, Box 1, 4th Infantry Division OR/LL, MACV Command Historian's Collection, MHI, 1–2.

80. Debriefing report, Charles P. Stone, 15 November 1968, Senior Officer Debriefing Reports, RG472, NARA. Operational Report—Lessons Learned for Quarterly Period Ending 31 January 1968, Box 1, 4th Infantry Division OR/LL, MACV Command Historian's Collection, MHI.

81. Debriefing report, Charles P. Stone, 15 November 1968, NARA.

82. Operations Report—Lessons Learned, 4th Infantry Division, 15 May 1967, MHI, 23. Operational Report—Lessons Learned for Quarterly Period Ending 31 January 1968, MHI, 51.

83. "Good Neighbor Program," "CI" File Folder, Box 1, Richard M. Lee Papers, MHI, 1.

84. On the Good Neighbor program, see Faris Kirkland, "Cultural Dynamics of Civic Action in the Central Highlands of Vietnam, 1967–1968," *Armed Forces and Society*, Vol. 26. No. 4 (Summer 2000): 547–560. Kirkland also argues that Americans "did not place a high value on long-term intercultural relations. The civic action programs were a short-term means to an end," 557.

85. Gabriel and Savage, *Crisis in Command*, 80. See also Martin van Creveld, *Command in War* (Cambridge, MA: Harvard University Press, 1985), 236; and Charles C. Moskos Jr., *Soldiers and Sociology* (United States Army Research Institute for Behavioral and Social Sciences, 1988), 7.

86. Just, *To What End*, 169.

87. Duiker, *The Communist Road to Power*, 291. Larry Cable, *Unholy Grail: The US and the wars in Vietnam, 1965–8* (London: Routledge, 1991), 195. On Dak To, see Edward F. Murphy, *Dak To: The 173d Airborne Brigade in South Vietnam's Central Highlands, June–November 1967* (Novato, CA: Presidio, 1993).

88. "The Battle for Dak To," Box 7, William R. Peers Papers, MHI. Senior Officer debriefing transcript, Box 12, William R. Peers Papers, MHI, 56–58. See also Hay, *Tactical and Materiel Innovations*, 79–80.

89. Willard Pearson, Post Mortem on Vietnam Strategy, 6 September 1968, Historian's Files, US Strategy, Vietnam, 1965–1975, CMH, 4.

90. On mixed messages, see Chris Argyris, *On Organizational Learning* (Cambridge, MA: Blackwell, 1993), 42. On "fighting a whole series of company actions," see Col. Eugene P. Forrester, VNIT Folder 206, CMH, 14.

91. MACV Monthly Evaluation Report, February 1966, MHI. On learning processes, see Jack S. Levy, "Learning and Foreign Policy: Sweeping a Conceptual Minefield," *International Organization*, Vol. 48, No. 2 (Spring 1994): 297.

92. CPT Mike Perkins quoted in Michael Takiff, *Brave Men, Gentle Heroes: American Fathers and Sons in World War II and Vietnam* (New York: Morrow, 2003), 305. This idea seemed fairly well understood at the time. See Julian Paget, *Counter-Insurgency Operations: Techniques of Guerrilla Warfare* (New York: Walker, 1967), 156.

93. Bergerud, *The Dynamics of Defeat*, 132. Yitzhak Klein, however, argues that strategy "formulates goals in general, conceptual terms" and the business of operations is "execution, not conceptualization." In "A Theory of Strategic Culture," *Comparative Strategy*, Vol. 10, No. 1 (January 1991): 11.

94. Remarks by General W. C. Westmoreland to Correspondents, 13 September 1966, Folder 524-2, Box 42, Westmoreland Personal Papers, RG 319, NARA. Palmer, *The 25-Year War*, 57. Confusion over objectives in Deputy Chief of Staff for Military Operations, "A Program for the Pacification and Long-Term Development of South Vietnam" (Department of the Army, March 1966), 46; Brownlee and Mullen III, *Changing an Army*, 138; and William B. Rosson, "Four Periods of American Involvement in Vietnam: Development and Implementation

of Policy, Strategy and Programs, Described and Analyzed on the Basis of Experience at Progressively Senior Levels" (Ph.D. diss., University of Oxford, 1979), 187.

95. Domestic support in Carter Malkasian, *A History of Modern Wars of Attrition* (Westport, CT: Praeger, 2002), 193. Blaming Westmoreland in Lewis Sorley, *Westmoreland: The General Who Lost Vietnam* (Boston: Houghton Mifflin Harcourt, 2011), 107.

96. "Command Emphasis on Revolutionary Development/Civic Action Programs," 22 October 1966, Folder 10, Reel 7, WCWP. "Simply confusing" in "The War: The New Realism," *Time*, 18 February 66. On Westmoreland understanding public opinion, see William Conrad Gibbons, *The U.S. Government and the Vietnam War: Executive and Legislative Roles and Relationships, Part III: January-July 1965* (Princeton, N.J.: Princeton University Press, 1989), 355. Formless war in Lloyd B. Lewis, *The Tainted War: Culture and Identity in Vietnam War Narratives* (Westport, CT: Greenwood Press, 1985), 70–71.

97. Maxwell D. Taylor, *Swords and Plowshares* (New York: W.W. Norton, 1972), 340. Harry McPherson also agreed. "You had to try to get the American people behind a half-war. It's terribly hard to do." Interview by T. H. Baker, 16 January 1969, LBJL, 14.

98. MACV leaders realized the difficulties of wresting control from the enemy. See MACV Command History, 1966, NARA, 31. On tasks related to nation building, see "CINCPAC Measurement of Progress in Southeast Asia," 23 February 1968, Folder 9, Box 10, Larry Berman Collection (Presidential Archives Research), TTUVA, 2.

99. Department of the Army, Field Manual 31-16, *Counterguerrilla Operations*, February 1963, 2. On modifying tactics, see Carland, *Stemming the Tide*, 358, and Robert H. Scales Jr., *Firepower in Limited Warfare*, rev. ed. (Novato, CA: Presidio, 1995), 81.

100. Command philosophy in MACV Command History, 1966, NARA, 341. Douglas Kinnard, *The War Managers: American Generals Reflect on Vietnam* (Hanover, NH: University Press of New England, 1977; DaCapo Press, 1991), 58. Richard A. Hunt, "Strategies at War: Pacification and Attrition in Vietnam," in *Lessons from an Unconventional War: Reassessing U.S. Strategies for Future Conflicts*, ed. Richard A. Hunt and Richard H. Shultz Jr. (New York: Pergamon Press, 1982), 27.

101. Dennis J. Vetock, *Lessons Learned: A History of US Army Lesson Learning* (Carlisle Barracks, PA: US Army Military History Institute, 1988), 97, 104, 106. On the role of knowledge sharing and learning, see M. Leann Brown, Michael Kenney, and Michael Zarkin, eds., *Organizational Learning in the Global Context* (Burlington, VT: Ashgate, 2006), 11

102. Browne, *The New Face of War*, ix. On the requirement for different methods, see Mark Moyar, *A Question of Command: Counterinsurgency from the Civil War to Iraq* (New Haven, CT: Yale University Press, 2009), 5.

Chapter 5

1. Westmoreland to Wheeler, 4 November 1965, Folder 6, Box 18, Series I, Official Correspondence, W. C. Westmoreland Collection, MHI.

2. Lewis Sorley, *Westmoreland: The General Who Lost Vietnam* (Boston: Houghton Mifflin Harcourt, 2011), 103. On pacification being an "integral part of allied strategy," see Richard A. Hunt, *Pacification: The American Struggle for Vietnam's Hearts and Minds* (Boulder, CO: Westview Press, 1995), 1.

3. Bunker quoted in Robert Shaplen, *The Road from War: Vietnam 1965–1970* (New York: Harper and Row, 1970), 133. Pacification defined in "Handbook for Military Support of Pacification," February 1968, Folder 14, Box 5, United States Armed Forces Manual Collection, TTUVA; and USMACV Guide for Province and District Advisors, 1 February 1968, CMH, 2-1. Interdependent parts in McNamara memorandum, 17 November 1967, in *The Pentagon Papers: The Defense Department History of United States Decisionmaking in Vietnam* [Senator Gravel, ed.] (5 vols.; Boston: Beacon Press, 1971–1972), III: 368.

4. Eric M. Bergerud, *The Dynamics of Defeat: The Vietnam War in Hau Nghia Province* (Boulder, CO: Westview Press, 1991), 5. Frank E. Vandiver, *Shadows of Vietnam: Lyndon Johnson's Wars* (College Station: Texas A&M University Press, 1997), 177. On 22 September 1966, McNamara highlighted the point. "Central to success, both in ending the war and in winning the peace, is the pacification program." *FRUS, 1964–1968*, IV: 659.

5. U. S. Grant Sharp and William C. Westmoreland,*Report on the War in Vietnam* (Washington, DC: US Government Printing Office, 1969), 229. On the role of security, see MACV, Blueprint for Vietnam, 1967, General Holdings, MHI, p. 1745. As a counterargument, Gabriel Kolko maintains that "the counterinsurgency and pacification efforts became interchangeable conceptions, centering on the military and technical means for physically securing the population." *Anatomy of a War: Vietnam, the United States, and the Modern Historical Experience* (New York: Pantheon Books, 1985), 131.

6. On local forces' roles, see RVNAF Counterinsurgency Roles and Missions, 4 February 1965, Folder 4, Box 53, Series II, Official Papers, W. C. Westmoreland Collection, MHI, p. 3. MACV asked the Rand Corporation to study rural Vietnamese villages for a better understanding of the evolution from insurgent control through pacification to government control. See R. Michael Pearce, *Evolution of a Vietnamese Village—Part I: The Present, after Eight Months of Pacification* (Santa Monica, CA: Rand, April 1965). On balancing development and security, see James M. Carter, *Inventing Vietnam: The United States and State Building, 1954–1968* (New York: Cambridge University Press, 2008), 112.

7. William C. Westmoreland, interview by Martin L. Ganderson, 1982, Box 1, Senior Officer Oral History Program, William C. Westmoreland Papers, MHI, 148. William C. Westmoreland, *A Soldier Reports* (Garden City, NY: Doubleday, 1976), 82. Bergerud, *The Dynamics of Defeat*, 115. Westmoreland was not alone in believing pacification could not change the face of the war on its own. See Richard Holbrooke in William Conrad Gibbons, *The U.S. Government and the Vietnam War: Executive and Legislative Roles and Relationships, Part IV: July 1965–January 1968* (Washington, DC: US Government Printing Office, 1994), 712–713.

8. Secretary McNamara's Meeting with General Thieu, Chairman, National Leadership Council, 11 October 1966, Folder 9, Reel 7, WCWP. On Westmoreland understanding pacification, see John M. Carland, "Winning the Vietnam War: Westmoreland's Approach in Two Documents," *Journal of Military History*, Vol. 68, No. 2 (April 2004): 554; Dale Andrade and James H. Willbanks, "CORDS/Phoenix: Counterinsurgency Lessons from Vietnam for the Future," *Military Review*, Vol. 86, No. 2 (March–April 2006): 13; and *The Pentagon Papers*, II, 491.

9. Chester L. Cooper et al., "The American Experience with Pacification in Vietnam, Volume III: History of Pacification," March 1972, Folder 65, ps. 206–207, U.S. Marine Corps History Division, Vietnam War Documents Collection, TTUVA. Command History, United States Military Assistance Command, 1966, Entry MACJ03, Box 3, RG 472, NARA, p. 501. *The Pentagon Papers*, II, 254–255. Hunt, *Pacification*, 25.

10. Sir Robert Thompson, *Defeating Communist Insurgency* (St. Petersburg, FL: Hailer, 2005; originally published 1966), 55. Thompson would later criticize the American effort for its "lack of control" in coordinating pacification programs. *No Exit from Vietnam* (New York: David McKay, 1969), 157. See also The BDM Corporation, "A Study of Strategic Lessons Learned in Vietnam," Volume V, Planning the War, General Holdings, MHI, 5–7

11. Department of the Army, Field Manual 31–16, *Counterguerrilla Operations*, February 1963, 31. On alluring analogies, see Richard E. Neustadt and Ernest R. May, *Thinking in Time: The Uses of History for Decision-Makers* (New York: Free Press, 1988), 48. In truth, the unique aspects of the Malayan situation were far different from those in South Vietnam.

12. Colonel Wilson quoted in Robert W. Komer, *Organization and Management of the "New Model" Pacification Program—1966–1969* (Santa Monica, CA: Rand, 1970), 17. On lack of coordination among agencies, see John Schlight, ed., *The Second Indochina War: Proceedings of a Symposium Held at Airlie, Virginia, 7–9 November 1984* (Washington, DC: Center of Military History, 1986), 127; and George C. Herring, *LBJ and Vietnam: A Different Kind of War* (Austin: University of Texas Press, 1994), 69. On clear and hold, see Department of the Army, Field Manual 31-73, *Advisor Handbook for Counterinsurgency*, April 1965, 58–61; Lessons Learned, 35: Clear and Hold Operations, 10 January 1964, General Westmoreland Reading File, Box 1, Paul L. Miles Papers, MHI; and Phillip B. Davidson, *Vietnam at War: The History: 1946–1975* (Novato, CA: Presidio, 1988), 321.

13. Long An Province Policy Review, 31 July 1964, Box 4, Robert M. Montague Papers, MHI. Admiral Felt to JCS, 22 February 1962, *FRUS*, 1961–1963, II: 167–169.

14. MACV, Monthly Report of Pacification Progress and Population and Area Control, 15 July 1964, Box 27, MACV Adjutant General Admin. Services Division, Box 27, RG472, NARA. See also Graham A. Cosmas, *MACV: The Joint Command in the Years of Escalation, 1962–1967* (Washington, DC: Center of Military History, 2006), 139.

15. Edward Miller, *Misalliance: Ngo Dinh Diem, the United States, and the Fate of South Vietnam* (Cambridge, MA: Harvard University Press, 2013), 218. Miller contends that the basic approach which Westmoreland and most of his colleagues endorsed was fundamentally "high modernist" in conception. On the definition of high modernism, see p. 57.

16. Sharp and Westmoreland, *Report on the War in Vietnam*, 86. Westmoreland, A Soldier Reports, 101. James William Gibson, *The Perfect War: The War We Couldn't Lose and How We Did* (New York: Vintage Books, 1986, 1988), 270–271. On nonmilitary aspects, see Psychological Requirements of Hop Tac, 13 July 1965, Folder 6, Box 13, Douglas Pike Collection, Unit 03: Insurgency Warfare, TTUVA. On sequential steps, see The Techniques of Pacification, 22 September 1965, 1965 Folder, Box 4, William E. DePuy Papers, MHI.

17. Official quoted in The BDM Corporation, "A Study of Strategic Lessons Learned in Vietnam," 5–37. *Hop Tac* problems in Cosmas, *MACV*, 143; and *The Pentagon Papers*, II: 482–483. Underscoring the cultural divides in these types of operations, Westmoreland noted of *Hop Tac* that the "ability to organize a project, execute it step by step, and supervise it to insure that things are done properly, is not typical of the Vietnamese mentality." History Notes, 30 August 1965, Box 12, Military Papers, WPUSC.

18. John J. McCuen, *The Art of Counter-Revolutionary War: The Strategy of Counterinsurgency* (St. Petersburg, FL: Hailer, 2005), 108. Ngo Quang Truong, "Territorial Forces," in *The Vietnam War: An Assessment by South Vietnam's Generals*, ed. Lewis Sorley (Lubbock: Texas Tech University Press, 2010), 209. See also History Notes, 2 September 1965, Box 12, Military Papers, WPUSC; and Peter Paret and John Shy, *Guerrillas in the 1960's* (New York: Frederick A. Praeger, 1962), 49.

19. Andrew Wiest, *Vietnam's Forgotten Army: Heroism and Betrayal in the ARVN* (New York: New York University Press, 2008), 74–75. On problems assessing pacification progress, see MACV Comments on Supplemental Information from Sector Advisors, 29 July 1964, Historians Background Material Files, 206–02, Mission Council Meetings, 1964, Box 2, RG 472, NARA, 5–6.

20. Operational Report for Quarterly Period Ending 31 October 1966, USARV Command History ORLLs, II Field Force Vietnam, Box 17, RG472, NARA. Resentment in Stathis N. Kalyvas, *The Logic of Violence in Civil War* (New York: Cambridge University Press, 2006), 123; and William R. Polk, *Violent Politics: A History of Insurgency, Terrorism & Guerrilla War, from the American Revolution to Iraq* (New York: HarperCollins, 2007), 172–173.

21. Reports and Evaluation Division, CORDS, "The Vietnamese Village in 1967," January 1968, Command Information Publications, 1967–1972, HQ MACV, Box 7, RG472, NARA. On concerns over organizing the civilian population, see Franklin A. Lindsay, "Unconventional Warfare," *Foreign Affairs*, Vol. 40, No. 2 (January 1962): 270; and James Eliot Cross, *Conflict in the Shadows: The Nature and Politics of Guerrilla War* (Garden City, NY: Doubleday, 1963), 17.

22. Long An Province Policy Review, MHI. Trip Report to I Corps, 18 May 1964, Folder J64, Box 3, Correspondence, 1956–1965, William E. DePuy Papers, MHI. On National Pacification Plan, see *FRUS, 1964–1968*, I: 86–87.

23. JCS History, JCSHO, 10–27.

24. Lodge to Westmoreland, 17 December 1965, in Gibbons, *The U.S. Government and the Vietnam War*, IV, 184–185. On NLF infrastructure, see Command History, United States Military Assistance Command, 1965, Entry MACJ03, Box 1, RG 472, NARA, 4.

25. William C. Westmoreland, interview by Charles B. MacDonald, 25 July 1985, LBJL, 4. Cosmas, *MACV*, 399.

26. McNamara quoted in Douglas S. Blaufarb, *The Counterinsurgency Era: U.S. Doctrine and Performance, 1950 to Present* (New York: Free Press, 1977), 236–237. On the Honolulu Conference, see Cosmas, *MACV*, 353. On the president and pacification, see Lloyd C. Gardner, *Pay Any Price: Lyndon Johnson and the Wars for Vietnam* (Chicago: Ivan R. Dee, 1995), 55.

27. The term "revolutionary development" broadly defined included the key tasks of population security and nation building programs. Jeffrey J. Clarke, *Advice and Support: The Final Years, 1965–1973* (Washington, DC: Center of Military History, 1988), 172.

28. "Increased Emphasis on Rural Construction," 27 December 1965, Correspondence, 1965–1966, Box 35, Jonathan O. Seaman Papers, MHI. PROVN report in *FRUS*, 1964–1968, IV: 596. See also Andrew J. Birtle, "PROVN, Westmoreland, and the Historians: A Reappraisal," *Journal of Military History*, Vol. 72, No. 4 (October 2008): 1213–1247.

29. Robert M. Montague, "Pacification: The Overall Strategy in South Vietnam," Student Essay, U.S. Army War College, 22 April 1966, Robert M. Montague Papers, Box 1, MHI, 5. On Westmoreland's views, see "Command Emphasis on Revolutionary Development/Civic Action Programs," 22 October 1966, Folder 10, Reel 7, WCWP; "Strategic Guidelines for 1967 in Vietnam," 14 December 1966, CSA (W.C.W.) Statements Folder, Reel 18, WCWP; and Sharp and Westmoreland, *Report on the War in Vietnam*, 132.

30. On single manager concept, see Cosmas, *MACV*, 357. Embassy fears in Herring, *LBJ and Vietnam*, 77–78.

31. OCO evolution in Hunt, *Pacification*, 82–84; Thomas W. Scoville, *Reorganizing for Pacification Support* (Washington, DC: US Army Center of Military History, 1999), 44–46; and Schlight, *The Second Indochina War*, 131.

32. Westmoreland, *A Soldier Reports*, 255. On inability of a civilian-led program to cope, see Andrade and Willbanks, "CORDS/Phoenix: Counterinsurgency Lessons from Vietnam for the Future," 12. On Knowlton, see Komer, *Organization and Management of the "New Model" Pacification Program*, 44.

33. Cosmas, *MACV*, 354. Scoville, *Reorganizing for Pacification Support*, 54. On local security being the "absolute prerequisite to the success of pacification," see Frank L. Jones, *Blowtorch: Robert Komer, Vietnam, and American Cold War Strategy* (Annapolis, MD: Naval Institute Press, 2013), 132.

34. National Security Action Memorandum No. 362, 9 May 1967, *FRUS*, 1964–1968, V: 398.

35. Westmoreland, *A Soldier Reports*, 260. "Single manager" concept in Komer, *Organization and Management of the "New Model" Pacification Program*, 55. For background on Komer, see Jones, *Blowtorch*, and his shorter article, "Blowtorch: Robert Komer and the Making of Vietnam Pacification Policy," *Parameters*, Vol. 35, No. 3 (Autumn 2005): 103–118. On CORDS responsibilities, see Hunt, *Pacification*, 89–90.

36. R. W. Komer, *Bureaucracy Does Its Thing: Institutional Constraints on U.S.-GVN Performance in Vietnam* (Santa Monica, CA: Rand, 1972), 115. On CORDS staff, see Scoville, *Reorganizing for Pacification Support*, 66–67 and Cosmas, *MACV*, 361.

37. CORDS programs in Schlight, *The Second Indochina War*, 133 and Hunt, *Pacification*, 90–94. Responsibilities delineated in MACV Dir. 10–12, Organizations and Functions for Civil Operations and Revolutionary Development Support, 28 May 1967, Folder 3, Box 1, John B. O'Donnell Collection, TTUVA; and MACV Commanders' Conference, 21 May 1967, Box 5, Paul L. Miles Papers, MHI, 5.

38. Corps organization in Hunt, *Pacification*, 94. Civilian and military advisor numbers in Cooper et al., "The American Experience with Pacification in Vietnam," TTUVA, 271.

39. John H. Cushman, "Pacification: Concepts Developed in the Field by the RVN 21st Infantry Division," *Army*, Vol. 16, No. 3 (March 1966): 26. While Cushman's experiences pre-dated CORDS, the requirements of pacification had not changed between 1966 and 1967. See MACV, Blueprint for Vietnam, 1967, MHI, 1743.

40. Westmoreland, *A Soldier Reports*, 260. Numbers of officials in CORDS from Herring, *LBJ and Vietnam*, 81. Of note, CORDS overwhelmingly was staffed with military personnel.

41. Blaufarb, *The Counterinsurgency Era*, 240. Herring, *LBJ and Vietnam*, 64. Jones notes that "Westmoreland's support was crucial…he backed Komer at numerous critical moments during CORDS' early days, signaling that Komer's and his organization's role would not be weakened." *Blowtorch*, 150.

42. On problems measuring the progress of pacification, see Gregory A. Daddis, *No Sure Victory: Measuring U.S. Army Effectiveness and Progress in the Vietnam War* (Oxford: Oxford University Press, 2011), chapter 5. Command History, United States Military Assistance Command, 1967, Entry MACJ03, Box 5, RG 472, NARA, 317. On CORDS bringing no

major conceptual innovations, see Thomas L. Ahern Jr., *Vietnam Declassified: The CIA and Counterinsurgency* (Lexington: University Press of Kentucky, 2010), 241. Cross purposes within U.S. operations in Marc Jason Gilbert, "The Cost of Losing the 'Other War' in Vietnam," in *Why the North Won the Vietnam War*, ed. Marc Jason Gilbert (New York: Palgrave, 2002), 179.

43. Cooper et al., "The American Experience with Pacification," 273. Similarly, one former intelligence officer complained that "counterinsurgency in Vietnam emphasized military considerations over political ones, enforcement of 'physical security' over more subtle questions of social change and psychological loyalties." David G. Marr, "The Rise and Fall of 'Counterinsurgency': 1961–1964," in *The Pentagon Papers*, V: 203. CORDS failing to come to grips with fundamental problems in Herring, *LBJ and Vietnam*, 87.

44. Komer, *Organization and Management of the "New Model" Pacification Program*, 246–247. Still, an "efficient and better-managed U.S. organization was not sufficient. If the South Vietnamese did not carry the main burden, the program could not succeed." Jones, *Blowtorch*, 151.

45. Operational Report for Quarterly Period Ending 31 January 1967, 25th Infantry Division, Box 2, MACV Command Historian's Collection, MHI, 21. Battalion percentages from Andrew Birtle, "The U.S. Army in Vietnam: Shifting Paradigms" (lecture, United States Military Academy, West Point, NY, 26 April 2010). These percentages are derived from the OSD Systems Analysis Monthly Report, September 1967, Folder 93, Thomas Thayer Papers, CMH.

46. MACV General 1967 Command History, Part 2, Folder 1, Box 00, Bud Harton Collection, TTUVA, 559.

47. Goodpaster to DePuy, 18 April 1967, *FRUS*, 1964–1968, V: 321.

48. III Corps MACCORDS Provincial Report, December 1967, CMH.

49. Robert H. Williams, "A Construct of Insurgency-Counterinsurgency in Vietnam," USMACV Command Information Publications, 1967–1972, Box 1, RG472, NARA, 7. Stathis N. Kalyvas and Matthew Adam Kocher, "The Dynamics of Violence in Vietnam: An Analysis of the Hamlet Evaluation System (HES)," *Journal of Peace Research*, Vol. 46, No. 3 (2009): 338.

50. David Halberstam, "Return to Vietnam," *Harper's*, Vol. 235, No. 1411 (December 1967): 48. On government weakness, see Lawrence E. Grinter, "The Pacification of South Vietnam: Dilemmas of Counterinsurgency and Development" (Ph.D. diss., University of North Carolina at Chapel Hill, 1972), 621.

51. David W. P. Elliott, *The Vietnamese War: Revolution and Social Change in the Mekong Delta, 1930–1975*, concise ed. (Armonk, NY: M.E. Sharpe, 2003, 2007), 99. Objective in Civic Action and Counterinsurgency, 22 March 1962, Folder 7, Box 1, Vladimir Lehovich Collection, TTUVA. See also Charles B. Flood, *The War of the Innocents* (New York: McGraw-Hill, 1970), 239.

52. On control and collaboration, see Kalyvas, *The Logic of Violence in Civil War*, 119. One representative MACV report argued "Area control . . . is not precise and is, at best, a rough approximation." Monthly Report of Revolutionary Development Progress: Population and Area Control from Period 1 July to 31 July 1966, 16 August 1966, MHI. Fallacious assumptions from Roger Spiller, comments to author, 14 January 2013.

53. John V. Tunney, *Measuring Hamlet Security in Vietnam: Report of a Special Study Mission* (Washington, DC: US Government Printing Office, 1969), 2.

54. On this point, see Henry A. Kissinger, "The Viet Nam Negotiations," *Foreign Affairs*, Vol. 47, No. 2 (January 1969): 214–215. For a similar discussion in relation to the US war in Afghanistan, see Bing West, *The Wrong War: Grit, Strategy, and the Way out of Afghanistan* (New York: Random House, 2011), 177, 242.

55. Peter Scott quoted in Mark Moyar, *Phoenix and the Birds of Prey: Counterinsurgency and Counterterrorism in Vietnam* (Lincoln: University of Nebraska Press, 1997, 2007), 295. On Phoenix, see Dale Andradé, *Ashes to Ashes: The Phoenix Program and the Vietnam War* (Lexington, MA: Lexington Books, 1990) xi, 72, 81; and Ahern, *Vietnam Declassified*, 261. Police action in G. C. Reinhardt, *Guerrilla-Combat, Strategy, and Deterrence in Southeast Asia* (Santa Monica, CA: Rand, 1964), 15.

56. Westmoreland, interview, LBJL, 7. Phillip B. Davidson, interview by Ted Gittinger, 30 March 1982, LBJL, 30. On army officers working with police, see Andrew F. Krepinevich Jr., *The Army and Vietnam* (Baltimore, MD: Johns Hopkins University Press, 1986), 12.

57. Tran Dinh Tho, "Pacification," in Sorley, *The Vietnam War*, 248. J. M. Carrier and C. A. H. Thomson, *Viet Cong Motivation and Morale: The Special Case of Chieu Hoi* (Santa Monica, CA: Rand, 1966), 16. See also Thomas C. Thayer, *War without Fronts: The American Experience in Vietnam* (Boulder, CO: Westview Press, 1985), 195.

58. Lucian W. Pye, *Observations on the Chieu Hoi Program* (Santa Monica, CA: Rand, 1969), 8. MACV General 1967 Command History, TTUVA, 599, 601. HQUSMACV, Chieu Hoi Returnees in Support of Counterinsurgency Operations, 29 April 1967, Chieu Hoi Exploitation Folder, Box 1, Richard M. Lee Papers, MHI.

59. Assessment of Refugee Problem, CORDS/Refugee Division, Folder 06, Box 31, Douglas Pike Collection: Unit 03-Refugees and Civilian Casualties, TTUVA. On the NLF role in population displacement, see Louis A. Wiesner, *Victims and Survivors: Displaced Persons and Other War Victims in Viet-Nam, 1954–1975* (Westport, CT: Greenwood Press, 1988), 58–59.

60. Maxwell Taylor quoted in Jonathan Schell, *The Military Half: An Account of Destruction in Quang Ngai and Quang Tin* (New York: Alfred A. Knopf, 1968), 71. Social worker quoted in "Vietnam's 1.5 Million Refugees," *U.S. News & World Report*, 3 June 1968, 59. Komer, *Organization and Management of the "New Model" Pacification Program*, 183. On elected officials, see James F. Ray, "The District Advisor," *Military Review*, Vol. 45, No. 5 (May 1965): 5; and Samuel L. Popkin, "Politics and the Village," *Asian Survey*, Vol. 10, No. 8 (August 1970): 665.

61. Stephen T. Hosmer and Sibylle O. Crane, *Counterinsurgency: A Symposium, April 16–20, 1962* (Santa Monica, CA: RAND, 1963, 2006), 141. On measuring progress in pacification, see Daddis, *No Sure Victory*, 118–122.

62. "A Systems Analysis View of the Vietnam War: 1965–1972, Vol. 9-Population Security," Geog. V. Vietnam-319.1, CMH, 28, 35. OSDHO, 9 January 1968, 8. On HES, see Erwin R. Brigham, "Pacification Measurement in Vietnam: The Hamlet Evaluation System," Folder 18, Box 3, Glenn Helm Collection, TTUVA; and Anders Sweetland, "Item Analysis of the HES (Hamlet Evaluation System)" (Santa Monica, CA: Rand, 1968).

63. Peter M. Dawkins, "The United States Army and the 'Other' War in Vietnam: A Study of the Complexity of Implementing Organizational Change" (Ph.D. diss., Princeton University, 1979), 99. Hamlet Evaluation System Study, 1 May 1968, Command Information Publications, Folder #101222, Box 19, RG472, NARA, 22. Ahern, *Vietnam Declassified*, 253.

64. Hearts and minds in Mark Baker, *Nam: The Vietnam War in the Words of the Men and Women Who Fought There* (New York: William Morrow, 1981), 73. Soldier quoted in Michael Herr, *Dispatches* (New York: Alfred A. Knopf, 1968, 1978), 29.

65. Timothy J. Lomperis, *The War Everyone Lost—and Won: America's Intervention in Viet Nam's Twin Struggles* (Washington, DC: CQ Press, 1993), 7. Robert Shaplen, "Viet Nam: Crisis of Indecision," *Foreign Affairs*, Vol. 46, No. 1 (October 1967): 102.

66. "Frustration Points in the Vietnamese and Free World Military System as noted by RF/PF Advisors," H. W. Lange, 29 June 1967, CMH.

67. McCuen, *The Art of Counter-Revolutionary War*, 152. On construction-destruction, see John Ellis, *A Short History of Guerrilla Warfare* (New York: St. Martin's Press, 1976), 182–183. For a criticism of MACV's failure in this area, see Thompson, *No Exit from Vietnam*, 149.

68. Vietnam Special Studies Group quoted in Birtle, "PROVN, Westmoreland, and the Historians," 1227. See also Warren Wilkins, *Grab Their Belts to Fight Them: The Viet Cong's Big Unit War against the U.S., 1965–1966* (Annapolis, MD: Naval Institute Press, 2011), 139.

69. Andrade and Willbanks, "CORDS/Phoenix," 12. On MACV, understanding these interrelationships and the challenges associated with them, see USMACV Guide for Province and District Advisors, CMH, 2–4; and Command History, United States Military Assistance Command, 1964, Entry MACJ03, Box 1, RG 472, NARA, 5.

70. Mark Atwood Lawrence, *The Vietnam War: A Concise International History* (New York: Oxford University Press, 2008), 118.

71. COMUSMACV, Role of ARVN Division in CORDS, 3 August 1967, #19 History File, Reel 10, WCWP. Combat Operations After Action Report, HQ, USARV Command Historian

After Action Reports, Box 33, NARA, 27. John M. Carland, *Stemming the Tide: May 1965 to October 1966* (Washington, DC: Center of Military History, 2000), 358.

72. USMACV Command History, 1967, Office of Secy, Joint Staff, Mil. Hist. Branch, Entry MACJ03, Box 5, RG 472, NARA, 108–109. Phillip B. Davidson, *Secrets of the Vietnam War* (Novato, CA: Presidio, 1990), 151.

73. See as an example, Robert J. Donovan, "Pessimism over Vietnam War Outcome Rises in Washington," *Los Angeles Times*, 9 June 67; and Thompson, *No Exit from Vietnam*, 67.

74. The best overview of Tet planning from Hanoi's perspective is Lien-Hang T. Nguyen, *Hanoi's War: An International History of the War for Peace in Vietnam* (Chapel Hill: University of North Carolina Press, 2012), 87–108. James J. Wirtz, *The Tet Offensive: Intelligence Failure in War* (Ithaca, NY : Cornell University Press, 1991), 20. See also William S. Turley, *The Second Indochina War: A Short Political and Military History, 1954–1975*, 2d ed. (Lanham, MD: Rowman and Littlefield, 1986, 2009), 141.

75. Lien-Hang T. Nguyen, "The War Politburo: North Vietnam's Diplomatic and Political Road to the Tết Offensive," *Journal of Vietnamese Studies*, Vol. 1. Nos. 1–2 (2006): 25. Merle L. Pribbenow II, "General Võ Nguyên Giáp and the Mysterious Evolution of the Plan for the 1968 Tết Offensive," *Journal of Vietnamese Studies*, Vol. 3 (Summer 2008): 12. Elliott, *The Vietnamese War*, 215.

76. Westmoreland to Wheeler, 20 December 1967, Folder 4, Box 22, Series I, Official Correspondence, W. C. Westmoreland Collection, MHI. Ronnie E. Ford, *Tet 1968: Understanding the Surprise* (London: Frank Cass, 1995), 100. USMACV Quarterly Evaluation Report, December 1967, MHI, 2.

77. Westmoreland to Wheeler, 10 December 1967, Folder 6, Box 1, Veteran Members of the 109th Quartermaster Company Collection, TTUVA. *Southeast Asia Analysis Report*, December 1967, MHI, 21.

78. Joint Chiefs of Staff to President Johnson, 29 January 1968, *FRUS*, 1964–1968, VI: 69. William J. Duiker, *The Communist Road to Power*, 2nd ed. (Boulder, CO: Westview Press, 1981, 1996), 283. William Thomas Allison, *The Tet Offensive: A Brief History with Documents* (New York: Routledge, 2008), 30–33.

79. Wirtz, *The Tet Offensive*, 138. Willard Pearson, *The War in the Northern Provinces, 1966–1968* (Washington, DC: US Government Printing Office, 1975), 30, 34, 94.

80. MACV General 1967 Command History, TTUVA, 596–597.

81. John Prados, *The Hidden History of the Vietnam War* (Chicago: Ivan R. Dee, 1995), 139. Davidson, *Vietnam at War*, 430, 435. Westmoreland, *A Soldier Reports*, 390. President Johnson recalled "Our intelligence sources indicated the enemy's next attacks in the winter–spring offensive would be launched around the Tet period, the Vietnamese holiday season during the Lunar New Year." *The Vantage Point: Perspectives on the Presidency, 1963–1969* (New York: Holt, Rinehart and Winston, 1971), 380–381.

82. Peter Lisagor, "Vietcong Smash Myth: Winning People's Favor," *Philadelphia Inquirer*, 6 February 1968. *FRUS*, 1964–1968, VI: 74. For senior officers blaming the media for distorting Tet, see Davidson, *Vietnam at War*, 441.

83. Westmoreland to Sharp, 3 February 1968, *FRUS*, 1964–1968, VI: 117. USMACV Quarterly Evaluation Report, January–March 1968, MHI, 2. Don Oberdorfer, *Tet!* (Garden City, NY: Doubleday, 1971), 238–239. Casualty figures from George Donelson Moss, *Vietnam: An American Ordeal*, 5th ed. (Upper Saddle River, NJ: Pearson Prentice Hill, 1990, 2006), 278. William J. Duiker believes MACV estimates were slightly exaggerated and 30,000 casualties seems to be more valid. *Sacred War: Nationalism and Revolution in a Divided Vietnam* (Boston: McGraw-Hill, 1995), 213.

84. Westmoreland quoted in Peter Braestrup, *Big Story: How the American Press and Television Reported and Interpreted the Crisis of Tet 1968 in Vietnam and Washington*, Vol. 2 (Boulder, CO: Westview Press, 1977), 155. TTU27. See also Westmoreland, *A Soldier Reports*, 427–428

85. Westmoreland to Wheeler, 9 February 1968, Folder 2, Box 39, Veteran Members of the 109th Quartermaster Company Collection, TTUVA.

86. Interview with Westmoreland, 23 October 1972, in Herbert Y. Schandler, *The Unmaking of a President: Lyndon Johnson and Vietnam* (Princeton, NJ: Princeton University Press, 1977), 106.

87. Westmoreland to Wheeler, 9 February 1968, TTUVA. See also Schandler, *The Unmaking of a President*, 106. For Westmoreland's perspective on this period, see "The Origins of the Post-Tet 1968 Plans for Additional American Forces in RVN," Box 24, WPUSC. The general argued the plan submitted to Washington was not "an 'emergency request for battlefield reinforcements.' Instead, it was a prudent planning exercise designed to generate the military capability to support future tactical and strategic options," p. 28.

88. Wheeler quoted in Graham A. Cosmas, *MACV: The Joint Command in the Years of Withdrawal, 1968–1973* (Washington, D.C.: Center of Military History, 2007), 91. Cosmas treats the reinforcement request beginning on p. 88.

89. Westmoreland to Sharp and Wheeler, 12 February 1968, *FRUS, 1964–1968*: VI: 185. John B. Henry II, "February, 1968," *Foreign Policy* No. 4 (Autumn 1971): 13. On recovery measures, see Project Recovery, 2 February 1968, Reel 12, #29 History File, 1–29 February 1968, WCWP.

90. Westmoreland, *A Soldier Reports*, 432. "Force package requirements" in Schandler, *The Unmaking of a President*, 110. Increment numbers in Henry, "February, 1968," 16–17. According to Cosmas, when he returned to Washington "Wheeler made no mention of reconstitution of the national reserve or expanded operations in Southeast Asia. Instead, he gave the impression that the Military Assistance Command needed all 206,000 additional troops merely to defeat the enemy offensive and restore the allies' pre-Tet position." Cosmas, *MACV: The Joint Command*, 96.

91. Hedrick Smith and Neil Sheehan, "Westmoreland Requests 206,000 More Men, Stirring Debate in Administration," *New York Times*, 10 March 1968.

92. MACV Commanders Conference, 19 May 1968, Pacification Overview, Conclusions Folder, Historian's Files, CMH. On Tet not destroying the NLF, see Samuel A. Adams, interview by Ted Gittinger, 20 September 1984, LBJL, 19; and Ngo Vinh Long, "The Tet Offensive and Its Aftermath" in *The Tet Offensive*, ed. Marc Jason Gilbert and William Head (Westport, CT: Praeger, 1996), 107. Vacuum in Robert W. Komer, interview (III) by Paige E. Mulhollan, 15 November 1971, LBJL, 68.

93. Cooper et al., "The American Experience with Pacification in Vietnam," TTUVA, 292. USMACV Quarterly Evaluation Report, January–March 1968, MHI, p. 4. Johnson's pessimism in Walter LaFeber, *The Deadly Bet: LBJ, Vietnam, and the 1968 Election* (Lanham, MD: Rowman and Littlefield, 2005), 25.

94. "Big Setback for U.S. in the Countryside," *U.S. News & World Report*, 4 March 1968. On Vietnamese perspectives, see Don Oberdorfer, interview (II) by Ted Gittinger, 17 September 1981, LBJL, 21.

95. DoD analysis in Schandler, *The Unmaking of a President*, 146. COL Marvin D. Fuller, VNIT 277, CMH, 18. For examples of media criticisms, see Ward Just, "Guerrillas Wreck Pacification Plan," *The Washington Post*, 4 February 1968; and Stanley Karnow, "Future of Pacification Is Questioned," *The Washington Post*, 16 February 1968.

96. F. J. West and Charles Benoit, "A Brief Report from Rural Vietnam," 31 October 1968, Strategy File #1, Folder 24, Thayer Papers CMH, 2. Duiker, *Sacred War*, 214.

97. "Text of Ambassador Komer's News Conference on the Hamlet Evaluation System, 1 Dec.," HES Newsletter #2, HES Briefing for the Press, 1 Dec 67, Amb. Komer to News Media Representatives in Saigon, Center of Military History Refiles, RG 319, NARA. William Tuohy, "Pacification Is Tied to Security," *Washington Post*, 27 June 1968. Project Takeoff Summary, Folder 65, US Marine Corps History Division Vietnam War Documents Collection, TTUVA, II-3. The BDM Corporation, "A Study of Strategic Lessons Learned in Vietnam," EX-8.

98. Thang quoted in Charles Mohr, "Gains Recorded in Pacification Despite Terrorism," *New York Times*, 31 March 1967. Problems with GVN and pacification in CIA Monthly Report, The Situation in South Vietnam, 4 June 1965, Folder 1, Box 2, Larry Berman Collection (Presidential Archives Research), TTUVA, 7; Hunt, *Pacification*, 131.

99. Komer, *Organization and Management of the "New Model" Pacification Program*, 252. LTC James C. Swain, VNIT 30, CMH.

100. Jeffrey Race, *War Comes to Long An: Revolutionary Conflict in a Vietnamese Province* (Berkeley: University of California Press, 1972), 226, 263. David Hunt, *Vietnam's Southern Revolution: From Peasant Insurrection to Total War* (Amherst: University of Massachusetts

Press, 2008), 9. Maurice E. Jessup, "The Validity of the Civic Action Concept," 24 January 1968, Course 4, Army War College Student Papers, MHI, 2.

101. MACV Fact Book 41, Viet Cong Strategy and Tactics, 22 October 1968, General Holdings, MHI. Martin Clemis, Temple University, kindly provided me with a copy of this document.

Chapter 6

1. As an example of criticizing Westmoreland, see Mark Moyar, *A Question of Command: Counterinsurgency from the Civil War to Iraq* (New Haven, CT: Yale University Press, 2009), 166. MAAG emphasis in 1954 in *The Pentagon Papers: The Defense Department History of United States Decisionmaking in Vietnam* [Senator Gravel, ed.] (5 vols.; Boston: Beacon Press, 1971–1972), I: 215.

2. Conference at Nha Trang, 24 October 1965, US Strategy, Vietnam 1965–76, Historian's Files, CMH, 5. Westmoreland to Wheeler, 30 October 1967, Policy/Strategy File, Box 6, Paul L. Miles Papers, MHI. On relation to political stability, see William C. Westmoreland, *A Soldier Reports* (Garden City, NY: Doubleday, 1976), 309; and Jeffrey J. Clarke, *Advice and Support: The Final Years, 1965–1973* (Washington, DC: Center of Military History, 1988), 81.

3. Ward Just, *To What End: Report from Vietnam* (Boston: Houghton Mifflin, 1968; New York: Public Affairs, 2000), 32–33.

4. G. C. Reinhardt, *Guerrilla-Combat, Strategy, and Deterrence in Southeast Asia* (Santa Monica, CA: Rand, 1964), 1. Governmental changes in JCS History, Part II, JCSHO, 27–14. Leverage in *The Pentagon Papers*, I: 279.

5. Robert W. Komer, *Bureaucracy Does Its Thing: Institutional Constraints on U.S.-GVN Performance in Vietnam* (Santa Monica, CA: Rand, 1972), 94. On diverse missions, see RVNAF Counterinsurgency Roles and Missions, 4 February 1965, Folder 4, Box 53, Series II Official Papers, W. C. Westmoreland Collection, MHI; and Clarke, *Advice and Support*, 93. Jurisdictional conflict in Debriefing Report, Colonel Charles H. Reidenbaugh, 15 June 1966, Box 14, Senior Officer Debriefing Reports, HQ UARV Command History, RG 472, NARA.

6. On Saigon refusing to have Vietnamese forces under US command, see George L. MacGarrigle, *Taking the Offensive: October 1966 to October 1967* (Washington, DC: Center of Military History, 1998), 5; *The Pentagon Papers*, I, 498–499; and Robert W. Komer, *Bureaucracy at War: U.S. Performance in the Vietnam Conflict* (Boulder, CO: Westview Press, 1986), 103. Problems in South Vietnam's army, which were noticeable even in the 1950s, in Mark Moyar, *Triumph Forsaken: The Vietnam War, 1954–1965* (New York: Cambridge University Press, 2006), 81.

7. John Prados, *Vietnam: The History of an Unwinnable War, 1945–1975* (Lawrence: University Press of Kansas, 2009), 40. Dong Van Khuyen, "The RVNAF," in *The Vietnam War: An Assessment by South Vietnam's Generals*, ed. Lewis Sorley (Lubbock: Texas Tech University Press, 2010), 12.

8. *The Pentagon Papers*, I: 77–78, 87. David M. Toczek, *The Battle of Ap Bac, Vietnam: They Did Everything but Learn from It* (Westport, CT: Greenwood Press, 2001), 28–29. On Diem, see Ronald H. Spector, *Advice and Support: The Early Years, 1941–1960* (Washington, DC: Center of Military History, 1983), 252–253.

9. *The Pentagon Papers*, I: 216–217. Prados, *Vietnam*, 64. "O'Daniel Starts Vietnam Training," *New York Times*, 13 February 1955. The article noted that the South Vietnamese "army will be, above all, according to American ideas on the subject, a police force capable of spotting Communist guerrillas and Communist efforts at infiltration."

10. Spector, *Advice and Support*, 264–265. On debate after O'Daniel's tour, see *The Pentagon Papers*, II: 432–433; and McGarr to Lemnitzer, 7 June 1961, *FRUS*, 1961–1963, I: 207–208. On Korean War influences, see "A Systems Analysis View of the Vietnam War: 1965–1972, Vol. 7-Rep. of Vietnam Armed Forces," Geog. V. Vietnam-319.1, CMH, 45–54.

11. Report from James Farmer, *Counter-Insurgency: Viet-Nam 1962–1963* (Santa Monica, CA: Rand, 1963), 9. On roles of the local forces, see James W. Dunn, "Province Advisers in Vietnam, 1962–1965," in *Lessons from an Unconventional War: Reassessing U.S. Strategies for Future Conflicts*, ed. Richard A. Hunt and Richard H. Shultz Jr. (New York: Pergamon

Press, 1982), 8–9; and Charles J. Timmes, "The Naïve Years," *Army*, Vol. 27, No. 5 (May 1977): 36. Balancing against conventional threat in Basic Counterinsurgency Plan for Viet-Nam, 4 January 1961, *FRUS, 1961–1963*, I:3. Force levels in James Lawton Collins Jr., *The Development and Training of the South Vietnamese Army, 1950–1972* (Washington, DC: US Government Printing Office, 1975; repr. 2002), 10.

12. The authors of *The Pentagon Papers* believed Diem, spurred by fears of a coup d'état, saw the Civil Guard as little more than a counterweight to a potentially disloyal army. In *The Pentagon Papers*, II: 456. Edward Miller, however, maintains Diem treated the Guard as a "core element of his counterinsurgency strategy in the countryside throughout the 1950s." *Misalliance: Ngo Dinh Diem, the United States, and the Fate of South Vietnam* (Cambridge, MA: Harvard University Press, 2013), 192-194. Spector, *Advice and Support*, 322. US financing in Lawrence S. Kaplan, Ronald D. Landa, and Edward J. Drea, *The McNamara Ascendancy, 1961–1965* (Washington, DC: Office of the Secretary of Defense Historical Office, 2006), 277.

13. John H. Cushman, "Pacification: Concepts Developed in the Field by the RVN 21st Infantry Division," *Army*, Vol. 16, No. 3 (March 1966): 27. McGarr to McNamara, 30 October 1961, *FRUS, 1961–1963*, I: 447. Courses in Cao Van Vien, et al., "The US Advisor" in Sorley, *The Vietnam War*, 705. Vung Tau in Harry McPherson, *A Political Education: A Washington Memoir* (Boston: Houghton Mifflin, 1988), 406–407.

14. James Joes, *The War for South Viet Nam, 1954–1975*, rev. ed. (Westport, CT: Praeger, 2001), 89. Leadership problems in *FRUS, 1961–1963*, II: 525. For Westmoreland's take on training, see U. S. Grant Sharp and William C. Westmoreland, *Report on the War in Vietnam* (Washington, DC: US Government Printing Office, 1969), 212.

15. Collins, *The Development and Training of the South Vietnamese Army*,18. Maxwell D. Taylor, *Swords and Plowshares* (New York: W.W. Norton, 1972), 238. Kevin Ruane, *War and Revolution in Vietnam, 1930–75* (London: UCL Press, 1998), 56.

16. Durbrow quoted in Jack Schulimson, *The Joint Chiefs of Staff and the War in Vietnam, 1960–1968*, Part I (Washington, DC: Office of Joint History, 2011), 24. ARVN Order of Battle Report, April 1961, Folder 8, Box 1, Douglas Pike Collection: Unit 01-Military Operations, TTUVA. Christopher K. Ives, *US Special Forces and Counterinsurgency in Vietnam: Military innovation and institutional failure, 1961–1963* (London: Routledge, 2007), 117.

17. Lemnitzer to Taylor, 18 October 1961, Folder 3, Box 2, Douglas Pike Collection: Unit 01-Assessment and Strategy, TTUVA. On lack of a specific strategy, see *The Pentagon Papers*, II: 128.

18. Country Team Staff Committee Paper, 4 January 1961, Folder 12, Box 1, Douglas Pike Collection: Unit 02-Military Operations, TTUVA. Collins, *The Development and Training of the South Vietnamese Army*, 20–21.

19. Peter M. Dawkins, "The United States Army and the 'Other' War in Vietnam: A Study of the Complexity of Implementing Organizational Change" (Ph.D. diss., Princeton University, 1979), 218. Collins, *The Development and Training of the South Vietnamese Army*, 25.

20. *The Pentagon Papers*, II: 138, 146. Donald W. Hamilton, *The Art of Insurgency: American Military Policy and the Failure of Strategy in Southeast Asia* (Westport, CT: Praeger, 1998), 131.

21. McGarr quoted in Noam Chomsky, *Rethinking Camelot: JFK, the Vietnam War, and U.S. Political Culture* (Boston, MA: South End Press, 1993), 101. Reliance on ARVN in US Embassy Telegram, 14 August 1961, *FRUS, 1961–1963*: Vol. 1, 276–279. On links to training and pacification, see Charles A. Cannon Jr., Senior Officer Debriefing Report, 17 November 1967, Box 4, Richard M. Lee Papers, MHI.

22. Taylor and Vien quoted in George C. Herring, "'People's Quite Apart': Americans, South Vietnamese, and the War in Vietnam," *Diplomatic History*, Vol. 14, No. 1 (Winter 1990): 6. Combined training programs in Robert K. Brigham, *ARVN: Life and Death in the South Vietnamese Army* (Lawrence: University Press of Kansas, 2006), 37. Lack of overall plan in *The Pentagon Papers*, II: 720.

23. Peter Paret and John Shy, *Guerrillas in the 1960's* (New York: Frederick A. Praeger, 1962), 45. Brigham, *ARVN*, 37.

24. Martin J. Dockery, *Lost in Translation, Vietnam: A Combat Advisor's Story* (New York: Ballantine Books, 2003), 193. Collins, *The Development and Training of the South Vietnamese Army*, 33–34.

25. Vann quoted in Mark Moyar, *Triumph Forsaken: The Vietnam War, 1954–1965* (New York: Cambridge University Press, 2006), 194. Moyar argues that Ap Bac, though a tactical failure, "was a defeat for the Viet Cong in a strategic sense." For a more balanced over-view, see David M. Toczek, *The Battle of Ap Bac, Vietnam: They Did Everything but Learn from It* (Westport, CT: Greenwood Press, 2001), 120–127. Advisor quoted in David Halberstam, "Vietnam Defeat Shocks U.S. Aides," *New York Times*, 7 January 1963.

26. David Halberstam, *The Making of a Quagmire: America and Vietnam during the Kennedy Era* (New York: Alfred A. Knopf, 1964, 1988), 79. Ted Serong, "The Lessons of Ap Bac," *Conflict*, Vol. 9, No. 4 (1989): 339. For the enemy perspective, see *Victory in Vietnam: The Official History of the People's Army of Vietnam, 1954–1975*, trans. Merle L. Pribbenow (Lawrence: University Press of Kansas, 2002), 137.

27. DIA report, 13 December 1963, in *FRUS, 1961–1963*, IV: 707.

28. James Reston, "Saigon: The Tragic Paradox of Vietnam," *New York Times*, 29 August 1965. Taylor to President Johnson, 11 January 1965, *FRUS, 1964–1968*, II: 47. See also Herring, " 'People's Quite Apart,' " 4. Bruce Palmer Jr. recalled that the escalation "presented Hanoi with a propaganda prize: the Americans, they could claim, were pushing the South Vietnamese aside and fighting the war for selfish U.S. imperialist goals." *The 25-Year War: America's Military Role in Vietnam* (Lexington: University Press of Kentucky, 1984), 179.

29. "Courses of Action in South Vietnam," 22 March 1965, in Jeffrey P. Kimball, *To Reason Why: The Debate about the Causes of U.S. Involvement in the Vietnam War* (New York: McGraw-Hill, 1990), 228. See also G. C. Hickey, *The American Military Advisor and his Foreign Counterpart: The Case of Vietnam* (Santa Monica, CA: Rand, 1965).

30. Bui Diem quoted in William Conrad Gibbons, *The U.S. Government and the Vietnam War: Executive and Legislative Roles and Relationships, Part IV: July 1965–January 1968* (Washington, DC: US Government Printing Office, 1994), 65. Jeffrey Clarke, "Civil-Military Relations in South Vietnam and the American Advisory Effort," in *The Vietnam War: Vietnamese and American Perspectives*, ed. Jayne S. Werner and Luu Doan Huynh (Armonk, NY: M.E. Sharpe, 1993), 192.

31. Westmoreland, *A Soldier Reports*, 118. RVNAF objectives in Command History, United States Military Assistance Command, 1965, Entry MACJ03, Box 1, RG 472, NARA, 217. See also Ngo Quang Truong, "Territorial Forces," in Sorley, *The Vietnam War*, 200.

32. DePuy quoted in Harry Maurer, ed., *Strange Ground: Americans in Vietnam, 1945–1975, an Oral History* (New York: Henry Holt, 1989), 451. Collins, *The Development and Training of the South Vietnamese Army*, 72.

33. Westmoreland to Walt, 28 August 1965, Folder 2, Box 18, Series I Official Correspondence, W. C. Westmoreland Collection, MHI. See also Westmoreland to Wheeler, 25 June 1965, US Strategy in Vietnam, 1965–1975, Historian's Files, CMH, 12. Mutually reinforcing missions in Graham A. Cosmas, *MACV: The Joint Command in the Years of Escalation, 1962–1967* (Washington, DC: Center of Military History, 2006), 396.

34. Westmoreland to Wheeler, 21 November 1965, Folder 6, Box 18, Series I Official Correspondence, W. C. Westmoreland Collection, MHI. Westmoreland, *A Soldier Reports*, 263.

35. For arguments that MACV marginalized the South Vietnamese armed forces, see Brigham, *ARVN*, 6; and Andrew Wiest, *Vietnam's Forgotten Army: Heroism and Betrayal in the ARVN* (New York: New York University Press, 2008), 49.

36. The United States Army Special Warfare School, *Counterinsurgency Planning Guide, Special Text Number 31-176* (Fort Bragg, NC: US Army Special Warfare School, May 1964), viii. Civic action quoted in William J. Ankley, "Civic-Action—Marine or Army Style?" 11 January 1968, Student Essay, US Army War College, MHI, 2.

37. Westmoreland to Wheeler, 26 June 1965, US Strategy in Vietnam, 1965–1975, Historian's Files, CMH. See also Richard A. Hunt, "Strategies at War: Pacification and Attrition in Vietnam," in *Lessons from an Unconventional War: Reassessing U.S. Strategies for Future*

Conflicts, ed. Richard A. Hunt and Richard H. Shultz Jr. (New York: Pergamon Press, 1982), 25.

38. Saigon station chief, Gordon L. Jorgensen, 20 July 1965, in William Conrad Gibbons, *The U.S. Government and the Vietnam War: Executive and Legislative Roles and Relationships, Part III: January–July 1965* (Princeton, NJ: Princeton University Press, 1989), 378.

39. Lewis Sorley, *Westmoreland: The General Who Lost Vietnam* (Boston: Houghton Mifflin Harcourt, 2011), 131. Sorley conveniently makes no mention of the M14 in this chapter, which was both a semi- and fully-automatic rifle, just like the AK47. John M. Carland, *Stemming the Tide: May 1965 to October 1966* (Washington, DC: Center of Military History, 2000), 55, 65. For a Vietnamese perspective on this topic, see Khuyen, "The RVNAF," in Sorley, *The Vietnam War*, 60–61; and "RVNAF Logistics," in Sorley, *The Vietnam War*, 384–385. Khuyen notes that not until 1967 did all communist forces employ the AK47 as their standard weapon.

40. Thomas L. McNaugher, *The M16 Controversies: Military Organizations and Weapons Acquisition* (New York: Praeger, 1984), 122. McNaugher also highlights the early M16's tendency to jam in the field, which embroiled the new rifle in controversy. See pp. 135–142. Brigham, *ARVN*, xi. On ARVN issue plan, see USMACV Command History, 1967, Office of Secy, Joint Staff, Mil. Hist. Branch, Entry MACJ03, Box 5, RG 472, NARA, 203.

41. A Program against the VC Infrastructure, 27 July 1967, Box 4, Richard M. Lee Papers, MHI, p. 2. In late 1966, Westmoreland spoke at a Mobile Training Team Course and emphasized that "the bulk of the military support of Revolutionary Development must rest on the shoulders of the ARVN." 8 December 1966, Box 44, Speeches (1944–1969), WPUSC.

42. Harvey Neese and John O'Donnell, eds., *Prelude to Tragedy: Vietnam, 1960–1965* (Annapolis, MD: Naval Institute Press, 2001), 111. James William Gibson, *The Perfect War: The War We Couldn't Lose and How We Did* (New York: Vintage Books, 1986, 1988), 294–295.

43. Westmoreland to Wheeler, 25 August 1967, Folder 6, Box 21, Series I Official Correspondence, W. C. Westmoreland Collection, MHI, 6. Terry T. Turner, "Mobile Advisory Teams in Vietnam: A Legacy Remembered," *On Point: The Journal of Army History*, Vol. 16, No. 4 (Spring 2011): 36. On MATs, see also Senior Officer Debriefing Program Report of LTG Fred C. Weyand, 4 October 1968, MHI, Annex C.

44. Morgan Sincock quoted in Eric M. Bergerud, *Red Thunder, Tropic Lightning: The World of a Combat Division in Vietnam* (Boulder, CO: Westview Press, 1993), 248. Truong in Sorley, *The Vietnam War*, 168–169.

45. On numerous advisor tasks, see Robert M. Montague Jr., "Advising in Government: An Account of the District Advisory Program in South Vietnam," 18 February 1966, Student Essay, US Army War College, MHI, 27; and Guide for Subsector Advisors, 1966, Historian's Files, CMH, 6.

46. Cushman in Maurer, *Strange Ground*, 521. See also Dockery, *Lost in Translation*, 13; and William J. Lederer, *Our Own Worst Enemy* (New York: W.W. Norton, 1968), 26.

47. Westmoreland in Command History, 1966, HQ USMACV, Entry MACJ03, Box 3, RG 472, NARA, p. 547. On the RVNAF training system, see "A Systems Analysis View of the Vietnam War: 1965–1972, Vol. 7-Rep. of Vietnam Armed Forces," CMH, 7. Collins, *The Development and Training of the South Vietnamese Army*, 75.

48. Nguyen Ba Lien quoted in Edward P. Metzner, *More Than a Soldier's War: Pacification in Vietnam* (College Station: Texas A&M University Press, 1995), 21. On US impatience, see Command History, United States Military Assistance Command, 1964, Entry MACJ03, Box 1, RG 472, NARA, p. 125. Vietnamese perspective from Vien et al., in Sorley, *The Vietnam War*, 681–682. Leverage from Clarke, in Werner and Huynh, *The Vietnam War*, 194.

49. Giltner quoted in Bergerud, *Red Thunder, Tropic Lightning*, 222. USARV, Battlefield Reports: A Summary of Lessons Learned, 30 June 1966, NARA. See also Kyle Longley, *Grunts: The American Combat Soldier in Vietnam* (Armonk, NY: M.E. Sharpe, 2008), 103; and Al Santoli, *Everything We Had: An Oral History of the Vietnam War by Thirty-three American Soldiers Who Fought It* (New York: Random House, 1981), 49.

50. Soldiers quoted in Bernard Edelman, ed., *Dear America: Letters Home from Vietnam* (New York: Pocket Books, 1986), 109–110; and Bergerud, *Red Thunder, Tropic Lightning*,

222–224. Inclinations in 25th Division Commander's Combat Notes, 1968, In-Country Publications Folder, Vietnam Tactics & Techniques, Historian's Files, CMH.

51. Hickey, *The American Military Advisor*, viii. Herring, "'People's Quite Apart,'" 11. On language barriers adding to this problem, see Senior Officer Debriefing Program Report of LTG W. B. Rosson, 11 October 1968, MHI, p. 13; and MG Ben Sternberg, VNIT Folder 1055, CMH, 13.

52. Moyar, *Triumph Forsaken*, 335. For early issues with these problems, see USMACV Command History, 1964, NARA, 117.

53. Frederick Taylor, "Wanted: South Vietnam Army Heroes," *Wall Street Journal*, 17 July 1967.

54. On social issues, see Nguyen Duy Hinh and Tran Dinh Tho, "The South Vietnamese Society," in Sorley, *The Vietnam War*, 715. On American press, see William M. Hammond, *Reporting Vietnam: Media and Military at War* (Lawrence: University Press of Kansas, 1998), 63.

55. Romie L. Brownlee and William J. Mullen III, *Changing an Army: An Oral History of General William E. DePuy, USA Retired* (Carlisle Barracks, PA: US Military History Institute, 1986), Box 1, William E. DePuy Papers, MHI, 123.

56. USMACV Command History, 1964, NARA, p. 122. Robert H. Scales Jr., *Firepower in Limited Warfare*, rev. ed. (Novato, CA: Presidio, 1995), 148. On ARVN problems, see Jonathan Randal, "Vietnam's Army: Sometimes It only Seems to Fight," *New York Times*, 11 June 1967.

57. Soldier quoted in Santoli, *Everything We Had*, 43. Victor H. Krulak, *First to Fight: An Inside View of the U.S. Marine Corps* (Annapolis, MD: Naval Institute Press, 1984), 195. See also, Neil Sheehan, *A Bright Shining Lie: John Paul Vann and America in Vietnam* (New York: Random House, 1988), 90; and Longley, *Grunts*, 96.

58. MACV, Blueprint for Vietnam, 1967, General Holdings, MHI, 1732. Westmoreland's 1967 End of Year Report, Folder 95, Thomas C. Thayer Papers, CMH, p. 14. See also USMACV Command History, 1964, NARA, 31.

59. William C. Westmoreland, interview by Charles B. MacDonald, 25 July 1985, LBJL, p. 5. Earlier US Army officer frustrations in Lawrence Freedman, *Kennedy's Wars: Berlin, Cuba, Laos, and Vietnam* (New York: Oxford University Press, 2000), 306.

60. Westmoreland quoted in *The Pentagon Papers*, II, 394. Colonel Wilbur Wilson quoted in Clarke, in Werner and Huynh, *The Vietnam War*, 47.

61. Quoted in William Tuohy, "How to Get Vietnamese Army to Pull Load Perplexes U.S.," *Los Angeles Times*, 14 July 1967. The problem of ARVN leadership did not go away under Abrams's tenure. See Senior Officer Debriefing Program Report of LTG W. R. Peers, 23 June 1969, MHI, 10.

62. William E. DePuy, interview by Les Brownlee and Bill Mullen, 26 March 1979, Box 1, William E. DePuy Papers, MHI, 8. Westmoreland even had to worry about ARVN officers being purged for their religious or political affiliation. Westmoreland to Taylor, 6 September 1964, *FRUS*, 1964–1968, I: 736.

63. Captain James B. Lincoln, in *A Vietnam War Reader: A Documentary History from American and Vietnamese Perspectives*, ed. Michael H. Hunt (Chapel Hill: University of North Carolina Press, 2010), 66. Gabriel Kolko, *Anatomy of a War: Vietnam, the United States, and the Modern Historical Experience* (New York: Pantheon Books, 1985), 255.

64. Tram Buu quoted in Robert K. Brigham, "Dreaming Different Dreams: The United States and the Army of the Republic of Vietnam," in *A Companion to the Vietnam War*, ed. Marilyn B. Young and Robert Buzzanco (Malden, MA: Blackwell, 2002), 147. See also Hammond, *Reporting Vietnam*, 86. One survey found "protracted operations" and "isolation location" as the top reasons for desertion. "A Systems Analysis View of the Vietnam War: 1965–1972, Vol. 7-Rep. of Vietnam Armed Forces," CMH, 66.

65. Ngo Quynh qoted in Brigham, *ARVN*, 40. Ngo Quynh arguably glossed over the fact that South Vietnamese nationalism was in truth defined largely by anticommunism and thus was a form of nationalism, even if not one that Ngo Quynh embraced. On ARVN problems, see also Wiest, *Vietnam's Forgotten Army*, 40; and Khuyen, "The RVNAF," in Sorley, *The Vietnam War*, 34.

66. Phillip B. Davidson, *Vietnam at War: The History: 1946–1975* (Novato, CA: Presidio, 1988), 371. Westmoreland's views in USMACV Command History, 1966, NARA, 461.

67. Colonel A.L. Hamblin Jr., Deputy Senior Advisor, CG I Corps, 1 Mar 66–1 July 67, Senior Officer Debriefing Reports, Box 6, 1 July 67, RG 472, NARA. Puppet army in Warren

Wilkins, *Grab Their Belts to Fight Them: The Viet Cong's Big Unit War against the U.S., 1965–1966* (Annapolis, MD: Naval Institute Press, 2011), 160. Gerard J. DeGroot, *A Noble Cause? America and the Vietnam War* (Harlow, Essex: Longman, 2000), 97.

68. General Westmoreland's Historical Briefing, 1 January 1967, Reel 8, Folder 12 History File, 13 Dec 66–26 Jan 67, WCWP. Westmoreland, *A Soldier Reports*, 310. LTC J. R. Meese, interview, 30 July 1968, VNIT Folder 239, CMH. MACV Monthly Evaluation Report, May 1966, MHI, 8.

69. Villagers quoted in Richard Shultz, "Coercive Force and Military Strategy: Deterrence Logic and the Cost-Benefit Model of Counterinsurgency Warfare," *The Western Political Quarterly*, Vol. 32, No. 4 (December 1979): 463–464; and James Walker Trullinger Jr., *Village at War: An Account of Revolution in Vietnam* (New York: Longman, 1980), 85. See also Stanley Karnow, *Vietnam: A History* (New York: Viking Press, 1983), 238; and Anne Blair, *There to the Bitter End: Ted Serong in Vietnam* (Crows Nest, Australia: Allen and Unwin, 2001), 38.

70. Frances FitzGerald, *Fire in the Lake: The Vietnamese and the Americans in Vietnam* (Boston: Little, Brown, 1972), 122. Louis A. Wiesner, *Victims and Survivors: Displaced Persons and Other War Victims in Viet-Nam, 1954–1975* (Westport, CT: Greenwood Press, 1988), 32. Westmoreland's views in MACV Commanders' Conference, 28 August 1966, US Strategy, Vietnam, 1965–75, Historian's Files, CMH, 29–30.

71. Henry Kissinger, *Ending the Vietnam War: A History of America's Involvement in and Extrication from the Vietnam War* (New York: Simon and Schuster, 2003), 81–82. TTU41. W. Scott Thompson and Donaldson D. Frizzell, eds., *The Lessons of Vietnam* (New York: Crane, Russak, 1977), 242.

72. Williams quoted in Schulimson, *The Joint Chiefs of Staff*, 21. See also Building a Strong National Vietnamese Army, an address by MG Samuel L. Myers, 17 April 1959, Folder 9, Box 6, Douglas Pike Collection: Other Manuscripts—American Friends of Vietnam, TTUVA. Harkins in Kaplan, Landa, and Drea, *The McNamara Ascendancy*, 281.

73. Wheeler to Westmoreland, 20 May 1966, *FRUS, 1964–1968*, IV: 394–395. For an example of this public criticism, see R. W. Apple Jr., "Saigon's Army: A U.S. Challenge," *New York Times*, 12 December 66.

74. Westmoreland to Wheeler and Sharp, 12 December 1966, Folder 7, Box 20, Series I Official Correspondence, W. C. Westmoreland Collection, MHI. On realizing limits of ARVN and RF/PF, see Analysis of Republic of Vietnam Armed Force (RVNAF), CY 1966, 27 April 1967, ARVN Strength, Org, Ability Folder, Historian's Files, CMH, A-14; and *The Pentagon Papers*, II: 381.

75. General Westmoreland's Historical Notes, 27 March 1967, Reel 19, Folder 15 History File, 13 Mar–30 Apr 67, WCWP. On 1967 campaign plan, see *The Pentagon Papers*, II: 493–497 and *The Pentagon Papers*, IV, 379. ARVN's role in RD in MACV General 1967 Command History, Part 2, Folder 1, Box 00, Bud Harton Collection, TTUVA, p. 605.

76. Westmoreland to Wheeler, 30 October 1967, Box 6, Paul L. Miles Papers, MHI. Sharp and Westmoreland, *Report on the War in Vietnam*, 215. The JCS official history noted that building up the RVNAF "remained high on the list of US goals even after US forces took over the principal burden of the fighting." JCS History, Part III, JCSHO, 51–1.

77. Westmoreland to Wheeler, 25 August 1967, Folder 6, Box 21, Series I Official Correspondence, W. C. Westmoreland Collection, MHI. MACV Monthly Evaluation Report, September 1967, MHI, p. 11. In March 1967, 40 percent of ARVN infantry battalions were in direct support of RD. MACV Monthly Evaluation Report, March 1967, MHI, 3.

78. "South Viet Nam," *Time*, 4 August 1967. Heintges to Westmoreland, 21 April 1967, Folder 6, Box 5, Series I Official Correspondence, W. C. Westmoreland Collection, MHI. MACV Quarterly Evaluation Report, December 1967, MHI, 19.

79. MACV General 1967 Command History, TTUVA, 576.

80. JCS History, Part III, JCSHO, p. 51–3. General Westmoreland's Historical Notes, 1 February 1968, Reel 12, Folder 29 History File, 1–29 Feb 69, WCWP.

81. Statement by General Westmoreland at LBJ Ranch, 30 May 1968, Reel 18, Analysis of Public Statements Folder III, WCWP, 30 May 1968. James H. Willbanks, *The Tet Offensive: A Concise History* (New York: Columbia University Press, 2007), 80–81.

82. Sharp and Westmoreland, *Report on the War in Vietnam*, 169. Bunker quoted in Lewis Sorley, ed., *Vietnam Chronicles: The Abrams Tapes, 1968–1972* (Lubbock: Texas Tech University Press, 2004), 98. Press Briefing, 1968 Tet Offensive in II CTZ, 17 April 1968, Folder 1, Bud Harton Collection, TTUVA, 7. *FRUS, 1964–1968*, VI: 477.

83. Robert W. Komer, *Organization and Management of the "New Model" Pacification Program—1966–1969* (Santa Monica, CA: Rand, 1970), 81. Debrief Report-Deputy Senior Advisor, II Corps Tactical Zone (BG John W. Barnes), 15 December 1968, Box 1, Senior Officer Debriefing Reports, HQ USARV Command History, RG472, NARA 10-38. Vietnamization in Herring, " 'People's Quite Apart,' " 15; and W. W. Rostow, *The Diffusion of Power: An Essay in Recent History* (New York: Macmillan, 1972), 520.

84. Notes of the President's Meeting with the Senior Foreign Affairs Advisory Council, 10 February 1968, *FRUS, 1964–1968*, VI: 179.

85. Historical Document 1968 Tet Offensive Actions in the II Corps Tactical Zone, 9 April 1968, Box 33, HQ USARV Command Historian After Action Reports, RG 472, NARA.

86. Senior Officer Debriefing Report, COL Gus S. Peters, Box 14, HQ USARV Command History Senior Officer Debriefing Reports, RG 472, NARA. See also USMACV Command History, 1968, Office of Secy, Joint Staff, MACV, Mil. Hist. Branch, Entry MACJ03, Box 6, RG 472, NARA, 26. The role of the media during Tet is still hotly contested among historians. For competing interpretations, see Charles Mohr, "Once Again—Did the Press Lose Vietnam?" in *The American Experience in Vietnam: A Reader*, ed. Grace Sevy (Norman: University of Oklahoma Press, 1989),150; Clarence R. Wyatt, *Paper Soldiers: The American Press and the Vietnam War* (New York: W.W. Norton, 1993), 183; and James Landers, *The Weekly War: Newsmagazines and Vietnam* (Columbia: University of Missouri Press, 2004), 191. Daniel C. Hallin, argues sensibly that even after Tet the media continued to "rely heavily on official information and to avoid passing judgment on official policy and statements." In "The Media, the War in Vietnam, and Political Support: A Critique of the Thesis of an Oppositional Media," *Journal of Politics*, Vol. 46, No. 1 (February 1984): 6.

87. Collins, *The Development and Training of the South Vietnamese Army*, 85–86. *FRUS, 1964–1968*, VI: 477. Thomas C. Thayer, "How to Analyze a War without Fronts: Vietnam, 1965–72," *Journal of Defense Research*, Series B: Tactical Warfare Vol. 7B, No. 3 (Fall 1975): 812. Willbanks, *The Tet Offensive*, 66. Clarke, *Advice and Support: The Final Years*, 313.

88. JCS History, Part III, JCSHO, p. 51–23.

89. LTC Robert Wagner quoted in Scales, *Firepower in Limited Warfare,*152. Clarke, *Advice and Support: The Final Years*, 333.

90. Eric Bergerud, "The Village War in Vietnam, 1965–1973," in *The Columbia History of the Vietnam War*, ed. David L. Anderson (New York: Columbia University Press, 2011), 271.

91. "War Take-Over by South Vietnam—When?"*U.S. News & World Report*, 13 May 1968. See also David F. Schmitz, *The Tet Offensive: Politics, War, and Public Opinion* (Lanham, MD: Rowman and Littlefield, 2005), 109; and Brian M. Jenkins, *The Unchangeable War*, RM-6278-ARPA, November 1970, CMH Library, v.

92. Melvin Zais, interview by William L. Golden and Richard C. Rice, 1977, Senior Officers Oral History Program, Melvin Zais Papers, MHI, pp. 475–476. The BDM Corporation, "A Study of Strategic Lessons Learned in Vietnam," Volume II, South Vietnam, General Holdings, MHI, EX-8.

93. Chiang Kai-shek quoted in William B. Hopkins, *The Pacific War: The Strategy, Politics, and Players That Won the War* (Minneapolis, MN: Zenith Press, 2008), 161.

94. Theodore H. White, *In Search of History: A Personal Adventure* (New York: Warner Books, 1978), 74, 83. For a more recent yet similar discussion, see Ahmed S. Hashim, *Insurgency and Counterinsurgency in Iraq* (Ithaca: Cornell University Press, 2006), 299.

95. George McTurnan Kahin and John Wilson Lewis, *The United States in Vietnam*, rev. ed. (New York: Dial Press, 1969), 339. Lawrence E. Grinter, "Bargaining between Saigon and Washington: Dilemmas of Linkage Politics during War," *Orbis*, Vol. 18, No. 3 (Fall 1974): 837. Bernard Brodie argued that it was "impossible from the beginning to succeed" because we "were supporting a government that not only did not deserve that

support but which could not benefit from it." *War and Politics* (New York: Macmillan, 1973), 173.

96. Kahin and Lewis, *The United States in Vietnam*. USMACV Command History, 1966, NARA, 7. Komer to President Johnson, 13 April 1966, *FRUS, 1964–1968*, IV: 346.

97. DePuy to Westmoreland, 6 February 1965, Folder D65, Box 4, William E. DePuy Papers, MHI. Operational Guidelines for Advisory Support of Revolutionary Development Cadre, 13 June 1966, Revolutionary Development Folder 2, Box 1, Richard M. Lee Papers, MHI, 2.

98. DePuy to Westmoreland, 1 February 1965, Folder D65, Box 4, William E. DePuy Papers, MHI. See also "People's War in Vietnam," 28 April 1965, Congressional Records-Senate, Lansdale Folder, Box 249, OSDHO.

99. *The Pentagon Papers*, II: 164.

100. Thomas J. Barnes, Thoughts on Pacification, Advisory, 1965–73 Folder, Historian's Files, CMH, John L. Throckmorton, interview by Paul Fisher and David H. Harris, 1978, Senior Officer Oral History Program, Box 1, J. L. Throckmorton Papers, MHI, 4. Kahin and Lewis, *The United States in Vietnam*, 363. Halberstam, *The Making of a Quagmire*, 7.

Conclusion

1. Lee Leseaze, "Westmoreland Sees No Early Viet Victory," *Washington Post*, 11 June 1968. John Maffre, "Military Color Sets Off New Army Chief of Staff," *Washington Post*, 4 July 1968. On being "kicked upstairs," see Larry Berman, *Lyndon Johnson's War: The Road to Stalemate in Vietnam* (New York: W.W. Norton, 1989), 191; and Phillip B. Davidson, *Vietnam at War, the History: 1946–1975* (Novato, CA: Presidio Press, 1988), 479–480.

2. Peter Braestrup, "The Abrams Strategy in Vietnam," *The New Leader*, 9 June 1969, 4. See also Graham A. Cosmas, *MACV: The Joint Command in the Years of Withdrawal, 1968–1973* (Washington, D: Center of Military History, 2007), 108.

3. MACV Lesson Learned 80, U.S. Combat Forces in Support of Pacification, 1970, in Andrew J. Birtle, *U.S. Army Counterinsurgency and Contingency Operations Doctrine, 1942–1976* (Washington, DC: Center of Military History, 2006), 367. Bernard Weinraub, "Abrams for Westmoreland—A Sharp Contrast," *New York Times*, 16 June 1968. The topic of consistency versus change in MACV continues to arouse heated debate. For those advocating a change, see Lewis Sorley, *A Better War: The Unexamined Victories and Final Tragedy of America's Last Years in Vietnam* (New York: Harcourt Brace, 1999); and John A. Nagl, "Counterinsurgency in Vietnam: American Organizational Culture and Learning," in *Counterinsurgency in Modern Warfare*, ed. Daniel Marston and Carter Malkasian (New York: Osprey, 2008), 143. On the more plausible argument of consistency, see Ronald H. Spector, "William C. Westmoreland and Creighton W. Abrams: Leadership and Innovation in Vietnam," in *Military Leadership and Command: The John Biggs Cincinnati Lectures, 1988*, ed. Henry S. Bausum (Lexington, VA: VMI Foundation, 1989), 127–138; and Robert Komer in *The Lessons of Vietnam*, ed. W. Scott Thompson and Donaldson D. Frizzell (New York: Crane, Russak, 1977), 79. Neither Ambassador Komer nor General Philip Davidson, both of whom served under Westmoreland *and* Abrams, believed there was a change in strategic concepts. McGeorge Bundy noted in 1966 that Westmoreland had "set the shape of MACV so firmly that any successor will be guided by many of his standards." Bundy to President Johnson, 16 February 1966, *FRUS, 1964–1968*, IV: 233.

4. Abrams to Wheeler, 24 June 1968, Abrams Messages #766, CMH. Abrams to Wheeler, 28 July 1968, Abrams Message #969, CMH. At one meeting in 1967, Abrams, for instance, "brought up the subject of development of a killer instinct in all U.S. and F.W. combat forces." CIIB Meeting, 7 October 1967, Body Counts File, History Division Safe 78/1, CMH.

5. Ronald H. Spector, *After Tet: The Bloodiest Year in Vietnam* (New York: Free Press, 1993), 116. Dale Andrade, "Westmoreland Was Right: Learning Wrong Lessons from the Vietnam War," *Small Wars & Insurgencies*, Vol. 19, No. 2 (June 2008): 148.

6. Eliot A. Cohen, "Will There Be an Afghanistan Syndrome?" *Washington Post*, 27 June 2010. See also John Nagl, *Learning to Eat Soup with a Knife: Counterinsurgency Lessons from Malaya and Vietnam* (Chicago: University of Chicago Press, 2002), 126.

7. Post Mortem on Vietnam Strategy, 6 September 1968, US Strategy, Vietnam 1965–1975, Historian's Files, CMH, 3.

8. Holbrook quoted in Lewis Sorley's *Westmoreland: The General Who Lost Vietnam* (Boston: Houghton Mifflin Harcourt, 2011), 67. For an example of the flawed narrative in which the army failed to adapt its "shallow" strategy, see Cincinnatus, *Self-Destruction: The Disintegration and Decay of the United States Army during the Vietnam Era* (New York: W.W. Norton, 1981), 9.

9. "A Symposium on Province Operations in South Vietnam, June 13–17 1966," Command Information Publications, Folder 101217, Box 18, RG 472, NARA, p. 8. "Tactical Standing Operating Procedure for Counterinsurgency Operations," Headquarters, 1st Brigade, 101st Division, published 1 June 1966, VNI Folder 17, CMH, vii.

10. "Ideas for Discussion with General Weyand," Box 7, Arthur S. Collins Papers, MHI. For a counterargument, see Herbert Y. Schandler, "America and Vietnam: The Failure of Strategy," in *Regular Armies and Insurgency*, ed. Ronald Haycock (London: Croom Helm, 1979), 84.

11. This point expressed by Lloyd Gardner, email with author, 16 February 2012. See also David J. Lonsdale, "Strategy," in *Understanding Modern Warfare*, ed. David Jordan et al. (New York: Cambridge University Press, 2008), 53. On "lessons," see John Prados, *The Hidden History of the Vietnam War* (Chicago: Ivan R. Dee, 1995), ix.

12. For an example acknowledging US limitations, see William S. Turley, *The Second Indochina War: A Short Political and Military History, 1954–1975*, 2nd ed. (Lanham, MD: Rowman and Littlefield, 1986, 2009), 241. MACV conceded in 1966 "there was no magic solution to the VC/NVA threat." Command History, United States Military Assistance Command, 1966, Entry MACJ03, Box 3, RG 472, NARA, 65.

13. Ho Chi Minh quoted in *Major Problems in the History of the Vietnam War*, 2d ed., ed. Robert J. McMahon (Lexington, MA: D.C. Heath, 1995), 303. Underestimating the enemy in Edward J. Drea, *McNamara, Clifford, and the Burdens of Vietnam, 1965–1969* (Washington, DC: Office of the Secretary of Defense Historical Office, 2011), 114; and Mark Atwood Lawrence, *The Vietnam War: A Concise International History* (New York: Oxford University Press, 2008), 99.

14. Pickett quoted in Jordan, *Understanding Modern Warfare*, 31. On strategic interactions and reciprocity, see Colin S. Gray, *Fighting Talk: Forty Maxims on War, Peace, and Strategy* (Westport, CT: Praeger Security International, 2007), 66; and Hew Strachan, *Clausewitz's On War: A Biography* (New York: Atlantic Monthly Press, 2007), 84.

15. *Victory in Vietnam: The Official History of the People's Army of Vietnam, 1954–1975*, trans. Merle L. Pribbenow (Lawrence: University Press of Kansas, 2002), 153. War Experiences Recapitulation Committee of the High-Level Military Institute, *The Anti-U.S. Resistance War for National Salvation 1954–1975: Military Events* (Hanoi: People's Army Publishing House, 1980), 72. "A Systems Analysis View of the Vietnam War: 1965–1972, Vol. 4–Allied Ground and Naval Operations," Geog. V. Vietnam-319.1, CMH, 50.

16. Lien-Hang T. Nguyen, *Hanoi's War: An International History of the War for Peace in Vietnam* (Chapel Hill: University of North Carolina Press, 2012), 3. Robert K. Brigham, *Guerrilla Diplomacy: The NLF's Foreign Relations and the Viet Nam War* (Ithaca, NY: Cornell University Press, 1999), x. Gabriel Kolko, *Anatomy of a War: Vietnam, the United States, and the Modern Historical Experience* (New York: Pantheon Books, 1985), 138–141.

17. Larry Cable, *Unholy Grail: The US and the Wars in Vietnam, 1965–8* (London: Routledge, 1991), viii. William J. Duiker, *Sacred War: Nationalism and Revolution in a Divided Vietnam* (Boston: McGraw-Hill, 1995), 184. Mai Elliott, *RAND in Southeast Asia: A History of the Vietnam War Era* (Santa Monica, CA: Rand, 2010), 157. On Hanoi's long-term goals, see John Prados, *Vietnam: The History of an Unwinnable War, 1945–1975* (Lawrence: University Press of Kansas, 2009), 144.

18. Vo Nguyen Giap, *People's War, People's Army* (Honolulu: University Press of the Pacific, 1961, 2001), 46. War Experiences Recapitulation Committee of the High-Level Military Institute, 30. Nguyen, *Hanoi's War*, 40–43. It is important to note that the dynamic of war did not always reflect Party dictates. See David W. P. Elliott, *The Vietnamese War: Revolution and Social Change in the Mekong Delta, 1930–1975*, concise ed. (Armonk, NY: M.E. Sharpe,

2003, 2007), 17; and David Hunt, *Vietnam's Southern Revolution: From Peasant Insurrection to Total War* (Amherst: University of Massachusetts Press, 2008), 29.

19. Lieutenant General Fred C. Weyand, Senior Officer Debriefing Reports, Box 17, RG 472, NARA, 2–3.

20. General W. C. Westmoreland, interview by Paul L. Miles Jr., 10 April 1971, Box 1, Paul L. Miles Papers, MHI, p. 10. Richard A. Hunt, "Strategies at War: Pacification and Attrition in Vietnam," in *Lessons from an Unconventional War: Reassessing U.S. Strategies for Future Conflicts*, ed. Richard A. Hunt and Richard H. Shultz Jr. (New York: Pergamon Press, 1982), 28. Robert S. McNamara, James G. Blight, Robert K. Brigham, et al., *Argument without End: In Search of Answers to the Vietnam Tragedy* (New York: Public Affairs, 1999), 213.

21. William B. Rosson, "Four Periods of American Involvement in Vietnam: Development and Implementation of Policy, Strategy and Programs, Described and Analyzed on the Basis of Experience at Progressively Senior Levels" (Ph.D. diss., University of Oxford, 1979), 192. David W. P. Elliott, *NLF-DRV Strategy and the 1972 Spring Offensive* (Ithaca, NY: Cornell University International Relations of East Asia Project, 1974), 2. David W. P. Elliott, "Hanoi's Strategy in the Second Indochina War," in *The Vietnam War: Vietnamese and American Perspectives*, ed. Jayne S. Werner and Luu Doan Huynh (Armonk, NY: M.E. Sharpe, 1993), 67. Marc Jason Gilbert, "Introduction," in Why *the North Won the Vietnam War*, ed. Marc Jason Gilbert (New York: Palgrave, 2002), 27.

22. George A. Carver, "The Faceless Viet Cong," *Foreign Affairs*, Vol. 44, No. 3 (April 1966): 348. Advanced Research Projects Agency, "Village Defense Study—Vietnam," CORDS Historical Working Group Files, 1967–1973, Box 3, RG 472, NARA, 8. MACV Monthly Evaluation Report, April 1966, MHI, 2. War Experiences Recapitulation Committee of the High-Level Military Institute, 46.

23. Douglas Pike quoted in Davidson, *Vietnam at War*, 22. Jeffrey Race, *War Comes to Long An: Revolutionary Conflict in a Vietnamese Province* (Berkeley: University of California Press, 1972), 205.

24. Giap, *People's War, People's Army*, 47. See also George K. Tanham, *Communist Revolutionary Warfare: From the Vietminh to the Viet Cong* (Westport, CT: Praeger Security International, 1961, 2006), 33.

25. Johnson quoted in Jeffrey Record, *The Wrong War: Why We Lost in Vietnam* (Annapolis, MD: Naval Institute Press, 1998), viii. Ang Cheng Guan, *The Vietnam War from the Other Side: The Vietnamese Communists' Perspective* (New York: Routledge Curzon, 2002), 114. John Prados, *The Blood Road: The Ho Chi Minh Trail and the Vietnam War* (New York: John Wiley, 1999), 86.

26. Peter Arnett, "Viet Cong Forced to Shift Strategy," *Christian Science Monitor*, 8 February 1967. Warren Wilkins, *Grab Their Belts to Fight Them: The Viet Cong's Big Unit War Against the U.S., 1965–1966* (Annapolis, MD: Naval Institute Press, 2011), 128. Brigham, *Guerrilla Diplomacy*, 41.

27. The BDM Corporation, "A Study of Strategic Lessons Learned in Vietnam," Volume II, Conduct of the War, General Holdings, MHI, 2–32. Thomas C. Thayer, "How to Analyze a War without Fronts: Vietnam, 1965–72," *Journal of Defense Research, Series B: Tactical Warfare*, Vol. 7B, No. 3 (Fall 1975): 835.

28. Strachan, *Clausewitz's* On War, 142.

29. John M. Gates, "Vietnam: The Debate Goes On," in *Assessing the Vietnam War: A Collection from the Journal of the U.S. Army War College*, ed. Lloyd J. Matthews and Dale E. Brown (Washington, DC: Pergamon-Brassey's International Defense Publishers, 1987), 53. See also Wilkins, *Grab Their Belts to Fight Them*, 10.

30. "Kennedy on Vietnam: An Unwinnable War," *U.S. News & World Report*, 19 February 1968. Tom Wickers, "Kennedy Asserts U.S. Cannot Win," *New York Times*, 9 February 1968. Townsend Hoopes to the Secretary of Defense, "The Infeasibility of Military Victory in Vietnam," 14 March 1968, Folder 1, Box 11, Larry Berman Collection (Presidential Archives Research), TTUVA, 12. Barbara W. Tuchman, *Practicing History* (New York: Ballantine Books, 1981), 257. Essay originally published in *Newsday*, 8 March 1968.

31. Bruce Palmer, interview (I) by Ted Gittinger, 28 May 1982, LBJL, I-30. Maurice E. Jessup, "The Validity of the Civic Action Concept," 24 January 1968, Student Paper, Course 4, US Army War College, MHI, 5.

32. James S. Olson, *The Vietnam War: Handbook of the Literature and Research* (Westport, CT: Greenwood Press, 1993), 106.

33. G. C. Hickey, *The American Military Advisor and His Foreign Counterpart: The Case of Vietnam* (Santa Monica, CA: Rand, 1965), 10. Hickey was speaking of "Americans" in general. McNamara, *Argument without End*, 24. On impatience, see Boyd T. Bashore, "Organization for Frontless Wars," *Military Review* Vol. 44, No. 5 (May 1964): 9; Lieutenant Colonel Charles P. Graham, interview by Peter L. Sawin, 29 June 1968, VNIT 3, CMH, p. 4. On time-space relationships, see Dima Adamsky, *The Culture of Military Innovation: The Impact of Cultural Factors on the Revolution in Military Affairs in Russia, the US, and Israel* (Stanford, CA: Stanford Security Studies, 2010), 51.

34. Quach Hai Luong quoted in McNamara, *Argument without End*, 191. Douglas S. Blaufarb, *The Counterinsurgency Era: U.S. Doctrine and Performance, 1950 to Present* (New York: Free Press, 1977), 91.

35. Allan E. Goodman, "South Vietnam: Neither War nor Peace," *Asian Survey*, Vol. 10, No. 2 (February 1970): 112. J. Menkes and R. G. Jones, "Pacification in Vietnam," June 1967, CORDS Historical Working Group Files, 1967–1973, Box 1, RG 472, NARA, 22. James H. Lebovic, *The Limits of U.S. Military Capability: Lessons from Vietnam and Iraq* (Baltimore, MD: Johns Hopkins University Press, 2010), 37. For a GVN official's perspective on these problems, see Nguyen Thai, *Is South Vietnam Viable?* (Manila, Philippines: Carmelo and Bauermann, 1962), 71, 77–82.

36. The BDM Corporation, Conduct of the War, MHI, p. vii. Robert Taber, *The War of the Flea: The Classic Study of Guerrilla Warfare* (New York: Lyle Stuart, 1965; Washington, DC: Potomac Books, 2002), 18. See also Robert E. Osgood, *Limited War Revisited* (Boulder, CO: Westview Press, 1979), 37; and Lawrence, *The Vietnam War*, 109.

37. On this point, see Edward Miller, *Misalliance: Ngo Dinh Diem, the United States, and the Fate of South Vietnam* (Cambridge, MA: Harvard University Press, 2013), 311, 325.

38. Taylor quoted in William Conrad Gibbons, *The U.S. Government and the Vietnam War: Executive and Legislative Roles and Relationships, Part III: January–July 1965* (Princeton, NJ: Princeton University Press, 1989), 158. Hanson Baldwin reported, "The War in South Vietnam—Is Victory for the West Possible," *New York Times*, 16 February 1964. Jeffrey Race, "How They Won," *Asian Survey*, Vol. 10, No. 8 (August 1970): 629. Seth Jacobs, *Cold War Mandarin: Ngo Dinh Diem and the Origins of America's War in Vietnam, 1950–1963* (Lanham, MD: Rowman and Littlefield, 2006), 181.

39. Edward G. Miller, comments to author, 27 August 2013. Laurence E. Grinter, "How They Lost: Doctrine, Strategies and Outcomes of the Vietnam War," *Asian Survey*, Vol. 15, No. 12 (December 1975): 1115. Daniel Moran, *Wars of National Liberation* (London: Cassell, 2001), 207. For a counterargument, see Westmoreland to Wheeler, 25 August 1967, Folder 6, Box 21, Series I Official Correspondence, W. C. Westmoreland Collection, MHI. Westmoreland thought the "country is coming alive in the political sense. See also Anthony James Joes, *The War for South Viet Nam, 1954–1975*, rev. ed. (Westport, CT: Praeger, 2001), xiii.

40. Michael V. Forrestal, interview by Paige E. Mulhollan, 3 November 1969, LBJL, I-8.

41. Douglas Pike, interview by Ted Gittinger, 4 June 1981, LBJL, p. I-13. On leverage, see Lebovic, *The Limits of U.S. Military Capability*, chapter 5.

42. Arthur Schlesinger Jr., "A Middle Way Out of Vietnam," *New York Times Magazine*, 18 September 1966.

43. Senior Officer Debriefing Program Report of LTG Fred C. Weyand, 4 October 1968, MHI, 4.

44. Dennis A. Leach, interview by Brian C. Bade, 1983, Senior Officer Oral History Program, Box 21, Company Command in Vietnam, MHI, p. LVII-13. John V. Tunney, *Measuring Hamlet Security in Vietnam: Report of a Special Study Mission* (Washington, DC: US Government Printing Office, 1969), 2.

45. Barbara W. Tuchman, *The March of Folly: From Troy to Vietnam* (New York: Alfred A. Knopf, 1984), 329. See also James L. Trainor, "What Business Does the Military Have in Pacification/Nation-Buidling?" *Armed Forces Management* (August 1967): 32–33, 71–72.

46. David Halberstam, *The Best and the Brightest* (New York: Random House, 1969), 552. Sickness in Malcolm W. Browne, *The New Face of War*, rev. ed. (Indianapolis: Bobbs-Merrill, 1968), 280. Rupert Smith, *The Utility of Force: The Art of War in the Modern World* (New York: Alfred A. Knopf, 2007), 7.

47. Brian M. Jenkins, *The Unchangeable War*, RM-6278-ARPA, November 1970, CMH Library, 4. See also Jeffrey S. Milstein, *Dynamics of the Vietnam War: A Quantitative Analysis and Prediction Computer Simulation* (Columbus: Ohio State University Press, 1974), 151.

48. John H. Hay Jr., end of tour interview, 20 July 1968, VNIT Folder 205, CMH, 26.

49. U. S. Grant Sharp and William C. Westmoreland, *Report on the War in Vietnam* (Washington, DC: U.S. Government Printing Office, 1969), 132.

50. Stanley Karnow, *Vietnam: A History* (New York: Viking Press, 1983), 464. Dave R. Palmer, *Summons of the Trumpet: U.S.-Vietnam Perspective* (San Rafael, CA: Presidio Press, 1978), 15–16. Michael D. Pearlman, *Warmaking and American Democracy: The Struggle over Military Strategy, 1700 to Present* (Lawrence: University Press of Kansas, 1999), 338.

51. William E. DePuy, "Vietnam: What We Might Have Done and Why We Didn't Do It," *Army* (February 1986): 31. See also Smith, *The Utility of Force*, 217.

52. William C. Westmoreland, *A Soldier Reports* (Garden City, NY: Doubleday, 1976), 255. Bruce Palmer Jr., exit interview, 26 June 1968, VNIT Folder 185, CMH. Lawrence E. Grinter, "The Pacification of South Vietnam: Dilemmas of Counterinsurgency and Development" (Ph.D. diss., University of North Carolina at Chapel Hill, 1972), 87.

53. Robert S. McNamara, *In Retrospect: The Tragedy and Lessons of Vietnam* (New York: Times Books, 1995), 322. Cable, *Unholy Grail*, 48.

54. William E. DePuy, interview by Les Brownlee and Bill Mullen, 26 March 1979, Box 1, William E. DePuy Papers, MHI, 14.

55. Eliot A. Cohen and John Gooch, *Military Misfortunes: The Anatomy of Failure in War* (New York: Vintage Books, 1990), 23. On Westmoreland's views of this problem, see Herbert Y. Schandler, *The Unmaking of a President: Lyndon Johnson and Vietnam* (Princeton, NJ: Princeton University Press, 1977), 62.

56. Jon Tetsuro Sumida, *Decoding Clausewitz: A New Approach to* On War (Lawrence: University Press of Kansas, 2008), 147. Carl von Clausewitz rightly stated "effects in war seldom rise from a single cause." *On War*, ed. and trans. Michael Howard and Peter Paret (New York: Alfred A. Knopf Everyman's Library, 1976, 1993), 182.

57. Neil Sheehan, "Realism in Saigon," *New York Times*, 28 February 1966.

58. On this general point, see John Lewis Gaddis, *The Landscape of History: How Historians Map the Past* (New York: Oxford University Press, 2002), 65, 71.

59. D. H. Armsby, "Proposed Study Project on Indicators of Political Success in South Vietnam," 2 September 1966, Folder 86, War Indicators SVN, Thomas C. Thayer Papers, CMH.

60. Eugenia C. Kiesling, discussion with author, 4 December 2012.

61. James McAllister, "Who Lost Vietnam? Soldiers, Civilians, and U.S. Military Strategy in Vietnam," *International Security*, Vol. 35, No. 3 (Winter 2010/11): 121. Gilbert, *Why the North Won the Vietnam War*, 3.

62. On this point see Colin S. Gray, *Modern Strategy* (New York: Oxford University Press, 1999), 44.

63. Halberstam, *The Best and the Brightest*, 550. "Notably stupid" in Thomas E. Ricks, "What Ever Happened to Accountability?" *Harvard Business Review* (October 2012): 97.

INDEX

Abrams, Creighton, 78, 85, 90, 110, 120, 155, 164, 170–171
air war, 11, 60, 96, 97
Algeria, 19, 25, 27, 29, 33, 34
Alsop, Joseph, 62, 79
American University, 29
Annam, 40
Ap Bac, battle of, 153
Army of the Republic of Vietnam (ARVN), xx, 12, 47– 49, 51, 59, 61, 75, 80, 88, 138, 148, 152, 155, 156, 161–163, 167, 181
    combined operations, 99, 106, 107, 110, 115
    criticism of, 52
    desertions, 98, 103, 142, 159, 161, 166
    divisions
        5th, 101
        7th, 49, 153
        22nd, 166
        25th, 103, 170
    and performance in Tet, 164–165, 166
    under MAAG training, 45, 149, 150
    and US advisors, 152–153, 157–160, 162, 169, 177
Arnett, Peter, 175–176
attrition, ix, xix, xx, xxi, xxiv, 9–10, 13–14, 75, 77, 78, 86, 91, 94, 106, 115, 116, 138, 167, 172, 182
August Revolution, 44

Badenov, Boris, 31
Baldwin, Hanson, 13, 178
Ball, George, 62, 69, 72
Bergerud, Eric, 121
Berlin, 21, 65
Biggio, Charles, 32–33
Birtle, Andrew, 8
body counts, ix, xix, 8, 9, 82–83, 93, 94, 98, 111, 112, 172
Braestrup, Peter, 170

Browne, Malcolm W., 100, 118–119
Buddhists, 53
Bundy, McGeorge, xxii, 62, 69, 207n93
Bundy, William, 60, 207n93
Bunker, Ellsworth, 86, 120, 165
Buu, Tram, 161

CBS, xxi
Cambodia, 50, 83, 95, 98, 102, 103, 106, 109, 111, 113, 143
Cao Dai, 148
Carver, George A. Jr., 175
Central Highlands, 95, 96, 98, 102, 103, 109, 110, 117, 126
Central Intelligence Agency (CIA), 32, 42, 43, 49, 51, 52, 60, 68, 84, 85, 122, 127, 128, 129, 141, 155, 175, 181
Central Office for South Vietnam, (COSVN), 106, 173
Chiang Kai-Shek, 167
Chien Thang plan, 122
Chieu Hoi, 135, 136
China, 20, 25, 39, 42, 46, 59, 68, 70, 71, 74, 167, 173
Chinese Civil War, 15, 18, 28, 31
Chinh, Phan Trong, 87
Chinh, Truong, 173
civic action, 24, 27, 36, 80, 93, 99, 101, 106, 112, 114, 115, 121, 127, 138, 162
    definition of, 34–35, 155
civil affairs, xxii, 33, 34, 36, 84, 101
Civil Guard, 46, 48, 149–150, 154
civil-military relations, 5, 19
Civil Operations and Revolutionary Development Support (CORDS), 128, 129, 130, 131, 132, 134, 136, 137, 138, 140, 143, 144, 171
Clausewitz, Carl von, xxiii, 3–4
clear and hold operations, 48, 104, 122, 125

Clifford, Clark M., 89
Cochinchina, 40
Cohen, Eliot A., 181
Cold War, xx, 3, 6, 9, 11, 14, 16, 17, 20, 21, 22,
        23, 30, 35, 36, 43, 60, 62, 74, 90, 93, 117,
        148, 172, 173, 181
Collins, Arthur S., 92–93, 109, 110, 112
Collins, Harold K., 119
Colonialism, French, 31, 40, 41, 126, 161, 162
Combined Action Platoons (CAPs), 80–81, 104
Combined Civil Action Coordination Center
        (CACC), 107
Combined Intelligence Center (CIC), 107
Combined Lightning Initial Project, 104
Commander in Chief, Pacific
        (CINCPAC), 11, 72
communism, xxii, 1, 17, 19, 21, 31, 39, 43, 111,
        147, 161, 162
containment, 16, 19, 38, 44, 62, 179
Continental Army Command, 26
Cosmas, Graham, 8
Counterguerilla Operations, 24, 25
counterinsurgency, xxiii, 2, 16, 21, 22, 23, 26, 27,
        28, 34, 48, 79, 95, 100, 116, 122, 144,
        149, 151, 155, 162, 179, 180
    definitions of, 24, 27, 92
Counterinsurgency Plan (CIP), 49, 151
Crean, John, 129
Cushman, John H., 150, 157
Cyprus, 17, 29
Czechoslovakia, 17

Dak To, 113, 114, 140
Darling, Kenneth, 34
Davidson, Phillip B., 11
Dawkins, Peter M., 151
Decker, George H., 30
decolonization, 10, 14, 15, 17, 20, 22, 36,
        141, 172
Defense Intelligence Agency, 153
Delbrück, Hans, 9
Democratic Republic of Vietnam (DRV), 41, 42,
        (*see also* North Vietnam)
DePuy, William E., 80, 99–100, 101, 160–161,
        168, 180, 181
Diem, Bui, 154
Diem, Ngo Dinh, 42, 43, 44, 47, 48, 49, 50, 52,
        53, 54, 122, 148, 149, 151, 152, 177–178
Dien Bien Phu, 32, 38, 42, 140
Dockery, Martin J., 153
doctrine, US Army, 6, 11, 16, 17, 22, 23, 25, 46,
        50, 75, 85, 117, 122, 124, 132, 145, 180
Durbrow, Elbridge, 151

economic development, ix, 23, 25, 35, 36, 47, 68,
        84, 123, 130, 144, 155
Eisenhower, Dwight D., 1, 11, 19, 20, 21, 43, 172

Elliott, David, 134
enclaves, xxv, 61, 78–79, 80, 213n58
Enthoven, Alain, 88

Falkenhayn, Erich Von, xix
Fall, Bernard, 34, 53
Field Service Regulations, 6, 17, 21, 22
firepower, 8, 9, 20, 26, 82, 92–93, 94, 95, 101,
        112, 159, 175
Fitzgerald, Frances, 108, 162
flexible response, 21
Forrestal, Michael V., 178
Fort Bragg, 29, 58
Fort Campbell, 2
Fort Knox, 29
France, 21, 27, 29, 40
free fire zones, 96, 105, 106, 179
Free World Forces, 81, 114, 1137, 164
French-Indochina War, 32, 33, 42, 44, 45,
        159, 160

Gaddis, John Lewis, xxiii
Gallagher, Wes, 142
Galula, David, 25, 26, 30, 57
Gavin, James M., 79
Geneva Accords (1954), 36, 42, 43, 45, 159
Giap, Vo Nguyen, 16, 26, 73, 139, 173, 174, 175
    in French-Indochina War, 42, 44
Giltner, Thomas, 158
Gooch, John, 181
"Good Neighbor" program, 112–113
Government of South Vietnam (GVN), xx,
        xxv, 12, 44, 46, 47, 56, 59, 72, 76, 83,
        102, 108, 117, 121, 122, 125, 131,
        132, 135, 136, 147, 152, 160, 166, 168,
        177, 202n31
Grant, Ulysses S., xix, 185n1
Gray, Colin, 4–5
Great Britain, 21
Great Society, 60, 68, 69, 86
Greece, 17, 19, 20
guerilla warfare, 16, 18, 22, 25, 27, 31, 32, 41, 46,
        61, 176
guerre révolutionnaire, 28, 33
Guevara, Ché, 16
Gulf of Tonkin, 58, 59

Halberstam, David, 133, 153, 179, 183
Hamlet Evaluation System (HES), 136–137
Hammer, Ellen, 47
Hanoi, 32, 43, 44, 46, 50, 57, 58, 60–62, 65–68,
        70, 72, 74, 76, 81, 83, 86, 89, 90, 96,
        98, 117, 119, 138, 139, 141, 172, 173,
        174, 175
Hao Hao, 148
Herr, Michael, 137
Harkins, Paul, 50, 51, 52, 53, 54, 55, 56, 163

Hilsman, Roger, 23, 51–52
Ho Chi Minh, xxii, 31, 33, 40–41, 42, 73, 81, 172
Ho Chi Minh Trail, 84, 86, 96
Holbrook, Willard Jr., 171
Honolulu Conference, 82, 126
Hoopes, Townsend, 176
Hop Tac program, 124
Howard, Michael, 5
Huk campaign, 29, 32
Huntington, Samuel, 107

Ia Drang, battles of, 74, 94, 97, 98, 114, 120, 147,
    155, 180
India, 10, 44
Indochina, 17, 18, 27, 32, 33, 34, 36, 39, 40
Indochinese Communist Party (ICP), 40, 41
Indonesia, 44, 62
Industrial College of the Armed Forces, 26
Infantry, 34
Iron Triangle, 105, 106, 107
"irregular warfare," 22

Japan, 30, 32, 41, 167
Jenkins, Brian M., 180
Johnson, Harold K., 27, 36, 63, 71, 83, 88–89
Johnson, Lyndon B., xxii, xxiii, 2, 7, 38, 44, 54,
    56, 58, 59, 60, 62, 65–69, 72, 76, 82, 85,
    86, 88, 90, 105, 126, 127, 128, 131, 137,
    139, 165, 175
Joint Chiefs of Staff (JCS), 11, 25, 29, 44, 48, 49,
    58, 59, 67, 68, 70, 71, 72, 73, 75, 77, 85,
    86, 92, 109, 120, 140, 151, 155, 163
Just, Ward, 10, 93, 113, 147

Kanh, Nguyen, 57
Kennan, George F., 6, 16, 18
Kennedy, Edward, 108
Kennedy, John F., 2, 21, 23, 39, 48, 49, 50, 54,
    71, 152
Kennedy, Kenneth, 27
Kennedy, Robert F., 23, 176
Khe Sanh, 140
Khrushchev, Nikita, 19, 20
Kinnard, Harry W., 97
Kissinger, Henry, 19, 20
Knowlton, William A., 104–105, 128
Komer, Robert W., 128, 129, 130, 131, 137, 143,
    144, 145, 148, 165
Korean War, xx, 1, 5, 8, 9, 15, 18, 20, 26, 35, 44,
    45, 48, 56, 68, 110, 149, 170
Krepinevich, Andrew F., 94
Krulak, Victor, 61, 79, 80, 81, 159–160, 213n60
Ky, Nguyen Cao, 82

Laird, Melvin, 163
Lange, H. W., 137
Lansdale, Edward, 32, 34, 47

Larsen, Stanley R., 109–110
Lao Dong Party Resolution 12, 73
Laos, 21, 42, 44, 50, 83, 143
learning organizations, 5, 8, 14
Lebanon Crisis, 2
Le Duan, 43, 47, 73, 95, 139, 141, 173, 174, 176
Lemnitzer, Lyman, 25
Lenin, Vladimir, 16
Liddell hart, Basil H., 4, 6, 67, 173
limited war, 15, 19, 20, 171, 175, 208n5
Lippman, Walter, 87
Lodge, Henry Cabot, 10, 53, 54, 75, 95, 124
Luong, Quach Hai, 177

MACV, *see* US Military Assistance Command,
    Vietnam
Magsaysay, Ramon, 32
Malaya, 2, 7, 19, 29, 33, 34, 52, 57, 122, 128, 130
Malayan Communist Party (MCP), 33
Man, Chu Huy, 95, 97, 98
Manila Conference, 92
Mao Tse-tung, 15–16, 28, 31
    writings of, 18, 27, 32, 47, 60, 61, 76, 175
Maple, Hugh L., 133
Marshall, George C., 41–42
McGarr, Lionel C., 30, 48, 49, 50, 150, 152
McNamara, Robert S., xxii, 10, 35, 61, 69, 70, 82,
    85, 124, 127, 181, 188n18
    assessments of progress, 66, 71, 165
    trips to Vietnam, 55, 58, 65, 98
    on victory in Vietnam, 7
McPherson, Harry C., 44, 225n97
Mekong Delta, 39, 51, 84, 95, 103, 153
metrics, ix, 7, 131
Military Assistance Training Advisor Course, 29
Military Review, 29, 33
Miller, Edward, 124
Minh, Duong Van, 58
Mobile Advisory Teams, 156–157
Mohr, Charles, 82
Moltke, Helmuth Graf von, 5, 6
Montague, Robert M. Jr., 28
Montgomery, Bernard Law, 7
Moore, Harold G., 97, 99
Munich analogy, 62, 88
My Lai, 110

Nagl, John, 22, 92, 218n4
Napoleon, 4
Napoleonic Wars, 3
nation building, xxiii, 84, 89, 92, 93, 107, 112,
    116, 132, 134, 136, 138, 161, 178
National Liberation Front (NLF), xxii, 43, 44,
    47–51, 54, 58, 59, 63, 66, 73, 79, 82, 93,
    98, 100, 102, 104, 108, 112, 121, 123,
    124, 125, 133, 135, 144, 146, 150, 152,
    154, 158, 161, 168, 173, 177, 180

National Liberation Front (NLF) (*Cont.*)
9th PLAF Division, 102
and propaganda, 52
and strategic hamlets, 53
National Military Program, 1
National Pacification Plan, 125, 126
National Security Action Memorandums
(NSAMs)
NSAM 273, 54, 58
NSAM 288, 65
National Security Council (NSC), 17, 23, 38,
128, 138, 163, 178
National Security Council Paper 68 (NSC
68), 17, 18
"New Look" policy, 19, 21
New York Times, xxv, 55, 74, 143
Nguyen dynasty, 39
Nguyen, Lien-Hang, 173
Nhu, Ngo Dinh, 52–53, 122
Nixon, Richard M., 163, 172
Nolting, Frederick E. Jr., 43, 53
North Vietnam, xxii, xxiv, 7, 67, 68, 71, 73, 75,
98, 180, (*see also* Democratic Republic
of Vietnam)
North Vietnam Army (NVA), 25, 32, 44, 60, 76,
82, 84, 96, 98, 100, 110, 111, 113, 121,
138, 140, 158, 161, 174, 179
infiltration of, 49, 50, 53, 60, 76, 84–87, 96,
98, 109, 11, 138, 139, 140, 158
nuclear weapons, 1, 5, 10, 15, 19, 20, 175

O'Daniel, John W., 46, 149
Office of Civil Operations (OCO), 127, 128, 129
Office of National Security Studies, 182
"operational art," 3
Operations (US and Allied)
Attleboro, 102
Cedar Falls, 106, 107
Explosion, 51
Fairfax, 106–107
Flaming Dart, 60
Junction City, 106, 107, 222n65
Lam Son II, 101
Recovery, 143
Rolling Stone, 101–102
Rolling Thunder, 60
"orthodox" history, xxii
Osgood, Robert, 19, 32
"Outline of Counterinsurgency Operations," 39

Pacific Command, 54, 66, 68, 71, 72, 92,
141, 142
pacification, xix, xxiii, 8, 11, 12, 28, 52, 58, 65, 77,
81, 84, 89, 98, 99, 104, 105, 109, 120, 121,
124, 125, 126, 130, 131, 134, 135, 137,
138, 143, 145, 147, 151, 162, 164, 171, 180
definitions of, 12, 120–121, 144
under MAAG, 48

Palmer, Bruce, xxiv, 27, 176, 210n26
Palmer, Dave R., 22
Peers, William R., 110, 111, 112, 113, 114,
165, 166
Pentomic divisions, 1–2
people's war, 20, 26, 44, 113, 174
Philippines, 19, 28, 29, 32, 34, 62
Phoenix program, 135
Picket, George, 173
Pike, Douglas, 39, 178
Pleiku, 60, 95, 102, 109, 110, 112
Politboro (Hanoi), 43, 73, 81, 139, 173,
175, 197n79
political stability, ix, 12, 34, 36, 47, 49, 53, 61, 82,
102, 121, 134, 153, 180
Popular Forces, 80, 124–125, 130, 137, 140, 148,
154, 156, 159, 164
population security, ix, 50, 76, 86, 90, 101, 102,
115, 121, 123, 136, 143
Posen, Barry, 6
Prados, John, 8
Program for the Pacification and Long Term
Development of South Vietnam
(PROVN), 83–84, 127
Pye, Lucien W., 57

Quynh, Ngo, 161

Rand Corporation, 30, 33, 59, 105, 136
refugees, 42, 83, 87, 103, 107, 108, 132, 136,
143, 179
Regional Forces, 80, 124–125, 130, 137, 140,
148, 154, 156, 159, 164
Republic of Vietnam Armed Forces (RVNAF),
11, 12, 52, 67, 71, 77, 78, 80, 88, 95, 142,
148, 151, 154, 160, 163, 167, 168
Reserve Officers' Training Corps
(ROTC), 28, 29
Reston, James, xxv, 74, 75, 153
"revisionist" history, xxii
Revolutionary Development (RD), xxii, xxiv, 11,
82, 84, 86, 101, 103, 104–105, 115, 127,
131, 141, 150, 155, 157, 164
definitions of, 35, 228n27
revolutionary warfare, 15, 16, 27, 33, 39, 67, 93
RGD, *passim*
Ridgway, Matthew B., 5, 18–19, 20
Rogers, Bernard W., 107
Rosson, William B., 73, 174
Rostow, Walt W., 2, 50, 57, 88, 124
Rusk, Dean, 69, 82, 124

60 Minutes, xxi
Saigon
government of, *see* Government of South
Vietnam (GVN)
battle of (1955), 43
Sanders, Ralph, 26

Seaman, Jonathan O., 87
search and destroy, xix, xxii, 9, 13, 79, 98, 101,
        106, 107, 111, 114
security, 6, 12, 23–24, 35, 43, 45, 48, 51, 61, 68,
        77, 80, 84–85, 92, 101, 101, 108, 112,
        121–124, 130, 132, 148, 149, 174 (*see
        also* population security)
    territorial, 12, 46, 89, 121, 166
Self-Defense Corps, 46, 48, 148, 149–150, 154
Shaplen, Robert, 13
Sharp, U.S.G., 68, 72, 84, 92, 142, 212n38
Sheehan, Neil, 182
Shin, Chae Myung, 87
Smithers, Samuel Jr., 35
Sorley, Lewis, 155
Southeast Asia, xxiv, 6, 7, 9, 10, 26 27, 30, 32, 37,
        38, 44, 48, 57, 58, 62, 65, 71, 90, 134,
        147, 148, 172, 179
South Vietnamese Army, *see* Army of the
        Republic of Vietnam (ARVN)
Soviet Union, 16–17, 18, 21, 36, 41, 46, 68,
        70, 173
Special Forces, 21, 95
Spector, Ronald, 171
"spectrum of conflict," 21
Starry, Donn A., 33
Stilwell, Richard G., 57
Stone, Charles P., 111–112, 113, 114
Strachan, Hew, 176
strategic hamlet program, 27, 52–53
strategy
    competing definitions of, 3–6, 21, 22, 39
    enclave, 61, 78, 79
    grand, xx, xxii, 4, 6, 39, 43, 54, 60, 63, 65, 117,
        179, 183, 188n15
    military, xx, xxiii, 6, 10, 18, 20, 22, 39, 58,
        61, 65, 69, 127, 151, 172, 176, 179,
        181, 183
    US, xxii, 168
Sumida, Jon, xxiii, 182

Taber, Robert, 26
"Tactics & Techniques of Counter-Insurgent
        Operations," 48, 150
Taylor, Maxwell D., 1, 19, 21, 50, 57, 116,
        152, 178
    as US ambassador, 9, 55, 58, 59, 70
Tet offensive (1968), 89, 90, 107, 111, 113, 114,
        136, 138, 141–145, 164, 165, 166, 170,
        171, 176, 180
Thailand, 62
Thang, Nguyen Duc, 145
Thanh, Nguyen Chi, 95
Thieu, Nguyen Van, 82, 121, 166
Thompson, Robert, 30, 122
Time, xx, xxi
Tonkin, 40
Treaty of Pressburg, 4

Trinquier, Roger, 30
Truman, Harry S., 17, 18, 20, 32, 41, 59, 68
Truong, Ngo Quang, 107
Tuchman, Barbara, 179

United Nations, 20
US Army, xxi, xxii, xxiv, 8, 15, 16, 21, 30, 45, 137,
        149, 175, 177, 181
    and 12-month tours, 110, 113
    brigades
        173rd Airborne, 61, 118
    criticisms of, 22, 46, 92, 94
    and counterinsurgency, xxiii, 16, 21, 24,
        29, 122
    divisions
        1st Cavalry, 94, 95, 96, 97, 98, 102, 103, 109
        1st Infantry, 99, 100, 101, 102, 104, 106,
            107, 155, 180
        4th Infantry, 92–93, 110, 112, 113, 114
        9th Infantry, 109
        25th Infantry, 102, 103, 104, 105, 106, 108,
            109, 132, 158
        82nd Airborne, 142
        101st Airborne, 1, 2, 57
    and learning, xxiii, 26, 37, 98, 99, 105, 112,
        114, 118, 147, 158, 171, 188n21
    regiments
        11th Armored Cavalry, 106
        Special Forces, 21, 95
US Agency for International Development
        (USAID), 122, 127, 128, 129
US Army Command and General Staff College,
        30, 34, 48
US Information Agency (USIA), 122, 128, 129
US Army War College, 10, 18, 27, 31, 34,
        57, 127
US Embassy in South Vietnam, 12, 45, 56, 75,
        89, 127, 141
US Marine Corps, 24, 60–61, 79–80, 96, 109,
        110, 116, 142
    Westmoreland critique of, 214n66
US Military Assistance Advisory Group
        (MAAG), 30, 45–50, 148, 149, 150,
        152, 163
US Military Assistance Command, Vietnam, xix,
        xxiii, xxiv, 11, 39, 59, 72, 78, 83, 86, 107,
        116, 161, 171, 174, 179
    Campaign Plans, 51, 87, 89, 131, 132, 163
    concept of operations, 12, 51, 93, 114
    formation and mission of 50, 67
    and intelligence, 52, 53, 60, 76, 103, 133,
        135, 140
    and measuring progress, 123–124, 131,
        136, 139

Vann, John Paul, 49, 153
Verdun, xix
Vien, Cao Van, 12, 152, 162

Vietcong, 8, 10, 43, 49, 54, 56, 61, 89, 105, 121, 133, 135, 165, (*see also* National Liberation Front)
  infrastructure, 44, 85, 101, 104–105, 106, 108, 112, 124-126, 130-133, 135, 138–139, 141, 145, 156, 157
Viet Minh, 31, 41, 44, 45, 48, 161
Viet Nam Doc Lap Dong Minh Hoi, 41
Viet Nam Quoc Dan Dong (VNQDD), 40
Vietnam War
  mosaic nature of, 11, 93, 109, 110, 118
Vietnamese National Army, 45
Vietnamese nationalism, xxii, 14, 17, 33, 35, 40, 44, 117, 162, 178
Vietnamization, 163, 165

Walt, Lewis, 79, 80, 81, 213n62
War Zone C, 106, 107, 109
Warner, Volney, 83
Westmoreland, William C., xix, xxiii, xxiv, 24, 38
  as 101st Division Commander, 1–2
  assistance to ARVN, 12, 107, 153, 154, 164
  and attrition, 67, 75, 77, 78, 81, 84, 90, 115, 118, 179
  authority of, 72
  and civilian casualties, 96, 109, 213n55
  command philosophy, 118
  and CORDS, 128-129, 228n41
  critics of, 8, 14, 22, 36, 74, 83 92, 94, 101, 114, 120, 138, 147, 155–156, 166, 171, 176, 181, 182
  as Deputy MACV Commander, 55, 56, 126
  faith in military force, 35, 36, 61, 90, 134, 160, 177, 181
  and ground war, 7, 12, 74, 88, 100, 105, 109, 117, 126, 132, 136, 212n43,
  on Lodge, Henry Cabot, 10
  on Malaya, 34
  on nature of the threat, 12, 73, 75–77, 86, 93, 96, 109, 114, 118, 125, 140, 158, 164
  on offensive operations, 82
  and order of battle controversy, 85
  on pacification, 12, 28, 57, 58, 86, 120–121, 124, 125, 126, 130, 131, 132, 138, 141, 154, 176
  on political war, 75, 206n81
  professional background of, 56–57
  and problems with communication, 91, 114–115, 116, 117, 118
  on protracted war, 57, 64, 71, 75, 77, 78, 88, 108
  and public opinion, 116, 141–142
  and relations with Vietnamese, 135, 138, 147, 155, 160, 162, 163, 166, 227n17
  and requests for manpower, 61, 69, 89, 142–143
  revolutionary development, 11, 82, 84, 86, 99, 116, 127, 163
  as Secretary of General Staff, 1
  strategic concept of, 46, 49, 66, 67, 73, 75, 76, 77, 87, 91, 93, 95, 100, 113, 115, 127, 138, 154, 157, 164, 169, 177, 182
  on strategy, 7, 11, 36, 39, 63, 69, 92, 142
  as Superintendant, USMA, 2, 28, 30, 57
  three phased campaign, 78
  Time Man of the Year, xx-xxi
  US Army Chief of Staff, 170
  and US escalation, 59, 60, 73, 76, 154
West Point, xx, 2, 22, 28, 29, 57, 151
Weyand, Frederick C., 13, 103, 104, 105, 174, 179
Wheeler, Earle, 59, 79, 84, 85, 88, 90, 99, 120, 140, 142–143, 163, 195n47, 232n90
White House, xxii, 18, 53, 67, 71, 72, 129
White, Theodore H., 167–168
"whiz kids," 69
Wickham, Kenneth, 170
Williams, Samuel T., 45–46, 48, 163
Williamson, Ellis W., 118
World War I, xix, 4, 9, 17
World War II, xx, 1, 5, 8, 9, 10, 11, 15, 17, 18, 23, 26, 29, 30, 32, 33, 35, 39, 41, 48, 56, 110, 111, 149, 171
Wyles, Eugene J., 55

Yarborough, William, 58
Yugoslavia, 17

Zais, Melvin, 167
Zorthian, Barry, 159